Judges and Democratization

This second edition examines judicial independence as an aspect of democratization based on the premise that democracy cannot be consolidated without the rule of law of which judicial independence is an indispensable part.

It pays particular attention to the restraints placed upon judicial independence and examines the reforms which are being applied, or remain to be adopted, in order to guard against the different kinds of interference which prevent judicial decisions being taken in a wholly impartial way. Focusing on the growing authoritarianism in the new democracies of Eastern Europe, Latin America, Asia and Africa, the book analyses the paradox of judicial activism arising from the independence endowed upon the judiciary and the rights bestowed on citizens by post-authoritarian constitutions. Finally, it asks how judicial accountability can be made compatible with the preservation of judicial independence when the concept of an accountable, independent judiciary appears to be a contradiction in terms.

This book will be of key interest to scholars and students of judicial studies, democratization and autocratization studies, constitutionalism, global governance, and more broadly comparative government/politics, human rights and comparative public law.

B. C. Smith is Emeritus Professor of Political Science, University of Dundee, UK.

Democratization and Autocratization Studies

Series Editors

Luca Tomini

CEVIPOL, Université libre de Bruxelles, Belgium, and Seraphine

and

F. Maerz

Goethe University Frankfurt, Germany

This series offers a space to those interested in recent regime transition and transformation processes globally, both empirically and theoretically. It considers sole- or jointly authored, and edited, volumes, both full-length and shorter, as well as handbooks.

Innovations, Reinvented Politics and Representative Democracy
Edited by Agnès Alexandre-Collier, Alexandra Goujon and Guillaume Gourgues

Nationalism, Referendums and Democracy
Voting on Ethnic Issues and Independence, 2nd edition
Edited by Matt Qvortrup

International Aid and Democracy Promotion
Liberalization at the Margins
Bann Seng Tan

The above titles were published in this series, formerly known as Democratization Studies.

Neo-militant Democracies in Post-communist Member States of the European Union
Edited by Joanna Rak and Roman Bäcker

The Effects of Rebel Parties on Governance, Democracy and Stability After Civil Wars
From Guns to Governing
Edited by John Ishiyama and Gyda M. Sindre

Judges and Democratization, 2nd edition
Judicial Independence in New Democracies
B. C. Smith

For more information about this series, please visit: www.routledge.com

Judges and Democratization

Judicial Independence in New Democracies

Second Edition

B. C. Smith

Routledge
Taylor & Francis Group
LONDON AND NEW YORK

Second edition published 2023
by Routledge
4 Park Square, Milton Park, Abingdon, Oxon OX14 4RN

and by Routledge
605 Third Avenue, New York, NY 10158

Routledge is an imprint of the Taylor & Francis Group, an informa business

First edition published by Routledge 2019

British Library Cataloguing-in-Publication Data
A catalogue record for this book is available from the British Library

ISBN: 978-1-032-36945-7 (hbk)
ISBN: 978-1-032-36949-5 (pbk)
ISBN: 978-1-003-33461-3 (ebk)

DOI: 10.4324/9781003334613

Typeset in Times New Roman
by Apex CoVantage, LLC

Contents

Illustrations

Figures

Table

Publications

B. C. Smith

Field Administration: An Aspect of Decentralization

Advising Ministers

Administering Britain (with J. Stanyer)

Policy-Making in British Government

Government Departments: An Organizational Perspective (with D. C. Pitt)

The Computer Revolution in Public Administration (with D. C. Pitt)

Decentralization: The Territorial Dimension of the State

Bureaucracy and Political Power

Progress in Development Administration

British Aid and International Trade (with O. Morrissey and E. Horesh)

Understanding Third World Politics (fourth edition)

Good Governance and Development

Introduction

It is a fundamental democratic principle that judiciaries should be politically impartial and immune from political interference. Such a judiciary is particularly important in countries trying to consolidate democracy following transition from authoritarian rule, whether in the form of military juntas, one-party systems, personal dictatorships or racial oligarchies. If democratic reforms are to be successful, it is essential that the judiciary is independent. Without an independent judiciary there can be no rule of law, and without the rule of law there can be no democracy.

It is, then, necessary to understand the role of the judiciary in the so-called 'third wave' of democratization which since the early 1970s swept across Southern and Eastern Europe and, to varying degrees, most less-developed regions of the world (Pinkney 1993). It increased the proportion of countries in the world with some form of democratic government from 28 per cent in 1974 to 60 per cent in 2011.

However, since 1980 the strength of democratization in post-authoritarian states has generally waned. What has been called a 'third wave of autocratization' began in earnest in 1990 as post-cold war democratization slowed down, spreading from Russia, Armenia and Belarus. By 2017 the states making democratic progress were outnumbered by those in regression (Lührmann and Lindberg 2019). This book is concerned with how the judiciary has fared during democratic deterioration, what its role has been in the process of democratization, and the reasons for the politicization of the judiciary in the new forms of authoritarianism.

The decline in the quality of democracy in Central and Eastern Europe has been so great since the beginning of the twenty-first century that by 2020 there were more authoritarian regimes than consolidated democracies. The democratic consolidation of the late 1990s and early 2000s had either stalled or been reversed (Freedom House 2021). By 2020 there were no 'full democracies' in Eastern Europe, a full democracy being one in which basic political freedoms and civil liberties are respected, a democratic political culture exists, the media are independent and diverse, the system of checks and balances is effective, the judiciary is independent, and judicial decisions are enforced.

While democracy in ten states in the region improved in 2020, in 17 others it declined. The gap between the highest-scoring countries – the Czech Republic and Slovenia – and the rest of the region became even more pronounced.

DOI: 10.4324/9781003334613-1

The only non-authoritarian state in Central Asia, the Kyrgyz Republic, moved closer to authoritarianism by registering the steepest democratic decline in Eastern Europe in 2020. Thirteen countries are classed as 'flawed democracies', or states which have free and fair elections, and basic civil liberties are respected, but significant weaknesses in governance, political culture and political participation persist.

Eight countries (including Ukraine, Moldova, Armenia, Georgia and the Kyrgyz Republic) have 'hybrid regimes', in which electoral irregularities prevent them from being free and fair, governments restrict opposition parties and candidates, a democratic political culture is weak, levels of political participation are low, corruption is widespread, the rule of law is weak, civil society is underdeveloped, journalists face constant harassment, and the judiciary lacks independence.

The remaining states in the region, including Belarus, Azerbaijan, Kazakhstan and Russia, are 'authoritarian regimes' where political pluralism is absent or heavily circumscribed, what few formal democratic institutions exist have little substance, elections (if they occur) are neither free nor fair, abuses and infringements of civil liberties are disregarded, the media are state-owned or controlled by groups connected to the government, the judiciary lacks independence, and criticism of the government is repressed or censored. The four Central Asian states (Kazakhstan, Tajikistan, Turkmenistan and Uzbekistan) are outright dictatorships (EIU 2021).

The Western Balkans have also developed a range of hybrid and autocratic regimes since the introduction of multiparty politics in the early 1990s, with none 'reaching the standing of fully consolidated liberal democracies' (Kmezić 2020: 183).

Latin America's level of democracy also continued to decline significantly between 2015 and 2020. In 2019 it was the worst affected region in the world. Although Latin America still has the best record for post-authoritarian democracy, there are only two full Third Wave democracies: Uruguay and Chile. The trend over the past decade has been towards authoritarianism, a development owing much to increasing anti-democratic politics in Bolivia and growing authoritarianism in Venezuela and Nicaragua. Decline has been driven by restrictions on political opposition, electoral participation, pluralism, civil liberties and effective government, undermining confidence in political institutions and democracy.

Asian states have also seen reversals in recent years. While South Korea and Taiwan became full democracies in 2020, the rest of the region's Third Wave democracies have become 'flawed', 'hybrid' or 'authoritarian'. South Korea's achievement was despite a reduction in civil liberties. In 2021 Myanmar reverted to military dictatorship following a coup. Thailand's military seized power in 2014. Democratic elections and political pluralism have benefitted Malaysia, but its democracy remains flawed owing to high-level corruption and restrictions on access to the media, electoral campaigning and freedom of assembly. Twenty years after the end of Suharto's authoritarian New Order regime, the quality of Indonesia's democracy has deteriorated significantly as the rights to freedom of speech and association have been watered down, electoral law has been manipulated, and the rule of law undermined by the weakening of law enforcement institutions such as the Corruption Eradication Commission (Satrio 2018).

Half of sub-Saharan Africa's regimes remain or have become authoritarian. None of the region's post-authoritarian states has consolidated its democracy, and 24 countries were rated authoritarian in 2020. The violence of jihadist groups such as Boko Haram, Islamic State and al-Qaeda offshoots has drawn responses from governments that have restricted civil liberties. Deterioration in the democratic quality of politics in the region is also a consequence of polling irregularities and constraints on legitimate opposition. In 2021 a military coup in Sudan destroyed the democratic gains made following the fall of the military government in 2019, and in Guinea the military ended the period of feeble democracy inaugurated in 2010.

The Middle East and North Africa saw very little effort to democratize until the 'Arab Spring' of 2011, and this soon atrophied so that by 2020 the region was the lowest ranking in the world in terms of the democratic quality of its regimes. Egypt's fleeting democratic experiment ended in 2013 when the military removed the president from power and suspended the 2012 Constitution. The region has become dominated by authoritarian regimes, with no full democracies and only one Third Wave regime, Tunisia, rated as a flawed democracy until 2021, when the president dismissed the prime minister and closed the legislature. Only Lebanon and Morocco have achieved hybrid status, leaving all other states in the authoritarian category. In 2021, uncompetitive parliamentary elections in Egypt, and the intimidation of civil rights activists and 'disappearances' of opposition figures in Lebanon, show how fragile democracy is in the region. It is difficult to see how this situation can be improved, given that there have been no true democracies or free societies in the Arab region, and few free or democratic states in countries where the population is predominantly Moslem (Keratnyky 2002).

Thus, the majority of 'third wave' countries have not established properly functioning democracy and suffer from varying levels of democratic deficit. While electoral democracy might be widely established (with the possibility of alternating governments based on electoral choices), it is not necessarily accompanied by liberal democracy and the protection of individual and group freedoms, pluralism, accountability, the rule of law, and judicial independence. Though the number of electoral democracies has grown, levels of political and civil freedom have declined.

Consequently, a study of the judiciary in new democracies has to include the experiences of states whose transition from authoritarianism stalled from the start, leaving them to be democracies in name only. This is because, first, their departures from their previous authoritarianism were characterized by new constitutional arrangements indicating that liberal democracy was the objective, however small the steps taken towards it. For example, the former Soviet republics of Kazakhstan, Tajikistan, Turkmenistan and Uzbekistan that declared their sovereignty from the USSR from 1990 to 1991, and which today are among the least democratic of the 'Third Wave' states, began independence with constitutions that declared the state to be a democracy with the rights and freedoms of the individual as its highest values, governed by law, and recognizing the rights of man as 'unshakeable'. Such states were momentarily in transition and must be included among the post-authoritarian states of democracy's 'Third Wave'.

There is also a thin veneer of political pluralism in these autocracies which makes them relevant to the study of illiberal democracy and the role of the judiciary within it. Regular parliamentary elections are held in all four countries, albeit judged by international observers as neither free nor fair, with only parties supporting the incumbent president allowed to participate. In Kazakhstan, for example, the first parliamentary elections under the new Constitution were seen as a major step forward in the transition to democracy. Opposition parties and candidates campaigned and openly expressed their views. However, these efforts fell short of the standards 'necessary for the establishment of a pluralistic democratic system. The goal of free and fair elections in Kazakhstan was not reached' (OSCE 1994: 6). In a rare demonstration of judicial independence, the Constitutional Court subsequently ruled that the elections that had created the parliament were unconstitutional because the authorities did not comply with the Constitution in training election officials and counting votes and did not allow citizens living abroad to vote. Parliament then voted to suspend the Constitutional Court. The president dissolved parliament and ruled by decree for the rest of the year.

Second, inclusion of such failed transitions provides relevant information on how judiciaries can be transformed into weapons to be used by dominant political factions in their efforts to sustain their power. Despite constitutional guarantees of judicial independence, courts subject only to the law and the constitution, interference punishable by law, and functioning independently from the legislative and executive branches, politicization of the judiciary has been part of the transition from one form of autocracy to another.

The global and regional pictures conceal internal variations. In Eastern Europe, Poland and Hungary have suffered reversals, while Estonia has consistently improved. In Latin America Bolivia became more authoritarian while Chile continued to consolidate its democracy. In sub-Saharan Africa Angola recorded a strengthening of its democracy while Senegal's status declined. Furthermore, it is not necessarily the 'Third Wave' countries that are responsible for a region's decline in democratic status. For example, in 2019 the erosion of civil liberties in India contributed to Asia's democratic deterioration.

The authoritarianism found in a growing number of Third Wave democracies has given rise to a type of hybrid regime, variously known as 'illiberal democracies', 'defective democracies', 'competitive authoritarianism' and 'electoral authoritarianism'. Such regimes remain equipped with all the constitutional provisions of liberal democracy: fundamental civil rights and liberties, political pluralism, regular elections, political accountability and the separation of powers. However, governments in such regimes typically use their electoral strength and parliamentary majorities to consolidate their power by taking control of the judicial system and using it to the disadvantage of all forms of political opposition, whether political parties, associations representing opposing interests and values, or critical mass media. Contemporary 'autocratization' sees the gradual erosion of democracy by 'electoral autocrats' who secure political supremacy by the harassment or control of the media, civil society, political parties and electoral commissions. Autocracy is reached by deception, with democratic institutions left in place. Consequently 'contemporary democracies tend to erode gradually and under legal disguise' (Lührmann and Lindberg 2019: 1).

Illiberal politics also entails governing parties using their legislative majorities to change the constitution in order to remain in power indefinitely. 'The resulting regimes maintain competitive multiparty elections but are neither democratic nor fully authoritarian' (Kapidžić 2020: 3). More overt forms of authoritarianism are eschewed in favour of 'reforms' which appear to be in the spirit of constitutional democracy but which undermine the institutions which preserve it. Older forms of authoritarianism, such as the military coup or the one-party state, are too disruptive. 'Aspiring dictators do everything they can to avoid them; instead, they opt for a more comfortable solution, dismantling the safeguards of democracy and the rule of law gradually, evoking less resistance' (Jakab 2020: 7). The main institutional victim of the illiberal state is thus the rule of law (see Chapter 1).

This goes a long way to explaining why control of the judiciary is so important to illiberal democracies. If the regime needs to give a veneer of legitimacy to undemocratic constitutional changes, bans on political opposition, unlimited presidential terms, expanded executive power (especially over the judiciary), court 'packing', the nullifying of legislative powers, statutory limitations on basic freedoms of speech, association, assembly, the franchise and the media, or otherwise undermine liberal democracy, then 'abusive judicial review' can provide the answer:

> Regimes turn to courts to carry out their dirty work because, in doing so, they benefit from the associations that judicial review has with democratic constitutional traditions and the rule of law. Having a court, rather than a political actor, undertake an antidemocratic measure may sometimes make the true purpose of the measure harder to detect, and at any rate it may dampen both domestic and international opposition.
>
> (Landau and Dixon 2020: 1317)

The following study of judicial independence as an aspect of democratization is based on the premise that democracy cannot be consolidated without the rule of law of which judicial independence is an indispensable part. It pays particular attention to the restraints placed upon judicial independence, and the reforms which are being applied, or remain to be adopted, in order to guard against the different kinds of interference which prevent judicial decisions being taken in a wholly impartial way. It examines the paradox of judicial activism arising from the independence endowed upon the judiciary by post-authoritarian constitutions. Judicial activism raises concerns that the legitimate authority of elected legislatures might be usurped. Consequently, demands have been voiced to make the judiciary more accountable. This study asks how such accountability can be made compatible with the preservation of judicial independence when the concept of an accountable, independent judiciary appears to be a contradiction in terms.

The basic principles which together constitute the rule of law are set out in Chapter 1. This presents the case for seeing the rule of law as a necessary condition of democratic consolidation and takes issue with one particular conception which links the rule of law to specific types of public policy. It is shown how the rule of law can, when it is associated with fundamental civil and political rights, reconcile the legitimate authority of sovereign government with the supremacy of law. It was not until the preservation of fundamental rights became an object of law from the eighteenth century onwards that it appeared possible to legitimize the concept of a higher law to which political authority was subordinate. The rule of law is shown to be crucial to the practice of democratic government and politics, recognition of which being reflected in the constitutions of transitional states. While the perceived quality of public policies is not part of the rule of law, government action is required to alleviate poverty and inequality, both of which undermine the rule of law. When such action is prescribed by the inclusion of social and economic rights in the constitution, the judiciary is drawn, through judicial review, even further into the policy-making process.

None of the principles that together constitute the rule of law can be realized without judicial independence. Chapter 2 specifies what is required of judges if they are to be truly independent. The rules which protect the judicial function against bias are distinguished: judicial immunity, the principle of sub judice, disqualification from other offices of state, and the regulation of political activities. Judicial independence also entails insularity. The devices used to isolate the judiciary from pressures that threaten to undermine justice are described, including the delegation of judicial management to judicial councils.

Judicial independence is also protected by the exclusive competence to adjudicate given to the courts. This is part of the separations of powers which in a democracy exclude legislatures and executives from performing judicial functions. Such exclusion raises the question of whether special tribunals to deal with specific types of dispute will inevitably have a detrimental effect on judicial independence. Special courts are increasingly advocated as alternative and preferable mechanisms for resolving disputes, leading to concerns about whether some traditional dispute resolution procedures lack the qualities required by the rule of law. Judicial independence may also need to be supported by measures designed to ensure compliance with judgements so that judicial decisions are respected and enforced. Chapter 2 explains why judicial independence serves democracy by protecting electoral competition, civil rights, minority interests and legality in government and by encouraging the development of a democratic political culture. The chapter concludes by showing how post-authoritarian constitutions have empowered judiciaries to undertake these tasks.

Despite the new constitutions of post-authoritarian states explicitly confirming the independence of the judiciary, protecting this independence has proved extremely difficult. The next two chapters describe how judicial independence is to varying extents compromised in many transitional states. Chapter 3 examines different types of 'undue influence': structural constraints, when the non-judicial branches of government try to secure decisions favourable to their political interests by altering judicial institutions; managerial methods which enable judicial careers to be used to limit impartiality; administrative influence through external control of court administration, especially the assignment of cases; and 'direct approaches', when threats, bribes, media campaigns and private intimations from government representatives influence the outcome in specific cases.

Political interference in the appointment and tenure of judges, making them vulnerable to political pressures, compromises the independence of the judiciary, as can control of a judge's career. Independence can also be indirectly curbed by appointments to the judicial councils which have been set up to provide self-management for the judiciary. Manipulating the resources allocated to the judicial branch can also be used to undermine the ability of the judiciary to deliver justice. Judges can be subjected to harassment and even violence when challenges to executive action or powerful economic interests come before the courts. Executive power can be protected by limiting the scope of judicial review and the use of exceptional courts. Governments sometimes make their expectations public by issuing 'guiding' or 'steering' statements to drive courts in the desired direction. When direct pressure cannot secure judicial outcomes favourable to the government, court decisions can be nullified by the non-implementation of judgements. Each of these practices is illustrated by examples from transitional states. Taking control of the judiciary enables it to be used as a weapon that can be wielded against political critics and opponents when it is difficult to ignore constitutional restraints on political repression.

Chapter 4 shows how a lack of judicial impartiality can be affected by factors other than external political interference in the course of justice. Court proceedings may be biased and so violate the principle of equality before the law and the right to a fair trial. There may be no presumption of innocence. Proceedings may fail to observe the rules of natural justice or due process. Judges may be biased by their own preferences, prejudices, political affiliations and ideological leanings when interpreting and applying the law, and conducting hearings. Inefficiencies within the judiciary due to lack of resources can compromise the principles embedded in the rule of law and amount to a denial of natural justice and basic rights. Chapter 4 also examines the problem of corruption within the judiciary, when justice is enjoyed by the highest bidder, and the judiciary's ability to offer impartial adjudication is destroyed. The possible causes of judicial corruption, and the reasons why it is of such significance in newly democratizing countries, are discussed. Particular attention is paid to the effect of judicial corruption on a democratic political culture, and finds that, contrary to expectations, perceptions of corruption do not appear to be strongly related to support for democratic values.

The reforms needed to protect the judiciary from political interference in the judicial process are examined in Chapters 5 and 6. These chapters focus on reforms which address the main sources of threats to judicial independence. Chapter 5 assesses the reforms which are designed to deal with problems arising from political interference in the judiciary, the intimidation of judges and other lawyers, limitations on judicial review, the use of exceptional courts and the non-enforcement of judgements. While conventional safeguards are crucial to providing the judiciary with immunity from political manipulation, political competition is arguably the most important prerequisite of judicial independence. For politicians to be concerned about the electoral consequences of political interference in judicial appointments, careers and decision-making, elections must be free and fair. However, the relationship between electoral competition and judicial independence in post-authoritarian states in Europe, Latin America, Asia and Africa is far from straightforward. This chapter also notes the importance of public opinion and civil society for the political accountability necessary if judicial independence is to be protected. In addition, civil society can become directly involved in the administration of justice.

If parliamentarians and civil society are to scrutinize the judiciary effectively, there has to be transparency in the way the judiciary is managed. Accountability also requires legislative institutions which can force members of the executive to explain and justify the use made of the powers over the judiciary entrusted to them by constitution and statute. The constraints on such legislative oversight under contemporary political conditions are noted. Reforms are also directed at protecting judges and other lawyers against different forms of intimidation and improving the security of the courts. Pro-democracy reforms have included the abolition of exceptional courts, though what is known as alternative dispute resolution has been tried in order to provide quicker, cheaper and more socially acceptable justice through the use of less-formal mechanisms than the regular courts. Reforms seeking to ensure the proper enforcement of court decisions have had to address the need for money, personnel and accountability.

Chapter 6 examines reforms which address problems of judicial capacity, biased proceedings, biased judges, and corruption. It thus deals with obstacles to independent judicial decision-making that arise from within the judiciary itself, as distinct from those that are imposed from other parts of the political system. Judicial capacity-building involves the development of politically neutral methods of evaluating performance by objective criteria, free from unwarranted external political influence. Capacity-building also calls for the modernization of judicial institutions, especially courts, to increase efficiency in the processing of cases and reduce the delays which feed public dissatisfaction with the judiciaries of many new democracies. Training programmes for judicial personnel, especially judges, court officials and public prosecutors, also feature among law reforms designed to strengthen judicial capacity.

Biased proceedings obviously violate the right to a fair trial. The major areas of concern in transitional states are the need for information about basic legal rights and the ability of people brought before the courts to understand the proceedings. Constitutional and statutory provisions have been put in place, including trial by jury, widely regarded as contributing to public confidence in, and support for, democracy. However, experience of jury trials varies greatly from one post-authoritarian country to another. Chapter 6 examines the conflicting views on this method of participatory justice.

A widely adopted yet controversial method of dealing with judicial bias carrying over from the pre-democratic regime has been 'lustration'. The risks associated with this process are examined. A system of appeals is recognized as an essential method for dealing with bias on the part of individual judges, though it is also possible to require judges to declare personal interests in a case before standing down. Judges can also be prohibited from holding other public offices or being members of political organizations. National codes of conduct or judicial ethics are also popular devices to ensure judges act and decide fairly.

Judicial corruption raises exceptionally difficult problems, partly because the judiciary is itself intrinsic to the eradication of corruption generally and partly because of the danger that the prevention of corruption might become an opportunity for political interference.

Two broad approaches to the reform of corrupt judiciaries have been adopted in new democracies. One is sociopolitical in that it requires a civil society of organizations capable of rigorously scrutinizing and monitoring the judiciary. Associated reforms within the judiciary are designed to make it more transparent and open to public scrutiny, thus making it more difficult to hide corruption. The other approach is to change the institutional environment within which the judiciary functions by making corruption more dangerous and costly for those who seek to benefit from it. Chapter 6 examines the relative importance of pressure groups, the media and the political will of government to reform. Reforms to improve the transparency of all aspects of the judicial process include the publication of performance measures, explicit anti-corruption rules, monitoring of anti-corruption strategies, freedom of information laws, independent anti-corruption agencies and stronger incentives to behave honestly and professionally.

Chapter 6 concludes with an examination of the politics of law reform since the main obstacles to reform which support judicial independence and the rule of law are political. This is because judicial reform ultimately affects the distribution of power between state institutions (the executive, legislative and judicial branches of government) and between political interests and social strata.

Judicial reform has also been directed at the management of the judiciary. Chapter 7 examines the role of different institutions in judicial management and assesses their compatibility with judicial independence. This is especially important when executives and legislatures are involved. Two highly generalized models are distinguished – self-management and executive management – in order to provide a broad context in which to clarify the role of other branches of government. The risks attended upon the delegation of administrative powers to the judiciary itself, through judicial councils, are discussed.

The executive model assigns power to administer the judiciary to the executive branch, although there are usually varying levels of involvement from other institutions, including members of the judiciary itself, and this model certainly does not necessarily encroach upon judicial independence. There is much sharing of responsibility for the management of the judiciary. Some legislatures have acquired significant powers. However, the theoretical benefits of parliamentary involvement are often negated by the partisan nature of parliamentary decision-making, which draws the management of the judiciary into party conflicts. Strict party discipline within a parliament can serve to reinforce the power of the executive in relation to the judiciary by politicizing managerial processes which ought to reflect professional merit rather than party allegiance.

Post-authoritarian constitutions endow the judiciary with exceptional powers. The factors which encourage 'judicial activism' are examined in Chapter 8. Activism involves the judiciary in the definition of constitutional rules, the amendment of constitutions, challenges to the legality of policy decisions, adjudicating on the constitutionality of the political process, and judicial review of administrative action. Such activism draws judges into political conflicts, inevitably attracting hostility from sections of society whose interests are adversely affected by judicial interpretations of legislative and administrative actions. This raises the question of whether risk-averse 'abstentionism' might be conducive to the consolidation of democracy. Whatever the wisdom of such a strategy, it is easy to understand why the question of judicial accountability has come to the fore.

The power granted to the judiciary in many post-authoritarian constitutions has led to accusations that the legitimate authority of parliaments and therefore voters is being usurped. This power enables the judiciary to adjudicate in disputes about the constitutional powers of governments, the interpretation of statutes and the application of precedents. Judges then appear to be making the law rather than just administering it. Acceptance of the human rights dimension of the rule of law and enshrining extensive positive social and economic rights in constitutions inevitably involve interpretation by the courts, obliging justices to make judgements about public policy. In some jurisdictions, judicial review of administrative decisions and procedures has evolved into a right to good administration.

The feeling that judicial review represents a challenge to the will of the people, as enunciated by their elected representatives through legislation, by an unelected and elitist body has led to calls for the judiciary to be made more accountable, demands which have been given added impetus by a number of other features of contemporary judiciaries. Two propositions are given special attention: that judges do not have the legitimacy to intervene in the implementation of economic, social and cultural rights; and that they have neither the professional nor institutional capacity to intervene in conflicts over such rights.

Chapter 9 asks how such accountability can be made compatible with the preservation of judicial independence when the concept of an accountable, independent judiciary appears to be a contradiction in terms. The need for accountability is perceived as arising not only from the extensive powers of constitutional and administrative review bestowed upon the judiciary but also by judicial self-management, corruption, political bias, inefficiency and inaccessibility. Explanations for the 'accountability gap' are offered before ways of conceptualizing accountability in the context of judicial independence are proposed. It is argued that accountability is best thought of as stimulating appeals against judicial errors on points of fact or law. The legislative process can respond to judicial review that alters public policy. The functions and selection processes of judicial councils can be redesigned to provide greater accountability. Publicity for judicial decisions facilitates public scrutiny. Professionalism in all aspects of judicial work, and the systematic assessment of judicial performance, can both be made consistent with judicial accountability. When accountability is applied to the judiciary, it is important that it be demanded from those responsible for the defects. Transparency is the key to knowing who should be accountable to whom.

The final chapter summarizes the conclusions of previous chapters and draws attention to the problems inherent in preserving the separation of powers when constitutions endow judiciaries with the task of protecting a wide range of citizens' rights, a responsibility which then prompts demands for judicial accountability lest the powers of democratic policy-making bodies be usurped. What has to be preserved here is the reciprocal relationship between democracy and judicial independence. Independent judges protect the political and civil rights on which democracy rests, while the democratic political process makes interference in the judiciary politically dangerous for those who indulge in it. Though the more mature the democracy, the stronger judicial independence and the rule of law, there is everywhere the risk of corrosion in these key institutions of the democratic regime.

My thanks to the editorial staff, reviewers and copy-editors at Routledge and Apex CoVantage, especially Andrew Taylor, Sophie Iddamalgoda and Venkatesh Sundaram, for their support and efficiency in bringing this revised edition to fruition.

References

EIU (2021), *Democracy Index 2020: In Sickness and in Health?*, London: Economist Intelligence Unit.

Freedom House (2021), *Freedom in the World: Democracy Under Siege*, New York: Freedom House.

Jakab, A. (2020), 'What can constitutional law do against the erosion of democracy and the rule of law? On the interconnectedness of the protection of democracy and the rule of law', *Constitutional Studies*, vol. 6, no. 1.

Kapidžić, D. (2020), 'The rise of illiberal politics in Southeast Europe', *Southeast European and Black Sea Studies*, vol. 20, no. 1.

Keratnyky, A. (2002), 'Muslim countries and the democracy gap', *Journal of Democracy*, vol. 13, no. 1.

Kmezić, M. (2020), 'Rule of law and democracy in the Western Balkans: addressing the gap between policies and practice', *Southeast European and Black Sea Studies*, vol. 20, no. 1.

Landau, D. and R. Dixon (2020), 'Abusive judicial review: courts against democracy', *UC Davis Law Review*, vol. 53, no. 3.

Lührmann, A and S. I. Lindberg (2019), 'A third wave of autocratization is here: what is new about it?', *Democratization*, vol. 26, no. 7.

OSCE (1994), *Report on the Elections in Kazakstan 7 Mach 1994*, Helsinki: Organization for Security and Co-operation in Europe.

Pinkney, R. (1993), *Democracy in the Third World*. Buckingham: Open University Press.

Satrio, A. (2018), 'Constitutional retrogression in Indonesia under President Joko Widodo's Government: what can the Constitutional Court do?', *Constitutional Review*, vol. 4, no. 2.

1 The rule of law and democracy

Introduction

An independent judiciary is indispensable if countries in transition from authoritarianism to democracy are to develop and consolidate a democratic regime. The importance of judicial independence here lies in its relationship to the rule of law. Without an independent judiciary there can be no rule of law. And without the rule of law there can be no development in any of its dimensions – economic, social or political – for transitional polities. This makes judicial independence fundamental to human development in general and democratic political development in particular.

Countries in transition from authoritarian rule have to deal with a legacy in which the rule of law was regularly undermined. This legacy has meant that the independence of the judiciary has frequently been compromised by political interference in the appointment and the tenure of judges, making them vulnerable to political pressures. In many transitional states the ideal of 'due process', entailing the impartial application of the laws, the availability of appropriate remedies, provision for appeals, access to legal assistance, and open and efficient judicial procedures, either has not been effectively pursued or has been intentionally disregarded. Outside of the courts of law, the maltreatment of suspects and detainees remains all too common. Those held on remand can spend so long in detention that even when found innocent they have effectively served the sentence prescribed for the guilty or are found guilty simply in order to legitimize the length of detention (Stotzky and Nino 1993). In many newly democratizing states fair trials are something of a luxury. These and other abuses of the judicial system will be examined further in Chapters 3 and 4.

This chapter shows how the rule of law is a necessary condition of democratic consolidation. It begins with an exploration of the principles underpinning the rule of law and the extent to which the association of the rule of law with certain approaches to public policy makes it a contested concept. Next, it relates the rule of law to the practice of democratic government. Then it explains how constitutional reforms in new democracies have built the rule of law into the fundamental principles of government. Finally, it returns to the relationship between the rule of law and public policy by showing how poverty and inequality undermine the rule

DOI: 10.4324/9781003334613-2

of law which thus becomes dependent upon the willingness of governments to address the structure of economy and society.

The rule of law and public policy

Before governance can be said to be based on the rule of law, a number of judicial principles have to be applied. The rule of law combines different concepts of justice – regular, equal, ubiquitous and natural – all of which demand judicial independence. This makes the rule of law a complex constitutional arrangement and to some extent a contested concept, though this problem mainly arises when the concept is stretched to encompass not only the quality of public policies supported by legislation but also human rights. This poses the question of whether the rule of law implies the existence of 'good' laws (Carlin and Sarsfield 2012; Merkel 2013). If not, cannot the rule of law be said to feature in repressive, authoritarian and totalitarian regimes? What concerns some proponents of constitutional democracy and the role of the judiciary within it is that the rule of law might apply to the administration of laws that violate democratic principles by, for example, outlawing political opposition, providing the state with control over the mass media or limiting freedom of speech. Laws may deny human rights, discriminate on grounds of race or gender and persecute minorities yet still conform to the rule of law: 'The law may, for example, institute slavery without violating the rule of law' (Raz 1979: 221).

The possibility that a repressive and unjust regime might function according to the rule of law has prompted the argument that there is no rule of law unless the law promotes ethical behaviour. For example, in 1959 the International Commission of Jurists (ICJ) extended its definition of the rule of law beyond the advancement of civil and political rights to include the establishment of the social, economic and cultural conditions needed for 'legitimate aspirations and dignity' to be realized (Allen 1985: 114). At a conference organized by the ICJ in 1965 in Bangkok it was agreed that the rule of law 'is endangered by the continued existence of hunger, poverty and unemployment, which tend to make a truly representative form of government impossible and promote the emergence of systems of government opposed to the principles of the Rule of Law'. Consequently social, cultural and economic goals became regarded as 'necessary to the smooth operation of the Rule of Law'. These are contained within the Universal Declaration of Human Rights, and include the right to work, to free choice of employment, to protection against unemployment, to just and favourable conditions of work and remuneration 'which will ensure to the worker and his family an existence worthy of human dignity', to security and social protection, and 'to the satisfaction and enrichment of his intellectual and cultural faculties' (International Commission of Jurists 1966). The World Bank defined the rule of law as a system of laws which guarantees private property rights (World Bank 1997). The United Nations has continued to promote a rights-based approach to the rule of law through the 1993 Vienna Declaration, the Secretary-General's report to the Security Council in 2004 and the Declaration adopted by the General Assembly in

2012 (Rishmawi 2018). For the Secretary-General the rule of law required laws that are not only 'publicly promulgated, equally enforced and independently adjudicated' but also 'consistent with international human rights norms and standards' (United Nations 2004: para. 6).

Legal theory also supports the inclusion of expanded human rights in the definition of the rule of law. For example, the legal philosopher Ronald Dworkin has dismissed what he called the 'rule book' conception in favour of a 'rights conception' which requires the law to have morally defensible content (Dworkin 1985: 11). Tom Bingham (Lord Bingham, former Master of the Rolls, Lord Chief Justice and Senior Law Lord of the United Kingdom) also rejected a procedural understanding of the rule of law in favour of a 'thick' definition which encompasses the protection of human rights (Bingham 2011: 67). Definitions of the rule of law have been made even 'thicker' by including substantive values that extend well beyond the judicial system, such as the separation of powers, constitutional checks and balances, participation in decision-making, citizens' consent to the content of laws, cultural rights, freedom from crime, the dignity of citizens and even democracy itself (Bedner 2018).

This conception of the rule of law creates numerous problems. The first is that associating the rule of law with a social philosophy detracts from its role in securing protection against arbitrary political power: 'the adoption of a fully substantive conception of the rule of law has the consequence of robbing the concept of any function which is independent of the theory of justice which imbues such an account of law' (Craig 2016: 116). What is sometimes called the 'thick' conception of the rule of law confuses definition of the concept with the benefits to society which flow from it, such as the protection of human rights, freedom of expression and association, and toleration of conflicting political orthodoxies. Defining the rule of law in a way which envelopes many admirable political values (and these have included public order, respect for human rights and democracy) creates 'too thick a conception of the rule of law which not only prevents treating some of the defining attributes as potential causes or consequences of the rule of law but may also empty the concept of its distinct meaning, as to become a term which means everything and means nothing' (Moller and Skaaning 2014: 26). Too often the rule of law comes close to being akin to a buzzword 'with only positive connotations – stronger economies, safer societies, open and predictable politics' (Carlin 2012: 169).

In contrast, 'a procedural approach to the rule of law stands a good chance of yielding institutions that are both strong and worthy of popular legitimacy' (Trebilcock and Daniels 2008: 25). Furthermore, while it is possible that what some regard as bad public policy can coexist with the rule of law, it is unlikely that a systematically repressive and unjust regime will satisfy the other principles on which the rule of law is based, such as making all state officials subject to the law, ensuring the law is enforced consistently, guaranteeing equality before the law, and ensuring the judiciary is independent of the law makers.

Second, identifying the rule of law with 'good' law enables the concept to be captured by highly ideological positions. For example, definitions of the rule of law which excluded the conferring of discretionary power on government ministers were long ago perceived as opposition to the welfare state and other forms of government intervention (Venice Commission 2011). Hostility to discretionary power in government and administration has been derived from antipathy to collectivism and an interventionist state (Jowell 2011). Neoliberal insistence that the rule of law requires an economic system characterized by minimal state intervention, the sanctity of private property and the maximum freedom for market forces also confuses the rule of law with a particular economic system. It is obviously possible for an economy to be partly managed by the state, with government intervention extending to the provision of social welfare while preserving the tenets of the rule of law. Equally, there are many instances of unbridled capitalism operating alongside severe breaches of the rule of law. Consequently we find even the World Bank contrasting an economy in which private property rights and free markets are enshrined not with a managed economy operating according to the rule of law but with a regime characterized by 'arbitrary government actions – ranging from unpredictable, ad hoc regulations and taxes to outright corruption' (World Bank 1997: 41). In other words, the rule of law comprises principles which are independent of public policy and economic system.

In addition, linking the rule of law to substantive outcomes such as 'good' law requires complex subjective judgements and risks, making the concept too vague or even redundant: 'Why should we bother talking about whether a society has or doesn't have the "rule of law" when what we really are asking is whether the society is good or not?' (Stephenson 2005). This problem occurs when the rule of law is found to be incompatible with the inequality common in modern societies. Political power, being unequally distributed, leads to the law being used to the benefit of 'a few well-organized social networks' which 'monopolize political access and turn law into an instrument increasingly useful to themselves but decreasingly useful to fellow citizens who belong to poorly organized and politically voiceless strata'. Consequently, 'a nominally liberal government, while continuing to rule *through* law, is retreating from the rule *of* law' (Holmes 2003: 23). Equating the rule of law with equality of power, which itself is dependent upon the distribution of material resources among social strata, severely underestimates the contribution which the rule of law can make in reducing some of the harmful effects of inequality. Creating a more equal and therefore more just society is a wholly admirable project. However, the cause of equality is not helped by assuming that a failure to redress inequality necessarily entails a retreat from the rule of law.

The main problem with substantive definitions of the rule of law is that they define it away by restricting it to specific social and economic systems. The rule of law should coexist with all economic systems and not be dependent upon the level of state intervention in the economy. Nor should it be associated with a particular set of human rights, especially since the concepts of social, economic and community rights are themselves highly controversial and contested. The rule of law should be respected regardless of whether a particular government is able to provide the public policies necessary to satisfy the political demands which lie behind many of the rights claimed by different sectional interests. The application of the rule of law should not have to be dependent upon agreement on what are highly contested concepts (Sampford 2005). This difficulty will be returned to in the discussion of judicial activism in Chapter 8.

One way of resolving this conflict between the 'thick' and 'thin' versions of the rule of law is to see it as a necessary but not sufficient condition of democratic government, and to understand that, while it might not guarantee democracy, it is highly unlikely that an authoritarian regime, whether of a military junta or totalitarian political party, or even a democracy which introduces repressive legislation such as South Africa's Protection of Information Act, or Uganda's restrictions on freedom of association, will rigorously and consistently observe the formal precepts of the rule of law such as equality before the law, fair and impartial adjudication or the use of judicial review to test the legality of official acts and decisions. Those who argue that oppressive, authoritarian regimes can rule according to the rule of law fail to recognize that government may be by law but will not be according to the rule of law unless people have access to justice in disputes with the state: 'the most important defining feature of a state based upon the rule of law is that a person in a rule of law state has the opportunity of challenging the government of the day with a reasonable prospect of success in an appropriate case' (Jowell 2015: 6). Legal empowerment of this type is never present in authoritarian regimes.

Furthermore, a regime which uses public policy to violate human rights is unlikely to practise the tenets of the rule of law in its judicial system. Authoritarian leaders may use laws to govern, but the rule of law entails non-arbitrariness: 'The rule of law obtains only when law is unavailable as an instrument of control by any particular actor but rather functions as a contractual benchmark for all members of society' (Helmke and Rosenbluth 2009: 348). The rule of law also embodies a number of basic human rights and does not just exist alongside them. Substantive values are embedded in the formal definition: the civil rights protected by rules governing police procedures; the protection of legal rights inherent in judicial review; the rules guaranteeing a fair trial. The rules which constitute the 'thin' rule of law are both procedural and substantive. The rule of law can never be rendered entirely formalistic (Foran 2019). It embodies fairness and justice which in turn derive from the fundamental right of equality before the law.

So a formal definition, which ascribes specific qualities to a legal system, is preferable to a substantive definition, though the former still conveys essential principles which are dependent upon the rule of law, such as fairness and justice. These are the principles mentioned earlier and which must now be elaborated on in order to establish the importance of judicial independence for their validity. So what does the rule of law prescribe for the judicial system?

Ubiquity

The first principle of the rule of law requires the law to be ubiquitous. There can be neither offence nor penalty without a law. Aristotle's axiom that 'it is preferable that the law should rule rather than any single one of the citizens' (Aristotle 1962:

143) became the first principle of the rule of law for the Victorian jurist A. V. Dicey, whose systematic exposition of the concept assigned 'absolute supremacy' to regular law 'as opposed to the influence of arbitrary power, and excludes the existence of arbitrariness, of prerogative, and even of wide discretionary authority on the part of the government . . . a man may be punished for a breach of law, but he can be punished for nothing else' (Dicey 1885: 189). Thus, under the rule of law no one can be harmed physically or financially by the whim of a state official such as a police officer or tax collector. More recently Tom Bingham universalized Dicey's thinking as follows:

> If anyone – you or I – is to be penalized it must not be for breaking some rule dreamt up by an ingenious minister or official in order to convict us. It must be for a proven breach of the established law of the land.
>
> (Bingham 2011: 2)

This principle is enshrined in Article 7 of the European Convention on Human Rights: 'No one shall be held guilty of any criminal offence on account of any act or omission which did not constitute a criminal offence under national or international law at the time when it was committed.' Only the law can define an offence and prescribe a penalty (*nullum crimen, nulla poena sine lege*). According to the European Court of Human Rights it follows that

> [o]ffences and penalties must be both accessible and foreseeable in order to prevent any arbitrariness by the domestic courts. First the law must be sufficiently clear for individuals to conduct themselves in accordance with its commands and, secondly, where there is judicial development of the law, any changes must be predictable.
>
> (Council of Europe/European Court of Human Rights 2019: 1)

The definition of an offence must make its meaning clear enough for its effects to be foreseeable so that people can regulate their conduct in advance. Clarity also provides a safeguard against arbitrary prosecution, conviction and punishment.

Consequently, extra-legal behaviour by the police, courts or security services, such as corruption, arbitrary arrest, forced confessions, collusion with criminals, failure to produce warrants, the restriction of access to a lawyer, prolonged remand beyond the legal limit or despite the granting of bail, and illegal searches and seizures, all violate the rule of law.

However, for Dicey, Bingham and other jurists the ubiquity of law has implications for a prominent feature of modern public administration: the delegation of discretionary powers to public officials or special tribunals. This understanding of the rule of law implies that it is incompatible with both. The role of special tribunals in the context of judicial independence will be considered in Chapter 5. As far as administrative discretion is concerned, questions of legal rights should normally be decided by law. This does not mean that the rule of law makes administrative decision-making so inflexible that considerations of humanity and fairness are ruled out. The rule of law does not constrain with such rigidity that 'those in power can exercise no initiative, flexibility, judgement, wisdom, or attention to substance or particulars' (Krygier 2018: 78). Nevertheless, discretion should not be unconstrained and should be testable before the courts for illegality, arbitrariness or unreasonableness (i.e. its procedural and substantive content) (Bingham 2011).

Procedures are thus needed to prevent the abuse of discretionary powers. The rule of law demands that a law which confers a discretionary power to a public body must indicate the scope of that discretion and how it should be exercised rather than left unfettered so that adequate protection against arbitrariness is given to those to whom discretionary decisions apply. If justice requires flexibility and discretion, consequent decisions must be according to rules limiting their scope. This became the widely accepted view of the relationship between the rule of law and discretionary power by the middle of the twentieth century:

> Discretion was accepted, but nevertheless should be constrained by the letter and purpose of the power-conferring law, as well as by other elements of the rule of law, such as that everyone have access to fair procedures before an impartial and independent court, and that the law be applied consistently, equally and in a manner that is not arbitrary or devoid of reason.
>
> (Venice Commission 2011)

The link between this facet of the rule of law and judicial independence is obvious: any breach of law must be established 'before the ordinary courts of the land, not a tribunal of members picked to do the government's bidding, lacking the independence and impartiality which are expected of judges' (Bingham 2011: 4).

Consistency

The rule of law next requires the law to be administered with regularity and consistency. When judges apply the appropriate legal rules, or interpret the law correctly, they serve the rule of law. Consistency here does not refer to the desirability of different statutes affecting the same policy area not being contradictory. It means that all laws should be applied consistently regardless of the nature and status of the parties seeking a judgement. Inconsistency in the application of the law undermines equality and fairness and leaves it unclear as to what penalties will be incurred if the law is broken.

> Simply put, the rule of law requires the law to be clear and to be correctly applied in the right circumstances. Inconsistent judgments that purport to create or apply legal standards breach both requirements. . . . Inconsistent judgments are contradictory at worst or, at best, generate incongruence between the law and its application.
>
> (Higgins 2019: 737, 745)

It follows that judges must be free from bias when applying the law to ensure that the law is predictable and the administration of the law leads to decisions that are regarded as just by all involved, including the general public. In this way arbitrary power is replaced by a system of law: 'If deviations from justice as regularity are too pervasive, a serious question may arise whether a system of law exists as opposed to a collection of particular orders designed to advance the interests of a dictator or the ideal of a benevolent despot' (Rawls 1972: 236).

Consistency in the application of the law is lost if judges are subjected to external pressures, such as political threats or corruption, when applying and interpreting the law in individual cases. Similarly, if judges are swayed by personal prejudices, then the individual will again be uncertain about how to obtain recourse to the law. When verdicts are determined before trials begin, evidence consists of forced confessions, illiterate defendants sign statements without being told their contents or crimes go unprosecuted, the consistency of law is undermined. The absence of legal consistency also allows discrimination against specific groups, especially the poor, ethnic minorities and those lacking political connections.

As with the ubiquity of law, legal consistency also requires laws to be clearly framed and understandable by the layperson. In addition, laws must create general categories. Law is general in that it 'indicates a general type of conduct and applies to a general class of persons who are expected to see that it applies to them and to comply with it' (Hart 1961: 21). The only particular orders which are consistent with the rule of law are rules which govern the application of the law to particular individuals appearing before the courts: '[T]he system must have techniques for the rule-governed application of the law to particulars by the institutions of the system, chiefly to impose the rule of law on its own operation' (Endicott 2013: 8).

Certainty

The rule of law also prescribes that the law should be certain so that actions and transactions are carried out in full knowledge of the legal consequences. Legal certainty requires the law to be easily accessible and legal rules to be clear and precise, allowing legal relationships to be foreseeable. Jurists, especially of the realist persuasion, generally recognize that there can be no absolute certainty of judicial outcomes. Clearly drafted legal provisions must inevitably be subjected to some degree of judicial interpretation. The more the rule of law is identified with the quality of government policies as measured by constitutional provisions (as in its 'thicker' versions), the less certain will be judicial decisions (May 2018), hence the idea that the law should be predictable and foreseeable rather than certain (Linarelli 2017).

Foreseeability means that the law must be proclaimed before it is implemented and predictable in its effects. It should be precise rather than ambiguous so that the citizen knows what is illegal and what legal. Laws must be clear enough to allow citizens to adapt their social and economic behaviour in advance. The wording of relevant provisions, assisted by judicial interpretation and legal advice, should be sufficient for the individual to know what acts or omissions will make her liable to litigation (Council of Europe/European Court of Human Rights 2019).

Foreseeability also offers protection to the rights of the citizen against the state. It means that the courts can decide fairly and impartially on the procedural or substantive 'legitimate expectations' of citizens arising from the state's undertakings, for example to consult before changing a public policy. Laws should not be used to mollify one group by prescribing action that is ineffective in practice so that another group, favoured by the state, can continue to behave in a way which is supposedly illegal but which, because of the poor formulation of the law, can be claimed as legal. Legal certainty also demands coherence in case law to avoid conflicting decisions within supreme or constitutional courts.

Certainty also requires the law to be prospective. Ex post facto law is prohibited by the rule of law. Actions should not be punished retroactively: 'Certainty cannot exist in the criminal law where the law, or the penalty for its breach, is retrospective. Retroactive legislation, especially in criminal matters, is inconsistent with the Rule of Law' (International Commission of Jurists 1966). This principle, enshrined in Article 7 of the European Convention on Human Rights, provides that no one shall be held guilty of any criminal offence on account of any act or omission,

> which did not constitute a criminal offence under national or international law at the time when it was committed. Nor shall a heavier penalty be imposed than the one that was applicable at the time the criminal offence was committed.

However, whether retrospective law fails to respect expectations depends on the extent of the change imposed on existing law. Furthermore, the guidance provided by the law may be reinforced if retrospective law closes loopholes or other unintended interpretations. Strong arguments can be made against a wholesale prohibition of retrospective law (Sampford 2006).

Such arguments have long been made in the case of retributive justice in transitional states, where punishment is sought for those who committed acts under the authoritarian regime which, though morally indefensible, were legal at the time. Retroactive punishment has been defended on the grounds that even under authoritarian regimes abuses perpetrated by agents of the state were often prohibited by law and had to be covert (e.g. in South Africa under apartheid) or that failure to punish extreme immorality such as torture, rape, murder or crimes against humanity would be a greater evil than ignoring the principle that the law should only be prospective (Lenta 2019).

In addition, legal certainty requires respect for the principle of *res judicata* (a matter decided) which prescribes that a matter already settled in court cannot be raised again. Final judgements by domestic courts should not be called into question. Precluding endless litigation guards against injustice, confusion and waste of resources arising from constant reconsideration of a decision: 'Courts are not one's pocket army: their aim is to resolve conflicts and not to maintain them indefinitely' (Gusarov and Terekhov 2019: 8). The quashing of final judgements without reasons of public interest is incompatible with the principle of legal certainty. In this respect the rule of law contrasts with the judicial systems of authoritarian regimes, such as those of the former Soviet bloc. Here different understandings of the rule of law allowed prosecutors to revoke decisions to ensure uniformity in the application of law, courts to review decisions until substantive truth was established, and court presidents to exercise discretionary powers to quash final court decisions (Gusarov and Terekhov 2019).

For the law to be predictable the final judgements of the courts have to be enforceable. Legal certainty or predictability implies that the law can be implemented. For this it has to be implementable. Under the rule of law it is the responsibility of law makers to assess whether the law is implementable in practice and to review how effectively it has been applied.

Natural justice

The rule of law also demands that the law be administered according to the rules of natural justice. These rules govern not only court procedures but also state officials and appointees empowered to take quasi-judicial decisions. Trials and hearings should be conducted in an orderly manner where rules of evidence guarantee rational procedures of inquiry. No one may be 'judge in his own cause'. Trials must be fair and open. Both sides to a case must be heard (*audi alteram partem*). Anyone appearing in court has the right to know the case being made against them and to be given opportunities to respond to it. Judges must be independent and impartial, again underlying the importance of an independent judiciary. Natural justice also requires that the reasons for a judicial decision should be made known to the interested parties. Article 6 (1) of the European Convention on Human Rights stipulates that, following a fair and public hearing by an independent and impartial tribunal established by law, judgement shall be pronounced publicly. Whether the rule of law exists thus depends upon how the law is administered in courts and tribunals rather than how it appears in the statute books.

Equality

Finally, the rule of law entails equality before the law. Under Article 7 of the 1948 Universal Declaration of Human Rights '[a]ll are equal before the law and are entitled without any discrimination to equal protection of the law'. Article 14 of the 1976 International Convention on Civil and Political Rights stipulates that all persons shall be equal before courts and tribunals: 'In the determination of any criminal charge against him, or of his rights and obligations in a suit at law, everyone shall be entitled to a fair and public hearing by a competent, independent and impartial tribunal established by law.'

Equality before the law requires judges to treat like cases alike, only discriminating when the law endorses it.

> Any unjustified unequal treatment under the law is prohibited and all persons have guaranteed equal and effective protection against discrimination on any ground such as race, colour, sex, language, religion, political or other opinion, national or social origin, property, birth or other status.
>
> (Venice Commission 2011: para. 63)

Legal equality is assisted by reasoned arguments for judgements made by reference to the relevant legal rules and principles. Judges cannot depart arbitrarily from the law, a principle which underlines the importance of a judiciary which is not subject to external pressures from politicians, internal prejudices or corrupt links with private interests when deciding how the law should be interpreted.

Equality before the law also means the equality of all persons and classes, including government officials. As a constitutional principle the rule of law means that 'all persons and authorities within the state, whether public or private, should be bound by, and entitled to the benefit of, laws publicly and prospectively promulgated and publicly administered in the courts' (Bingham 2006). No one is above the law, and all are subject to the ordinary courts. This particularly applies to government officials, whether elected or appointed. The legality of their decisions must be subject to judicial review by courts acting independently of the executive and bureaucracy. Thus, citizens need only fear 'the office of the law, not its administrators' (Shklar (quoting Montesquieu) 1998: 23). This applies to both judicial and administrative officials. Pressure on judges to discriminate in favour of the state constitutes arguably the most serious departure from the rule of law.

Judicial review enables challenges to be mounted in court to test whether the decisions and actions taken by servants of the state involve the misuse of public powers. The rule of law allows three such tests: legality, fairness and reasonableness. Decisions or actions may be declared illegal if a legal duty has not been performed or if powers have been exceeded and the public body responsible is ultra vires. Fairness requires procedures prescribed by legislation, as well as the rules of natural justice to have been followed. Decision-makers must thus act impartially and without conflicts of interest. Such procedural propriety 'requires decision-makers to be unbiased and to grant a fair hearing to claimants before depriving them of a right or significant interest' (Jowell 2015: 27). Abuse of power might here include a failure to exercise a statutory duty to consult specified groups, including any with a 'legitimate expectation' of being consulted. A legitimate expectation may also preclude reneging on a promise to provide some benefit.

Finally, judicial review may test the reasonableness, rationality or proportionality of administrative decisions. A court may quash a decision if it considers it so unreasonable as to constitute 'irrationality' or 'perversity' on the part of the decision-maker. Proportionality requires the interests of the community and the legitimate aims of the state to be balanced against the protection of the individual's rights and interests. These concepts will be examined further in the discussion of judicial activism in Chapter 8.

Reference to the 'ordinary courts' in discussions of common law systems may be thought to rule out the use of administrative courts applying a body of administrative law, found in many countries. However, there is no reason to assume that, when the citizen is in conflict with the state, independent adjudication cannot be provided by specialized administrative courts which offer the benefits of a coherent body of law, specialist expertise in the review of administrative action, comprehensive coverage by a small number of easily understood remedies, uniformly applied law, and inexpensive and simple procedures (Brown et al. 1998). Rules of evidence can be relaxed in order to bring out, through an inquisitorial rather than adversarial procedure, all relevant information – from experts as well as citizens and their representatives and the government agencies involved – with hearings taking place within a shorter time frame than is usual for the normal courts (Kmieciak 2013). The acceptability of 'exceptional courts' will be returned to in Chapter 5.

Despite its centrality in the rule of law, judicial review is nevertheless a contentious concept. For if judges rule on political and administrative decisions taken under existing statutes, they run the risk of imposing their own interpretation of the law's intentions over those of the legislature. As will be shown in Chapter 8, this is especially problematic when judicial review extends to constitutional issues such as whether a legislature is entitled to make law in a particular area or seek particular objectives through statutory enactments. This power is often given to the judiciary, through either a constitutional court (in the civil law tradition) or the ordinary courts (in the common law tradition). The practice also varies according to whether the courts can only adjudicate if a dispute is brought before them, or can express a view on proposed legislation, or can investigate any matter which they believe constitutes a violation of human rights. In all cases the courts are inevitably brought into the policy-making process, raising fears about the power of an unelected body to override that of a democratically composed legislature.

The rule of law and the development of democracy

The history of Western political thought since classical antiquity is replete with attempts to justify the subordination of government to the law. Centuries before the modern concept of a democratic state was formulated, the rule of law was regarded as a prerequisite of liberty. Graeco-Roman civilization espoused the belief that 'government must be subject to law, that any other kind of government is tyranny with no sanction behind it but bare force' (Lindsay 1943: 52). The Athenian philosopher Plato argued that the state would collapse without the authority of law. For Aristotle the law represented reason as distinct from the desires and passions perverting the minds of rulers. Supporters of Athenian democracy believed government under law protected society against tyrants, aristocrats and oligarchs. This understanding affected government in over 1,500 city states. 'From a political point of view, the shared commitment to the rule of law soon became a key trait of Greek identity, and therefore the ultimate measure of the legitimacy of any political regime' (Canevaro 2017: 230). During the final years of the Roman Republic in the first century BC, it was possible for the republican scholar Cicero to contrast the rule of law with autocracy.

During the Medieval period in the West, tension between church and state led to 'dynamic interpretations of Roman law and Aristotle . . . symptoms of a social order in which factors pertaining to the rule of law could flourish' (Møller 2017). The concept of law was developed into a restraint on the sovereign's divine authority by identifying it with divine or natural law. It became widely accepted that natural law required monarchs to obey the law in the interest of Christian justice (Tamanaha 2004). In 1215 England's Magna Carta, though originating in the economic interests of the nobility, nevertheless laid 'some cornerstones of English liberty' (Feiling 1952: 160), pronouncing the ubiquity of law in its demand that there be no penalty except by lawful judgement. Building on this foundation, Bracton's treatise on the laws of England (c. 1260) affirmed the rule of law principle that the lawgiver is bound by the law.

As the significance of natural law and divine law waned, absolute monarchy, claiming Divine Right, attempted to free itself from the constraints of law. This trend was obstructed by appeals to the rule of law. Thus, in the early seventeenth century, England's Chief Justice Coke claimed that the law, not the monarch, ruled the kingdom, a claim which clearly implied the rule of law (Gooch 1959: 55). Puritan political thought during the English Civil War advocated the equality of all before the law, impartial adjudication and the abolition of special courts. John Locke's defence of the 1688 Revolution declared that 'whatever form the commonwealth is under, the ruling power ought to govern by declared and received laws, and not by extemporary dictates and undetermined resolutions'. Government under law ensures

> that both the people may know their duty, and be safe and secure within the limits of the law, and the rulers too kept within their due bounds. . . . Wherever law ends tyranny begins . . . whosoever in authority exceeds the power given him by the law, and makes use of the force he has under his command to compass that upon the subject which the law allows not, ceases in that to be a magistrate.
>
> (Locke 1690: 69, 99)

The 1689 Bill of Rights asserted the supremacy of law as delivered by parliament so that 'the Britain which emerged from the Glorious Revolution was one where the rule of law, imperfectly and incompletely, held sway' (Bingham 2011: 25).

In the eighteenth century Montesquieu's *Spirit of the Laws*, published in 1748 and widely regarded as 'the political masterpiece of the age' (Plamenatz 1963: 253), associates the rule of law with the liberty of the individual which suffers unless penalties are imposed only when known laws are broken, judicial procedures protect the innocent, courts are independent, and individual rights can be enforced against executive power: 'by the laws making for freedom as they relate to the citizen, Montesquieu means what is usually meant by the phrase the rule of law' (Plamenatz 1963: 278). The eighteenth century also produced a philosophical innovation which justified the subordination of political power to the law by reference to human rights (Tamanaha 2004). Rights became essential to the rule of law, especially when enshrined in constitutions, notably the American Constitution of 1787, followed in 1789 by ten amendments, collectively known as the Bill of Rights, and in 1868 by the Fourteenth Amendment which prohibits the denial of equal protection of the law, and life, liberty or property without due process of law. The French Declaration of the rights of Man and the Citizen of 1789 declared rights to be natural, inalienable and sacred.

By the early nineteenth century the rule of law was such an important part of democratic government that Alexis de Toqueville found it 'hardly necessary to say that, in a free country like America, all the citizens have the right of indicting public functionaries before the ordinary tribunals, and that all the judges have the power of convicting public officers'. This aspect of the rule of law was 'so natural a one, that it cannot be looked upon as an extraordinary privilege' (Toqueville 1835: 76–77).

In the twentieth century A. D. Lindsay chose the universality and certainty of law as defining features of the modern democratic state: 'If men are to enjoy rights and use the opportunities for life which rights provide, they must be certain that their rights will be protected. One of the greatest virtues a law can have lies in the certainty of its operations.' The 'necessary universality' of law provides 'rules which are known, definite, certain, and promptly enforced' (Lindsay 1943: 207–210).

Throughout the history of Western civilization philosophers have sought to reconcile the legitimate authority of sovereign government with the supremacy of law. It was not until the preservation of fundamental rights became an object of law from the eighteenth century onwards that it appeared possible to square the circle. Rights would be enshrined in constitutions, and the rule of law would protect them through judicial review of legislative enactments. Consequently 'the most frequent solution proposed by the rule of law doctrines is to leverage the judicial control of political decisions. If the political power (the parliamentary majorities in modern democracies) is the danger, defence appears to come from the judiciary' (Costa 2018: 148). The rule of law, to which the rule of the sovereign is subordinated, rests upon those civil and political rights which are preserved by the content of law and its administration. The rule of law underpins both liberties and procedural justice. It prescribes the right to life and liberty and to freedom of thought, speech, association, assembly, religion and the press. It represents political equality. In the administration of the law it stands for a set of principles that embody justice.

However, what appears to make sovereign political authority compatible with the sovereignty of law immediately creates another problem: the reconciliation of judicial power to test new laws against constitutional principles with the authority of democratic government. The more extensive the concept of human rights, the more the judiciary is politicized as it is required to judge whether legislation conflicts with the rights built into the constitution. The lasting effect was to draw judges into the political process as it became necessary for them to test new laws against inviolable rights. As will be shown in Chapter 8, the equation of the rule of law with human rights has endowed judiciaries with powers that have drawn hostility from proponents of democracy and attempts by governments to constrain judicial activism. How the controversial political significance of judicial review of an elected government's legislative programme has affected democracy in post-authoritarian states will be examined further.

Analysis of democratic consolidation in states in transition from authoritarian government has revealed the significance of the rule of law in this process, as well as the setbacks which have been witnessed in most regions of the world. In Latin America democratic consolidation is recognized as dependent upon the protection of universal rights and access to justice, necessary for effective citizenship and the legitimacy of the new regime. The role of the courts is crucial in all this, 'as it is the judiciary that underpins the establishment of rule of law and legal accountability to constitutional norms' (Domingo 1999: 153). In Asia the rule of law is seen as a symbol of the state's transition from authoritarianism: 'The formal submission of political power to the dictates of the rule of law is one of a package of institutions designed to express the break with the past' (Ginsburg 2003: 26). By holding decision-makers accountable to the democratic process through the rule of law, the courts in new democracies 'are important for the working and consolidation of democratic regimes' (Gloppen et al. 2004: 1).

When the rule of law provides a justiciable legal framework for the protection of human rights, consisting of national constitutions, laws, and international treaties, the promotion of human rights and therefore democracy in transitional states becomes more effective. Studies of weak democracies, such as Nepal, Malaysia, Indonesia and Timor Leste, show that a legal framework which protects the political mobilization in non-governmental organizations of poor and marginalized groups and their supporters, and gives such groups access to the courts when rights are infringed by government policies or the forces of law and order, strengthens the realization of human rights, 'even in the context of weak court systems and unresponsive political institutions' (Rosser 2015: 190). If judiciaries are weak, new democracies are unlikely to 'ensure a healthy arrangement of checks and balances on elected officials who may at times test the bounds of constitutionalism' (Prillaman 2000: 2).

The rule of law also enabled the courts in newly formed democracies to educate citizens in the new constitutional rules governing the state by guaranteeing rights and freedoms, especially freedom of speech and assembly, a fair trial and due process. The courts marked a clear departure from the authoritarian past and showed how state power was now limited (Baudoin 2017; Oliveira 2020; Gajduschek 2017), even when the new legal systems were transplanted from Western Europe or the USA and lacked national cultural roots.

The rule of law further supports the consolidation of democracy by protecting the citizen against arbitrary government and ensuring that state officials and institutions operate within the law and constitution. By ruling on the legality of administrative decisions and the constitutionality of legislative acts the courts provide citizens with judicial means of calling officials, both appointed and elected, to account, thereby augmenting the electoral and legislative accountability which underpins democracy. The protection given to human rights by the rule of law and an independent judiciary working within it sustains the individualism which is part of democratic theory. The rule of law is 'linked with the fight of the individual against the absolute power of the State' (Friedmann 1953: 423). The freedom of the individual is dependent upon the rule of law. This includes freedom to associate with others to achieve aims and objectives that cannot be achieved by individuals acting in isolation.

Consequently, most constitutions in transitional countries provide means by which private individuals and groups (and governments themselves in federations) can seek rulings from a judicial authority on the legality or constitutionality of government policies and administrative decisions. Both statutes and decisions made under them can be challenged if their legality is in doubt. Constitutional courts have been set up to evaluate laws challenged before the ordinary courts. In some cases even draft laws may be referred for review. Some constitutions stipulate a separation of powers between executive and judiciary to ensure that disputes with the state are resolved independently of any political interference. Judicial review is sometimes provided for by the establishment of administrative courts to review the legality of official decisions on applications from private individuals, as in Lithuania.

The rule of law also reduces the risk that the sanctions which inevitably support the law do not infringe the citizen's basic human rights. Public policy in a democracy will usually benefit some interests at the expense of others. The rule of law ensures that those who are disadvantaged by collective action feel that it is the result of properly applied decision-making rules. This particularly applies to the election of decision-makers and the operation of the legislative process. Impartial adjudication when elections are thought to be flawed is vital to a democracy. The legality of election campaigns, voter registration, candidate nominations, campaign expenditure, the registration of political parties, the conduct of ballots and counts, and petitions to have a result annulled can all be ruled on to ensure that election results reflect the electorates intentions. If in so doing the courts demonstrate independence and fairness, their legitimacy will be enhanced, which in turn strengthens trust in the electoral process and democracy in general (Kerr and Wahman 2020). For this reason the refusal of the courts to examine complaints about the falsification of the presidential election result in 2008, which the organization for security and co-operation in Europe found to be seriously flawed, seriously undermined the legitimacy of Georgia's government and triggered a political crisis (Georgia Times 2009).

Democracy requires social order, based on a consensus that political procedures are lawful and constitutional. The rule of law helps sustain support for democratic principles by protecting human rights, preventing state officials from placing themselves above the law, and boosting public confidence in the law and the institutions responsible for administering it. The rule of law, together with democratic accountability, constrains power. When society is not protected against arbitrary, oppressive or corrupt decision-making and adjudication, the costs of social disorder as attempts are made to secure reform may seem worth bearing. Conversely, the rule of law will curb anti-social attitudes by resolving conflicts fairly (Testa et al. 2017).

In countries in transition from authoritarianism the rule of law represents a clear break with the past and signifies the emergence of a political culture in which there is respect for the law and those who make and enforce it. Thus, public trust in the South African judiciary, revealed in opinion polls in 2007 which recorded no less than 77 per cent of respondents expressing confidence in the judicial system and the courts, boosts the rule of law in South Africa (Gallup 2008). In contrast, the lack of public confidence in the judiciary to secure basic rights and hold the government to account has undermined the credibility of democratic institutions in Guatemala (Sieder 2004).

Figure 1.1 shows the close relationship between democracy and the rule of law.[1] However, this does not show the direction of causality. In the transition from authoritarianism to democracy, the establishment of democratic constitutions and institutions will invariably include rules and procedures necessary for the rule of law, especially judicial independence and commitment to respect for fundamental civil rights. During democratic consolidation the rule of law supports democracy by ensuring free and fair elections, the legality of government decisions and the protection of human rights.

In both phases the rule of law has the capacity to support democracy. Nevertheless, the principles and institutions which represent the rule of law, especially judicial independence, have proved to be fragile. Democracy requires other defences than the rule of law, and if public support for democracy weakens, perhaps in response to the attractions of zero-sum populist politics, the rule of law is

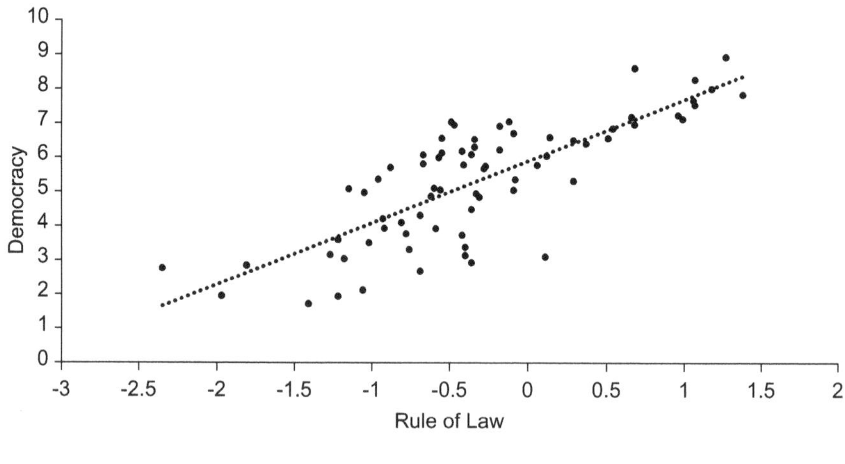

Figure 1.1 Democracy and the Rule of Law, 2020

likely to be an early casualty. Democracy needs to be reinforced by other social and political values and organizations, notably toleration, forbearance, consensus, non-violent protest and a well-developed civil society: 'law has only a weak role in preventing a breakdown of constitutional democracy when democracy is not the only game in town and when democratic support for constitutional checks and balances is eroding' (Bugaric 2019: 450).

Democratic constitutions and the rule of law

A crucial feature of the transition from authoritarianism to democracy has been the removal of violations of the rule of law from the authoritarian statute books and constitutional documents in order to put an end to practices by the political executive which undermined the independence of the judiciary. Such practices included merging the judiciary and the executive (in Uruguay in the 1970s), changing the terms of employment in order to remove uncooperative justices (as in Bangladesh in 1977), suspending the operation of courts, refusing to execute court judgements, using the law to punish critics and opponents (Burma), pre-empting judicial resolution of disputes by constitutional amendment, passing retroactive legislation to reverse judicial decisions, using ad hoc tribunals which ignore the protections offered by the ordinary courts, and allocating cases in order to affect their outcome (Shetreet 1985).

In order to distance themselves from their authoritarian predecessors, the constitution-builders in transitional countries incorporated the rule of law as basic principles enshrined in constitutional documents. When specific reference is made to the rule of law it is usually either as a defining characteristic of the state or presented in its constituent parts. Examples of the former are Armenia where, in an attempt to 'to come closer to the European standards in the areas of the rule of law and the judiciary' (Mouradian 2012: 1197), Article 1 of the 1995 Constitution describes the Republic of Armenia is a sovereign, democratic, social, and rule of law state. Post-authoritarian constitutions in Belarus, Estonia, and Indonesia also create states founded on the rule of law. Article 1 of the 1991 Constitution of Romania envisions a democratic and social state, governed by the rule of law, 'a natural consequence of the declared shift of political orientation, and also a requirement for the country's acceptance as a potential member of the European organisations' (Selejan-Gutan 2016). The 1993 Constitution of the Czech Republic defines the state as sovereign, unitary, and democratic and governed by the rule of law. In addition, Articles 37–40 contain the prescription of due process. Article 1 of Egypt's 2014 Constitution describes a democratic republic based on citizenship and the rule of law, reasserted in Article 94 which makes the rule of law 'the basis of governance in the state'.

A number of constitutions include fundamental human rights as part of the rule of law, including positive social and economic rights in addition to civil and political rights. For example, the Fundamental Law of Hungary makes the state responsible for the application of individual and collective rights: 'The inviolable and inalienable fundamental rights of man shall be respected. It is the primary obligation of the State to protect these rights' (Article 1). The Constitution guarantees fundamental rights to everyone without discrimination, in particular on grounds of race, colour, sex, disability, language, religion, political or other opinion, national or social origin, property, birth or any other status. The Hungarian Constitutional Court can be asked to establish whether the government is in breach of constitutionally enshrined rights by *failing* to legislate. When the 1996 South African Constitution was adopted as the supreme law of the Republic, it also established a society based on fundamental human rights and freedoms, including equality, human dignity, security, and freedom of religion, belief and opinion. Chapter 2 contains a Bill of Rights which applies to all law and binds the legislature, the executive, the judiciary and all organs of state. Amendments to the Constitution of Argentina in 1994 also guarantee full enjoyment of political rights.

In addition to civil and political rights, the post-authoritarian constitutions have often included declarations of social and economic rights. For example, the Polish Constitution guarantees the right to equal compensation for work of similar value, to social security, a minimum level of remuneration, safe and hygienic conditions of work, statutorily specified days free from work, as well as annual paid holidays, social security for unemployment and old age, health care, and education. Public authorities are further required to ensure special health care to children, pregnant women, handicapped people and persons of advanced age; combat epidemic illnesses; prevent the negative health consequences of degradation of the environment; support the development of physical culture, particularly among children and young persons; and provide aid to disabled persons. The state, in its social and economic policy, is also required to take into account the good of the family. Families in social and material difficulty, particularly those with many children or a single parent, have the right to special assistance from public authorities.

South Africa's Bill of Rights includes access to adequate housing, health care, sufficient food and water, social security, and basic education, including adult basic education and further education. The response of constitution builders in Morocco, Tunisia and Egypt to the escalation of protests during the Arab Spring of 2011 was to add to the list of rights, reinforcing existing political rights and extending social, economic and community rights. For example, the new Constitution of Tunisia recognizes rights to strike, work, equal pay, a safe work environment, health care, education, water, support for the disabled, protection of the family, scientific and technological research, culture, and sport. Special attention is given to the rights of women, children and minorities in all three Constitutions. The Moroccan states that men and women enjoy equally the rights and freedoms of a civil, political, economic, social, cultural and environmental character (Porras-Gómez 2020).

Some constitutions make specific reference to the individual principles which comprise the rule of law, especially due process and judicial independence. For example, the 1997 Constitution of Poland devotes numerous articles to rule of law principles: no one shall be compelled to do that which is not required by law; all persons shall be equal before the law; only a person who has committed an act prohibited by a statute in force at the moment of commission shall be held criminally responsible; deprivation or limitation of liberty may be imposed only in accordance with principles and under procedures specified by statute; and everyone shall have the right to a fair and public hearing, without undue delay, before a competent, impartial and independent court: 'Thus, in the area of personal and political rights, an entirely new system of law emerged, providing genuinely effective procedures to challenge official transgression of due process guarantees' (Brzezinski 1998: 110). Courts and tribunals constitute a separate power, independent of other branches of power, and provision is made for judicial review.

Similarly, the Bill of Rights in the 1996 Constitution of South Africa makes everyone equal before the law and prohibits arbitrary deprivation of freedom or detention without trial. It gives a right to administrative action that is lawful, reasonable and procedurally fair and to have any dispute that can be resolved by the application of law decided in a fair public hearing. The rights of arrested, detained and accused persons are specified. What constitutes a fair trial is described in detail. Article 165 provides for judicial independence and 172 for judicial review. The Constitution was regarded as having entrenched human rights 'as a cornerstone of South African democracy' and provided 'a basis for developing a human-rights culture in South Africa' (Sarkin 1999: 86).

Trends in the rule of law

Despite legal and constitutional reforms to enshrine the rule of law generally and the independence of the judiciary in particular in transitional democracies, protecting the rule of law has proved to be one of the most difficult tasks in the context of growing authoritarianism.

The strength of the rule of law is dependent on a number of factors. Consequently, departures from the rule of law take many different forms. Problems for the rule of law are not exclusively the result of political interference in judicial decision-making. Other factors include legalized discrimination against minorities and political opponents; the slavery of migrant workers; excessive periods spent in oppressive prison conditions for those on remand, including severe overcrowding and lack of access to healthcare; bad law enforcement practices, including arbitrary arrest and detention, detention without warrants, ill treatment at police stations, confessions obtained under duress, and an unwillingness to prosecute the rich and powerful; the involvement of the police with organized crime; abuses of the rights of suspects; procedural defects in pre-trial investigations; a lack of independence among state prosecutors; assumptions within judicial practice that defendants are guilty rather than innocent; and the low quality of the counsel to which poorer citizens have access. While in theory it is conceivable that judges could arbitrate fairly and independently on the basis of all the evidence, including that obtained illegally, it is difficult in practice to believe that judges could conduct hearings in ignorance of how the evidence before them was obtained. The ill treatment of suspects is thus another way of interference in judicial decision-making and distorting the course of justice.

A key factor associated with the anti-democratic resurgence during the past 20 years in post-authoritarian countries is a global decline in the rule of law. The independence and impartiality of judicial systems have been undermined. Human rights violations have further weakened the rule of law. Between 2005 and 2010 the dominant cause of democratic decline was the retreat from the rule of law (Diamond 2015). The rule of law suffered further decline in 2011 and 2012, 'reflecting a global erosion of judicial independence, unequal application of the law, arbitrary detention, and various other human rights violations by both state and non-state forces' (Puddington 2011). Between 2017 and 2020 more countries recorded a decline in the rule of law than achieving an improvement. In all regions of the world a majority of countries have either remained unchanged or regressed (World Justice Project 2020).

The post-communist states have recorded a persistent decline in the rule of law since 2000, especially in Eurasia. Eight of the 12 non-Baltic former Soviet republics are authoritarian regimes in which the rule of law is largely absent. The states of Central Europe, the Balkans and Eurasia continue to depart further from the rule of law or fail to recover ground lost since 2000. Political involvement in the management and financing of the courts, the appointment of judges, and disciplinary procedures account for most of the damage to the rule of law, but illegalities in police procedures have played an important part. The increasingly illiberal democracies of Eastern and Central Europe have devised numerous techniques to ensure their actions avoid veto by the courts: changing the composition of supreme and constitutional courts, lowering the retirement age for judges, dismissing and reassigning judges, altering appointment procedures, removing a court's powers and changing court procedures. The formal institutions of the rule of law remain but are fundamentally compromised (Sajo and Tuovinen 2018).

In Hungary the decline in the rule of law has taken not only the form of governmental interference in the administration of the courts but also political involvement in the National Judicial Office (NJO), responsible for the management and financing of the courts; and a lack of action on overcrowded and unhealthy prisons. In 2019 the Polish government pushed through legislation enabling political interference in the appointment of judges to the Constitutional Court, the membership of the National Council of the Judiciary, disciplinary procedures, judges' freedom of expression and association, and the participation of judges in the administration of justice. Although Ukraine's new government has embarked on reforms, the legal process can still be manipulated to their own advantage by people with wealth and political connections. In Belarus the courts are controlled by the executive branch, trials in political cases are rarely free and fair, the police act illegally with impunity and lawyers are subject to abuse from members of the government. In many parts of Eastern and Central Europe the courts have become instrument for attacking the political opposition. The governments of Belarus, Azerbaijan and Kazakhstan used control of the judiciary to punish political dissent inspired by the 'Arab Spring'.

The rule of law is equally fragile in the post-military regimes of Latin America. Courts have remained vulnerable to political interference, judicial proceedings are subject to corruption, police powers are abused, fair trials are jeopardized by long delays and shortages of defence lawyers for poor clients, and economic interests favoured by the government are allowed to break the law with impunity. A new form of militarism has evolved with detrimental effects on the rule of law. Civilian governments increasingly rely on the military to shore up their power. In the name of public order and security, governments have bestowed extra-legal powers on the military. Consequently, the rule of law falls victim to the empowerment of the military to adjudicate on, and prosecute in, civil cases, despite departures from due process and compromised impartiality (Rios-Figueroa 2019).

In Argentina, with the exception of the federal Supreme Court, the courts remain vulnerable to political interference, judicial proceedings are subject to delays and corruption, and the police abuse their powers arbitrarily. In Brazil the rule of law has been compromised by judicial corruption, and the police in the larger cities have been involved with organized crime and local private militias that extort protection money from residents. Fair trials are jeopardized by long delays, a shortage of defence lawyers for poor clients and the use of military courts for trials of military personnel accused of offences against civilians. Mexico introduced significant judicial reforms in the mid-1990s, including judicial review, but the criminal justice system is still affected by corruption, inefficiency and the failure of police to investigate offences. Party political influence over the judiciary is strong in Nicaragua, and due process is compromised by the abuse of police powers and procedures.

The former Asian autocracies that are attempting to create democratic regimes are also finding it hard to protect the rule of law. The transition from military rule to democracy in Burma was checked by political control of the judiciary, widespread interference in the administration of justice, and administrative powers which allow suspects in special cases to be held without charge, legal counsel or trial for a maximum of five years. Democratic gains in Indonesia since 1998 have been offset by judicial corruption, religious interference in the judicial process, and abuse of police powers affecting arrests, interrogations and access to legal representation. The rule of law is compromised in Cambodia by corruption and politicization in the judiciary and abuse of police powers. In Thailand emergency powers, political interference in the judiciary and the use of *lese majeste* laws have limited the support which the rule of law can give to human rights (Thompson and McCarthy 2020).

A small number of democratic reforms in the Middle East and North Africa have had mixed results for the rule of law. It has been a victim of the military coup in Egypt in 2013 with the new authoritarian government characterized by increased presidential powers over judicial appointments and discipline, the use of emergency powers and expansion of the civil jurisdiction of military courts which regularly disregard the rules of due process. Civilians can also be tried in Tunisia's military courts, a practice which constitutes a departure from the rule of law despite democratic progress following the revolution of 2011. In addition, both the Supreme Council of the Judiciary and the Supreme Council of Magistrates remain too closely aligned with the executive.

Post-authoritarian Africa has seen significant reforms, but the fair administration of justice is adversely affected by poverty and abuse of due process. The rule of law in Nigeria is compromised by corruption and other forms of misconduct by sitting judges, and state-level courts are vulnerable to political pressures.

In Uganda, the rule of law is obstructed by corruption, political pressure on prosecutors and the appointment of judges on political criteria. Growing political interference in South Africa's courts threatens to weaken the substantial autonomy enjoyed in the post-apartheid era. In Tanzania, the rule of law is compromised by the presidential appointment of all judges and 'weak procedures of judiciary appointment, inadequate resources and poor remuneration of judicial personnel' (Legal and Human Rights Centre 2013: 41). In Zimbabwe, the rule of law struggles against the politicization of the judiciary. Though stipulated by the constitution, the rules and principles of due process are not enforced. Police and security personnel

> frequently ignore basic rights regarding detention, searches, and seizures, and accused persons are often held and interrogated for hours without legal counsel or explanation of the reason for their arrest. Lawyers also face detention and arrest on spurious charges. Perceived opponents of the regime faced arrests and detentions throughout 2020.
>
> (Freedom House 2021)

Because the principles embodied in the rule of law entail the involvement of many different organizations, individual countries can exhibit internal variations in the quality of different facets of the rule of law. So while Indonesia ranks fairly high on the clarity of its laws, the rule of law is weak when measured by corruption and access to civil justice. In Brazil the system of civil justice is accessible, but court decisions are difficult to enforce. In Argentina there is political interference in the judiciary, but the courts are accessible, giving people better access to legal counsel in civil disputes than in some more developed democracies. The Philippines also presents contrasts, especially between the independence of the judiciary compared with deficient enforcement mechanisms, corruption among judges and law enforcement officers, and the lengthy duration of cases. In the Czech Republic the courts are independent but very slow. Croatia's judicial system, while generally accessible, also operates too slowly and in addition is subject to political influence and corruption. In Ghana the system of justice is relatively independent but still inaccessible to most people (Agrast et al. 2011). Instances of all such defects can be found among the newly democratizing countries and may be found even when judicial independence is strong.

The will to reform on the part of political leaders and the demand for reform of international donors has meant that the legal framework for democratic governance has improved. Yet in many countries there is a yawning gulf between laws and implementation, whether because of scarcity of resources, lack of institutional capacity or lack of political will, especially if political leaders fear the threat to their power posed by strong judicial institutions.

The rule of law and social inequality

It would be a mistake to think of the rule of law as dependent solely upon institutional factors. It can be undermined by social factors, especially poverty and inequality. In fact, inequality before the law is in large measure a function of poverty. Social inequality undermines the rule of law in many new democracies. Corruption, political bias on the part of individual judges and inefficiency in the management of cases, all found in a large number of democratizing states, violate the principle of equality before the law because they are disproportionately burdensome for the poor. The poor provide most of the victims of departures from the rule of law. This can mean that large sectors of the population believe there is no equality before the law. In 2019 only 19 per cent of respondents agreed that the courts in Georgia treat all citizens equally (Thornton and Turmanidze 2020).

Corruption impedes equal access to justice because the poor are unable to purchase favourable decisions or hire good lawyers capable of pleading their cause successfully without having to bribe judges. Bias within the judiciary usually means that political and business elites can prolong the judicial process through appeals or even halt proceedings altogether with the support of sympathetic judges. The poor have no such opportunities.

Inefficiency due to a lack of resources amounts to a denial of natural justice and basic rights, despite constitutional guarantees of due process, fair trials and legal representation. In particular, shortages of defence lawyers mean that those without resources, including political connections, have great difficulty obtaining a fair hearing. In Brazil, there is an acute shortage of public defenders on which the poor depend for independent legal representation. Some 10,000 additional public defenders are needed if adequate legal representation is to be available to those on low incomes. This problem has been exacerbated in some countries when the legal profession has been subject to repression because its human rights work has been in opposition to government policy. Restrictive legislative changes and punitive measures targeting individual lawyers in Azerbaijan, Tajikistan, Kazakhstan and Crimea have undermined the right of equal access to justice (Freedom House 2018).

Even where corruption is absent, judges are impartial and the administration of justice reasonably efficient, equality before the law is still restricted by poverty. The cost of hiring a lawyer is beyond most people in the poorer transitional countries, and few poor countries can afford to provide legal aid. In Albania, despite a constitutional guarantee that in criminal proceedings free defence will be provided to those without sufficient means, legal counsel is not always provided to those that cannot afford their own. In Hungary, where the cost of litigation is relatively high, access to legal aid is limited, and there are concerns about the quality of lawyers appointed for poorer defendants. In Brazil defendants who are unable to afford a lawyer are not always provided with counsel by the state, contributing to problems of access to justice in a country with a high level of income inequality. The right to legal counsel in Chile is constitutionally guaranteed, but poor defendants do not always receive effective legal representation. Many defendants in Zambian courts lack access to legal aid because of limited resources in the judiciary. As South Africa's Justice Makume points out, we live in 'a time when people around the globe, especially poor persons, are denied access to justice as they are unable to afford lawyers or if they can afford, their funds may dry out as such persons cannot sustain the costs associated with continued litigation'.

These costs include fees for filing documents and the often unregulated tariffs charged by legal practitioners. Civil justice may be more problematic than criminal. In South Africa, for example, 85 per cent of the budget of legal aid is spent on criminal legal services (Klaaren 2019).

In criminal justice Systems the rich are less likely than the poor to be arrested, prosecuted and convicted, partly because they can afford to hire good lawyers and bribe legal officers and partly because the poor have insufficient education to understand legal procedures, especially when conducted in English (Balogun 2020). A lack of basic knowledge of the justice system 'is a serious impediment to accessing justice, in particular for the poor who are less likely to be familiar with their rights' (Lima and Gomez 2020: 9). Other barriers to justice for the poor include the location and design of court premises and the jargon used in legal proceedings. Those dependent on state welfare benefits may well have to consider the risk of provoking retaliation by legal challenges to those in authority (Abregu 2001).

The attitudes of the legal profession towards the poor constitute another barrier to justice. Traditional attitudes often undermine legal provisions designed to assist disadvantaged groups such as those outlawing polygamy, child marriages and 'honour' killings, for example. New laws protecting human rights often remain unimplemented. Patronage, kinship and other social connections, rather than legal rules, influence the decisions of judges to the disadvantage of those not well placed in the social hierarchy. Legal traditions sometimes emphasize social control and the suppression of dissent rather than the protection of rights. Consequently the poor and other marginalized groups view the law with resignation, scepticism or indifference and as something traditionally used against them and in the interests of the wealthy. So even when the rule of law is given prominence in the objectives of national governments, 'it remains an alien concept to the majority of the world's poor' (Asian Development Bank 2001: 30).

The detrimental effect of poverty on the rule of law shows that while a particular policy agenda should not be equated with the rule of law, some policy interventions may be required before the benefits of the rule of law are accessible to all. If the law is to protect all equally, it may be necessary for governments to ameliorate poverty and inequality so that they no longer constitute obstacles to justice. Public policies may further be needed to ensure that the protection from discrimination enshrined in the Universal Declaration of Human Rights is guaranteed.

Consequently, the United Nations, in planning the post-2015 sustainable development goals (SDGs), has identified the rule of law as necessary for socio-economic development, poverty reduction and access to justice (SDG 16). The rule of law is thus understood to be in a reciprocal relationship with social development, providing access to justice for marginalized sections of society and being in turn facilitated by social conditions which support the judicial processes central to the rule of law. Initially, member states appeared agreed that the post-2015 development agenda should promote, among other values, the rule of law, recognizing it is essential for sustainable socio-economic development and poverty reduction. However, in 2014 a number of governments, including China, India and Russia, withdrew support for the rule of law as an internationally agreed goal, preferring instead 'access to justice', or making it easier for people to get into court, but without guarantees of due process, a fair trial in criminal cases, or an independent and impartial judge.

The rise of authoritarianism has had an adverse effect globally on progress in the implementation of SDG 16. A lack of political will is a major cause of failure to promote the rule of law generally and equal access to justice in particular. A failure to devote adequate resources to these objectives explains why in many countries public awareness of rights remains low, and judicial systems lack sufficient numbers of trained personnel to ensure the efficient investigation and adjudication of cases. Of particular concern is the rate of pre-trial detention and the vulnerability of detainees to torture, extortion, disease and arbitrary violations of police procedures. Little progress has been made in promoting the rule of law or increasing access to justice (Hope 2020).

* * *

The rule of law is crucial to the practice of democratic government and politics. This is reflected in the constitutions of transitional states. While the rule of law should not be defined in terms of particular public policies, its association with fundamental civil and political rights can reconcile the legitimate authority of sovereign government with the supremacy of law. The preservation of fundamental rights has become an object of law, making it possible to legitimize the subordination of political authority to a higher law. However, the inclusion of social and economic rights in post-authoritarian constitutions inevitably draws the judiciary, through judicial review, into the policy-making process, leading to accusations that judges are usurping the powers of democratically elected representatives.

Nevertheless, judicial independence is a prerequisite for each of the constituent principles of the rule of law. Ubiquitous law entails breaches of the law being established by independent and impartial judges if there are to be no offences or punishments other than prescribed by law. Certainty presupposes that judgements will be determined by the law and not personal prejudice. Regularity requires judges to apply laws that are appropriate to the case, free from bias induced by external pressures or their own world views. Judges must be independent if the law is to be applied consistently, regardless of the social standing, political status or economic power of the litigants. Only independent judges will ensure that the rules of natural justice are observed in court proceedings. Equality before the law assumes judges will discriminate only when the law endorses it. The next chapter dismantles the concept of judicial independence in order to better understand its relationship to the consolidation of democracy.

Note

1 The chart is derived from scores awarded by the World Bank and Economist Intelligence Unit. The World Bank's Worldwide Governance Indicators (WGI) project reports aggregate and individual governance indicators for 215 economies over the period 1996–2020, for six dimensions of governance: voice and accountability; political stability and absence of violence; government effectiveness; regulatory quality; rule of law; and control of corruption. These aggregate indicators combine the views of a large number of

enterprise, citizen and expert survey respondents in industrial and developing countries. They are based on over 30 individual data sources produced by a variety of survey institutes, think tanks, non-governmental organizations, international organizations, and private sector firms. The composite measures of governance range from −2.5 to 2.5, with higher values corresponding to better governance.

The Economist Intelligence Unit's Democracy Index provides a snapshot of the state of democracy worldwide for 165 independent states and two territories. The Democracy Index is based on five categories: electoral process and pluralism, civil liberties, the functioning of government, political participation and political culture. Each category has a rating on a 0-to-10 scale, and the overall index of democracy is the simple average of the five category indexes. The category indexes are based on the sum of the indicator scores in the category, converted to a 0-to-10 scale. See Economist Intelligence Unit 2020.

References

Abregu, M. (2001), 'Barricades or obstacles: the challenges of access to justice' in R. V. Van Puymbroeck (ed.), *Comprehensive Legal and Judicial Development*, Washington, DC: The World Bank.

Agrast, M., J. Botero and A. Ponce (2011), *WJP Rule of Law Index 2011*, Washington, DC: The World Justice Project.

Allen, T. R. S. (1985), 'Legislative supremacy and the rule of law: democracy and constitutionalism', *Cambridge Law Journal*, vol. 44, no. 1.

Aristotle (1962 edition), *The Politics*, translated with an Introduction by T. A. Sinclair, Harmondsworth: Penguin Books.

Asian Development Bank (2001), *Legal Empowerment: Advancing Good Governance and Poverty Reduction*, Manila: ADB.

Balogun, V. (2020), 'Realising access to justice for the poor: lessons from working with rural communities' in E. Durojaye and G. Mirugi-Mukundi (eds.), *Exploring the Link Between Poverty and Human Rights in Africa*, Pretoria: Pretoria University Press.

Baudoin, M.-E. (2017), 'Constitutional Law as a mirror of transition to liberal democracy and its backsliding in Eastern Europe' in F. Balázs and G.-O. Fruzsina (eds.), *Central and Eastern European Socio Political and Legal Transition Revisited*, Central and Eastern European Forum for Legal, Political and Social Theory Yearbook, Frankfurt am Main: Peter Lang.

Bedner, A. (2018), ' The promise of a thick view' in C. May and A. Winchester (eds.), *Handbook on the Rule of Law*, Cheltenham: Edward Elgar.

Bingham, T. (2006), 'The Rule of Law', lecture to the Centre for Public Law, University of Cambridge, www.cpl.law.cam.au.uk/past_activities

Bingham, T. (2011), *The Rule of Law*, London: Penguin Books.

Brown, L. N., J. Bell and J.-M. Galabert (1998), *French Administrative Law*, Oxford: Oxford University Press.

Brzezinski, M. (1998), *The Struggle for Constitutionalism in Poland*, Basingstoke: Macmillan.

Bugaric, B. (2019), 'Can law protect democracy? Legal institutions as "speed bumps"', *Hague Journal on the Rule of Law*, vol. 11, nos. 2–3.

Canevaro, M. (2017), 'The Rule of Law as the measure of political legitimacy in the Greek city states', *Hague Journal on the Rule of Law*, vol. 9, no. 2.

Carlin, R. E. (2012), 'Rule of Law typologies in contemporary societies', *Justice System Journal*, vol. 33, no. 2.

Carlin, R. E. and R. Sarsfield (2012), 'Rethinking the Rule of Law: concepts, measures, and theory', *Justice System Journal*, vol. 33, no. 2.

Costa, P. (2018), 'The rule of law: an outline of its historical foundation' in C. May and A. Winchester (eds.), *Handbook on the Rule of Law*, Cheltenham: Edward Elgar.
Council of Europe/European Court of Human Rights (2019), *The 'Quality of Law' Requirements and the Principle of (Non)-Retrospectiveness of the Criminal Law under Article 7 of the Convention*, Strasbourg: Council of Europe.
Craig, P. P. (2016), 'Formal and substantive conceptions of the rule of law: an analytical framework', in R. Bellamy (ed.), *The Rule of Law and the Separation of Powers*, Abingdon: Routledge.
Diamond, L. (2015), 'Facing up to the democratic recession', *Journal of Democracy*, vol. 26, no. 1.
Dicey, A. V. (1885), *An Introduction to the Study of the Law of the Constitution*, 2009 edition, Charleston, SC: Bibliobazaar.
Domingo, P. (1999), 'Judicial independence and judicial reform in Latin America' in A. Schedler, L. Diamond and M. F. Plattner (eds.), *The Self-Restraining State: Power and Accountability in New Democracies*, London: Lynne Rienner.
Dworkin, R. (1985), *A Matter of Principle*, Cambridge: Cambridge University Press.
Endicott, T. (2013), 'The generality of law' in L. D. Almeida, A. Dolcetti and J. Edwards (eds.), *Reading the Concept of Law*, Oxford: Hart Publishing.
Feiling, K. (1952), *A History of England*, London: Macmillan.
Foran, M. P. (2019), 'The rule of good law: form, substance, and fundamental rights', *The Cambridge Law Journal*, vol. 78, no. 3.
Freedom House (2018), *Freedom in the World, Democracy in Crisis*, New York: Freedom House.
Freedom House (2021), *Freedom in the World: Democracy Under Siege*, New York: Freedom House.
Friedmann, W. (1953), *Legal Theory*, 3rd edition, London: Stevens.
Gajduschek, G. (2017), '"The opposite is true . . . as well": inconsistent values and attitudes in Hungarian legal culture: empirical evidence from and speculation over Hungarian survey data' in F. Balázs and G.-O. Fruzsina (eds.), *Central and Eastern European Socio-political and Legal Transition Revisited*, Central and Eastern European Forum for Legal, Political and Social Theory Yearbook, Frankfurt am Main: Peter Lang.
Gallup (2008), 'In South Africa, high level of confidence in judiciary', www.gallop.com/poll/south-africa
Georgia Times (2009), 'Conservatives will appeal against election results', 6 January, www.georgiatimes.info/en
Ginsburg, T. (2003), *Judicial Review in New Democracies: Constitutional Courts in Asian Cases*, Cambridge: Cambridge University Press.
Gloppen, S., R. Gargarella and E. Skaar (eds.) (2004), *Democratization and the Judiciary: The Accountability Function of Courts in New Democracies*, London: Frank Cass.
Gooch, G. P. (1959), *English Democratic Ideas of the Seventeenth Century*, Cambridge: Cambridge University Press.
Gusarov, K. and V. Terekhov (2019), 'Finality of judgments in civil cases and related considerations: the experience of Ukraine and Lithuania', *Access to Justice in Eastern Europe*, vol. 4, no. 5.
Hart, H. L. A. (1961), *The Concept of Law*, London: Oxford University Press.
Helmke, G. and F. Rosenbluth (2009), 'Regimes and the rule of law: judicial independence in comparative perspective', *Annual Review of Political Science*, vol. 12.
Higgins, A. A. (2019), 'The Rule of Law case against inconsistency and in favour of mandatory civil legal process', *Oxford Journal of Legal Studies*, vol. 39, no. 4.

Holmes, S. (2003), 'Lineages of the Rule of Law' in J. M. Maravall and A. Przeworski (eds.), *Democracy and the Rule of Law*, Cambridge: Cambridge University Press.

Hope, K. R. (2020), 'Peace, justice and inclusive institutions: overcoming challenges to the implementation of Sustainable Development Goal 16', *Global Change, Peace and Security*, vol. 32, no. 1.

International Commission of Jurists (1966), *Human Rights and the Rule of Law: Principles and Definitions*, Geneva: International Commission of Jurists.

Jowell, J. J. (2011), 'The Rule of Law and its underlying values' in J. Jowell and D. Oliver (eds.), *The Changing Constitution*, Oxford: Oxford University Press.

Jowell, J. J. (2015), 'The rule of law: a practical and universal concept' in J. J. Jowell, J. C. Thomas and J. van Zyl Smit (eds.), *The Importance of the Rule of Law in Promoting Development*, Singapore: Singapore Academy of Law and Bingham Centre for the Rule of Law.

Kerr, N. and M. Wahman (2020), 'Electoral rulings and public trust in African courts and elections', *Comparative Politics*, vol. 53, no. 2.

Klaaren, J. (2019), 'What does justice cost in South Africa? A research method towards affordable legal services', *South African Journal on Human Rights*, vol. 35, no. 3.

Kmieciak, Z. (2013), 'The efficiency of administrative courts (in the light of European and Polish experience)', *Comparative Law Review*, vol. 15, no. 1.

Krygier, M. (2018), 'Arbitrary power and the ideal of the rule of law' in C. May and A. Winchester (eds.), *Handbook on the Rule of Law*, Cheltenham: Edward Elgar.

Legal and Human Rights Centre (2013), *Tanzania Human Rights Report 2012*, Dar es Salaam: Legal and Human Rights Centre.

Lenta, P. (2019), 'Transitional justice and retributive justice', *Ethical Theory and Moral Practice*, vol. 22, no. 1.

Lima, V. and M. Gomez (2020), 'Access to justice: promoting the legal system as a human right' in W. Leal Filho et al. (eds.), *Peace, Justice and Strong Institutions Peace*, Cham: Springer International Publishing.

Linarelli, J. (2017), 'Legal certainty: a common law view and a critique' in M. Fenwick, M. M. Siems and S. Wrbka (eds.), *The Shifting Meaning of Legal Certainty in Comparative and Transnational Law*, Oxford: Hart Publishing.

Lindsay, D. A. (1943), *The Modern Democratic State*, 1962 edition, Oxford: Oxford University Press.

Locke, J. (1690), *The Second Treatise of Civil Government*, 1948 edition, Oxford: Blackwell.

May, C. (2018), 'The centrality of predictability to the rule of law' in C. May and A. Winchester (eds.), *Handbook on the Rule of Law*, Cheltenham: Edward Elgar.

Merkel, W. (2013), 'Measuring the quality of Rule of Law: virtues, perils, results' in M. Zürn, A. Nollkaemper and R. Peerenboom (eds.), *Rule of Law Dynamics in an Era of International and Transnational Governance*, Cambridge: Cambridge University Press.

Møller, J. (2017), 'Medieval origins of the Rule of Law: the Gregorian reforms as critical juncture?', *Hague Journal on the Rule of Law*, vol. 7, no. 2.

Moller, J. and S.-E. Skaaning (2014), *The Rule of Law: Definitions, Measures, Patterns and Causes*, Basingstoke: Palgrave Macmillan.

Mouradian, G. (2012), 'Independence of the judiciary in Armenia' in A. Seibert-Fohr (ed.), *Judicial Independence in Transition*, Berlin: Springer.

Oliveira, M. R. (2020), 'Constitutional courts in transitions to democracy: limits, critiques and possibilities in Brazil and Argentina', *Latin American Law Review*, no. 5.

Plamenatz, J. (1963), *Man and Society*, vol. 1, London: Longmans.

Porras-Gómez, A. (2020), 'The new Arab Bills of Rights: a study on the Constitutions of Egypt, Morocco and Tunisia', *Global Journal of Comparative Law*, vol. 9, no. 1.
Prillaman, W. C. (2000), *The Judiciary and Democratic Decay in Latin America: Declining Confidence in the Rule of Law*, London: Praeger.
Puddington, A. (2011), 'Freedom in the world 2011: the authoritarian challenge to democracy' in *Freedom in the World 2011*, New York: Freedom House.
Rawls, J. (1972), *A Theory of Justice*, Oxford: Oxford University Press.
Raz, J. (1979), *The Authority of Law: Essays on Law and Morality*, Oxford: Oxford University Press.
Rios-Figueroa, J. (2019), 'The "new militarism" and the rule of law in Latin American democracies' in R. Sieder, K. Ansolabehere and T. Alfonso (eds.), *Routledge Handbook of Law and Society in Latin America*, Abingdon: Routledge.
Rishmawi, M. (2018), 'The rule of law and human rights' in C. May and A. Winchester (eds.), *Handbook on the Rule of Law*, Cheltenham: Edward Elgar.
Rosser, A. (2015), 'Realising rights in low quality democracies: instructive Asian cases', *Asian Studies Review*, vol. 39, no. 2.
Sajo, A. and J. Tuovinen (2018), 'The rule of law and legitimacy in emerging illiberal democracies', *Osteuropa Recht*, vol. 64, no. 4.
Sampford, C. (2005), 'Reconceiving the rule of law for a globalizing world' in S. Sifcak (ed.), *Globalisation and the Rule of Law*, London: Routledge.
Sampford, C. (2006), *Retrospectivity and the Rule of Law*, Oxford: Oxford University Press.
Sarkin, J. (1999), 'The drafting of South Africa's final constitution from a human-rights perspective', *American Journal of Comparative Law*, vol. 47, no. 1.
Selejan-Gutan, B. (2016), *The Constitution of Romania: A Contextual Analysis*, Oxford: Hart Publishing.
Shetreet, S. (1985), 'Judicial independence: new conceptual dimensions and contemporary challenges' in S. Shetreet and J. Deschenes (eds.), *Judicial Independence: The Contemporary Debate*, Dordrecht: Martinus Nijhoff.
Shklar, J. N. (1998), *Political Thought and Political Thinkers*, Chicago: University of Chicago Press.
Sieder, R. (2004), 'Renegotiating "law and order": judicial reform and citizen responses in post-war Guatemala' in S. Gloppen, R. Gargarella and E. Skaar (eds.), *Democratization and the Judiciary: The Accountability Function of Courts in New Democracies*, London: Frank Cass.
Stephenson, M. (2005), 'Rule of Law as a goal of development policy', World Bank Brief, Washington: The World Bank, worldbank.org/wbsite/external/topics/extlawjustinst
Stotzky, I. P. and C. S. Nino (1993), 'The difficulties in the transition process' in I. P. Stotzky (ed.), *Transition to Democracy in Latin America: The Role of the Judiciary*, Boulder, CO: Westview.
Tamanaha, B. Z. (2004), *On the Rule of Law*, Cambridge: Cambridge University Press.
Testa, A., J. K. Young and C. Mullins (2017), 'Does democracy enhance or reduce lethal violence?', *Homicide Studies*, vol. 21, no. 3.
Thompson, M. R. and S. McCarthy (eds.) (2020), *Governance and Democracy in the Asia Pacific*, Abingdon: Routledge.
Thornton, L. and K. Turmanidze (2020), *Public Attitudes in Georgia*, Washington: National Democratic Institute.
Toqueville, A. de (1835), *Democracy in America*, Part I, 1956 edition, New York: Mentor Books.

Trebilcock, M. J. and R. J. Daniels (2008), *Rule of Law Reform and Development: Charting the Fragile Path of Progress*, Cheltenham: Edward Elgar.
United Nations (2004), 'The rule of law and transitional justice in conflict and post-conflict societies', Report of the Secretary-General, Doc. S/2004/616, 23 August.
Venice Commission (European Commission for Democracy Through Law) (2011), *Report on the Rule of Law*, Study No. 512/2009, Strasbourg: Council of Europe.
World Bank (1997), *World Development Report 1997: The State in a Changing World*, Washington: The World Bank.
World Justice Project (2020), *The World Justice Project Rule of Law Index 2020*, Washington: World Justice Project.

2 The rule of law and judicial independence

Introduction

There has been much international effort to specify the standards of judicial independence which nation states, including those in transition from authoritarianism to democracy, are expected to endorse. The most important agreement was produced by the World Conference on the Independence of Justice held in Montreal in 1983, at which representatives of 26 international bodies, including the United Nations, the International Commission of Jurists and the four international courts, unanimously adopted a Universal Declaration on the Independence of Justice. Covering the treatment of both judges and advocates, it declares that judges should be impartial and free from 'any restrictions, influences, inducements, pressures, threats or interferences, direct or indirect, from any quarter or for any reason'. This declaration was followed in 1985 by the Basic Principles on the Independence of the Judiciary promulgated by the Seventh United Nations Congress on the Prevention of Crime and the Treatment of Offenders and endorsed by the General Assembly (Shetreet and Deschenes 1985). These principles stipulate that the state should guarantee the independence of the judiciary, enshrining it in the constitution or the law.

> It is the duty of all governmental and other institutions to respect and observe the independence of the judiciary. . . . There shall not be any inappropriate or unwarranted interference with the judicial process, nor shall judicial decisions by the courts be subject to revision.

In this chapter the prerequisites of judicial independence are differentiated as impartiality, insularity, exclusive competence and compliance. The rules which help to sustain an impartial judiciary – immunity, the sub judice principle and disqualification from holding other governmental or political positions – are explained with illustrations from a range of different transitional regimes. The second section shows how, through judicial councils and security of tenure, judiciaries may be insulated against improper influences. The significance of departures from the principle of exclusive competence is then examined, followed by an explanation of how failure to comply with or enforce judicial decisions negates

DOI: 10.4324/9781003334613-3

judicial independence. The final section of the chapter discusses the relationship between judicial independence and democracy.

Impartiality

For the judiciary to be independent, judges have to be impartial in their rulings. Impartiality means that judges are unbiased. Personal interests have no influence on the outcome of cases brought before them. The judge is a neutral third party, detached from the litigants who are equal before the law. All new democracies are bound by the Universal Declaration of Human Rights, which enshrines the right to a fair and public hearing by a competent, independent and impartial tribunal established by law. Article 14 of the International Covenant on Civil and Political Rights, ratified by most new democracies (Malaysia being a notable exception), also stipulates that everyone shall be entitled to a fair hearing by an impartial tribunal established by law. Such principles, though lacking enforcement mechanisms, stand as authoritative yardsticks by which the performance of national judiciaries can be measured.

In 1981 the International Commission of Jurists defined judicial independence as meaning that 'every judge is free to decide matters in accordance with his (sic) assessment of the facts and his understanding of the law' (Vyas 1992: 135). In 2002 the Consultative Council of European Judges, emphasizing the importance to an effective judicial system of public confidence in, and respect for, the judiciary, defined impartiality as requiring judges to discharge their duties without any favouritism, prejudice or bias and reach decisions without taking into consideration anything which falls outside the application of the law. Impartiality also implies that a judge will not make any observations which could suggest pre-judgement of the resolution of the dispute or which might influence the fairness of the proceedings. 'They should show the consideration due to all persons (parties, witnesses, counsel, for example) with no distinction based on unlawful grounds or incompatible with the appropriate discharge of their functions' (CCEJ 2002: para. 23).

The impartiality of judges applies to both adjudications between private parties and disputes between the state and the citizen. It takes on particular significance when the citizen is in dispute with the state itself (as in criminal trials and judicial review). This is why 'the protection of judicial impartiality through strong guarantees of independence became one of the most important traits of constitutionalism' (Guanieri and Pederzoli 2020), especially in the transition from authoritarianism to democracy.

Impartiality normally requires judges to renounce commitments to political party, race, class, caste, community, tribe and religion when judicial powers are exercised. Under an impartial judiciary, decisions are determined exclusively by the law, rather than by judicial predisposition to declare government actions lawful. Thus, under the South African constitution, '[t]he courts are independent and subject only to the Constitution and the law, which they must apply impartially and without fear, favour or prejudice' (Article 165). Recognition of the potential for bias is reflected in the unusual requirement that 'the racial and gender composition of South Africa must be considered when judicial officers are appointed' (Article 174).

Many post-authoritarian states have found it difficult to secure the autonomy from ideology and social connections required for judicial independence after years of political infiltration of the judiciary. In communist Central and Eastern Europe, for example, judges wishing to join the communist party were welcomed, and membership was necessary for career advancement. Such membership was compulsory in the USSR. The proportion of party-affiliated judges in the higher courts was much greater than that in the lower courts, and all Supreme Court justices were party members. In Bulgaria, judges were members of the *nomenklatura* and as such 'shared political attitudes with other officials; and, furthermore, they viewed themselves as bureaucrats. . . . Therefore, it was usually unnecessary for party leaders to pick up the phone to suggest what might be favorable dispositions of cases. In most instances, the judges knew what was expected of them' (Melone 1996: 238). Although communist ideology supported the idea of an independent judiciary, the power of state and party made such an ideal impossible to realize in practice: 'Until the very end of the Communist regimes, neither law nor the practice of its application assured genuine judicial independence' (Kuhn 2011: 62).

Under military regimes the judiciary was often in sympathy with the aims of the regime and actively sought to legitimize it. The impartiality of the judiciary was further compromised by the extended use of military tribunals and by purges which removed judges who were ideologically suspect. For example, during Chile's 17 years of military rule, Supreme Court decisions were heavily influenced by the political ideology of the regime. The powers of military courts were broadened and the jurisdiction of civilian courts subjected to restrictions and interference. Fear of reprisals, combined with a willingness on the part of many judges to enforce the junta's decrees, restricted their impartiality and led to extensive violations of human rights.

If the judicial function is to be discharged impartially, that is, subject only to the law, it has to be supported by rules which help guard against bias. The most significant of these are judicial immunity, disqualification from holding legislative or executive office, and the regulation of political activities. It is also generally accepted that judges should disqualify themselves from hearing cases in which they have a personal interest or close relationship with litigants, lawyers or witnesses. This procedure, known as recusal, can also be instigated by either party to a case if they perceive a conflict of interest on the part of the judge.

Judicial immunity protects judges from liability for civil damages provided they have jurisdiction over the subject matter before the court. This is a controversial and therefore contested concept in both theory and practice, especially when the immunity is believed to be absolute. Absolute immunity supports a judge's freedom to act independently and without fear of vexatious litigation which could impair independent and impartial adjudication. Should immunity lead to misconduct, such decisions can always be reviewed on appeal. However, critics of absolute immunity fear that releasing judges from all personal responsibility can mean that victims of incompetent or malicious judicial decisions lose any chance of redress. Even when judicial immunity can be lifted, it may not mean that judicial misbehaviour will be disciplined. If judges enjoy full immunity, the investigation of corruption cases can be obstructed and discouraged.

As a common law concept, judicial immunity is rarely found enshrined in constitutions. This can lead to conflict between the protection of individual freedom provided by a constitution and the protection provided for judges by judicial immunity. For example, the Nigerian Constitution gives anyone who believes their civil rights to have been infringed the right to seek redress and damages in the High Court. Judicial actions are not excluded. On the other hand, no exception is understood to the principle of judicial immunity, which is derived from common law, including violations of constitutionally guaranteed rights. 'There is thus a potential conflict between the principles of judicial immunity and the constitution', leaving unsettled the constitutionality of judicial immunity (Olowofoyeku 1991: 50).

Maintaining a public image of impartiality demands that judges have carefully circumscribed extra-judicial activities (Shetreet 2019). International standards for extra-judicial conduct have been spelt out in the Mount Scopus International Standards of Judicial Independence, approved in 2008 and consolidated in 2018 by the International Association of Judicial Independence and World Peace. Articles 16–18 specify that judges shall enjoy freedom of expression and association, though only if exercised in a manner that is compatible with the judicial function and does not affect judicial independence or impartiality. Judges are expected to maintain the confidentiality of deliberations and not comment extra-judicially upon pending cases. Appropriate restraint should be shown in commenting extra-judicially upon judgements and procedures of their own and other courts. Judges should not engage in extra-judicial activity that is incompatible with their judicial function, the efficient functioning of the court of which they are members, or their independence and impartiality. They should not exercise any political function. Courts should give guidance to judges on extra-judicial activities and provide appropriate means by which parties to proceedings may raise concerns.

The doctrine of the separation of powers reinforces the principle that normally judges are disqualified from holding other offices of state. Judicial independence generally rules out the holding of positions in the executive or legislature. According to the resolutions adopted by the International Bar Association, '[j]udges may not, during their term of office, serve in executive functions, such as ministers of the government, nor may they serve as members of the Legislature or of municipal councils, unless by long historical traditions these functions are combined' (IBA 1982: para. 35).

However, not all transitional democracies ban political activities outright. In the Czech Republic, for example, only Constitutional Court judges are banned from joining political parties or movements, though under the 1991 Law on Courts and Judges all judges are required to 'refrain from anything that might discredit the dignity of the judicial office or threaten the trust of independent, impartial and fair judicial decision-making' (OSI 2001: 24). In Romania it is a disciplinary offence for a judge to carry out public political activities or express their political opinions in exercising their professional duties. Under Article 95 of the Brazilian Constitution no judge is allowed to engage in political activity. Judges in Thailand are prohibited under Section 197 of the Constitution from holding any political position. It is accepted in most judiciaries that while the educated and informed people who become justices are bound to have opinions on political matters and cannot be totally neutral, they should nevertheless be totally impartial when adjudicating, regardless of political and other affiliations prior to being appointed to the bench.

Some activities related to politics are, however, regarded as consistent with a judicial career. These generally include writing, lecturing, teaching and participating in activities such as appearing at public hearings concerning the law, the legal system and the administration of justice; and serving as a member of an official body or other government commission, committee or advisory body, when such membership is not inconsistent with judicial impartiality and political neutrality. These rights are spelt out in the Bangalore Principles of Judicial Conduct, adopted by the United Nations' Judicial Group on Strengthening Judicial Integrity in 2002. This may entail defending the legal system and the rule of law against incursions by governments, as in Poland in recent years (Gersdorf and Pilich 2020).

The situation is further complicated by the general acceptance that judges, like other citizens in a democracy, should enjoy freedom of speech and association. Members of the judiciary therefore have the right to form professional bodies to represent their interests, including the protection of professional standards. An example is Albania's National Judicial Conference, established in 1999 as a voluntary, professional association of judges that aims to strengthen the rule of law and the efficiency of the judiciary. It has adopted a code of judicial ethics, which gives guidance on conflicts of interest, ex parte proceedings and inappropriate political activity. While the association cannot sanction judges for misconduct, it does have the right to elect 9 of the 15 judges of the High Council of Justice. In Pakistan the Supreme Court Bar Association represents the country's legal profession and aims to ensure the Constitution of Pakistan is upheld, to defend justice, and promote professional excellence and respect for the rule of law.

Insularity

Judicial independence also entails insularity. According to the United Nations' Basic Principles on the Independence of the Judiciary, judges should decide matters before them 'without any restrictions, improper influences, inducements, pressures, threats or interferences, direct or indirect, from any quarter or for any reason'. An independent judiciary is thus insulated against political interference in the composition of courts, the tenure of judges, their methods of appointment, their remuneration and, of course, their judgements. To this end international declarations require the political executive to guarantee the physical security of all lawyers when engaged in litigation (Frankel 1993).

Judicial insularity also means collective independence, enabling the judiciary to act as a corporate body with a role in the management of budgets, court personnel and premises (though there are many variations in the way such responsibilities can be shared with the executive). Ideally, executive control should be limited to the minimum requirements of executive accountability to the legislature. There are a large number of choices to be made in this respect, such as how to make judicial appointments, which disciplinary procedures to adopt and how to ensure judicial accountability (the subject of Chapter 9).

In an attempt to distance the judiciary from the executive branch of government and protect it against political interference, a large number of constitutions and laws in new democracies delegate the management of the judiciary to judicial councils consisting of judges and representatives of other branches of government and lawyers' associations. According to the United Nations Special Rapporteur on the independence of judges and lawyers 'judicial councils play an essential role in guaranteeing the independence and the autonomy of the judiciary. The underlying rationale for their creation is the need to insulate the judiciary and judicial career processes from external political pressure' (UN 2018).

Such councils have been set up to protect the independence of judges whose appointment, promotion and discipline might otherwise be subjected to political manipulation. They are among the judicial reforms supported by the World Bank and other donor agencies (Garoupa and Ginsburg 2009). The majority of countries in the world now have an institution of this type to strengthen the independence of the judiciary and improve the administration of the courts (Hammergren 2002). This includes about half the countries in Latin America and most in Eastern Europe.

Judicial insularity is also commonly protected by the tenure given to judges. International opinion on judicial independence, such as that represented by the European Commission for Democracy through Law (informally known as the Venice Commission), usually recommends that judges be appointed permanently until retirement (Venice Commission 2010). It is assumed that the longer a judge has tenure, the lower the risk of political interference in the judicial process. When judges are appointed for life, or given tenure until retirement age, there are far fewer opportunities for the political executive to take political factors into account when making appointments than there are when judges are periodically assessed for renewal. Judges with tenure will also be less inclined to please the politicians than those concerned about their future careers. Short terms of service make judges more sensitive to the political pressures that politicians, the media and interest groups can be tempted to exert. They make it possible to remove judges on inappropriate grounds, rather than for incapacity or gross misconduct, the only grounds for removal consistent with judicial independence. It follows that when terms of office are short, clear and stringent rules on re-appointments and disciplinary procedures are needed.

The tenure enjoyed by judges in new democracies nevertheless varies from one judiciary to another, as well as within the judicial systems of individual countries, partly reflecting the extent to which the court's business draws it into political controversy. In Romania, for example, the tenure given to judges is either 65 or 68 years according to the type of court. However, Supreme Court judges are appointed for only six years (renewable) and Constitutional Court judges for nine. The Brazilian Constitution, in contrast, guarantees tenure until retirement at the age of 70 for all judges, including the Supreme Federal Court. Judges can only be dismissed in the public interest, which is determined by a decision supported by an absolute majority of the relevant court or the National Council of Justice. Providing judges with guaranteed life tenure under the Constitution was part of the attempt to strengthen their independence following 20 years of authoritarianism: 'the Constituent Assembly of 1986–88 considered that the restoration of the judiciary's credibility and legitimacy necessarily entailed securing its political independence' (Santiso 2004: 164).

In some new democracies judges are appointed for life. In South Africa a judge can only be removed from office by act of parliament. If the Judicial Service Commission finds a judge to be incapacitated, grossly incompetent or guilty of gross misconduct, the National Assembly may pass a resolution, supported by a two-thirds majority, calling for the judge to be removed from office. However, Constitutional Court judges hold office for non-renewable terms of twelve years or until they attain the age of 70, whichever occurs first.

Where judges do not receive lifetime appointments, reappointment is usually possible, as in South Korea. Justices of the Supreme Court serve for six years and other judges for ten. At the same time, no judge may be removed from office except by impeachment or as a result of being sentenced to imprisonment. Disciplinary action may lead to a judge being suspended from office, a reduction in salary or other unfavourable treatment. A judge may also be retired because of serious mental or physical impairment, within legally prescribed circumstances.

Insularity from improper influences is also sought through restrictions on public discussion of cases currently before the courts. The sub judice rule, part of common law relating to contempt of court, is designed to ensure that public statements about legal proceedings do not usurp the court's proper functioning by prejudging matters or prejudicing a trial while a case is being heard. This includes comments by people in political office. The mass media are also capable of prejudicing the outcome of a case by flouting the sub judice rule, a development which has caused considerable concern in South Africa in recent years. Trial by the media and the televising of court cases mean that the sub judice rule is all but extinct. Even the Venice Commission offered no more than a feeble injunction in an opinion on judicial independence issued in 2010:

> In order to shield the judicial process from undue pressure, one should consider the application of the principle of 'sub judice', which should be carefully defined, so that an appropriate balance is struck between the need to protect, the judicial process on the one hand and freedom of the press and open discussion of matters of public interest on the other.
>
> (Venice Commission 2010: para. 64)

One possible reason why the principle lacks strong support is that it can be manipulated to restrict public discussion, protect judges from criticism, and delay or prevent criticism of government in the legislature, media and other public forums (Solomon 2019).

Exclusive competence

The third prerequisite of independence is found in an exclusive competence to adjudicate, a key feature of the separation of powers in a democracy, excluding both legislature and executive from performing judicial functions. The independence of the judiciary becomes, at the very least, suspect if either of the other two branches of government takes over judicial functions. This principle has its origins in Montesquieu's consideration of liberty in *The Spirit of Laws*:

> When the legislative and executive powers are united in the same person, or in the same body of magistrates, there can be no liberty; because apprehensions may arise, lest the same monarch or senate should enact tyrannical laws, to execute them in a tyrannical manner. Again, there is no liberty if the judiciary power be not separated from the legislative and executive. Were it joined with the legislative, the life and liberty of the subject would be exposed to arbitrary control; for the judge would be then the legislator. Were it joined to the executive power, the judge might behave with violence and oppression. There would be an end of everything, were the same man, or the same body, whether of the nobles or of the people, to exercise those three powers, that of enacting laws, that of executing the public resolutions, and of trying the causes of individuals.
>
> (Montesquieu 1748: Book XI, Ch. VI)

The principle of exclusive competence rules out the establishment of ad hoc or special tribunals. To be independent the judiciary must have the authority to deal with the application and interpretation of the law and to make decisions immune from revisions by the other two powers. The judiciary should be 'constitutionally recognized as a separate and independent body with an exclusive mandate to handle judicial matters according to the law' (Dung 2003: 13; Larkins 1996; Shetreet 2021). To this end Paraguay's 1992 Constitution stipulates that '[i]n no case will members of other branches of government or other officials claim to have judicial powers' (Article 248). According to Article 162 of Armenia's Constitution 'justice shall be administered solely by courts in accordance with the Constitution and laws'. In Bulgaria, specialized courts may be set up 'by virtue of law', but 'there shall be no extraordinary courts' (Article 19). In Estonia, '[j]ustice shall be administered solely by the courts' (Article 146).

One way of limiting the scope of ordinary courts and of involving the executive branch in adjudication is to create special administrative tribunals to deal with specific types of dispute relating to particular areas of public policy. It is often thought that this will have a detrimental effect on judicial authority and the independence of the adjudication made available in this way, especially when military tribunals are empowered to hear criminal, civil, commercial and administrative cases which should be entrusted to the ordinary courts.

This need not necessarily be the case. Special tribunals can be constituted so that they dispense justice cheaply and quickly but in ways which nevertheless preserve the rules of natural justice. They can therefore be important means of improving access to justice, especially for the poor. They can be particularly effective in resolving disputes between the citizen and public authorities, as well as between private parties, such as employers and employees. Such informal, quasi-judicial entities can deliver impartial, open and fair judgements following an appeal against a discretionary decision by a public body. In principle they can provide specialized, inexpensive and informal adjudication as an alternative to the ordinary courts, where challenging an administrative decision can prove expensive, protracted and intimidating. Adjudication by an independent body, which hears both sides of the dispute before making a legally binding decision, either endorsing that made by the administrative agency or substituting its own, reflects the importance of bureaucratic decisions in many countries, especially when there is no structure of administrative courts to hear such disputes.

As their name implies, administrative tribunals usually consist of a panel of three adjudicators drawn from different walks of life to ensure a balance of attitudes and opinions. So a tribunal in the field of industrial or employment policy might consist of representatives of business and labour, with a lawyer in the chair. At hearings, representatives of the agency against which the appeal has been made and of the appellant present their sides of the case, with the rules of evidence applied flexibly so that both interested parties feel that everything of relevance to their case has been heard. Appellants may wish to present their own cases or be represented by someone from a support group such as a trade union or voluntary body, rather than a lawyer. Costs and formalities are thus reduced, of particular benefit to poorer appellants.

However, it is crucial for judicial independence that special courts, especially if based on traditional forms of dispute resolution, recognize the indispensability of the rules of natural justice and reasoned, transparent decisions. It remains absolutely indisputable that any such mechanisms provide no acceptable alternatives to the ordinary courts if they fail to operate according to the rule of law. The use of 'exceptional courts' will be examined further in Chapter 5.

Compliance

The World Bank, a major sponsor of legal and judicial reform in developing and transitional countries, adds a fourth dimension to judicial independence: *compliance.* Judicial decisions have to be respected and enforced by either compliance or legal coercion. This is definitely a problem in some transitional societies. Failure to enforce judgements undermines the independence of the judiciary and weakens public support for the principle of judicial independence, as in Hungary. Erratic implementation of court decisions is a major weakness in a judicial system. Ineffective rulings mean that state institutions do not respect court decisions and do not compensate individuals who have been successfully defended against prosecution. The lack of an effective bailiff organization can mean that many court decisions remain un-enforced, as in Latvia. A government may fail to comply with court rulings which are themselves suspect because of corruption in the judiciary, as in Indonesia. The executive branch may both ignore court rulings and treat others as mere recommendations, as in Nigeria. Compliance, or the lack of it, is clearly a widespread problem.

However, compliance extends the concept of judicial independence beyond the behaviour of magistrates to encompass the willingness and ability of state agencies to enforce the law. This can remain a problem even if judicial independence has not been called into question. Nevertheless, it is important to recognize that justice is undermined if a fair and impartial decision remains un-enforced, leaving successful litigants deprived of their rights. Furthermore, weak state capacity to ensure that judicial decisions are enforced undermines public willingness to comply with the law. The more legal rulings can be ignored, the more a culture of disobedience is cultivated. A key element in the rule of law is thus enforcement: 'without good enforcement of impartial rules, no rule of law can be established' (Bergman 2012: 174). A competent and autonomous judiciary needs to be supported by effective enforcement of the law.

Other conditions necessary for judicial independence have been proposed, including respect for decisions once rendered; insulation from judicial colleagues who might seek to exert influence over the administrative, procedural or substantive stages of adjudication; and freedom from pressures of public opinion, especially that mobilized and articulated by the mass media (Shetreet 1985; Domingo 1999).

Any given judiciary is likely to vary in the extent to which the different conditions for independence are present. Judges may be impartial but not insulated from political interference and with little scope to challenge the actions of state agencies. Or there may be little political interference, but equally little impartiality or scope of authority, so that judges are inclined to act in support of political power. Or courts may be given wide scope but lack impartiality and insularity (Larkins 1996). The rule of law is only fully served when judicial independence is enjoyed by judges with the authority to adjudicate in all areas of public and private law.

Consequently, it is difficult to measure how independent a judiciary is. The constituent elements of judicial independence do not necessarily all move together in the same direction. Weighting the different elements is complex (e.g. highly politicized judicial appointments yet minimal post-appointment interference, compared with selecting judges on merit but promoting them on political criteria). Judicial independence within a single country may also vary depending on the type of case, especially since formal and technical provisions (such as the judicial budget, the selection process and tenure) are routinely ignored or manipulated in many countries. Nevertheless, the International Commission of Jurists has produced a list of indicators by which the judicial independence of different countries can be compared, including direct efforts by governments to influence judicial decisions and the executive's role in the 'personnel management' of the judiciary (Widner 1999).

Judicial independence and democracy

It is clear why judicial independence is seen as a prerequisite of democracy. First, the conflicts of interest within society need to be resolved through representative government and not by judges biased in favour of a particular class or occupational interest. Free and fair elections to a legislature determine which political group or groups shall be dominant until the next opportunity for the electorate to pronounce on how well the state has been managed since the last election. Independent courts are essential if these and other democratic procedures are to be protected against those in authority who might seek to prolong their hold on power by manipulating the rules of the democratic political game.

Hence the significance of Kenya's Supreme Court's ruling following the General Election of 2013. The Court was petitioned to declare the outcome fundamentally flawed but unanimously upheld the result. Despite being criticized for not adopting a more reflective, remedial and reconstructive approach to its task, the Court's adjudication prevented a recurrence of the violence which followed the 2007 presidential election (Harrington and Manji 2015). In contrast, without an independent judiciary willing to enforce electoral laws, abuses such as illegal campaign finance and vote buying will undermine the democratic process, as in Mexico (Serra 2016).

Democracy is also nullified if political interference in, and control over, the judiciary means that it cannot perform its duty of protecting the constitution and the civil rights which guide democratic public participation. If politicians undermine the independence of the courts for political gain, they undermine the political freedoms and equality on which democracy rests. 'Subversive strategies' which transform an independent judiciary into a weapon against political opponents mean that politics becomes judicialized and the courts 'become actors in political strategies that alter the rules of democratic competition' (Maravall 2003: 262).

There is a wealth of evidence that the greater the judicial independence, the stronger the protection given to human rights, including those which form the foundation of democratic politics (Crabtree and Fariss 2015). Comparative analysis of the institutional foundations of personal freedom shows 'a positive and robust relationship between judicial independence and personal freedom', as indicated by the individual's security and safety and freedom of movement, religion, association, assembly, expression, information and identity:

> [J]udicial independence is a robust predictor of personal freedom in all its forms. The more power independent judges have to make legal decisions that 'bite', the higher is the degree to which people are free to make their own decisions in life.
>
> (Berggren and Gutmann 2020: 168, 183)

In post-authoritarian regimes independent courts perform another function supportive of democracy: providing those in opposition protection against 'majoritarian excess' by the new party of government following a general election. Constitutional courts, especially, by 'preserving the accountability of the leaders of today add an ingredient to the contemporary efforts to stabilize democracy through elections in seemingly inauspicious settings' (Issacharoff 2015: 13). This function of the judiciary has become particularly significant as a growing number of illiberal regimes attempt to control elections so that a political party maintains a perpetual majority in the legislature.

An independent court is thus particularly important under conditions of single-party dominance but will need to exercise strategic judgement over when to confront or defer to the legislature, especially when there is uncertainty about the legal status of constitutional review. This has been observed in South Africa where, in enforcing democratic rights under a major threat to democracy in the form of the African National Congress's parliamentary dominance, the Supreme Court has been 'highly sensitive to the long-term impact of their decisions on the Court's capacity to enforce democratic rights'. Avoiding attacks on its independence has been 'arguably a better outcome for South African democracy than the alternative course of robustly asserting its powers' (Roux 2016: 13). It has to be added here that the justices serving on constitutional courts have to be independent if they are to provide this service to democratization. It cannot be assumed that all constitutional courts will enjoy such independence.

There can, of course, be no guarantee that an independent judiciary will always be able to rein in a government which has majority support in the legislature and which is determined to render its decisions non-justiciable or introduce laws that permanently discriminate against a section of society. For example, Malaysia's three states of emergency declared between 1969 and 1977 remain unrevoked. When challenged over this, the government used its majority in parliament to amend the Constitution retrospectively to make declarations of states of emergency non-justiciable. The freedom of any judiciary to challenge such policies will at least form part of a process of politically educating the electorate in readiness for when the government's term expires.

Sometimes, local political conditions will prevent constitutional courts from promoting democratization, as in the Middle East. Following the Arab Spring of 2011, stronger judicial review was designed to entrench democratic reforms. However, the new courts did little to promote democratization, which duly stalled. A number of reasons account for this. Some of the new institutions were too weak or lacked independence. Others lacked popular legitimacy. Where politics deteriorated into warlordism (Libya) the political context became impervious to judicial review. Where senior justices felt the new regime threatened the social groups from which they were drawn, as in Egypt, the judiciary turned to an authoritarian alternative.

Judges give additional support to representative democracy by ensuring that the actions of the political executive are consistent with the legislation emanating from the legislature. Public policy must be determined by the people's elected representatives and not by subsequent arbitrary executive decision. A judiciary which is independent of the executive, despite the latter's unavoidable role in appointing judges and managing the justice system, is essential if the executive branch is to act only in ways intended by the legislature. The protection of civil rights may also require the judiciary to review legislation which appears to violate fundamental rights and freedoms, though it should be recognized that the scope of universal rights is far from uncontested and highly variable in the protection given by written constitutions (see Chapter 8). Nevertheless, independent judicial review represents a form of mutual restraint that sustains electoral democracy (Stephenson 2003; Hannssen 2004).

An independent judiciary also contributes to the development of a democratic political culture in post-authoritarian states. The consolidation of democracy requires attitudes which recognize the legitimacy of constitutional arrangements and a willingness to accept the outcomes when the rules of political life (especially electoral rules) have been adhered to. The values associated with democracy include moderation, co-operation, bargaining and accommodation. These are more likely to be absorbed and influence political behaviour by a legal system which is independent, fair and competent, rather than one which reinforces discrimination, exclusion and privilege. Thus, an independent judiciary contributes to democratic consolidation and stability by providing incentives for political leaders to avoid taking decisions that threaten to break constitutional rules and allowing potentially destabilizing political conflicts to be dealt with through established institutional relationships between the judicial and executive branches of government (Staton et al. 2015).

When judges act fairly, impartially and independently, rather than favouring partisan objectives or responding to powerful sectional interests, people are more likely to develop trust in political institutions than if they perceive the judiciary to be incapable and unwilling to offer protection to all equally against the abuse of power. Just as people only accept electoral outcomes that conflict with their beliefs and interests if the elections were free and fair, so they will accept losing a case before the courts only if the judicial process has been demonstrably fair and conducted by an independent and impartial judge. Credibility in the public mind, by appointments which are regarded as fair and representative and decision-making that is just and authoritative, turns the courts into 'credible arbiters of political disputes and brings them into the position to facilitate or even foster the consolidation of unlikely democracies' (Stroh 2019: 601).

Judicial independence is thus regarded by both scholars and liberal politicians as 'an added institutional safeguard for newly democratizing countries' (Larkins 1996: 606). Those who designed constitutions in post-communist Europe, for example, 'placed great reliance on their written constitutions to secure judicial independence. They have created governments predicated on the separation of powers and the rule of law' (Howard 2001: 98). In recognition of this, and in order to distance the new from the old regime, most post-authoritarian constitutions describe the judiciary as independent. Article 50 of the Hungarian Constitution, for example, stipulates that '[j]udges are independent and answer only to the law'. The 1973 Constitution of Pakistan, as amended in 2010 to reduce the executive powers accumulated under the country's military leaders, specifies that 'the independence of the judiciary shall be fully secured'. Similarly, courts in South Africa, according to section 165 of the Constitution, are 'independent and subject only to the constitution and the law' (Bridge 2007: 4).

Some new constitutions create a separation of powers between the three main functions of government – legislative, executive and judicial. The preservation of democracy requires that these powers should not fall into the same hands, thus preventing proper executive accountability to elected representatives and avoiding political interference in the administration of justice. Each governmental power needs to be balanced and checked by the others if autocracy is to be avoided. Since a fusion of powers often characterized the authoritarian systems of government from which new democracies are in transition, a number of constitutions explicitly base the organization of the state on the separations of powers. For example, Article 10 of the Polish Constitution declares that '[t]he system of government in the Republic of Poland shall be based on the separation of and balance between the legislature, executive and judicial powers'. The Lithuanian Constitution forbids state institutions from interfering in the activities of judges and courts, as well as members of parliament, political parties and other public organizations. Article 2 of the Brazilian Constitution describes the legislative, executive and judiciary as 'independent of and harmonious among each other'. Paraguay's 1992 Constitution 'guarantees' the independence of the judiciary and stipulates that '[i]n no case will members of other branches of government or other officials claim to have judicial powers' (Article 248). According to Articles 1 and 24 of Indonesia's amended Constitution 'the State of Indonesia shall be a state based on the rule of law' and 'the judicial powers shall be independent'.

It is less common to find Asian constitutions stipulating the separations of powers, though it is clear that in a number of cases this principle is implied. The Malaysian Constitution, for example, makes no mention of it, but according to a Constitutional Court judge, 'it is a common belief that the doctrine of the separation of powers has always been part and parcel of our constitutional fabric' (Bin Zakaria 2009: 31). The situation is similar in sub-Saharan Africa. For example, the separation of powers is not spelt out in South Africa's Constitution, but it was in the Interim Constitution of 1993 which stipulated that '[t]here shall be a separation of powers between the legislature, executive and judiciary, with appropriate checks and balances to ensure accountability, responsiveness and openness'. Since then, the separation of powers has, according to the Minister for Justice and Constitutional Development, been 'tacitly incorporated' in the Constitution and 'underlies the South African constitutional order' (Mabandla 2006). In Malawi the separation of powers is implied in references to the separate status, functions and duties of the three branches of government. However, Article 98 of Niger's Constitution explicitly states that 'the judiciary is independent of the legislature and the executive', judges being answerable only to the authority of the law (Article 100).

Such formal rules are important and more than mere 'parchment barriers' against political interference. De facto independence, or the political conditions necessary to restrain politicians from exerting undue pressure on the judiciary, is clearly important. But so is the formal protection provided by constitutional rules – de jure independence. Studies of constitutional reviews by high courts show that institutional protection for judges makes them less vulnerable to political threats, especially in political systems where power is highly concentrated, as in many of the presidential systems of transitional states (Carrubba et al. 2015).

Constitutional protection also provides a reference point for groups advocating the observance of constitutional rules. By insulating the judiciary from external interference, constitutional provisions also 'reduce the number of weapons at the disposal of the judiciary's enemies'. To this end, the provisions within the constitution need to be specific, particularly with regard to the selection and removal of judges. For example, one of the reasons why increases in de jure protection for judicial independence have not always been matched by greater de facto independence is that selection and removal procedures are rarely spelt out in the constitutions of new democracies. The results of one statistical analysis, comparing scores for de jure (constitutional) and de facto judicial independence, 'suggest that *de facto* judicial independence might be improved if countries without selection and removal procedures that insulate judges from other branches of government adopt such provisions' (Melton and Ginsburg 2013: 8, 24).

* * *

None of the principles that together constitute the rule of law can be realized without judicial independence. To protect its independence, the judiciary relies on judicial immunity, the principle of sub judice, disqualification from other offices of state and the regulation of political activities. Judicial independence also entails insularity. The devices used to isolate the judiciary from pressures that threaten to undermine justice include the delegation of judicial management to judicial councils.

Judicial independence is further protected by the exclusive competence to adjudicate given to the courts. This is part of the separations of powers. Democracy excludes legislatures and executives from performing judicial functions. Such exclusion raises the question of whether special tribunals to deal with specific types of dispute will have a detrimental effect on judicial independence. Special courts are increasingly advocated as alternative and preferable mechanisms for resolving disputes, leading to concerns about whether some traditional dispute resolution procedures lack the qualities required by the rule of law. Judicial independence may also need to be supported by measures designed to ensure compliance with judgements so that judicial decisions are respected and enforced.

A judiciary which meets all the requirements of independence signifies the replacement of a state governed by executive force by a state governed by law. When democracy is in part defined as a state governed by law, the significance of an independent judiciary immediately becomes apparent. Judicial independence serves democracy by protecting electoral competition, civil rights, minority interests, and legality in government and by encouraging the development of a democratic political culture. Post-authoritarian constitutions have empowered judiciaries to undertake these tasks.

However, as will be seen in Chapter 8, replacing a politicized judiciary with impartial and independent judges who test legislative and executive action against the law and the constitution can lead to the judicialization of politics. Then the courts can find themselves accused of usurping the role of the people's elected representatives, especially when the executive has the support of clear legislative majorities or when the courts find it necessary to strike down legislation, and thereby the will of parliament, on the grounds that it is unconstitutional. There may then be a move to limit the power of the judiciary which in turn threatens the very independence upon which democracy depends.

Countries in transition from authoritarianism had to remove violations of the rule of law from statute books and constitutional documents in order to put an end to practices by the political executive which undermined the independence of the judiciary. Political interference in the judicial process and other violations of the rule of law form a political legacy of authoritarianism which constitutional reforms purport to address. The constitutions of most post-authoritarian states explicitly confirm the independence of the judiciary. Despite this, protecting the independence of the judiciary has proved to be particularly difficult for transitional states. How judicial independence can be undermined is the subject of the next two chapters.

References

Berggren, N. and J. Gutmann (2020), 'Securing personal freedom through institutions: the role of electoral democracy and judicial independence', *European Journal of Law and Economics*, vol. 49, https://doi.org/10.1007/s10657-020-09643-9

Bergman, M. (2012), 'The rule, the law, and the rule of law: improving measurements and content validity', *The Justice System Journal*, vol. 33, no. 2.

Bin Zakaria, A. (2009), 'The relation between constitutional review organs, governments and the ordinary judiciary: Malaysian perspective' in C. Hill (ed.), *Constitutional Review and Separation of Powers: Sixth Conference of Asian Constitutional Court Judges 2009*, Singapore: Konrad Adenauer Stiftung.

Bridge, J. (2007), 'Constitutional guarantees of the independence of the judiciary', *Electronic Journal of Comparative Law*, vol. 11, no. 3.

Carrubba, C. J., M. Gabel, G. Helmke, A. D. Martin and J. K. Staton (2015), 'When parchment barriers matter: de jure independence and the concentration of power', 14 October, polisci.emory.edu/faculty/jkstato/resources/

CCEJ (2002), *Opinion No. 3 of the Consultative Council of European Judges (CCJE) to the Attention of the Committee of Ministers of the Council of Europe on the Principles and Rules Governing Judges' Professional Conduct, in Particular Ethics, Incompatible Behaviour and Impartiality*, Strasbourg: Consultative Council of European Judges.

Crabtree, C. D. and C. J. Fariss (2015), 'Uncovering patterns among latent variables: human rights and *de facto* judicial independence', *Research and Politics*, vol. 2, no. 3.

Domingo, P. (1999), 'Judicial independence and judicial reform in Latin America' in A. Schedler, L. Diamond and M. F. Plattner (eds.), *The Self-Restraining State: Power and Accountability in New Democracies*, London: Lynne Pienner.

Dung, L. T. (2003), *Judicial Independence in Transitional Countries*, Oslo: UNDP Governance Centre.

Frankel, M. E. (1993), 'Concerning the role the judiciary may serve in the proper functioning of a democracy' in I. P. Stotzky (ed.), *Transition to Democracy in Latin America: The Role of the Judiciary*, Boulder: Westview Press.

Garoupa, N. and T. Ginsburg (2009), 'Guarding the guardians: judicial councils and judicial independence', *American Journal of Comparative Law*, vol. 57, no. 1.

Gersdorf, M. and M. Pilich (2020), 'Judges and representatives of the people: a Polish perspective', *European Constitutional Law Review*, vol. 16, no. 3.

Guanieri, C. and P. Pederzoli (2020), *The Judicial System: The Administration and Politics of Justice*, Cheltenham: Edward Elgar.

Hammergren, L. (2002), *Do Judicial Councils Further Judicial Reform? Lessons From Latin America*, Rule of Law Working Paper 28, Washington: Carnegie Endowment for International Peace.

Hannssen, F. A. (2004), 'Is there a politically optimal level of judicial independence?', *American Economic Review*, vol. 94, no. 3.

Harrington, J. and A. Manji (2015), 'Restoring Leviathan? The Kenyan Supreme Court, constitutional transformation, and the presidential election of 2013', *Journal of Eastern African Studies*, vol. 9, no. 2.

Howard, A. E. D. (2001), 'Judicial independence in post-communist central and eastern Europe' in P. H. Russell and D. M. O'Brien (eds.), *Judicial Independence in the Age of Democracy: Critical Perspectives From Around the World*, Charlottesville, VA: University Press of Virginia.

IBA (1982), *Minimum Standards of Judicial Independence (Adopted 1982)*, London: International Bar Association.

Issacharoff, I. (2015), *Fragile Democracies: Contested Power in the Era of Constitutional Courts*, Cambridge: Cambridge University Press.

Kuhn, Z. (2011), *The Judiciary in Central and Eastern Europe: Mechanical Jurisprudence in Transformation?*, Leiden: Martinus Nijhoff.

Larkins, C. M (1996), 'Judicial independence and democratization: a theoretical and conceptual analysis', *American Journal of Comparative Law*, vol. 44, no. 4.

Mabandla, B., MP (2006), 'Separation of powers in Sub-Saharan Africa', address to the Konrad Adenauer Foundation's Rule of Law Conference, 8 November, Somerset West, South Africa.

Maravall, J. M. (2003), 'The Rule of Law as a political weapon' in A. Przeworski and J. M. Maravall (eds.), *Democracy and the Rule of Law*, Cambridge: Cambridge University Press.

Melone, A. P. (1996), 'The struggle for judicial independence and the transition toward democracy in Bulgaria', *Communist and Post-Communist Studies*, vol. 29, no. 2.

Melton, J. and T. Ginsburg (2013), 'Does de jure judicial independence really matter? A re-evaluation of explanations for judicial independence', in *Chicago Institute for Law and Economics Working Paper No. 612*, Chicago: Coase-Sandor Institute for Law and Economics.

Montesquieu, Charles Louis de Secondat (1748), 'The spirit of laws' in A. M. Cohler, B. C. Miller and H. S. Stone (eds.), *Cambridge Texts in the History of Political Thought 1989*, Cambridge: Cambridge University Press.

Olowofoyeku, A. A. (1991), 'Judicial liability and the Nigerian Constitution', *The International and Comparative Law Quarterly*, vol. 40, no. 1.

OSI (2001), *Judicial Independence in the Czech Republic*, Brussels: Open Society Institute.

Roux, T. (2016), 'Constitutional courts as democratic consolidators: insights from South Africa after 20 years, *Journal of Southern African Studies*, vol. 42, no. 1.

Santiso, C. (2004), 'Economic reform and judicial governance in Brazil: balancing independence with accountability' in S. Gloppen, R. Gargarella and E. Skaar (eds.), *Democratization and the Judiciary: The Accountability Function of Courts in New Democracies*, London: Frank Cass.

Serra, G. (2016), 'Vote buying with illegal resources: manifestation of a weak rule of law in Mexico', *Journal of Politics in Latin America*, vol. 8, no. 1.

Shetreet, S. (1985), 'Judicial independence: new conceptual dimensions and contemporary challenges' in S. Shetreet and J. Deschenes (eds.), *Judicial Independence: The Contemporary Debate*, Dordrecht: Martinus Nijhoff.

Shetreet, S. (2019), 'Reflections on contemporary issues of judicial independence' in P. Pinto de Albuquerque and K. Wojtyczek (eds.), *Judicial Power in a Globalized World*, Cham: Springer.

Shetreet, S. (2021), 'Democracy challenged' in S. Shetreet, H. Chodosh and E. Helland (eds.), *Challenged Justice: In Pursuit of Judicial Independence*, Leiden: Brill/Nijhoff.

Shetreet, S. and J. Deschenes (eds.) (1985), *Judicial Independence: The Contemporary Debate*, Dordrecht: Martinus Nijhoff.

Solomon, R. (2019), 'The subject of sub judice: an analysis of the sub judice rule in Uganda', *Commonwealth Law Bulletin*, vol. 45, no. 4.

Staton, J. K., C. Reenock and S. Lindberg (2015), *Bending But Not Breaking: Rule of Law Tensions and Regime Survival*, Emory University Working Paper, http://polisci.emory.edu/faculty/jkstato/resources/WorkingPapers/break.pdf

Stephenson, M. C. (2003), '"When the devil turns . . .": the political foundations of independent judicial review', *Journal of Legal Studies*, vol. 32, no. 1.

Stroh, A. (2019), 'Sustaining and jeopardising a credible arbiter: judicial networks in Benin's consolidating democracy', *International Political Science Review*, vol. 39, no. 5.

UN (2018), 'Judicial Councils: report of the special rapporteur on the independence of judges and lawyers', presented to the Human Rights Council at its 38th session, United Nations Human Rights Council, New York.

Venice Commission (2010), *Opinion on the Draft Constitution of the Kyrgyz Republic*, Opinion No. 582 (2010), Strasbourg: European Commission for Democracy Through Law.

Vyas, Y. (1992), 'The independence of the judiciary: a Third World perspective', *Third World Legal Studies*, vol. 11, Article 6.

Widner, J. (1999), 'Building judicial independence in common law Africa' in A. Schedler, L. Diamond and M. C. Plattner (eds.), *The Self-Restraining State: Power and Accountability in New Democracies*, London: Lynne Reinner.

3 Undermining judicial independence

Introduction

Although the countries in transition from authoritarianism have endorsed the principle of judicial independence, political interference in the judiciary persists. The consolidation of democracy has been undermined by the growing number of illiberal and authoritarian regimes. This and the following chapter describe the many types of 'undue influence' exposed by the comparative study of judiciaries and the constraints on their independence. These include structural constraints, when the non-judicial branches of government alter judicial institutions to secure favourable judicial decisions. Next, interference takes a managerial form when control of judicial careers is used to limit impartiality. Administrative influence occurs when the courts lose control of court administration, especially the assignment of cases. 'Direct approaches' include threats, bribes, media campaigns, and private intimations from government representatives designed to influence outcomes in specific cases (Russell 2001).

The importance of the courts for modern authoritarians is that government actions designed to rig the political system, and particularly elections, can obtain a veneer of legitimacy if endorsed by courts, especially courts with the power to review acts for their constitutionality. In the illiberal democracies governments distrust liberal institutions such as constitutional courts, supreme courts and ordinary courts yet rely on them to confer legitimacy: 'the formal legitimization of political decisions and the maintenance of the appearance of democracy and rule of law are important functions of the legal system' (Szente 2021: 26) which can nevertheless be controlled by informal means.

Political interference in the judicial process has five main objectives: to secure a judiciary which can be expected to favour the government when it is involved in litigation or otherwise has a political interest in the outcome of a case; to reduce the effectiveness of political opposition and dissent in both government (opposition deputies and MPs, governors and mayors at sub-national levels, and so on) and civil society (NGOs, human rights activists and investigative journalists); to punish specific individuals who have exposed abuses of executive power and corruption; to remove obstacles, in the form of judicial review, to a government's legislative programme; and to prolong an incumbent's term in office. A political system may offer examples of more than one objective over a period of time.

DOI: 10.4324/9781003334613-4

This chapter shows how different forms of intervention in the judicial process can be used to achieve these objectives, concentrating on how external factors reduce the independence and impartiality of the judiciary, specifically the powers assigned to other branches of government and the extra-constitutional influences that can be brought to bear on the judicial process. In the next chapter the focus is on the behaviour of judges themselves and the ways in which this can deviate from impartial and independent judicial decision-making, especially when the courts are used as a political weapon.

Powers of appointment to the judiciary

The most familiar way in which the independence of the judiciary can be compromised is through political interference in the appointment and tenure of judges, making them vulnerable to political pressures. This is usually the result of the powers granted to the political executive, and especially presidents, over recruitment to the judiciary and the deployment of judges within it. Despite the democratic rhetoric with which the constitutions of democratizing states were presented to the world, their content did not always afford sufficient protection against interference in the judiciary by the executive branch of government. Appointments to constitutional courts are particularly prone to political motivations, often reflecting the partisan choices of executives and legislators, even when justices are mainly recruited from the professional judiciary (Garoupa and Ginsburg 2015).

The powers of appointment assigned by the constitution can be divided into three categories. First there is the power to select lawyers to become judges and prosecutors. Then there are powers over judicial careers, including the assignment of judges to specific courts, especially constitutional courts. And finally, there is the power to appoint judges to membership of the judicial councils responsible for the management of the judiciary.

Excessive executive power of appointment to the judiciary itself is detrimental to democracy, as illustrated by the former Soviet Socialist Republic of Armenia, where sweeping powers were given to the office of president under the 1995 Constitution. As well as making the president dominant in relation to other branches of government, this Constitution entitled the president to appoint all judges, who then served for life. Amendments to the Constitution in 2005, though reducing some presidential powers over the judiciary (such as the scope of presidential appointment to the Council of Justice), left presidential powers of appointment to the judicial branch intact. Consequently, the Constitutional Court has never threatened presidential power in the political process and even endorsed fraudulent presidential elections. The ordinary courts also rarely find against the state when the use of executive or administrative power is challenged. As a result, a large majority of the population believe that political pressures on the courts make it impossible for them to protect citizens against the abuse of power (Freedom House 2003). Such powers of appointment can also undermine the equality of citizens before the law and the judiciary's ability to impartially interpret and enforce the constitution, as in Azerbaijan (Freedom House 2015a).

Executive power may extend to the composition of the legal profession itself, as in Belarus, where the Ministry of Justice controls the Collegium of Advocates which all attorneys must join if they wish to practise law and which dismisses those who offend the executive by, for example, defending human rights or the independence of the media. The president then appoints half the members of the Constitutional Court and some of the members of the Council of the Republic (the upper house of the National Assembly) which appoints the other half by rubber-stamping presidential nominations. The president also appoints and dismisses district and military judges as well as the entire Supreme Court. Members of the Constitutional Court can be removed by the president simply by 'notifying' the Council of the Republic. All such powers are endorsed by a constitution which stipulates that the judiciary should be independent but which allows the judicial system to be systematically used as a political instrument to suppress political opposition and dissent.

Such executive powers result in the judiciary having a poor record in cases relating to civil liberties, political freedom, the independence of the media and human rights, as in Kazakhstan where the president proposes nominees for membership of all courts, up to and including the level of the Supreme Court, to the Senate. These are chosen from recommendations made by the Supreme Judicial Council whose members are also appointed by the president. Consequently, convictions are secured in all politically motivated prosecutions, despite the absence of credible evidence or proper procedures. Control of the courts enables the executive to harass NGOs, opposition activists and journalists, as in Azerbaijan, where the courts serve 'as the primary weapon in the regime's escalating crackdown on dissent' (Freedom House 2015a).

In the more extreme cases, where there is no check on, or review of, presidential appointments by the legislature or other organ of government, the judicial system risks becoming a rubber stamp for presidential decisions and an instrument of political repression, putting fundamental rights, the rule of law and due process all at risk, as in Turkmenistan. Judges may be instructed by members of the executive on the rulings that should be handed down as happens frequently in Uzbekistan, where the president exercises powers of appointment and dismissal over judges and appoints a qualifications collegium which screens applicants to the lower courts. Criminal charges can be brought against judges if the public prosecutor or other official accuses them of violating the law or 'defaming' the judiciary. The rules of natural justice play no part in court proceedings. Consequently, the judiciary is unable to protect human rights or the rule of law and thus becomes a major contributor to the stalling of the democratic transition.

Malignant executive power allows ever more extreme forms of political manipulation, as in Kenya where a Chief Justice was appointed despite not being a practising advocate or sitting judge as required by the Constitution and despite having been dismissed twice previously from judicial offices on disciplinary grounds. He had, however, been active as Deputy Public Prosecutor in prosecuting critics of the government. In Paraguay appointments at all levels of the judiciary are made on the basis of political service and allegiance rather than professional merit, despite the separations of powers and the independence of the judiciary being built into the Constitution.

Other consequences of executive powers of appointment to the judiciary include the allocation of politically sensitive cases to junior judges rather than to more independent senior judges; the determination of supreme court judgements according to political rather than legal considerations; refusals to proceed with human rights petitions lodged by lawyers and civil society organizations with the supreme court; and the use of contempt of court proceedings to stifle criticism from the legal profession and the media.

Political bias in the appointment of senior judges can infect the whole of the judiciary. Latin American constitutions generally enshrine judicial independence while endowing the executive branch with excessive powers. Once political interference in appointments occurs at the higher levels of the judiciary, it is likely to percolate down if appointments to lower-level courts are determined by the judiciary itself. Consequently, it was found that '[i]f supreme court appointments are vitiated from the top . . . the likelihood that lower appointments would be subject to clientelism and patronage rather than merit-based criteria was greater' (Domingo 1999: 160).

Federalism offers a further possibility: that while the judiciary may operate independently at one level of government, political considerations can still affect appointments at lower levels of the judiciary. In Mexico, for example, the appointment and dismissal of judges at the federal level are largely unbiased. The president's nominees for justices of the Supreme Court have to be confirmed by the Senate. The careers, including initial appointment, of other federal judges are controlled by the Federal Council of the Judiciary. However, judges at state level are appointed and dismissed by state governors and lack security of tenure. Consequently, justice in state courts is heavily affected by state politics.

Similarly, in Nigeria, the independence of federal court judges is stronger than that at state level, where state governors' powers of appointment and financial allocations mean that the courts respond positively to political pressures from the executive branch of state government. In February 2012 the Chief Justice of Nigeria claimed that the lack of independence of the judiciary at the state level constitutes one of the greatest challenges facing the nation's judicial system. A major factor in this is the refusal of many state governors to comply with the provision of the constitution which requires funds for the judiciary to be paid to the National Judicial Council for disbursement to the heads of courts (Adesomoju 2012).

In addition to securing favourable judgements and restraining political opposition, control of the composition of the judiciary may lead to it being used for purposes of political retribution, as in Georgia where the prosecution of former political leaders in 2014 led to condemnation by the European Union and the United States government. The EU warned that it would closely monitor such legal proceedings against members of the former government and current opposition to ensure that the prosecutions were 'transparent, proportionate, free of political motivation, and adhering strictly to due process' (Reuters 2014).

Control of the judge's career

Once appointed, there is the question of who controls a judge's career and how far this is vulnerable to politically motivated interventions from the executive. Judges who are dependent on the executive for promotion and material benefits may be influenced by 'managerial' tactics used to bias judicial decisions, including suspending judges before challenges to executive action can be heard; appointing temporary judges who are more vulnerable to political influence (as in Pakistan, where the use of presidential powers to appoint judges to the High Court under Article 197 of the Constitution has frequently been used to test the political allegiances of candidates for permanent positions); and even biasing housing allocations to penalize magistrates ruling against city officials (as in Ukraine, where the perks of office are used to influence local court decisions: Popova 2012). The Polish and Hungarian governments' attacks on the judiciary have relied heavily on the manipulation of rules on judges' tenure and retirement, leading to references to the Court of Justice of the European Union seeking rulings in support of judicial independence (Bako 2020). In 2020 the Argentinian legislature passed a government bill creating new criminal courts to be staffed by temporary judges, despite the Supreme Court having ruled in 2015 that this undermined judicial independence (HRW 2022).

Power to appoint judges to specific courts provides opportunities for the political executive to determine both the general ideological approach to constitutional and policy issues and the outcome of specific cases. Control of appointments to constitutional and supreme courts provides opportunities for presidents to 'pack' the courts with politically biased judges (as in Argentina under President Menem in 1991 and Mexico under Zedillo in 1995) and undermines the courts' ability to offer protection against fraudulent elections and the arbitrary arrest of opposition activists (as in Azerbaijan, where the judiciary has been controlled by the Aliyev family, first under President Heydar Aliyev from 1993 and then by his son from 2003 (Lenke 2022)).

Presidents have sometimes dissolved supreme courts when rulings contrary to the political interests of the government were handed down. In 2020 Mali's president dissolved the Constitutional Court in an attempt to calm the civil unrest caused by the court's decision to overturn the provisional results for 30 parliamentary seats declared following a general election, which resulted in the president's party retaining its majority. In the same year the president of Ukraine submitted a draft law to parliament cancelling the decisions of the Constitutional Court, recognizing them as 'null and void' and without legal consequences and terminating the powers of the current Constitutional Court justices. This followed the court's rulings that the government's anti-corruption measures were unconstitutional.

Enlarging a supreme court, with politically biased appointees ensures that the majority of justices are ideologically oriented towards the values of the incumbent government, as in Argentina in 1990, where '[i]n the course of a very few months the Supreme Court shifted from a very liberal position to a very conservative one' (Gargarella 2004: 189).

Decisions on the assignment of justices to constitutional courts can become a weapon in political conflicts over the powers of the political executive itself. In 2011 the president of Ukraine replaced four members of the Constitutional Court with judges loyal to him before securing a ruling from the court that constitutional amendments passed in 2004 which limited the powers of the president should be annulled. The fact that this questioned the constitutional legitimacy of government between 2004 and 2011 was not lost on critics of the court's ruling.

The power to assign judges to hear specific cases can also be used as a political weapon, even when there are clear rules prescribing the correct procedure, as in Azerbaijan. In Russia the power given to the president to appoint court chairmen allows political pressure to be brought to bear, since chairmen control the assignment of cases to individual judges as well as personnel matters such as salary levels and housing benefits. As a result, the courts can be used to silence opponents of the government and others who challenge the political and economic elite, sacrificing 'the long-term interests of Russian society in favour of the short-term political interests of the leaders of the state. It is hard to imagine something more destructive for the legal institutions and judicial system' (Freedom House 2015b).

The assessment of judges for career purposes enables political loyalty to be used as a criterion, as in Kyrgystan, where independence and impartiality have been replaced by use of the judiciary as an instrument of government policy and a tool for silencing critics. Disciplinary procedures may also be used to secure court decisions favourable to the government and to punish judges who have made statements critical of political leaders, as in Slovakia (US Department of State 2014).

Disciplinary procedures have been heavily politicized in Poland, leading to a ruling from the European Court of Justice that the Polish Supreme Court's disciplinary body should be suspended on the grounds that the chamber could not be considered an impartial and independent judicial body as defined under EU law. The government agreed to comply but has failed to do so. Judges in Poland continue to face arbitrary disciplinary proceedings for raising concerns about the rule of law and judicial 'reforms' that directly interfere with their independence (HRW 2022).

Such powers motivate judges to consider the effects of their decisions on their futures in the judiciary. For example, control of a judge's career by the Algerian Ministry of Justice means that they are 'averse to making judicial decisions contrary to government expectations for fear of imperiling their careers' (Freedom House 2005: 7). Consequently, the Algerian's constitutional right to a fair trial is frequently undermined. Judges in Indonesia also tailor their decisions to what they feel will satisfy the government and thus protect their careers. The minister of justice uses powers of promotion, transfer and remuneration to reward or penalize judges depending on whether their rulings met with the minister's approval.

Conditions of service within the judiciary can also be used to influence judicial decisions. Judges that serve the interests of the government may be rewarded with promotions and valuable perks, widely regarded as a strategy to undermine the independence of the judiciary. When Senegal's president sought a third term of office in 2012, contrary to Article 27 of the Constitution which limits the head of state to two terms, opponents appealed to the Constitutional Court, whose members were originally appointed by the outgoing president. The court not only ruled in the president's favour but also barred an opposition candidate from standing in the coming election. This followed a doubling of the five constitutional judges' salaries by the president and the gift of a limousine each. The ruling led to violent protests in a country hitherto known for its democratic stability (Gueye 2012). In Zimbabwe Supreme Court judges have been given fully equipped, profitable and tax-free farms as part of the policy of awarding white-owned farms to ZANU-PF supporters. Senior judges of the High Court and Labour Court have also been given television sets, cars and generators (valuable, given the frequency of power failures in Zimbabwe) (Berger 2008).

Appointments to judicial councils

Even the establishment of a judicial council, designed to distance the appointment of judges and the management of the judiciary from the political process, will not guarantee judicial independence if the executive controls its membership. In Malaysia the prime minister appoints the majority of Judicial Appointments Commission (JAC) members who lack security of both tenure and remuneration. In this case the legislation setting up the JAC appears to have been 'carefully crafted to incapacitate the members of the Commission from performing their functions of selecting and recommending candidates for appointment as judges of the superior courts independently' (Bari et al. 2015: 248).

Judicial councils provide a measure of self-government within the judiciary, but the executive's powers of appointment can mean that judicial decision-making remains politicized, as in Kazakhstan where the Supreme Judicial Council is de facto controlled by the president through power of appointment. Consequently, the judiciary lacks independence, and the courts have been a major weapon used by the government against political opposition (Olcott 2010). In Tunisia presidential power was used in 2022 to dissolve the Supreme Judicial Council, following months of presidential criticism of the judiciary and the removal of council members' financial privileges. This was widely seen as an attempt to place the judiciary under presidential control, as part of a political purge of the judiciary, and the latest move by President Saied to tighten his grip on power, following suspension of parliament, dismissal of the prime minister and enlargement of executive power. The president appointed a new, temporary body, a move seen as a major regression, giving the executive power over the judiciary, as it was under the former authoritarianism, and removing the separation of powers enshrined in the 2014 Constitution.

There are also indirect methods by which controls can be exercised. In 2010 concerns were expressed when the Bulgarian government secured legislative backing for the requirement that members of the Supreme Judicial Council should have clearance from part of the security service. This was widely seen as risking executive interference in the judiciary.

Resources

The ability of the judiciary to deliver justice can be undermined when it is starved of resources. Whether this is the result of a deliberate attempt on the part of politicians to interfere in judicial decision-making depends on the circumstances of individual regimes. There are certainly occasions when ulterior political motives are suspected when the judiciary is inadequately resourced, and as a consequence judicial review is undermined. For example, in Zambia and Tanzania 'lack of adequate and secured funds seems to be a major factor limiting the ability and willingness of courts to hold the executive to account', motivating the judiciary to 'stay on good terms with the executive to keep what little they have' (Gloppen 2004: 128).

Resources may be so limited that judges have to perform administrative tasks, raising fears that judicial independence could again be compromised. If under-resourcing takes the form of low salaries, judges may be dependent on government for benefits such as subsidized housing, making them wary of offending government agencies (not to mention having an incentive to behave corruptly). A combination of heavy caseload and inadequate resources can create incentives to find in favour of the state in order to shorten proceedings, risking failure to observe procedures required by due process and a fair trial (as has happened in Algeria). Under-funding by the national government may leave the judiciary vulnerable to improper political influences from the local authorities to which the courts have to turn for resources, as in Russia (Rishmawi 2000).

Resource problems can extend to a lack of basic infrastructure, which can mean that trials have to be held in judges' offices instead of courtrooms, 'hindering the ability of the courts to carry out open trials and increasing opportunities for abuse and corrupt practices' (Freedom House 2013), as in Albania where there have been repeated reductions in budgetary allocations in recent years. The capacity of judges to make the fairest possible rulings is also limited by inadequate training prior to and during their careers and by the absence of law reports recording earlier judgements. For example, in Sierra Leone the lack of stenographers, even at Supreme Court level, means that

> [j]udges have to compile the transcript of each hearing themselves in long hand. The Judge's written record becomes the sole record of the trial. This system is extremely slow and cumbersome, with Judges and Magistrates essentially taking dictation from witnesses and barristers. Consequently the statements read into the record are delivered slowly and carefully to avoid mistakes in transcription. The potential negative consequences flowing from this practice are numerous and include unnecessarily lengthy and cumbersome procedures, potentially inaccurate recording of events and statements, as well as opening the door to allegations of bias or prejudice in terms of what is actually recorded by the Judge or Magistrate in a particular legal case.
>
> (Harris and Nicol-Wilson 2007: 14–15)

Intimidation

In addition to the formal powers which may be used to undermine judicial independence, there are many types of informal influence and pressure which can be brought to bear. These include personal threats to careers and physical safety, as well as the manipulation of patronage obligations, personal networks, bribery and material rewards (Llanos et al. 2015). Intimidation may be initiated by both agents of the state and groups of political activists.

Judges in many countries are subjected to harassment when challenges to executive action are heard in court. Intimidation comes from many different directions, including state agents, paramilitary groups, militias, and armed opposition groups. Intimidation of the judiciary in Guatemala reached such proportions in 2000 that judges and other legal professionals were unable to obtain life insurance (Sieder 2004). Others have been forced to flee the country. In 2015 the Pakistani judge who convicted the killer of the governor of Punjab, murdered because he advocated reform of the blasphemy law, was forced to flee the country following threats by religious conservatives.

The reprisals suffered by jurists for carrying out their professional duties include murder, disappearances, prosecutions, detention, physical abuse, verbal threats and professional obstruction. In 2001 an Indonesian Supreme Court justice was murdered after finding the president's son guilty of corruption (ICJ 2002). Lawyers defending opponents and critics of the government have been arrested, as in Belarus. Zimbabwe has become notorious for the harassment of judges, illustrated by the arrest of High Court Justice Benjamin Paradza in 2003, a judge with a history of passing judgements unfavourable to the government, such as ordering the release of opposition members abducted by supporters of the president and ruling as illegal the eviction orders served on some white farmers. Judges have been subjected to intimidation by corrupt para-military groups as well as the armed forces, as in Tajikistan, where courts have been turned into 'a tool to silence opposition figures' (Freedom House 2006b). In 2010 Ghanaian judges feared to attend their courts following statements by leading members of the government threatening a 'purge' of the judiciary, and violent demonstrations by ruling-party militants against a judicial decision that went against the government. Attempts by a judge in Rio de Janeiro to bring corrupt police officers to justice led to her murder in August 2011; more than 90 other Brazilian judges were found to be on a 'most wanted' death list. In the same year an Albanian judge, known for his integrity, was assassinated, and a record number of judges had to be placed under police protection. In 2013 the Chief Justice of Kenya was threatened with 'dire consequences' in a poison-pen letter from the Mungiki sect if the courts barred presidential candidate Uhuru Kenyatta from contesting the presidential election. Threats to the lives of justices presiding over criminal proceedings brought against prominent politicians have also been made in Nigeria. In 2020 the president of Colombia and other leading members of the Democratic Centre party made statements smearing the Supreme Court in order to undermine the legitimacy of its decision ordering the arrest for bribery of a political ally.

The intimidating atmosphere in South Africa became so pronounced that in 2015 the Chief Justice sought a meeting with the President in an attempt to end the attacks on the judiciary by government ministers and senior members of the African National Congress over recent years, especially following judgements unfavourable to the state. Public statements by prominent politicians have accused the courts of seeking to create 'chaos for governance', thereby undermining it (February 2015). In May 2012 the United Nation's Special Rapporteur on the independence of judges and lawyers expressed her concern about the number and nature of reported cases of serious threats and attacks on judges and lawyers in Pakistan. In Bosnia, domestic prosecutors and judges are vulnerable to intimidation by powerful individuals, particularly in the absence of adequate security measures so that prosecutors are sometimes reluctant to pursue war crimes and other cases against politically prominent suspects.

Lack of resources may also mean that the physical security of judges is compromised, making them more vulnerable to intimidation, as in Afghanistan where, despite legal guarantees of judicial independence, a lack of security for judges left them exposed to pressure and interference from armed groups, public officials and private individuals. In 2001 the South African Cabinet had to plan for the physical security of judges, magistrates, prosecutors and detectives involved in the investigation and prosecution of cases of urban terrorism in the Western Cape.

Intimidation can also be exercised through unwarranted legislative oversight, as when a subcommittee of the Hungarian parliament, investigating infringements of civil and political rights, summoned senior members of the judiciary to appear before it in September 2010 to answer questions about sentences handed down following anti-government riots in 2006. In the view of the Chief Justice of the Supreme Court, parliamentary investigation into specific rulings which held individual judges personally responsible constituted a severe threat to judicial independence.

The independence of the judicial process can also be undermined by the harassment and intimidation of lawyers, as in Belarus, where lawyers have been arbitrarily disbarred, lost their licenses, and faced criminal and administrative charges for defending human rights and representing clients in politically motivated cases. Official interference in the work of lawyers by recording confidential conversations with clients, sharing video recordings with governmental broadcasters, forcing acceptance of nondisclosure agreements, denying access to clients, and questioning clients without their lawyer present has violated fundamental due process. Since 2021 practising lawyers have had to be employed by regional bar associations controlled by the Ministry of Justice, further undermining the independence of the legal profession (HRW 2022). Serbia's accession to the European Union is currently jeopardized by inadequate guarantees against political influence over the judiciary, and attacks by government officials and members of parliament, public comments on ongoing court proceedings, and insults and attacks on individual judges, including during parliamentary debates on judicial elections, all of which negatively influence public opinion and trust in the judiciary (EU 2021).

Limiting the scope of judicial review

The scope of judicial review is heavily dependent upon executive, and especially presidential, powers. The courts are less likely to invalidate government decisions and more likely to support the executive when the president appears as an appellant, especially when seeking to have legislation restricting presidential power overturned. The stronger the executive power, when measured by the power to veto legislation, issue decrees, determine budgets and control cabinet membership, the more constrained is judicial review of legislation being tested for its constitutionality (Herron and Randazzo 2003).

Judicial review can also be restricted by impunity rules which inhibit lawyers from pursuing justice, as in Chad, where no action has been taken against members of the security forces responsible for human rights violations. Impunity and avoidance of justice can also be achieved by the infiltration of judicial institutions by military personnel, as in Guatemala, thereby ensuring human rights violations go unpunished. The military were able to create 'an extensive clandestine network operating throughout state institutions in the justice sector and the public security forces that works to systematically obstruct the course of justice' (Sieder 2004: 149). Judicial review of executive or administrative legality can also be limited by giving the executive powers to relieve citizens of criminal liability and withhold consent for the prosecution of senior public officials, as in Belarus.

In November 2012 a decree issued by President Morsi exempting all presidential edicts from judicial review until the ratification of a constitution brought renewed instability to Egyptian politics. Justified by the president as protecting the new regime against a judiciary packed with judges and prosecutors sympathetic to former President Mubarak, the edict declared that previous constitutional declarations, laws and decrees made by the president since he took office on 30 June 2012 were final and binding and could not be appealed until the constitution was approved and a new People's Assembly elected. 'Nor shall they be suspended or canceled and all lawsuits related to them and brought before any judicial body against these decisions are annulled' (Muftah 2012). In fact, the Egyptian judiciary under the previous regime had a reputation for independence and professionalism.

Ouster clauses further limit the jurisdiction of the courts, as in Zambia, where many basic human rights are unjusticiable and where the widespread use of derogation clauses 'has undermined the constitutional protection of rights' (Gloppen 2004: 124). Emergency powers can be used to restrict judicial review, thereby undermining constitutional guarantees and fundamental rights, as in Colombia (Uprimi 2004). The rule of law can be undermined by legislation which restricts the power of the courts to issue injunctions in support of challenges to government actions from civil society, as in Malawi in 2011.

Restricting the scope of judicial review can extend to constitutional as well as administrative matters. In 2010 the Hungarian government amended the Constitution so that the Constitutional Court no longer had jurisdiction over taxation, the national budget or property rights. The new constitution of 2012 provides for further reductions in the competences of the Constitutional Court, including the *actio popularis* rule which allowed citizens to request the court to determine whether a given regulation is constitutional. The Venice Commission found cause for concern in the weakening of the position of the Constitutional Court in the Hungarian system of checks and balances, arguing that large scale of competences is essential if the courts are to protect constitutionally guaranteed fundamental rights. 'Therefore, restricting the Court's competence in such a way that it would review certain state Acts only with regard to a limited part of the Constitution runs counter to the obvious aim of the constitutional legislature in the Hungarian parliament "to enhance the protection of fundamental rights in Hungary"' (Venice Commission 2011: para. 99).

Restricting constitutional review is usually motivated by a determination to remove obstacles to a government's legislative programme. This was the case when the Law and Justice government in Poland used its parliamentary dominance in 2015 to enact legislation requiring a two-thirds majority rather than a simple majority of justices before legislation can be deemed unconstitutional by the Constitutional Court. In addition, 13 justices are now required to be present for the most contentious cases, instead of the previous nine. The new law also makes it obligatory for three to six months to elapse between a request for a ruling being made and the court's verdict, compared with two weeks currently. The government also attempted to install five judges of its own choosing, refusing to recognize those appointed by the previous parliament. The Court claims the new law interferes with its independence, and the European Union has warned of the danger posed to the rule of law in Poland.

Judicial review can also be restricted by changes to the structure of courts. By merging the Supreme Arbitration Court and the Supreme Court in 2014 enabled the Russian government to remove members of the Arbitration Court known for their independence in the administration of commercial law. In addition to undermining consistency in the application of commercial law, the merger was predicted to 'block innovative efforts to reform the Russian judicial system, and instead create more opportunities for political leaders to intervene in the judicial process and advance their particular economic interests' (Freedom House 2015b).

Exceptional courts

As was pointed out in Chapter 2, the use of exceptional courts does not necessarily entail a loss of judicial independence and departure from the rule of law. Special tribunals can offer benefits such as low cost, informality and efficient conflict resolution without jeopardizing natural justice and impartiality.

Nevertheless, extraordinary courts are often prohibited under the constitution as contrary to the rule of law, as in Bulgaria and Yemen. Despite this, executive determination to secure greater control of the judicial process has led to departures from constitutional prohibitions. In 2010 the Bulgarian government defended its decision to set up specialized courts to deal with the prosecution of organized crime by reference to the need to speed up judicial proceedings and protect them against pressure from the criminal fraternity. The two-tier system, with a first-instance court for initial trials and an appeals court, began operations in January 2012. It was also intended that such courts should deal with corruption prosecutions, but this was dropped following criticism by the European Commission for Democracy through Law (the Venice Commission). Yemen also has two specialized courts, mainly for the prosecution of media offences, despite a constitutional prohibition against creating 'exceptional courts . . . under any conditions'. In 1999 a Specialized Criminal Court was established to hear cases related to crimes such as terrorism and piracy but had its jurisdiction widened in 2002 to include 'crimes against state security and serious economic and social crimes', which has allowed the prosecution of journalists. The Specialized Press and Publications Court was created in 2009 to enforce the press law, the penal code and any other laws as it sees fit.

Exceptional courts in post-authoritarian transitions are especially vulnerable to manipulation to secure outcomes favourable to state agencies. The use of exceptional courts can undermine the principles of natural justice, especially when military tribunals are allowed to hear civilian cases, as in Peru and the Democratic Republic of the Congo. In 2014 an International Commission of Jurists mission to Tunisia expressed concern that military courts have powers to hear cases of human rights violations against civilians (ICJ 2014).

The use of emergency laws is often associated with special courts such as Egypt's security courts and the referral of civilian cases to military tribunals. In 2011 more than 12,000 Egyptians were tried in military courts. In one case an Egyptian army doctor carried out forced 'virginity tests' on seven female protesters at a military prison but was found not guilty in 2012 of public indecency and disobeying military orders by a military court, despite an earlier administrative court ruling that such tests were illegal. Use of a military court enabled the doctor to evade a charge of administering illegal tests, leaving him accused only of conducting the test in an 'open space', a charge easily dismissed on the grounds of contradictory evidence from different victims. There is no appeal from a military court and no recourse is allowed to a civilian court. Egypt at the time had a caretaker military regime supposedly preparing the country for democracy (*The Guardian* 2012). It is generally agreed among jurists that there is no justification for allowing military tribunals to hear cases under criminal, civil, commercial or administrative law just because they happen to involve military personnel. And it is unlikely that civilians will be ensured a fair trial under this type of 'exceptional' jurisdiction.

The administration of customary law also entails the use of courts which are separate from the judiciary, as in Sierra Leone. They are often exposed to the political influence of local elites (including local and provincial government officials). Political loyalties can be more important than impartiality or expertise in the recruitment of local customary court officials. The separation of powers at the local level can be insufficient for customary courts to deliver impartial adjudication

(Freedom House 2012). Questions raised by exceptional courts, often considered as part of judicial reform, will be considered further in Chapter 5.

Steering the judiciary

Governments may resort to making public their expectations of the courts by issuing statements which 'guide' or 'steer' the courts in the desired direction. The most infamous type of informal influence and pressure on the judiciary is the system ironically named 'telephone justice' which has its roots in the Soviet judicial system. Telephone justice (or injustice) is 'a practice by which outcomes of cases allegedly come from orders issued over the phone by those with political power rather than through the application of law'. Though it often only applies to exceptional cases affecting the preservation of state power and the interests of those who wield it, rather than to more everyday litigation, it nevertheless 'strikes at the very heart of the traditional concept of the "rule of law". It calls into question both the independence of the judiciary and the universalistic nature of law' (Hendley 2009: 242, 258).

'Steering' takes a variety of forms. Public statements can be made about how the courts are expected to rule on policy issues such as energy tariffs and state pensions, as in Georgia in 2003. Presidents may comment publicly on current cases in attempts to influence decisions and appeals, especially those dealing with the return of property appropriated by the state during the communist regime, as in Romania (ABA 2002). Presidents may hold meetings with senior judges to discuss the government's policy objectives, including housing, taxation and reform of the judicial system itself, as in Russia. Judges here see nothing wrong in this in a culture in which they are 'susceptible to influence within a society that assumes policies are set at the top'. Since senior judges affect the decisions of lower courts through their influence on salaries and the allocation of cases, the president's suggestions 'undoubtedly trickle down through the judicial hierarchy' (Freedom House 2006a: 13).

'Steering' can in some circumstances result from attitudes engendered during recruitment. Procedures for appointing judges in Russia, involving vetting and clearance by government agencies, leave them in no doubt as to where their loyalties should lie and how they will be expected to adjudicate when they become judges. Candidates who demonstrate too much independence are unlikely to be appointed. The courts are part of a system of informal practices, unwritten rules and bonds of loyalty, which ensures that the government receives the judgements it needs (Ledeneva 2010).

Non-enforcement

If direct or indirect pressure is insufficient to secure favourable judicial outcomes, court decisions can be nullified by the non-implementation of judgements. It is commonly agreed that failure to implement decisions of the courts undermines judicial independence (Voigt et al. 2015). Selective enforcement of the laws can also undermine public trust in the impartiality of judicial decisions, judicial authority and the state itself (Kozyreva and Smirnov 2015).

This is one of the most common problems identified by the European Court of Human Rights and constitutes a refusal on the part of national governments to accept the rule of law. The non-execution of court judgements by the authorities constitutes a breach of the right to a fair trial or hearing. It is thus a serious human rights problem. It is also important that judgements delivered against the government are enforced. When political leaders invent pretexts for disregarding judicial decisions, and convey a lack of respect for the judiciary, the credibility of the judicial system is harmed. 'Members of the public who have placed their trust in the judicial system should obtain satisfaction, not only on paper but also in practice. To ensure full and prompt execution of court decisions is one of the hallmarks of a democratic society' (Hammarberg 2009).

The non-enforcement of court judgements particularly affects vulnerable groups when state agencies ignore judicial decisions on social benefits. Prominent among non-executed decisions in post-communist states have been those relating to the return of property nationalized by former governments.

Judicial rulings have sometimes been considered recommendations when members of the executive have been found guilty of wrongdoing, as in Nigeria, to the extent that 'the general disrespect for court orders by powerful institutions in the country erodes the credibility of the judicial system' (Freedom House 2004: 4). Albania's Constitutional Court has been required to rule on a number of dismissals by the president of prosecutors general, but its judgements have not been enforced. Here the cases of 'non-respect' for Constitutional Court decisions, coupled with the politicization of senior judicial appointments, challenge 'fundamental principles such as the independence of the judiciary and respect for the rule of law' (European Commission 2010: 6). The frequency of non-compliance with court orders on the part of government, which has also reduced the credibility of the system of justice in the eyes of the public in Malawi, (IBA 2012), is likely to damage the process of democratic consolidation.

Practices from the authoritarian era which obstruct the enforcement of court orders can be carried over and extended in the post-authoritarian period, as in post-Suharto Indonesia, where letters (*surat sakti*) from the Chief Justice of the Supreme Court to judges responsible for ensuring compliance with court decisions advise delay in their execution when they are hostile to government interests. These letters 'constitute illegal judicial-like decisions which undermine the independence to which all judges are legally entitled' (Butt 2008: 358).

Non-compliance may even extend to constitutional rulings. In 2008 the Supreme Court of Argentina declared unconstitutional an article in the Trade Union Act which restricted freedom of association and the principle of 'free and democratic union organization', both enshrined in Article 14 of the Constitution. The act was also found to be in conflict with the International Labour Organization's Freedom of Association and Protection of the Right to Organize Convention, 1948, giving this convention precedence over Argentinian law and therefore the status of constitutional law (Goldin 2009). The federal government did not comply with this ruling.

Evasion of court rulings may entail bringing political pressure to bear on a private body which has received a court ruling, such as in Azerbaijan where pressure was used in 2004 to stop an electricity company from restoring power to an independent publisher after an economic court had ordered supply to be resumed. However, it is usually public bodies which refuse to comply, as in Belarus in 2003 when the Central Electoral Commission refused to provide vote-counting documents when ordered to do so by the Constitutional Court, declaring that the court was incorrect in its judgement. Earlier, in 2002, when the court outlawed official restrictions on foreign travel, its ruling was ignored by the Ministry of the Interior which then successfully brought pressure to bear on the court to revise its judgement. In 2003 a ruling by the Constitutional Court of Georgia – that it was unconstitutional to require public demonstrations to obtain special permission – was ignored by the police who continued to disrupt protest rallies.

Sometimes non-compliance with judicial rulings is the result of scarce resources, inefficiency or lack of administrative capacity, as in Sierra Leone and South Africa, rather than defiance by government agencies or other powerful interests. The lack of an effective bailiff organization in Latvia has meant that many court decisions remain unenforced. In Russia, frequently delayed enforcement and non-enforcement of court decisions are in part the result of inadequate resources and an inefficient bailiff system (Provost 2015). The failure to enforce legal decisions in civil cases in Russia has created incentives for successful litigants to resort to private 'enforcers' who use illegal methods to obtain information and coerce debtors and others against whom the courts have ruled. This illegality works in partnership with the under-resourced bailiff organization (Favarel-Garrigues 2015).

Weaponizing the judiciary

Why do governments in illiberal democracies go to such lengths to undermine judicial independence? On reason is that under the new, post-authoritarian constitutions, the judiciary has been empowered to review the compatibility of government policies with constitutional guarantees and civil, social and economic rights. The ramifications of 'judicial activism' for democracy and judicial independence will be explored further in Chapter 8. The other is that governments have found in the courts a weapon that can be wielded against political critics and opponents.

When it is difficult to ignore constitutional restraints on political repression the judiciary has become an important means of ensuring that government policies can be driven through or political opposition suppressed. The new illiberal democracies have to look as if they are respecting human rights and the rule of law, including freedom of speech and association, when provision for these is written into the constitution and when scrutiny is being exercised by international watchdogs such as the European Union, Human Rights Watch, the International Court of Human Rights and the United Nations High Commission for Human Rights. It is much more difficult under democratic constitutional constraints to have opponents 'disappeared', as in some military dictatorships (though some post-authoritarian democracies have come close to perfecting the extra-judicial killing of hostile politicians and journalists). Opposition parties cannot be outlawed as in one-party states. It is not easy, given constitutional guarantees, to incorporate community groups, industrial unions, professional associations and advocacy groups into the state apparatus, as in totalitarian regimes. When constitutions endorse political pluralism and fundamental rights, repression has to be disguised as the rule of law. So the prosecution in the courts of opponents – leaders of opposition parties, investigative journalists, human rights activists, and even members of the judiciary itself – gives the appearance of deference to the rule of law but turns the courts into a weapon in political conflicts played out within constitutional constraints. The weaponization of law can be 'compatible with autonomous judiciaries and individual judges, who enjoy decisional independence' (Popova 2019: 17).

In illiberal democracies prosecutions are aimed at three types of critic: opposition leaders, journalists and human rights workers. In 2019 leaders of opposition parties and movements were imprisoned for a fabricated traffic offence (Azerbaijan); attempting to seize power illegally and being a national security threat (Belarus); money laundering (Georgia); sedition or accepting money from drug dealers (Philippines); and unlawful assembly, rioting and sedition (Tanzania). Opposition leaders in Kyrgyzstan repeatedly face politically motivated criminal investigations and prosecutions, reducing the legitimacy of the justice system in the eyes of the public. The many trumped-up or otherwise flawed cases brought against opposition activists in Azerbaijan is a major factor in the courts' lack of political independence. Arrested detainees find access to legal counsel restricted, evidence fabricated or withheld, and their confessions sought by physical abuse (Freedom House 2021). In Zimbabwe the Movement for Democratic Change and its supporters faced arrests and prosecutions following disputed elections in 2018.

Journalists are equally vulnerable to a weaponized judiciary. In 2020 Belarus recorded a significant increase in journalists fined, held in detention and criminally prosecuted. The government used anti-extremism legislation to curtail the media. At least 105 journalists were behind bars in Turkey, Azerbaijan, the Russian Federation and the Russian-controlled Ukrainian territory of Crimea. There was a significant increase in spurious and politically motivated legal threats and judicial harassment in Bulgaria and Poland. The politically motivated prosecutions included accusations of justifying terrorism, spreading false information and resisting pressures to reveal confidential sources. Governments sometimes seek to hide the punishment of critical reporting by bringing cases that appear unrelated to journalism such as drug offences. As some journalists are being brought to court on fabricated charges, others are denied justice when they are victims of attacks or abuse at the hands of public officials and the police (Council of Europe 2020).

In Latin America, 2020 witnessed an overall decline in respect for press freedom with government officials retaliating against critical reporting by accusing the media of spreading 'fake news' and threatening and jailing critical journalists. In Asia political criticism is also labelled 'false news', and journalists have been arrested for inciting 'panic' among communities. The situation here has been exacerbated by the decline of Myanmar from struggling democracy into military dictatorship, but it also reflects the arrest and conviction of journalists across Southeast Asia as part of a surge in state-backed attacks on freedom of expression. At the end of 2019 there were at least 63 journalists in prisons in Asia. The majority were in China, but Cambodia, Pakistan, Bangladesh, Indonesia and the Philippines also used the courts to stifle the media.

Journalists in Africa face prosecution for cybercrime, fake news or terrorism. Many countries have adopted new laws in recent years, with vague and draconian provisions on the pretext of combatting disinformation and hate speech, that are used to deter journalists from criticizing the authorities. African journalists have been arrested for calling the president 'anti-democratic' (Ghana); conspiracy and defamation for criticizing the local authorities' handling of the health crisis (Nigeria); the unlawful possession of classified drugs, following investigation by journalists into the illegal sale of government drugs (Uganda); and financial pretexts (such as non-payment of taxes) or defamation and sedition (Zambia). A journalist renowned for exposing corruption in government in Zimbabwe was arrested in 2020 for 'inciting violence'. Charges of treason are widely used to gag the Ugandan media.

As part of the general repression of dissent, illiberal governments regularly target human rights defenders who have exposed corruption, human rights violations or electoral fraud with intimidation and arbitrary detention. Human rights activists are prosecuted and imprisoned for vaguely worded offences, such as spreading misinformation, leaking state secrets and insulting authorities, or are labelled 'terrorists'. Criminalizing human rights defenders is a way to silence dissent and makes it difficult for them to work freely and safely (Amnesty International 2021).

In 2020 human rights workers in Eastern and Central Europe were prosecuted for defamation (following exposure of torture in Kazakhstan prisons), theft (following public criticisms of the Azerbaijan authorities), not carrying identity documents (for working on behalf of victims of torture in Kyrgyzstan), theft and burglary (for accusing the Polish government of manipulating Covid-19 statistics, and offending religious beliefs for allegedly possessing and distributing posters and stickers depicting the Virgin Mary with a rainbow halo), and non-payment of arbitrary fines in Russia. The Russian government regularly brings charges against human rights groups under a law which requires registration as a 'foreign agent' if the group receives external funding. In 2021 Poland's politicized Constitutional Tribunal ordered the dismissal of the country's commissioner for human rights, a frequent critic of the government's abuse of the rule of law and human rights, contrary to the constitution, since parliament had failed to appoint a successor.

In Africa attacks on human rights defenders have been particularly relentless, especially in countries that held or prepared for elections, including Burundi, Côte d'Ivoire, Guinea, Niger, Tanzania and Uganda. In Zimbabwe the government has abused the criminal process to stifle and intimidate human rights defenders. 'The arrest and subsequent denial of bail and prolonged pre-trial detention is undoubtedly and increasingly being used as a tool of repression in Zimbabwe' (ICJ 2021). Arbitrary detention has been employed against Latin American human rights workers in the Dominican Republic, Guatemala, Mexico, Nicaragua and Venezuela. In Asia human rights defenders had counter-terrorism measures used against them for their legitimate support for human rights.

Critics of illiberal governments fall foul of the law in different ways. First, dissidents may be subjected to fabricated prosecutions under perfectly reasonable laws designed to deter criminal activity such as money laundering, corruption and embezzlement. For example, in 2021 the Russian opposition leader Alexei Navalny was sentenced, following an assassination attempt by state agents, for violation of probation after having been convicted of embezzlement. The European Court of Human Rights condemned the original conviction as arbitrary and manifestly unreasonable, and in violation of the European Convention on Human Rights, to which Russia is signatory. Belarusian opposition leaders were arrested in 2020 under suspicion of destabilizing the country and harming national security, as part of what the government called an ongoing national security probe following strongly disputed election results which were not recognized by the European Union.

In 2017 a Philippine journalist was accused of tax evasion and then, in 2019, 'cyber-libel', for which she was convicted on the basis of an article she did not write. In 2019, 57 members of trade unions and civil society organizations were arrested and charged with illegal possession of firearms and explosives, charges condemned by local and international rights groups as bogus. Although there may be little chance of securing a conviction under such laws, it is often enough to secure the government's objectives to have the dissident activist arrested and held without bail for a prolonged period.

An alternative strategy is prosecution under special laws designed to stifle criticism of the incumbent government. For example, journalists in Bangladesh have been prosecuted under the notorious Digital Security Act which creates a wide range of vague and over-generalized offences, including destroying communal harmony, creating unrest or disorder, engaging in propaganda, disseminating information that hurts religious values, sending offensive information, and campaigning against the spirit of the liberation war, the father of the nation, the national anthem or the national flag (BBC 2021). In Thailand the Constitutional Court ruled in 2021 that calls for curbs on the power of the royal family by civil rights activists constituted an abuse of rights and freedoms under the country's draconian lese-majeste law and harmed the security of the state.

In 2021 the director of a film festival in Belarus was prosecuted and fined for 'protesting against the police'. Another criminal case is now being prepared, accusing her of 'raising money for protests'. Laws governing the organization of mass meetings were used against Armenian opposition leaders arrested in 2020, following protest at the agreement reached with Azerbaijan over the disputed territory of Nagorno-Karabakh. Laws defining 'unlawful assembly' were deployed against opposition leaders in Tanzania as part of a crack-down on political dissent, including a ban on party political activities before the National Electoral Commission announced the start of official campaigning for the 2020 elections. Charges of 'incitement to revolt' and 'mobilisation of protest' were brought against opposition party members and activists in Zimbabwe in 2020. A Nigerian human rights activist and former presidential candidate was arrested for treason in 2021 following a peaceful protest in the capital, Abuja.

Overly imprecise laws that violate the rule of law principles of regularity, consistency and certainty can also be weaponized, including Poland's insult laws, and laws on offending religious feelings or insulting the flags of Poland, which led in 2021 to a well-known writer being charged with committing an act of public insult for calling the president a moron on social media. Similarly, successive Bolivian governments have used the judiciary to persecute their opponents under an imprecisely broad definition of terrorism. Others were investigated for belonging to a criminal organization, dereliction of duty and other crimes, despite strong evidence that many cases were politically motivated. Case files against former President Morales contained no evidence he had committed acts that could be considered terrorism (HRW 2021). A charge of 'hooliganism' was brought against a prominent Azerbaijani opposition leader in 2020 in a long-standing pattern of trumped-up charges against government critics, according to Human Rights Watch.

Weaponizing the legal system and judiciary to wage political warfare against opposition to government policies and constitutional revisions has become an increasingly familiar aspect of authoritarianism in those Third Wave democracies in which control of the judiciary is part of the government's strategy to consolidate its hold on power. A compliant judiciary enables the governments of illiberal democracies to minimize the use of draconian laws in the knowledge that prosecutions of opposition and civil society activists based on doctored evidence and false testimony will succeed in the courts, and victims of excessive pre-trial detention and police violence will obtain no remedy. Leading officials of the governing party can also protect their corrupt interests in sectors of the economy by wrongfully investigating and charging enterprises, including foreign firms, that are able to offer better products or services to consumers. Hence the attraction of undermining judicial independence.

* * *

Protecting this independence of the judiciary has proved extremely difficult, in many 'Third Wave' states, despite constitutional provisions explicitly confirming the independence of the judiciary. This is increasingly explained by the use which can be made of the judiciary as a political weapon to be wielded by those in power against their political opponents. The scope for political interference to undermine independence is extremely wide: restructuring judicial institutions; managing judicial careers so as to limit impartiality; external control over court administration, especially the assignment of cases; and 'direct approaches', such as threats, bribes, media campaigns and private intimations from government representatives, all designed to influence the outcome in specific cases.

Political interference in the appointment and tenure of judges, control of a judge's career, appointments to the judicial councils, manipulation of the resources allocated to the judicial branch, harassment and violence when challenges to executive action or powerful economic interests come before the courts, limiting the scope of judicial review, the use of exceptional courts, 'guiding' and 'steering' statements by chief executives, and the nullification of court decisions by non-implementation leave judges vulnerable to political pressures and compromise their independence in the delivery of justice. Taking control of the judiciary enables it to be used as a weapon against political critics and opponents when it is difficult for governments to ignore constitutional restraints on political repression.

And yet interference in judicial decision-making is not the sole explanation for lost judicial independence. The independence of the judiciary can be compromised in more ways than by political interference in the course of justice by other branches of government. Court proceedings may be biased and so violate the principle of equality before the law and the right to a fair trial, a particular risk when courts are subservient for whatever reason to the government of the day. Judges may be biased by their own social and political values when interpreting and applying the law and conducting hearings. Inefficiency within the judiciary can compromise principles embedded in the rule of law. Corruption within the judiciary means that justice gives way to the highest bidder. These impediments to judicial independence will be examined in the next chapter.

References

ABA (2002), *Judicial Reform Index for Romania*, Washington: American Bar Association.

Adesomoju, A. (2012), 'Lack of independence of state judiciary dangerous: CJN', *Punch*, 10 February.

Amnesty International (2021), *The State of The World's Human Rights*, London: Amnesty International.

Bako, B. (2020), 'Judges sitting on the Warsaw-Budapest express train: the independence of Polish and Hungarian judges before the CJEU', *European Public Law*, vol. 26, no. 3.

Bari, M. E., E. M. Bari and S. Naz (2015), 'The establishment of the Judicial Appointments Commission in Malaysia to improve the constitutional method of appointing the judges of the superior courts: a critical study', *Commonwealth Law Bulletin*, vol. 41, no. 2.

BBC (2021), 'Fears for democracy as buoyant Bangladesh turns 50', *BBC News*, 24 March, www.bbc.co.uk/news/world-asia-56433279

Berger, S. (2008), 'Robert Mugabe lavishes gifts of plasma TVs and Mercedes on Zimbabwe's judges', *Daily Telegraph*, 1 August.

Butt, S. (2008), '*Surat Sakti*: the decline of the authority of judicial decisions in Indonesia' in T. Lindsey (ed.), *Indonesia: Law and Society*, Singapore: Institute of South East Asian Studies.

Council of Europe (2020), *Hands off Press Freedom: Attacks on Media in Europe Must Not Become a New Normal*, Strasbourg: Council of Europe.

Domingo, P. (1999), 'Judicial independence and judicial reform in Latin America' in A. Schedler, L. Diamond and M. C. Plattner (eds.), *The Self-Restraining State: Power and Accountability in New Democracies*, London: Lynne Reinner.

EU (2021), *Serbia 2021 Report*, Commission Staff Working Document, Strasbourg: European Commission.

European Commission (2010), *Commission Opinion in Albania's Application for Membership of the European Union*, Brussels: European Commission.

Favarel-Garrigues, G. (2015), 'A power horizontal: the public-private enforcement of judicial decisions in Russia', *Europe-Asia Studies*, vol. 67, no. 4.

February, J. (2015), *South Africa: The Judiciary and the Executive: At Peace, for Now*, Pretoria: Institute for Security Studies.

Freedom House (2003), *Nations in Transit: Armenia*, New York: Freedom House.

Freedom House (2004), *Countries and the Crossroads: Nigeria*, New York: Freedom House.

Freedom House (2005), *Countries at the Crossroads 2005: Algeria*, New York: Freedom House.

Freedom House (2006a), *Nations in Transit: Russia*, New York: Freedom House.

Freedom House (2006b), *Nations in Transition: Tajikstan*, New York: Freedom House.

Freedom House (2012), *Countries at the Crossroads, 2012: Sierra Leone*, New York: Freedom House.

Freedom House (2013), *Nations in Transit, 2013: Albania*, New York: Freedom House.

Freedom House (2015a), *Nations in Transit 2015: Azerbaijan*, New York: Freedom House.

Freedom House (2015b), *Nations in Transit 2015: Russia*, New York: Freedom House.

Freedom House (2021), *Azerbaijan: Freedom in the World 2021 Country Report*, New York: Freedom House, https://freedomhouse.org/country/azerbaijan/freedom-world/2021

Gargarella, R. (2004), 'In search of democratic justice: what courts should not do: Argentina 1983–2002', in S. Gloppen, R. Gargarella and E. Skaar (eds.), *Democratization and the Judiciary: The Accountability Function of Courts in New Democracies*, London: Frank Cass.

Garoupa, N. and T. Ginsburg (2015), *Judicial Reputation: A Comparative Theory*, Chicago: University of Chicago Press.

Gloppen, S. (2004), 'The accountability function of the courts in Tanzania and Zambia' in S. Gloppen, R. Gargarella and E. Skaar (eds.), *Democratization and the Judiciary: The Accountability Function of Courts in New Democracies*, London: Frank Cass.

Goldin, A. (2009), 'A Supreme Court challenge to Argentina's trade union model', *International Labour Review*, vol. 148, nos. 1–2.

The Guardian, UK (2012), 'Tahir Square women lose forced "virginity tests" case in military court', 12 March.

Gueye, M. (2012), 'Comment: tense times', *Development and Co-operation*, vol. 39, no. 3.

Hammarberg, T. (2009), 'Flawed enforcement of court decisions undermines the trust in State justice', Strasbourg: Council of Europe Human Rights Commission, www.coe.int/t/commissioner/Viewpoints/090831_en.asp

Harris, P. and M. Nicol-Wilson (2007), *The Feasibility of a Legal Aid System for Sierra Leone*, London: The British Council.

Hendley, K. (2009), '"Telephone Law" and the "Rule of Law": the Russian case', *Hague Journal on the Rule of Law*, vol. 1, no. 2.

Herron, E. S. and K. A. Randazzo (2003), 'The relationship between independence and judicial review in post-communist courts', *Journal of Politics*, vol. 65, no. 2.

HRW (2021), 'Bolivia should end revenge justice', Human Rights Watch, www.hrw.org/news/2021/03/22/bolivia-should-end-revenge-justice

HRW (2022), *World Report 2022*, New York: Human Rights Watch.

IBA (2012), *Rule of Law in Malawi: The Road to Recovery*, London: International Bar Association.

ICJ (2002), *Indonesia: Attacks on Justice 2002*, Geneva: International Commission of Jurists.

ICJ (2014), *Annual Report 2014*, Geneva: International Commission of Jurists.

ICJ (2021), *The 'Weaponization' of the Criminal Law in Zimbabwe*, Geneva: International Commission of Jurists.

Kozyreva, P. M. and A. I. Smirnov (2015), 'Difficulties in the development of the Russian courts, *Sociological Research*, vol. 54, no. 3.

Ledeneva, A. (2010), 'Is Russia's judicial system reformable?', *Open Democracy*, March, www.opendemocracy.net

Lenke, S. (2022), 'Judicial and prosecutorial independence in Europe: how politicized judges and prosecutors undermine the right to a fair trial in Eastern Europe and Central Asia' in S. Schiedermair, A. Schwarz and D. Steiger (eds.), *Theory and Practice of the European Convention on Human Rights*, Nomos: Baden-Baden.

Llanos, M., C. T. Weber, C. Heyl and A. Stroh (2015), 'Informal interference in the judiciary in new democracies: a comparison of six African and Latin American cases', *Democratization*, http://dx.doi.org/10.1080/13510347.2015.1081170.

Muftah (2012), 'President Mohamed Morsi issues new Constitutional Declaration', 22 November, http://muftah.org/egyptian-president-morsis-constitutional-decree-english-text/

Olcott, M. B. (2010), *Kazakhstan: Unfulfilled Promise?*, Washington: Carnegie Endowment for International Peace.

Popova, M. (2012), *Politicized Justice in Emerging Democracies: A Study of Courts in Russia and Ukraine*, Cambridge: Cambridge University Press.

Popova, M. (2019), 'The rise of weaponised legalism', paper to the European Consortium for Political Research Joint Sessions, April, Mons, Belgium.

Provost, R. (2015), 'Teetering on the edge of legal Nihilism: Russia and the evolving European human rights regime', *Human Rights Quarterly*, vol. 37, no. 2.

Reuters (2014), 'Court in Georgia orders arrest of ex-president Saakashvili', http://uk.reuters.com/article/uk-georgia-saakashvili-charges-id

Rishmawi, M. (2000), *Attacks on Justice: The Harassment and Persecution of Judges and Lawyers*, Geneva: Centre for the Independence of Judges and Lawyers.

Russell, P. H. (2001), 'Toward a general theory of judicial independence' in P. H. Russell and D. M. O'Brien (eds.), *Judicial Independence in the Age of Democracy: Critical Perspectives From Around the World*, Charlotteville: University Press of Virginia.

Sieder, R. (2004), 'Renegotiating "law and order": judicial reform and citizen responses in post-war Guatemala' in S. Gloppen, R. Gargarella and E. Skaar (eds.), *Democratization and the Judiciary: The Accountability Function of Courts in New Democracies*, London: Frank Cass.

Szente, Z. (2021), 'Populism and populist constitutionalism' in F. Gárdos-Orosz and Z. Szente (eds.), *Populist Challenges to Constitutional Interpretation in Europe and Beyond*, Abingdon: Routledge.

Uprimi, R. (2004), 'The Constitutional Court and control of Presidential extraordinary powers in Colombia' in S. Gloppen, R. Gargarella and E. Skaar (eds.), *Democratization and the Judiciary: The Accountability Function of Courts in New Democracies*, London: Frank Cass.

US Department of State (2014), Bureau of Democracy, Human Rights and Labour, *Country Reports on Human Rights Practices 2013: Slovakia*, www.state.gov/j/drl/rls/hrrpt/humanrightsreport

Venice Commission (2011), *Opinion on the New Constitution of Hungary*, Opinion No. 621 (2011), Strasbourg: European Commission for Democracy Through Law.

Voigt, S., J. Gutmann and L. P. Feld (2015), 'Economic growth and judicial independence, a dozen years on: cross-country evidence using an updated set of indicators', *European Journal of Political Economy*, vol. 38, June.

4 Judicial bias

Introduction

The ability of the courts to deliver judgements that are wholly impartial will be compromised if bias is introduced through proceedings which are unfair to one of the parties to a dispute or inefficient so that it is impossible to ensure equality before the law or adherence to the rules of natural justice. More obviously, the abuse of judicial powers prompted by personal bias or corruption on the part of individual judges and other judicial officials removes all of the qualities of judicial decision-making which make judicial independence meaningful. The independence of justice requires both independent justices and unbiased judicial processes. These qualities are particularly important in view of the evidence showing fairness strengthens social solidarity, self-respect, the legitimacy of the judiciary and obligation to obey the law, 'notwithstanding the fact that obedience may come at a personal cost' (Meyerson 2015: 82).

In this chapter, we first examine how structural defects in the system of justice – the organization and efficiency of the courts – can negate the power of judges to arrive at decisions based solely on the facts and the law, before looking at the ways judges themselves may be biased. Proceedings can be biased by the conduct of hearings, failure to observe a presumption of innocence, use of the 'common purpose' doctrine, language problems, the physical or psychological abuse of detainees, and discriminatory laws. The effect on the rule of law of inefficiency in the judicial process is then examined. Individual judges may be biased by cultural and ideological beliefs, links to earlier authoritarian practices, political affiliations and corruption. We examine the definition, measurement, perceptions and causes of judicial corruption before considering its effect on democratic consolidation.

Biased proceedings

Judicial independence disappears when proceedings in court are biased. This may arise because hearings are actually designed to favour one side in the case, as when defence lawyers are prevented from reviewing all the evidence presented against their clients. Judges may have to preside over proceedings in which prosecutors are given a higher status than defence lawyers. Or they enable prosecutors to be

DOI: 10.4324/9781003334613-5

more influential, despite them having equal standing under the constitution, because of their own subservience to the executive branch. For example, in Russia the prosecution services exercise undue influence in criminal proceedings with more weight given to the prosecution's arguments than to the defence's. Judges may face adverse consequences for their careers, including dismissal, if they are perceived as being insufficiently attentive to the prosecution's demands, refuse to order pre-trial detention, or grant too many acquittals (ICJ 2014).

Bias may also derive from structural defects in court proceedings. The first is failure to observe a presumption of innocence. When a case is brought before court, the party making the allegation bears the legal burden of proof. In criminal law the presumption of innocence means that everyone who has been charged shall be presumed innocent until proved guilty according to law. It is thus on the prosecution that the burden of proof falls, and unless legally admissible evidence and testimony convince judge or jury that the accused is guilty beyond reasonable doubt, the accused must be acquitted.

This presumption of innocence is guaranteed by the constitutions of many democratizing states, including Slovakia, Argentina, Nicaragua, South Africa, Sierra Leone, Uganda and Zimbabwe. However, the presumption of innocence is not consistently upheld when prosecutors are required to follow political priorities, or the law gives intelligence agencies powers to arrest and detain without the authorization of a court (as under Indonesia's Law on Intelligence adopted in October 2011). The presumption of innocence is compromised when the onus of proving their innocence is placed on the accused and when the accused has to prove he or she had a lawful reason for their action. Some provisions in Nigerian financial crime law prescribe forfeiture of assets prior to trial of persons arrested for financial crimes. The pronouncements of judicial authorities drawing inferences from an accused person's silence also threaten the presumption of innocence. Prolonged periods of remand, often in bad conditions, weaken the principle. Anti-corruption laws may reverse the presumption of innocence when it is presumed that a benefit received by a public official from certain categories of people has been received corruptly unless the contrary is proved (Chinyere 2021). New anti-drugs legislation in the Philippines sets out 30 legal presumptions allowing the authorities to impute criminal acts to people under presumption of importing or financing illegal drugs or protecting dealers contrary to Article 3, Section 14 of the Constitution, which states that in all criminal prosecutions, the accused is presumed innocent until proven guilty beyond reasonable doubt.

Providing the media with confidential information relating to ongoing investigations before the defence receives this information also adversely affects the application of the presumption of innocence principle, as do comments by politicians about ongoing criminal proceedings. The use of physical restraints on suspects and accused persons appearing in court compromises the presumption of innocence. Imputing use of the right to remain silent and not incriminate oneself to indicate guilt also negates the principle. Any shift of the burden of proof further constitutes an infringement of the presumption of innocence (FRA 2021). All such threats have been found in new democracies in recent years.

At the extreme, the presumption of innocence is totally lost when opponents of the state may be 'disappeared' by security forces empowered to act as prosecution, judge and executioner. The phenomenon of 'extra-judicial killings' may even become part of public policy in which the killing of suspects is justified as 'wanted criminals' resisting arrest or being caught in the 'crossfire' between the police and criminal gangs, as in the case of deaths during arrests or in custody caused by the Rapid Action Battalion established in Bangladesh in 2004 in response to spiralling crime and the rise of terrorism (Habib 2015).

The presumption of innocence can also be tenuous when the right to a defence lawyer is denied. Political detainees in Azerbaijan can have access to legal counsel restricted. Many defendants lack counsel in Bangladeshi courts. Defendants in Indonesia are sometimes denied proper access to legal counsel, even in death penalty cases. The Ghanaian government is not obliged to provide legal counsel, and those unable to afford lawyers are forced to represent themselves in court (Freedom House 2021).

The use of the 'common purpose' doctrine also violates the presumption of innocence, as in South Africa in 2012 when striking miners were prosecuted for the murder of 34 co-workers shot dead by police. They were declared complicit in the killings since they were arrested at the scene with weapons. The miners were accused of guilt by association and complicit in the killing of their colleagues by police. Common purpose means that any person who conspires with any other person to aid in the commissioning of a crime, or incites another person to commit a crime, will be found guilty if that person is found guilty. For it to be applicable to the miners' case the miners would have to be regarded as having commissioned the police to kill their colleagues.

Second, a fair hearing and due process are jeopardized when abuses are introduced into judicial proceedings. These may be conducted in a language that the majority of the population cannot understand. In Peru translation services are rarely provided for defendants who do not speak Spanish, leaving constitutional guarantees of due process unevenly upheld. The right to a fair public hearing is denied when suspects are abused physically or psychologically by police and prison officers. Defendants may be prevented from having access to relevant documents, as in Mexico. Verdicts unrelated to the evidence may be given. Defence motions on evidentiary questions may be arbitrarily rejected, and verdicts prepared before completion of the hearing (Kazakhstan). Bulgaria's constitutional rights to a fair judicial hearing are not always upheld, and major problems with the prosecution service have weakened due process and the rule of law. Despite constitutional guarantees of fairness in court hearings, political detainees in Azerbaijan can face arbitrary arrest, restricted access to legal counsel, fabrication and withholding of evidence, and physical abuse to extract confessions. Arbitrary arrests and detentions are common in Malawi and Honduras, which also suffers from a corrupt police force, many of whose officers engage in criminal activities including drug trafficking and extortion. Requests to investigate allegations that confessions have been extracted under duress can be refused, trials can be heard in secret (in Tajikistan), and fabricated evidence accepted, including testimony from 'witnesses' long since dead and others who could not have been present at the trial (Uzbekistan). In Belarus the right to a fair trial is rarely respected in cases with political overtones. Denial of natural justice enables political opponents to be harassed with punitive financial inspections by state agencies or trumped-up charges, including terrorism, illegal arms possession, accounting frauds or public obscenity (see Chapter 3).

Several existing security laws in Malaysia undermine constitutional guarantees of due process (Shor 2009; Freedom House 2021). Justice in Venezuela for victims of extrajudicial killings, arbitrary arrests and torture committed by security forces has been obstructed by courts using retrospective arrest warrants for illegal arrests, routinely ordering pre-trial detention on the basis of flimsy evidence, allowing significant procedural delays and interfering with the right to choose one's own lawyer (HRW 2022).

So, while the law itself may not be unjustly discriminatory, the judicial process may be, especially when particular groups are unaware of their legal rights, through illiteracy and lack of education, or differential burdens of proof are placed by criminal proceedings on men and women, as in Sharia law, again negating equality before the law. The discrimination practised by the courts against the Roma people throughout Eastern Europe, and minority language groups in Africa and Latin America, also undermines equality before the law.

Third, the judicial process is damaged when victims are left unprotected as a result of the non-enforcement of laws. This leaves the independence of the judiciary unaffected, since judges are not called on to rule on individual cases as none are brought before the courts for adjudication. For example, despite the enactment of the Afghan Law on the Elimination of Violence against Women in 2009, which criminalized child marriage, forced marriage, forced self-immolation and 19 other acts of violence against women, including rape, implementation of the law, in particular by police and prosecutors, has been limited: '[O]nly a small percentage of the cases of violence against women have been prosecuted or charged.' A majority of cases of violence against women reported to the police and or prosecutors' offices were dealt with outside the formal justice system, through mediation, pressure to withdraw complaints, and by elders in traditional dispute resolution mechanisms, mechanisms which too often fail to protect the rights of women or, significantly, enforce the new law (United Nations High Commissioner for Human Rights 2011: 30). As a consequence, millions of Afghan women continued to suffer from violence and abuse.

Fourth, proceedings are structurally defective when the law which judges are called upon to apply is itself unfairly discriminatory because it denies rights to a group without there being any reasonable grounds for so doing. Despite all new democracies having enshrined equality before the law in their constitutions, discrimination remains widespread. For example, millions of women live under systems of law which systematically discriminate against them in relation to property, inheritance, employment, freedom to enter and leave marriage, and domestic violence. Where traditional, religious and customary law is given a role in the judicial system it is often exempt from the non-discrimination requirement in the constitution. Progressive reform, where enacted, is often not implemented (Hallward-Driemeier et al. 2013; García-Moreno et al. 2015). Women's freedom of movement is limited by discriminatory legislation in many countries, requiring accompanied travel or prohibiting applications for passports. Nationality laws in many Middle Eastern and North African states deny women the equal right to confer nationality on their children. Discriminatory legal frameworks for judicial administration obstruct women's access to justice by denying them the same rights as men to bring cases, and to be present at, or to speak during, hearings. A woman's testimony may not carry the same evidentiary weight as a man in some types of court proceedings. Women's rights to own, use and manage property may be legally restricted. Women may be discriminated against by laws demanding obedience to husbands, restricting authority over her children, denying the same right as men to initiate divorce procedures, and limiting inheritance rights (European Parliament 2020).

In many countries customary, religious or traditional practices or laws discriminate against women's legal rights to provide testimony, sue or hold office. The 'moral crimes' applied to women in Afghanistan make it an offence to run away from an abusive husband or report a violent crime against themselves, including rape. More generally, there is empirical evidence that the influence of Islam causes discrimination in legal institutions against women and conflicts with judicial impartiality. Some Moslem countries have constitutions which contain specific inequalities between men and women, and legal systems based on religious doctrine of which judges are not the sole interpreters: '[L]egal institutions in Islamic states are clearly designed to disadvantage women' (Gutmann and Voigt 2015: 373). In Bangladesh Sharia law takes precedence over civil law in family matters, thereby rendering women's rights inferior to men's in cases concerning divorce, inheritance, child custody, violence against women and sexual harassment. In Jordan's Sharia courts 'the testimony of women is worth only half that of men in most matters' (Freedom House 2004).

In a number of countries the law discriminates against homosexuals. Same-sex sexual activity is illegal in many Third Wave states, including Tunisia (though legalization has been proposed by a presidential committee), Nigeria (with capital punishment in 12 states), Turkmenistan, Uzbekistan and Bangladesh (though for men only), Pakistan, and Malaysia. While same-sex relations are legal throughout Eastern Europe, Poland's law against inciting hatred does not cover crimes motivated by sexuality or gender identity, leaving public figures free to make slurs that would be prosecuted if targeted at other minority groups. In Hungary the Fidesz government has been increasingly discriminatory towards LGBT people with the parliament voting in 2020 to end the legal recognition of gender identity.

When adjudicating in such cases a judge's impartiality may remain unaffected though it might be thought that a judge who recognized the injustice embedded in the law might use discretion to reduce the harm as far as possible. However, this is where the judge's own prejudices come into play, or his or her level of support for basic social principles which entail justice. Or a judge may simply fear the personal consequences of not enforcing an unjust law, especially when there are extremists capable of violence to those who do not support their prejudices and Ministers of Justice capable of ending a judge's career.

Clearly the consequence of such structural judicial bias is destruction of judicial impartiality, a key component of an independent judiciary. Structural defects lead to failure to observe the rules of natural justice or due process. Though the constitutions of new democracies commonly guarantee the right to a fair hearing without undue delay, in practice this is frequently negated by biased proceedings. Violations of human rights are left without remedy. There is no redress against violations of due process or natural justice.

Inefficiency

Inefficiency in the judicial process amounts to a denial of natural justice and basic rights. It is not only caused by inadequate resources. It can also follow from a loss of judicial independence. The external political interference in the judicial process described in Chapter 3 not only undermines judicial independence. It also damages the efficiency of the judiciary. There is evidence that greater judicial independence stimulates competition among judges for professional advancement which, in the absence of rewards for political favours, can only be earned by skills and competence. This increases the individual efficiency of judges and prosecutors and improves the overall performance of the judiciary. It follows that political interference has a damaging effect on judicial efficiency (Melcarnel and Ramello 2015).

An under-resourced judiciary is the consequence of political decisions about budgets and, even when not driven by ulterior political motives, can still mean that justice is undermined. Whether a manifestation of political interference in the judiciary or not, inadequate funding, both budgetary (buildings, office equipment and support staff) and jurisprudential (training, case materials and law reports), adversely affects morale, the effective disposition of cases and the standing of judges in public opinion, none of which augurs well for the administration of justice or the consolidation of democracy.

The judiciary in transitional states is frequently hampered by a shortage of human resources and physical infrastructure (Afsah 2016), with damaging consequences for judicial independence and the rule of law. Shortages of qualified judges and magistrates mean that cases are misunderstood, laws misapplied and backlogs created, as in Zambia, all of which 'reduces public confidence in the system and the morale of those struggling to work within it' (Chikalanga et al. 2007: 289). Chronic underfunding for staff can lead to judges, prosecutors and lawyers having inadequate legal education and training in the fundamental principles of natural justice, the rule of law and international standards defining a fair trial. Shortages of staff also mean that cases can take many years to be decided, as in the Philippines. Mozambique needs hundreds of additional judges if the judicial system is to meet the demands on it. The backlog of court cases in Serbia in 2014 numbered over 2 million (Freedom House 2015b). Backlogs of pending cases in the criminal courts can leave suspects imprisoned on remand for excessive periods.

A lack of physical resources, including accommodation, computers, and up-to-date legal documentation (including recent legislation), also affects the efficiency of courts. In 2010 a report from the European Commission on Albania's application for membership of the European Union found that a lack of financial resources led to poor-quality court management, adequate organization and training of court administrators, unreasonable delays in judicial proceedings, and large backlogs of cases.

> Court proceedings are slow and the number of trial sessions for a case is high. In addition, proceedings are often delayed or outright stalled by defendants. Working conditions in courts remain poor and hearings often take place in judges' offices, hampering transparency and efficiency.
>
> (European Commission 2010: 20)

Inadequate documentation such as supplies of law reports can mean that courts make decisions without access to case law as determined by courts of appeal and supreme courts. In Uzbekistan there is a need to make court judgements accessible to the public, including online. Courthouses also need to be more accessible to the public, including persons with disabilities in order to ensure that justice is more accessible (ICJ 2021).

An under-resourced judiciary is not necessarily a sign that staff and facilities cannot be afforded. It may also reflect the political interests of those in power. Under-staffed courts in Uganda caused a backlog of 24,000 civil and 16,000 criminal cases in 2010. The problem was that vacancies on the Judicial Services Commission, responsible for appointing judges, had been left unfilled by President Museveni for political reasons (*The Observer*, Kampala 2012). In 2014 the government of Uganda was sued in the East African Court of Justice for the president's failure to appoint the required number of judges to the High Court, Constitutional Court and Supreme Court. The Chief Justices of Nigeria and South Africa have expressed fears that an under-funded judiciary makes political interference easier. In 2021 a nationwide strike of court workers in Nigeria demanded financial autonomy for courts, rather than relying on the often corrupt system of funding from state governors.

In some cases, resources appear to be restricted with the intention of making access to justice difficult. In Tajikistan, family members, court observers and the media face obstacles when they need to attend public hearings. It is difficult to obtain information about the schedule of hearings, as the timing of hearings is not always announced or published on court websites, and it is common for last-minute changes to be made. Judgements are not always publicly available so that members of the public cannot consult court decisions. The majority of court buildings do not have facilities large enough to hold public hearings, with judges holding hearings in their offices rather than court rooms which are too small to have adequate seating, and which are chosen for political and other sensitive cases, with the apparent aim of excluding members of the public. 'The lack of access to the final outcome of the judicial proceedings – the court judgment – does not serve the interests of justice and undermines trust in administering justice' (ICJ 2020: 67).

Thus, under-funding can be almost as damaging to the process of democratization as direct interference in judicial decision-making by politicians. When the system of justice is inefficient or inaccessible because of costs or an inadequate supply of judges, public defenders and courts staff, citizenship is limited and the public alienated from the institutions which make the law as well as those which administer it (Prillaman 2000). The delays in judicial decision-making which are the commonest outcome of under-resourcing undermine trust in both government and judiciary, as in Argentina where delayed appointments in 2011 left 20 per cent of seats in the federal courts vacant. Delayed judgements have prompted negative public attitudes towards the judiciary in Latvia. At the extreme, a weak judicial system can lead to people taking the law into their own hands, and indulging in vigilante behaviour, as in Guatemala which recorded 480 lynchings between 1996 and 2002 without a single perpetrator being convicted (Pena 2007). In South Africa the occasional appearance of lynch mobs, self-appointed vigilantes and kangaroo courts also reflects frustration with inaccessible justice among the poor (Hoffman 2012).

A judiciary that is under-resourced also exacerbates the inequality before the law already suffered by the poor. Shortages of staff and other resources undermine rights to a timely trial and legal counsel, especially among the poor and geographically isolated, as in parts of South Africa (Freedom House 2006).

Biased judges

A judge is by training and inclination a person with an interest in governance and public affairs. Judges are therefore to some degree political animals. They inevitably have their own preferences, prejudices and ideological leanings: '[J]udicial behaviour, like human behaviour more generally, departs from both pure rationality and from the sort of ideology-free objectivity that we might posit as the ideal' (Oldfather 2015: 155).

This is particularly significant when judges have to use discretion or apply imprecise legal rules. Judicial independence means not just proper relationships between the different branches of government, and freedom from improper pressures from outside the formal structures of government, such as the media, organized crime or powerful economic interests. It also means a 'capacity for independent thought and judgement' (Russell 2001: 6).

Bias in judicial thinking can occur in all systems because of either individual idiosyncrasies or systemic deviation from judicial independence. It may stem from culturally induced deference towards others in authority; resentment towards a government which fails to provide adequate resources (as in Russia in the 1990s); or ideological beliefs and assumptions. Realists know that 'judges come to their work with predispositions based on their pre-judicial experience and affiliations, and that these predispositions are not easily shed even if they are disciplined by new orientations after their appointment' (Russell 2001: 10).

For example, judicial decisions indicate that some judges in Hungary, Romania and Bulgaria are biased against members of the Roma community. Disparaging comments by jurists, alleging that Roma show disrespect for private property, provide unreliable witnesses, lack adaptability to social and moral norms, prefer a parasitic and criminal way of life, are culturally inherently inclined towards delinquency or crime, and are unable to understand the justice system because of cultural disassociation from the law, all have a direct impact on judicial decisions. Consequently, Roma defendants are presumed to be guilty during criminal proceedings and more likely to face custodial sentences or pre-trial detention than other citizens. When combined with anti-Roma prejudice among police officers and prosecutors, the bias of judges means that 'at every stage of criminal proceedings, from arrest until sentencing, they are vulnerable to discriminatory attitudes and biases that skew outcomes against them. The very system that is meant to impart fair and equal justice is, in fact, doing the opposite' (Fair Trials 2020: 6). Despite this, in 2020 Bulgarian law was amended to make it more difficult to bring discrimination lawsuits against any magistrate.

Judicial bias may be a legacy of earlier authoritarianism. Old habits die hard so that the independence of the judiciary has frequently been compromised by earlier political attachments. Remnants of the authoritarian regime (whether military, single party or communist) frequently held judicial office during efforts to consolidate democracy, especially when others did not have the requisite qualifications. In Central and Eastern Europe it was difficult to replace the old ruling-class members of the judicial branch, with its links to the authoritarian regime, with a new class eager to introduce values consistent with the need to keep the judiciary independent and subordinated exclusively to the law. Criteria for selection or confirmation in office based on a candidate's legal qualifications favoured those with experience acquired during the communist era, as in the Czech Republic. Consequently, the anti-democratic traditions in the judiciary persisted, leading courts to show leniency towards human rights violations during the authoritarian regime, as in Chile following the Pinochet regime, and risked judicial independence imperiling democracy by failing to respond to the need for justice for victims of repression. Fairness and impartiality in court hearings are lost when judges maintain patterns of behaviour required under the authoritarian regime as in Indonesia where under Suharto judges allied themselves with the police and state prosecutors.

Dependence on judges with close connections with the *ancien regime* can actually halt the transition from authoritarianism to democracy, as in Egypt when, in 2012, fresh protests broke out on the streets of Cairo following a ruling from the Constitutional Court, whose judges were appointed by former President Mubarak, that the previous year's parliamentary vote was unconstitutional, and calling for the dissolution of the lower house of parliament and fresh elections. According to the Muslim Brotherhood, power had been taken by 'one of the symbols of the previous era'.

The ideological preferences of judges may reflect strategic decision-making in response to incentives to show party loyalty. Such incentives include access to positions in other areas of government (election commission, national bank or legal advisor to the prime minister's office), consultancies, or reputational gains and enhanced academic prestige in the legal profession. This is the case in Poland, where nominations to the court come exclusively from the lower chamber of parliament, and judges with policy preferences shared by the parliamentary majority are sought (Kantorowicz and Garoupa 2016).

The political and ideological orientation of judges becomes particularly significant when courts are empowered to decide whether legislation, and therefore public policy, is consistent with a country's constitution. Changes to the composition of the courts which result in party political influence on appointments can lead to internal conflict, reflected in an increase in the number of dissenting opinions, as in Chile where, following constitutional reforms in 2005, 70 per cent of the members of the Constitutional Tribunal were appointed by elected politicians. Levels of dissent increased with patterns of conflict reflecting 'increasing political influence on the Tribunal, which in turn may have increased the possibility of politically oriented opinions and disagreement' (Tiede 2015: 21).

Similarly, the Constitutional Court in Hungary makes important policy choices, and is inevitably part of the political process. While professional qualities prevail in the selection of ordinary judges, the appointment of Constitutional Court justices is suffused with political considerations with the political preferences of the candidates of primary importance: '[I]t does not at all mean that candidates having an excellent profession record cannot be nominated, but it implies that political preferences can seriously distort the selection process as whole' (Fekete 2015: 183).

Political affiliations on the part of judges can have far-reaching consequences for the rule of law, enabling civil and military officials to engage with organized crime, abuse human rights, expropriate land and generally undermine justice, as in Guatemala in 2003 when the appeal court judges who overturned guilty verdicts against military officers for the murder of a bishop were found to have close ties with the military, and some Constitutional Court justices had connections with the governing party. Some federal judges in Argentina have close ties with political actors with implications for anti-corruption efforts (Freedom House 2021). Reforms to secure the independence of the judiciary have occasionally been rejected as threatening the social status of judges, as in Croatia, by judges appointed on the basis of party loyalty rather than professional merit during the Tudjman regime (1991–2000).

It is not always clear whether judicial bias arises from the personal prejudices of the judge or political pressure to arrive at a decision favoured by the government. Often the two forces cannot be separated, as in the trial, widely condemned as a travesty of justice, at Moscow's City Court in August 2012 of three members of the punk band Pussy Riot. Court officials prevented most of the defence witnesses from entering the courthouse, the judge then ruling that their absence meant that they could not be called to testify. The judge also refused to hear many of the objections raised by defence lawyers. The prosecution was allowed to question whether all defence witnesses were Orthodox believers, but the defence was not given the same privilege when cross-examining prosecution witnesses. In addition, President Putin had made it clear publicly during the trial that he expected the defendants to be found guilty.

Corruption

In many post-authoritarian states there is evidence of judicial corruption, which completely undermines the ability of the courts to provide impartial adjudication equally to all litigants and fuels demands for greater accountability. As the United Nations recognizes, the protection of all human rights is dependent upon the honest administration of justice. A corrupt judicial system thus negates the rule of law:

> If one of the parties has bribed the judge or other court official and obtained access to documents to which the other party has no access, or caused documents to disappear, there can be no equality of arms. A judge who has taken a bribe cannot be independent, impartial or fair. When a party to judicial proceedings offers a bribe to a judge or other officials, and the bribe is accepted, that party immediately acquires a privileged status in relation to other parties who have not offered, or are not in a position to offer, a bribe or inducement. The preferential treatment secured and the resulting discrimination, then, obliterates objectivity and neutrality from the judicial process. A legitimate aim is not being pursued. The fundamental precepts of human rights are violated rather than upheld.
>
> (UN 2001: 3)

One problem with the study of corruption is knowing how to measure it. Heavy reliance is placed in the study of judicial corruption on what people think the scale of the problem is in their country. This is easier to assess than finding out how many people actually pay bribes to judges. It will inevitably exaggerate the problem because every bribe-payer will be in contact with many who thus learn about corruption without having been directly involved in it. Consequently, levels of bribery in the judiciary seem invariably to be inflated in the minds of the public. The 2009 survey by Transparency International found that 49 per cent of respondents from 41 countries believed that the judiciary in their country was infected by corruption, but only 16 per cent reported actually having had to pay a bribe. In 2015 a majority of Zimbabweans perceived judges and magistrates to be involved in corruption, though only 21 per cent of survey respondents had paid a bribe (TI and Afrobarometer 2015).

In Asia 27 per cent of those surveyed in 2020 had little or no trust in the courts because of corruption, though only 17 per cent of people who used the courts had paid a bribe in the previous twelve months (TI 2020). In all regions in which are found countries struggling with the transition to democracy, fewer people experience corruption than believe it to afflict the judicial process.

It is important to establish what is meant by corruption in the context of judicial independence. Corruption needs to be distinguished from theft of state assets, extortion, influence peddling, nepotism, fraud and embezzlement. Some analysts extend the meaning of corruption to include all deviations from impartial adjudication, including politically motivated court rulings, party political activities, and judges' ideological and social-class biases (Brooks 2019). Such colloquial uses of 'corruption' obscure its formal, legal meaning and complicate the business of designing anti-corruption reforms. Corruption requires a definition relating to public office if it is to be distinguished from other forms of objectionable, immoral or illegal behaviour on the part of public officials. This must be built on a distinction between the public and private realms. Corruption occurs when public officials deviate from their formal public duties and abuse their power for private pecuniary gain through bribery.

For many people in Third Wave democracies corruption in the judicial process begins with the police, with the right to a fair trial undermined by bribes which purchase immunity from arrest or interference with evidence. They may then have to bribe court officials to interfere with files of written evidence, postpone or bring forward dates of hearings, ignore court judgements, and misinform litigants. A lack of knowledge among the general public of court procedures makes it easier for officials to extort bribes. In some countries even public prosecutors are able to extract bribes from litigants or the lawyers representing them. A bribe may persuade a prosecutor to discontinue a case, charge a defendant with less than their offence warrants, withhold evidence, present a weak challenge to defence evidence, or present weak arguments in support of conviction or penalty (Cowdery 2007).

Judges are bribed in order to manipulate the proceedings of their courts or judicial decision-making so that verdicts and other outcomes suit those paying the bribes. Such manipulation takes the form of abuse of discretion as applied to court procedures or rulings based on outdated or inappropriate law. Corrupt payments may induce judges to allow or exclude evidence, manipulate the dates of hearings, inaccurately summarize proceedings, distort testimony, and endorse applications for appeal. A corrupt judge may also grant conditional release to a prisoner who has served only a fraction of their sentence when such offenders are not eligible under the relevant law (Freedom House 2011).

Judicial corruption is a global phenomenon, but is worst in countries in transition from authoritarianism or regressing back to authoritarian status. In 2013 public opinion surveys in 20 countries attempting to consolidate democracy found the judiciary was believed to be the most corrupt part of government, with an average of 30 per cent of those who came into contact with the judiciary reporting having to pay a bribe. Since then, the situation has improved in all regions, though significant levels of judicial corruption persist. In 2020 between 22 and 26 per cent of people in the new democracies of Eastern Europe and Central Asia thought that judges and magistrates were highly corrupt. Corruption by powerful political and business elites undermined due process in Kosovo. In Kyrgyzstan corruption among judges was widespread, with corruption charges levelled against judges accused of issuing rulings favouring organized crime. Although public confidence in courts had been steadily improving in Lithuania since 2010, a judicial corruption scandal in 2019 involving eight senior judges (one a member of the Supreme Court) significantly damaged it. In Romania the right to a fair and timely trial is often undermined by corruption. Ukraine suffers from corrupt courts, and reform initiatives have stalled because judges persistently obstruct corruption investigations into senior members of the judiciary (Freedom House 2020).

Surveys in Asia in 2020 showed that the percentage of respondents who thought that most or all judges and magistrates are corrupt ranged from 9 per cent in the Philippines to 24 per cent in South Korea. In Bangladesh access to the justice system is compromised by widespread corruption in the lower courts where magistrates, attorneys and court officials frequently demand bribes from defendants. Indonesian courts remain plagued by corruption, and judicial independence is hampered by corruption in the Philippines. In South Korea and Taiwan corruption has led to demands for the introduction of jury trials in the belief that juries provide protection against judicial corruption and politicization (TI 2020).

In Africa 34 per cent of survey respondents in 2019 thought that most or all judges and magistrates were involved in corruption. The proportions ranged from 52 per cent in Nigeria to 16 per cent in Tunisia. The situation appeared to have improved between 2015 and 2019 in Ghana, Kenya, Tanzania, Zambia and Zimbabwe but deteriorated in Malawi, where 41 per cent believed the courts to be corrupt, and Nigeria, where the public perceived judges to be easily bribed, and many citizens receive requests from judicial officials for bribes to expedite cases or obtain favourable rulings. In Uganda, where 43 per cent believed most or all judges to be corrupt, Uganda's chief justice set up a task force in 2019 to investigate widespread allegations of judicial corruption (TI 2019a).

Trust in the courts is very low throughout Latin America where 42 per cent of those surveyed in 2019 believed most or all judges and magistrates to be involved in corruption. In a majority of countries the situation had deteriorated between 2017 and 2019. In Argentina, a 'vibrant representative democracy', the proportion rose from 39 per cent to 54 per cent. High court judges are especially at risk of corruption, though the problem stems from political control of the judiciary, leading to corruption cases being mishandled or shelved, rather than corrupt judges. The Brazilian judiciary has also been ineffective in combating corruption, partly owing to corruption in the courts themselves. In Peru the judiciary is perceived as one of the most corrupt institutions in the country, with 68 per cent of poll respondents believing judges to be corrupt, and despite the creation of a new National Board of Justice in 2018 charged with selecting, evaluating and disciplining judges. The worst Latin American case in 2019 was Venezuela where 80 per cent of respondents thought that most or all judges were corrupt. However, the 'corruption' referred to here largely takes the form of political control of the courts. In Mexico, where 58 per cent believe the courts to be corrupt, the justice system is plagued by corruption, and widespread bribery undermines the integrity of lower-level courts.

Judicial corruption poses numerous problems for democratic consolidation. The relationship between corruption and lack of trust in political institutions generally has been demonstrated by empirical analysis. A lack of trust in the honesty of the judiciary strengthens that malign relationship. This is why public perceptions of judicial corruption are significant, especially when they overestimate the scale of the problem. Rather than increasing support for, and trust in, contemporary political arrangements by reducing red tape and improving accessibility to public services, corruption is very damaging to trust in political institutions.

There is a strong relationship between perceptions of corruption and levels of trust in political arrangements, especially democratic institutions. Comparative household surveys conducted in 18 sub-Saharan African countries found that both experience of corruption and the belief that it is widespread, including 35 per cent of the population believing that most or all judges and magistrates are corrupt, had 'a negative impact on citizens' trust in political institutions' (Lavallée et al. 2008: 16). Research into African public opinion further confirmed that when trust in political institutions and processes is undermined, the development of attitudes supportive of democracy is inhibited: '[P]eople who trust the key executive and legislative institutions of the land are also likely to support democracy and be satisfied and patient with democracy's performance. If they think that public officials are corrupt, however, their satisfaction and patience with democracy are likely to decline'. Indeed, surveys have shown that trust in political institutions is *the* most important factor in explaining satisfaction and patience with democracy (Armah-Attoh et al. 2007: 17). Corruption can infect the electoral system, alienate citizens from political participation, violate civil rights such as equality and the right to a fair trial, weaken oversight of government, limit the ability of the state to provide security to its citizens, reduce the quality of public services, and destroy trust in the political system. It thus undermines 'the fragile balance between institutions, and rules and norms that provide trust and legitimacy of the system' (Drapalova et al. 2019: 7).

Bribery rates, defined as the proportion of those who had contact with public services in the past 12 months and had paid a bribe, can be compared with strength of democratic political culture, accepting that the latter is 'crucial for the legitimacy, smooth functioning and, ultimately, the sustainability of democracy' (EIU 2018: 63). Political culture is defined as the degree of popular support for democracy based on levels of consensus and perceptions of leadership, military rule, rule by experts, public order, economic performance under democracy, and the separation of church and state.[1]

Figure 4.1 lends a limited measure of support to the hypothesis that a democratic political culture becomes weaker, the more bribery is a fact of life for the population. This reflects the fact that in new democracies, and especially those of an increasingly illiberal character, lack of faith in democracy is driven by other factors such as the desire of sections of the community to prolong their access to power by limiting the rights of their opponents.

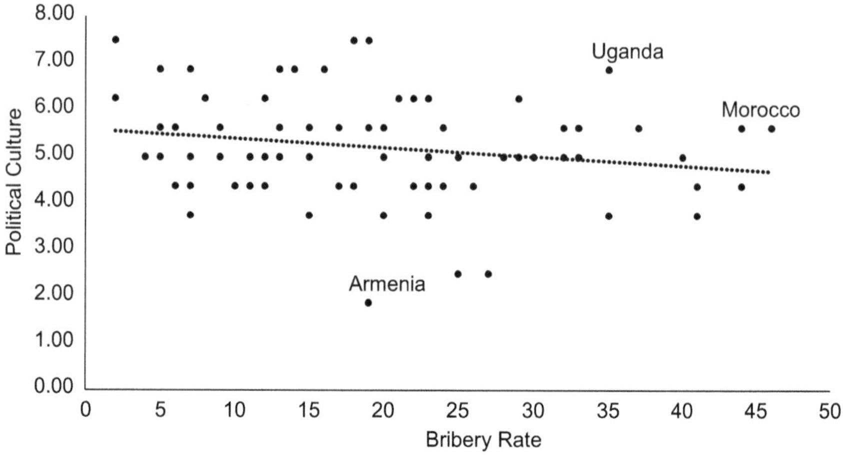

Figure 4.1 Bribery and Political Culture, 2017

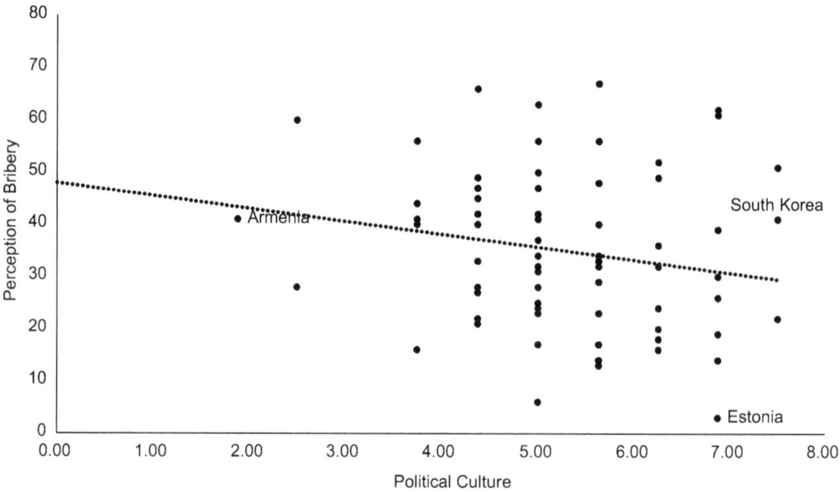

Figure 4.2 Perceptions of Bribery and Political Culture, 2017

Perceptions of judicial corruption are only part of the general view held by members of the public on the overall corruption level in their country. Contrary to expectations, such perceptions do not appear to be strongly related to support for democratic values. Figure 4.2 plots Transparency International's Global Corruption Barometer's results for the percentage of respondents who thought that most or all judges and magistrates in their country were involved in corruption against the Economist Intelligence Unit's ratings for political culture. This gives very little support to the proposition that the greater the perceived corruption, the less the support for democratic values. It is likely that, rather than damaging a democratic political culture, judicial corruption is taken as a symptom of democratic backsliding, best corrected by stronger democracy rather than authoritarianism.

There is also the fact that in many countries there is far worst corruption in other parts of the government system than in the judiciary. In no country surveyed in 2019–2020 was the judiciary believed to be the most corrupt part of government, though only in 14 countries was the judiciary found to be the least corrupt institution (see Table 4.1).

In Eastern Europe, while judges are rated as more corrupt than the police, they are generally seen as much less corrupt than parliamentarians. In Romania, for example, 22 per cent think that most or all judges and magistrates are corrupt, compared to 51 per cent for parliamentarians. In Latin America, presidents, prime ministers and parliamentarians are seen as most corrupt, and over half of respondents think most or all elected politicians are corrupt. Judges and magistrates are on average perceived as the least corrupt of all government institutions. In Guatemala, 44 per cent rate the judiciary as corrupt, compared to 71 per cent for the president. A high percentage of Peruvians think judges are corrupt (68 per cent), more than the executive, government officials and the police, but still considerably fewer than those who believe parliamentarians to be corrupt: 80 per cent (TI 2019b).

Table 4.1 Corruption in Government Institutions* 2019–2020. Selected Countries

Country	*President/ Prime Minister*	*MPs*	*Government Officials*	*Police*	*Judges*
Latvia	20	38	30	13	12
Romania	37	51	40	24	22
Brazil	57	63	54	38	34
Guatemala	71	59	56	51	44
Tunisia	25	30	31	23	16
Kenya	36	47	47	66	28
Malawi	47	43	44	54	41
South Africa	38	44	44	49	32
Zambia	32	36	37	54	28
Zimbabwe	28	37	36	57	25
Bangladesh	20	18	22	30	12
Malaysia	25	36	28	30	13
Taiwan	24	17	19	17	14
Thailand	47	39	30	37	12

*Percentage of people who think that most or all people in these institutions are involved in corruption.

Sources: TI (2019a), TI (2019b), TI (2020) and TI (2021).

Parliamentarians and government officials are seen as the most corrupt institutions in the Middle East and North Africa, with 44 per cent of people believing most or all parliamentarians and government officials to be corrupt, compared to 27 per cent for judges and magistrates. In the transitional democracies the chief executive, parliamentarians and bureaucrats are seen as more corrupt than the judiciary.

In Africa the problem of corruption is greatest in the police with 47 per cent identifying corruption in the police as more prevalent than in any other institution. Many Africans also believe most or all government officials and parliamentarians are corrupt (39 per cent and 36 per cent, respectively). In all the transitional democracies judges were believed to be less corrupt than the police. In Kenya, Malawi, South Africa, Zambia and Zimbabwe judges and magistrates are seen as the least corrupt of all parts of government.

Asian parliamentarians are seen by nearly one person in three as the region's most corrupt part of government. Judges and lawyers were rated the least corrupt public officials in Bangladesh, Malaysia, Taiwan and Thailand.

While the public may regard other institutions as more corrupt than the judiciary, democrats will be very aware that the effects of a corrupt judiciary is damaging to the establishment of democracy following a history of authoritarianism:

> [I]t erodes the ability of the international community to tackle transnational crime and terrorism; it diminishes trade, economic growth and human development; and, most importantly, it denies citizens impartial settlement of disputes with neighbours or the authorities. When the latter occurs, corrupt judiciaries fracture and divide communities by keeping alive the sense of injury created by unjust treatment and mediation. Judicial systems debased by bribery undermine confidence in governance by facilitating corruption across all sectors of government, starting at the helm of power.
>
> (TI 2007: xii)

A venal judiciary also destroys trust in democracy by failing to enforce the law fairly and effectively (Bailey 2009). Corrupt judiciaries and law enforcement agencies help governments to incapacitate political activists and eradicate the independent media. Judicial corruption also undermines judicial review, another pillar of democratic consolidation: '[A] corrupt judiciary is costly for democracy because it cannot credibly play the role of watchdog on constitutional values or monitor the honesty of the other branches of government. . . . An honest government administration will be difficult to establish if the judiciary is venal' (Rose-Ackerman 1999: 156–157).

Corruption also provides a means of evading the consequences of breaking the law and thereby reduces the laws deterrent effect. It provides a fertile environment for the growth of organized crime and corruption in other branches of government. It means that political and business elites can prolong the judicial process through appeals or even halt proceedings altogether with the support of sympathetic judges: 'Illicit interferences with justice can also be violent, particularly when perpetrated directly by members of organised crime. These forays are intended to secure specific objectives, such as the closing of a particular case, or the acquittal of a given individual' (García-Sayán 2018).

Finally, the elimination of corruption elsewhere in the political system is made all the more difficult to achieve when the legal process required to combat corruption is itself corrupt: 'Judiciaries that are corrupt or corruptible are not suited to the task of rooting out corruption in other government institutions' (Decker et al. 2006: 7). When the judiciary is corrupt, unusually light sentences will be handed down in anti-corruption trials, suspects may be released if they agreed to return corrupt payments, the misconduct of judges will rarely be investigated, and the courts will put up strong resistance to legislation designed to sanction judges who commit misconduct, as in Indonesia (Freedom House 2012). In Albania, weak anti-corruption efforts by the judiciary have failed to restore public trust in the courts. In contrast, when the courts are able to hand down significant verdicts in important corruption cases, as in Romania in 2014, it can do much to strengthen the credibility of the judiciary in the eyes of the public (Freedom House 2015a).

Causes of judicial corruption

Poor salary levels in the judiciary are thought to be the main cause of corruption, especially when salaries are too low to provide a decent standard of living: 'The salary of the judge must be sufficient to support the judge to an adequate standard, else the judge may be forced to turn to external funding sources, whether business activities, or more insidiously, through corrupt means. A sufficiently high judicial salary mitigates these threats' (McIntyre 2019: 211).

A number of newly democratizing countries, including Ecuador, Georgia, Nigeria and Peru, have increased judicial salaries significantly in order to reduce judicial corruption. However, it is difficult to prove a causal relationship between salary levels and corruption. The salaries of judges in Georgia increased by 400 per cent between 2005 and 2007, but public perceptions of corruption remained high (TI 2007). Nevertheless, judicial corruption is significantly less in countries if judges' salaries have not decreased in real terms (Voigt and Gutmann 2015).

Organizational matters are also relevant to understanding judicial corruption and to the development of reforms to combat it. First, corruption is facilitated by weak mechanisms by which the judiciary can be monitored and by 'an opaque judicial system where both litigants and the public have trouble finding out what is going on' (Rose-Ackerman 2007: 23). If rulings and justifications of court decisions are not extensively publicized, corruption is less visible and traceable. A lack of transparency and uncontrolled discretion among court officials further encourages corruption, by creating an environment in which lawyers can expect officials to perform 'an unmonitored task in exchange for an illicit fee with a low probability of being sanctioned' (Voigt and Gutmann 2015).

Second, complex court administration, marked by informal and unpredictable allocations of responsibilities to different court officials, also makes corruption easier. Similarly, if judges are given a wide range of administrative tasks such as strategic planning, personnel management, budgetary control and planning, and the administration of other resources, without formal guidelines, corruption is more difficult to control.

Third, corruption is encouraged by defective court information systems which distort judicial knowledge of jurisprudence, law and regulations and leads to abuse of substantive and procedural discretion. In such a context, 'the abuse of public office for private benefit is more likely and more difficult to detect' (Buscaglia 2001: 238–239). The problem of vague and contradictory laws necessitating judicial discretion, and so increasing incentives for corruption, is particularly acute in democratizing countries (Rose-Ackerman 1999).

Organizational factors, rather than low salaries for judges and their staff, are thus major causes of corruption, especially weak monitoring which reduces transparency, and poor information technology which cannot ensure consistency in the application of the law: 'organizational structures coupled with procedural and administrative patterns make judiciaries prone to the uncontrolled spread of systemic corrupt practices at every level' (Rose-Ackerman 1999: 238). When higher judicial salaries are found with levels of corruption, this is explained by organizational factors (Voigt 2007; Voigt and Gutmann 2015).

Another likely cause of judicial corruption are the delays resulting from an under-resourced judiciary which create incentives to pay and accept 'speed money'. Corruption in the judicial system of Pakistan means 'the operators of the legal system constantly expect "speed money" to push the process along; subsequently, the integrity of the judicial officers is doubtful' (Mehdi 2017: 221). 'Motivating' court officials with bribes is particularly prevalent in Latin America and not only speeds up the progress of cases through the courts but also affects the final outcomes (Rose-Ackerman 1999: 155; Voigt 2007). Such an environment also encourages magistrates to delay cases deliberately in order to encourage litigants to offer bribes, as in Tanzania.

There are also cases where corruption has been encouraged by criminal organizations which make the acceptance of bribes preferable to the alternative – violent death in the case of Colombian and Mexican drug cartels which offer a choice between *plato o plume*, silver or lead, money or bullet.

Social norms may also support corruption and create a culture of corruption in state institutions, including the judiciary. In addition to corrupt interference by politicians, business interests, and even organized crime, judges come under pressure from 'the looser, still potent informal networks formed by extended family, friends, neighbours and other groups with whom they associate'. Corruption then reflects 'local norms of networking, exchanging favours and gifts, and offering and receiving payoffs to ensure favourable outcomes' (Kurkchiyan 2007: 103).

However, popular protest against corruption shows it is not universally endorsed by cultural values and practices. In many democratizing countries it is regarded as unacceptable, regardless of culture. Public opinion regularly sees corruption as a serious problem. In Eastern Europe this view ranges from 69 per cent in Hungary to 92 per cent in Croatia. In Latin America between 85 per cent (Chile) and 96 per cent (Peru) see corruption as a big problem. The regional average for Asia is 74 per cent, with 92 per cent of Indonesians regarding corruption as a big problem for the country.

Tolerance of corruption is not the rule. Corruption is seen as representing a decline in public ethics. Even when seen as a necessary evil (simply for getting things done) it is still regarded as evil. People are able to distinguish between appropriate and inappropriate official, including judicial, behaviour (Rose-Ackerman 1998). Corruption is rarely endorsed as culturally acceptable or inevitable, especially by its victims.

Judicial corruption may also be caused by the absence of adequate controls over lower-level courts by higher institutional levels. In Latin America the hierarchical organization of the judiciary is relevant to the prevention of corruption at lower levels (where administrative corruption is most prevalent): '[C]orruption within the judiciary is higher where institutional levels of internal independence are also higher . . . because too many decentralized, poorly monitored, and unconstrained lower courts may increase the incentives for lower-court judges to accept bribes.' Inadequate supervisory resources create magistrates who are 'small emperors' (Rios-Figueroa 2012: 200).

* * *

Judicial impartiality and independence can be damaged by factors that extend beyond external political interference in the course of justice. Court proceedings may be biased, violating the principle of equality before the law and the right to a fair trial. Despite constitutional guarantees, in practice there may be no presumption of innocence. Proceedings may fail to observe the rules of natural justice or due process. Judges may be biased by their own preferences, prejudices, political affiliations and ideological leanings when interpreting and applying the law and conducting hearings. Inefficiencies within the judiciary due to lack of resources can compromise the principles embedded in the rule of law and amount to a denial of natural justice and basic rights. When corrupt justice is enjoyed only by the highest bidder the judiciary's ability to offer impartial adjudication is destroyed. The relationships between the causes of judicial corruption, its significance in newly democratizing countries, and its effect on a democratic political culture are complex, making the selection of appropriate reforms difficult.

Reforms designed to strengthen the independence and integrity of the judiciary have been launched in many post-authoritarian states, though these do not always address the political factors which render judicial independence vulnerable. These reforms will be considered in the following two chapters under categories corresponding to the main sources of threats to judicial independence. The next chapter will examine the reforms designed to deal with problems arising from politically motivated interference in judicial appointments and careers, including attempts to 'steer' judicial decision-making, the intimidation of judges and other members of the judiciary, limits on the scope of judicial review, the use of exceptional courts and the non-enforcement of verdicts. Chapter 6 will focus on judicial capacity, biased proceeding, inadequate resources and inefficiency in the judicial process, biased judges, and corruption.

Note

1 The political culture score is on a 0–to-10 scale. Source: EIU (2018), *Democracy Index 2017*, pp. 5–9.

For bribery rates and perceptions of bribery, see TI 2017 'Global Corruption Barometer Results 2017', GCB-2017-Global-Results(5).xlxs, Q3 and Q2G.

References

Afsah, E. (2016), 'Guides and guardians: judiciaries in times of transition' in M. Scheinin, H. Krunke and M. Aksenova (eds.), *Judges as Guardians of Constitutionalism and Human Rights*, London: Edward Elgar.

Armah-Attoh, D., E. Gyimah- Boadi and A. B. Chikwanha (2007), *Corruption and Institutional Trust in Africa: Implications for Democratic Development*, Afrobarometer Working Paper No. 81, East Lansing: Michigan State University.

Bailey, J. (2009), 'Corruption and democratic governability' in C. H. Blake and S. D. Morris (eds.), *Corruption and Democracy in Latin America*, Pittsburgh: University of Pittsburgh Press.

Brooks, G. (2019), *Criminal Justice and Corruption State Power, Privatization and Legitimacy*, Cham: Palgrave Macmillan.

Buscaglia, E. (2001), 'An analysis of judicial corruption and its causes: an objective governing-based approach', *International Review of Law and Economics*, vol. 21, no. 2.

Chikalanga, D., G. Lungu and N. Yezi (2007), 'Zambian judiciary struggles to modernise' in Transparency International (ed.), *Global Corruption Report 2007: Corruption in Judicial Systems,* London: Transparency International.

Chinyere, A. C. (2021), 'Emerging trends on the presumption of innocence and the right to silence in Nigeria', *Legalpedia*, https://legalpediaonline.com/

Cowdery, N. (2007), 'Judicial corruption from the prosecution's perspective' in Transparency International (ed.), *Global Corruption Report 2007: Corruption in Judicial Systems*, Cambridge: Cambridge University Press.

Decker, K., C. Sage and M. Stefanova (2006), 'Law or justice: building equitable legal institutions' in World Bank (ed.), *World Development Report 2006: Equity and Development*, Washington: The World Bank.

Drapalova, E., A. Mungiu-Pippidi, B. J. Palifka and J. Vrushi (2019), *Corruption and the Crisis of Democracy: The Link between Corruption and the Weakening of Democratic Institutions*, Berlin: Transparency International.

EIU (2018), *Democracy Index 2017: Free Speech under Attack*, London: Economist Intelligence Unit.

European Commission (2010), *Analytical Report*, staff working document accompanying the Communication from the Commission to the European Parliament and the Council on Albania's application for membership of the European Union, (com 2010, 680), Brussels: European Commission.
European Parliament (2020), *Discriminatory Laws Undermining Women's Rights*, Strasbourg: European Parliament.
Fair Trials (2020), *Uncovering Anti-Roma Discrimination in Criminal Justice Systems in Europe*, Brussels: Fair Trials.
Fekete, B. (2015), 'How to become a judge in Hungary? From the professionalism of the judiciary to the political ties of the Constitutional Court' in S. Turenne (ed.), *Fair Reflection of Society in Judicial Systems: A Comparative Study*, Cham: Springer International Publishing.
FRA (2021), *Presumption of Innocence and Related Rights*, Luxembourg: European Union Agency for Fundamental Rights.
Freedom House (2004), *Countries at the Crossroads 2004: Jordan*, New York: Freedom House.
Freedom House (2006), *Countries at the Crossroads 2006: South Africa*, New York: Freedom House.
Freedom House (2011), *Nations in Transit 2011: Turkmenistan*, New York: Freedom House.
Freedom House (2012), *Countries at the Crossroads 2012: Indonesia*, New York: Freedom House.
Freedom House (2015a), *Nations in Transit 201: Romania*, New York: Freedom House.
Freedom House (2015b), *Nations in Transit 2015: Serbia*, New York: Freedom House.
Freedom House (2020), *Country Profiles*, New York: Freedom House.
Freedom House (2021), *Freedom in the World 2021: Democracy Under Siege*, Country Data, https://freedomhouse.org/countries/freedom-world/scores
García-Moreno, C. et al. (2015), 'Addressing violence against women: a call to action', *The Lancet*, vol. 385, no. 9978.
García-Sayán, D. (2018), *Corruption, Human Rights, and Judicial Independence*, Vienna: United Nations Office on Drugs and Crime.
Gutmann, J. and S. Voigt (2015), 'The rule of law and constitutionalism in Muslim countries', *Public Choice*, vol. 162, nos. 3–4.
Habib, A. Z. M. A. (2015), 'Extrajudicial killing in Bangladesh: a murder of human rights', *OIDA International Journal of Sustainable Development*, vol. 8, no. 2.
Hallward-Driemeier, M., T. Hasan and A. B. Rusu (2013), *Women's Legal Rights Over 50 Years: What Is the Impact of Reform?*, Policy Research Working Paper 6617, Washington, DC: World Bank.
Hoffman, P. (2012), 'Vigilantism: the last resort of the unprotected', Washington: World Justice Project, worldjusticeproject.org/blog/vigilantism-last-resort-unprotected
HRW (2022), *World Report 2022*, New York: Human Rights Watch.
ICJ (2014), *Russian Federation: Country Profile Prepared by the ICJ Centre for the Independence of Judges and Lawyers*, Geneva: International Commission of Jurists, www.icj.org/cijlcountryprofiles/russian-federation/
ICJ (2020), *Neither Check Nor Balance: The Judiciary in Tajikistan: ICJ Mission Report*, Geneva: International Commission of Jurists.
ICJ (2021), *Accessing Economic and Social Rights in Uzbekistan: An Analysis of Selected Laws and Practices*, Geneva: International Commission of Jurists.
Kantorowicz, J. and N. Garoupa (2016), 'An empirical analysis of constitutional review voting in the polish constitutional tribunal, 2003–2014', *Constitutional Political Economy*, vol. 27, no. 1.

Kurkchiyan, M. (2007), 'Judicial corruption in the context of legal culture' in Transparency International (ed.), *Global Corruption Report 2007: Corruption in Judicial Systems*, Cambridge: Cambridge University Press.

Lavallée, E., M. Razafindrakoto and F. Roubaud (2008), *Corruption and Trust in Political Institutions in Sub-Saharan Africa*, Afrobarometer Working Paper 102, East Lansing: Michigan State University.

McIntyre, J. (2019), *The Judicial Function: Fundamental Principles of Contemporary Judging*, Singapore: Springer.

Mehdi, R. (2017), 'Lady judges of Pakistan: embodying the changing living tradition of Islam' in N. Sonneveld and M. Lindbekk (eds.), *Women Judges in the Muslim World: A Comparative Study of Discourse and Practice*, Leiden: Brill.

Melcarnel, A. and G. B. Ramello (2015), 'Judges' incentives and efficiency', *Review of Law and Economics*, vol. 11, no. 2.

Meyerson, D. (2015), 'Why should justice be seen to be done?', *Criminal Justice Ethics*, vol. 34, no. 1.

The Observer, Kampala (2012), 'Ogoola's judicial work well cut out', 29 January.

Oldfather, C. M. (2015), 'Of judges, law, and the river: tacit knowledge and the judicial role', *Journal of Dispute Resolution*, vol. 152, no. 1.

Pena, C. M. (2007), 'Judicial corruption and the military legacy in Guatemala' in Transparency International (ed.), *Global Corruption Report 2007: Corruption in Judicial Systems*, Cambridge: Cambridge University Press.

Prillaman, W. C. (2000), *The Judiciary and Democratic Decay in Latin America: Declining Confidence in the Rule of Law*, Westport, CT: Praeger.

Rios-Figueroa, J. (2012), 'Justice system institutions and corruption control: evidence from Latin America, *The Justice System Journal*, vol. 33, no. 2.

Rose-Ackerman, S. (1998), 'Corruption and the global economy' in UNDP/OECD Development Centre (ed.), *Corruption and Integrity Improvement Initiatives in Developing Countries*, New York: UNDP.

Rose-Ackerman, S. (1999), *Corruption and Government: Causes, Consequences and Reform*, Cambridge: Cambridge University Press.

Rose-Ackerman, S. (2007), 'Judicial independence and corruption' in Transparency International (ed.), *Global Corruption Report 2007: Corruption in Judicial Systems*, Cambridge: Cambridge University Press.

Russell, P. H. (2001), 'Toward a general theory of judicial independence' in P. H. Russell and D. M. O'Brien (eds.), *Judicial Independence in the Age of Democracy: Critical Perspectives from Around the World*, Charlotteville: University Press of Virginia.

Shor, J. (2009), 'Kazakhstan: human rights defender faces unfair trial', *Human Rights Brief*, Centre for Human Rights and Humanitarian Law, Washington: The American University.

TI (2007), *Global Corruption Report 2007: Corruption in Judicial Systems*, Cambridge: Transparency International.

TI (2019a), *Global Corruption Barometer Africa 2019 Citizens' Views and Experiences of Corruption*, Berlin: Transparency International.

TI (2019b), *Global Corruption Barometer: Latin America and the Caribbean, 2019. Citizens' Views and Experiences of Corruption*, Berlin: Transparency International.

TI (2020), *Global Corruption Barometer Asia 2020: Citizens' Views and Experiences of Corruption*, Berlin: Transparency International.

TI (2021), *Global Corruption Barometer, European Union 2021: Citizens' Views and Experiences of Corruption*, Berlin: Transparency International.

TI and Afrobarometer (2015), *People and Corruption: Africa Survey 2015*, Berlin: Transparency International.

Tiede, L. B. (2015), 'The political determinants of judicial dissent: evidence from the Chilean Constitutional Tribunal', *European Political Science Review*, available on CJO, doi:10.1017/S1755773915000090

UN (2001), Office for Drug Control and Crime Prevention, *Strengthening Judicial Integrity Against Corruption*, Vienna: United Nations Office on Drugs and Crime, www.unodc.org/dohadeclaration/en/news/2018/04/corruption-human-rights-and-judicial-independence.html

United Nations High Commissioner for Human Rights (2011), *A Long Way to Go: Implementation of the Elimination of Violence Against Women Law in Afghanistan*, Kabul: OHCHR and United Nations Assistance Mission in Afghanistan.

Voigt, S. (2007), 'When are judges likely to be corrupt?' in Transparency International (ed.), *Global Corruption Report 2007: Corruption in Judicial Systems*, Cambridge: Cambridge University Press.

Voigt, S. and J. Gutmann (2015), 'On the wrong side of the law: causes and consequences of a corrupt judiciary', *International Review of Law and Economics*, vol. 43, August.

5 Judicial reform

Introduction

Law reform has been a central feature of the democratization process in post-authoritarian states in Eastern Europe, Latin America, Asia and sub-Saharan Africa, though with highly variable levels of intensity, effort and success. Reforms have been widely supported with grants and technical assistance from multilateral and bilateral donors. For example, between 1994 and 2012 the World Bank invested $850 million in justice reform projects. In a number of post-communist countries, application for membership of the European Union has allowed the EU and the Council of Europe to insist upon the promotion of judicial independence as part of the accession process (Piana 2009; Hipper 2015). For example, in 2015 Bulgaria's lack of transparency and competition in the appointment of judges to the highest courts, including the Supreme Court of Cassation, was noted in a European Commission report to the European Parliament (European Commission 2015; Wetzel and Orbie 2015). Whether driven by domestic pressures or external funding, judicial reform has become a familiar part of the transition process.

This chapter starts by arguing that democratic political competition gives strong protection against interference in the judiciary by politicians, especially those with parliamentary majorities which give them control of the political executive. The contribution to judicial independence which civil society can make, and the reforms which empower civil society's role here, are assessed next. The following section explains the importance of legislative oversight of the judiciary and the features of contemporary politics which militate against this. The question of what might be done to protect judges against intimidation is then addressed, followed by an examination of reforms to protect the scope of judicial review and the different courts involved in this expanding role for the judiciary in democratizing states. This is followed by a discussion of how exceptional courts and alternative methods of dispute resolution might be kept consistent with judicial independence. Finally, the chapter asks what needs to be done to ensure that judicial independence is not undermined by failures to enforce and comply with the decisions of the courts.

DOI: 10.4324/9781003334613-6

Political competition

Political reform provides the firmest foundation for judicial independence, according to the 'insurance' theory of judicial independence. The best protection against political interference in the judiciary is political competition. Judicial independence is buoyed up by the expectations of governing parties under competitive conditions. Politicians have incentives to support judicial independence when the long-term pattern of electoral politics entails the prospect of regular transfers of power from one party to another. But if a party expects to remain in power indefinitely despite regular elections, its political leaders will calculate that there will be 'lower risk-adjusted costs to non-independent judiciaries'. So states with dominant parties are less likely to find that independent courts are respected (Ramseyer 1994: 747).

Strong and stable political competition also supports the independence of the judiciary through the incentives for mutual restraint which it creates for both government and opposition. A political party in power has incentives to respect judicial independence because of the constraints this would impose on the opposition, should it come to power. Even fragile multiparty democracies, as in some democratizing African states, achieve greater judicial independence, strengthening the view that 'the best safeguard of judicial independence is party competition' (Widner 1999: 185). Judicial independence is a form of political 'insurance' against some of the costs of losing power.

Judicial independence thus has part of its origins in the logic of sustained political competition, under which political actors that anticipate alternating in power over a period of time will adopt a pro-independence perspective. Though judicial independence reduces the benefits a party can accrue while in power, it also reduces the costs of being out of power, since its opponents are also constrained. Equally, politicians continue to 'play' the political game even when they are not in power because they have the opportunity to punish violators of judicial independence once they return to power.

Incentives to increase the autonomy of the courts when exercising powers of judicial review have also been found to be greater when the governing party has internal weaknesses and a low level of party unity, thus increasing the risk that it will not survive long in power (Yadav and Mukherjee 2014). This again reflects the calculations made by politicians who wish to see their opponents constrained by a judiciary which enjoys a large measure of independence from the executive branch. Political competition thus explains the paradox of executives and legislatures not limiting the power of judiciaries even when the courts frequently find *against* executive and administrative action, and when the judiciary is ultimately dependent upon politicians for organization, appointments, funding and enforcement. Politicians may be prepared to share rule-making with judges, allowing them to elaborate on the details of legislation or develop a whole area of law, because under competitive politics politicians calculate that they will be able to claim the credit for policies from their supporters while shifting blame from opponents on to the judiciary. It is thus in the interest of political decision-makers to delegate powers to an independent judiciary because 'this delegation assists in maximizing their political support and chances of re-election' (Salzberger 1993: 350).

Rotating the exercise of power through electoral competition is one mechanism protecting judicial independence. If power is concentrated, reducing the frequency with which power alternates between competing parties, judicial independence may still be preserved by political 'fragmentation', the result of laws which divide authority over the judiciary between different agencies, thus making a concerted attack on the judiciary difficult: 'When divided government obtains, impeaching judges, packing courts, or replacing judges with others more closely aligned with the executive is less likely. For this reason, fragmentation should protect the stability of justices' (Leiras et al. 2015). However, fragmentation here was investigated in a very specific context relating to only one dimension of judicial autonomy: the stability of office-holding among provincial Supreme Courts justices in Argentina between 1984 and 2008. The conclusions drawn may not apply to other forms of political interference in other contexts.

Politicians may also be favourably disposed towards judicial independence because of concerns about corruption in government and business, the effect of a collapse of the rule of law on party cohesion or business confidence, or the need to establish a new regime's legitimacy. Judicial independence, and thus the rule of law, is protected by stable political competition and its correlative values, such as a willingness to compromise.

Political competition thus might explain why judicial independence in the Czech Republic is greater than might be expected, given the powers exercised over the judiciary by the political executive (see Chapter 7). There have been regular, free and fair elections since the Republic's creation in 1993 with regular rotations of power. Consequently, 'no one doubts the fairness of the electoral process, and reports never surface of intimidation, fraud or any other type of manipulation on the part of the authorities' (Freedom House 2005: 6). Political opposition is strong at all levels of government, and the multiparty system is firmly established. The mass media are not subject to government control, since they are not all owned by the government, and those that are have the status of independent public service institutions.

In Romania, in contrast, most elections are free and fair in the organization of polling, and incumbents have been successfully rejected by the electorate. But some elections have been marred by fraudulent practices. It has also proved difficult to establish a meaningful and constructive political opposition, reducing the incentive for government leaders to respect the independence of the judiciary. Successive governments have resorted to emergency ordinances as a means of legislating. Extensive rural poverty in areas controlled by 'local predatory elites' means that elections in much of the country are not based on free choices. Parliament has blocked investigations into electoral fraud and failed to improve the law governing elections. The quality of Romania's electoral system is consequently rated as worse than in the Czech Republic, as is its level of judicial independence. A habit of political interference is strongly embedded in political and judicial cultures. It is significant that the European Court of Human Rights and the EU have provided the main pressures for judicial reform in Romania, rather than domestic political forces.

Elsewhere, levels of political competition are associated with judicial independence. In Georgia a strong ruling party and weak opposition have prevented the other branches of government from developing into effective checks and balances, leaving the executive dominant over the judiciary. In Hungary, where since 2010 the government coalition has held more than two-thirds of the seats in the legislature, parliament does not serve as a significant check on the executive, enabling it to introduce legislation which exposes the judiciary to government influence. The presidential government in Russia has eliminated, marginalized or harassed most of the organized political opposition's leadership. The media, business leaders, regional governors, political parties and civil society have been brought under centralized control, and the judiciary lacks independence, especially in politically important cases.

However, Figures 5.1 to 5.4,[1] which compare electoral competition with judicial independence in post-authoritarian states in Europe, Latin America, Asia and Africa, show that the relationship is far from straightforward. In post-communist states in particular there are countries labelled 'authoritarian' by the Economist Intelligence Unit with surprisingly high levels of judicial independence: Azerbaijan, Kazakhstan and Tajikistan. Then there are countries with competitive electoral processes but low judicial independence scores, for example Poland and Slovakia. Africa too shows a weaker relationship with low levels of political competition combined with relatively strong judicial independence. In Latin America and Asia the correlation is stronger.

How might a combination of autocratic qualities and judicial independence be explained?

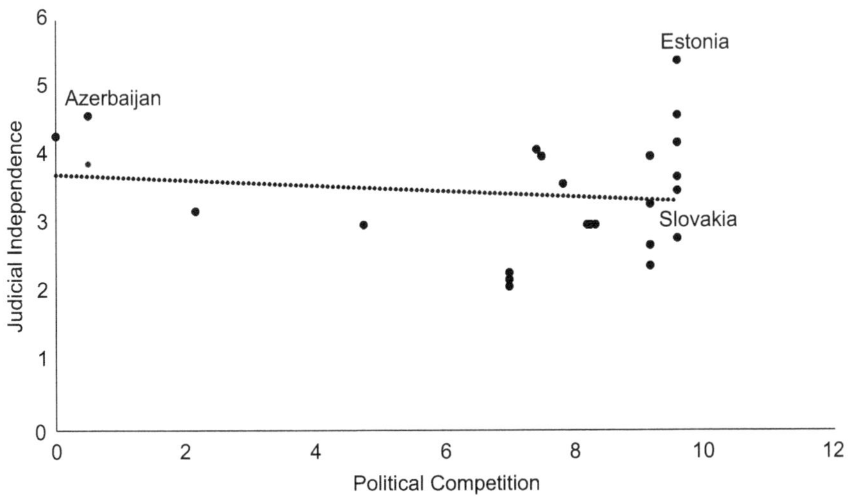

Figure 5.1 Electoral Competition and Judicial Independence, Eastern Europe, 2020

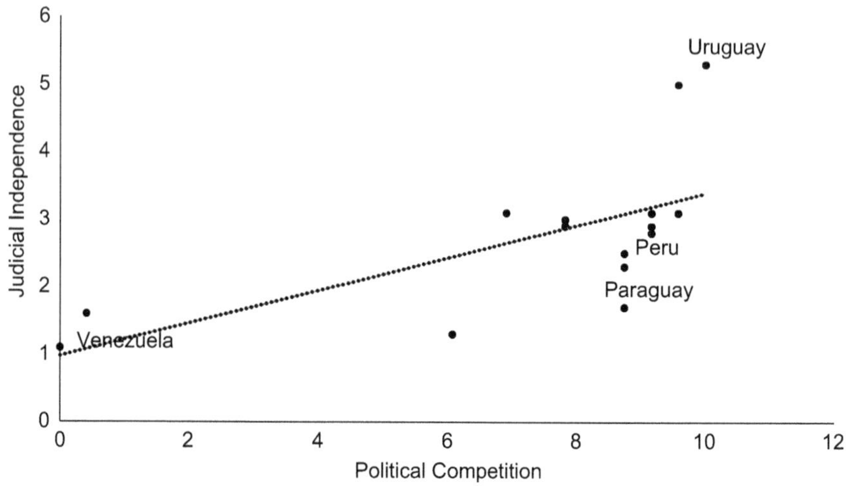

Figure 5.2 Electoral Competition and Judicial Independence, Latin America, 2019

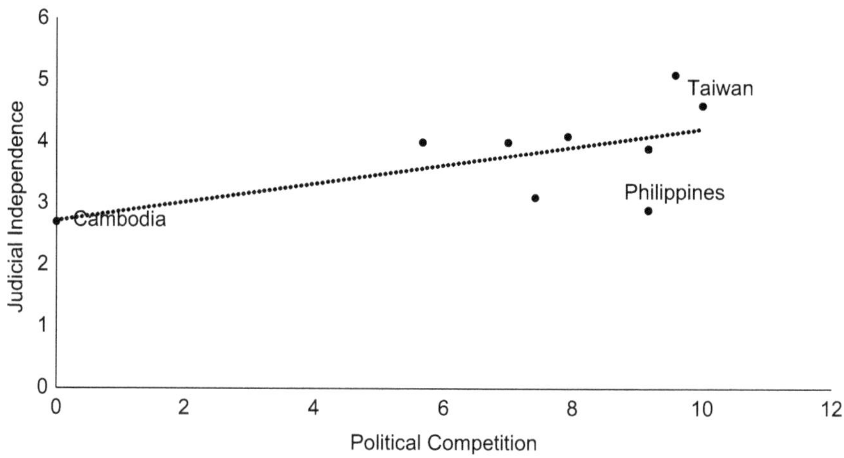

Figure 5.3 Electoral Competition and Judicial Independence, Asia, 2019

First, it may reflect difficulties in creating quantifiable measures of the relevant variables. These are notoriously difficult phenomena to measure, and different methodologies will produce different estimates. To measure judicial independence Freedom House uses a combination of on-the-ground research, consultations with local contacts, and information from news articles, non-governmental organizations, governments, and a variety of other sources. The World Economic Forum

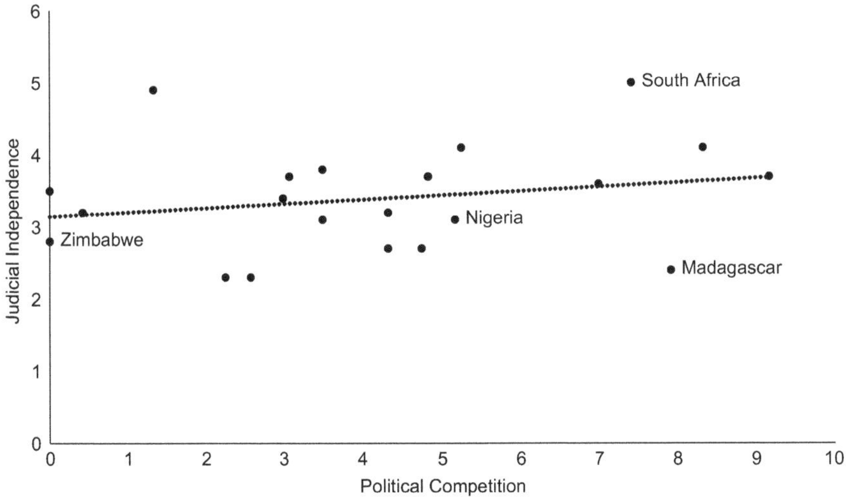

Figure 5.4 Electoral Competition and Judicial Independence, Africa, 2019

measures judicial independence by responses to the question 'In your country, how independent is the judicial system from influences of the government, individuals or companies?' in a survey of business executives from representative sectors of the economy with wide geographical coverage (WEF 2020). So while the World Economic Forum scores Azerbaijan 4.6 out of a possible 7 for judicial independence, Freedom House gives 0 out of 4, describing its judiciary as 'subservient to the executive'. Tajikistan also scores zero, and Kazakhstan, with a judiciary 'effectively subservient to the executive branch', scores 1. Egypt also scores only 1 in freedom House rankings due to the executive branch exerting influence over the courts, which protect the interests of the government and military. Using Freedom House scores would thus show stronger support for the insurance theory of judicial independence.

Second, authoritarian regimes might seek to maintain independent courts in order to attract foreign investment, improve government legitimacy, make the bureaucracy more compliant, or, as in the case of Russia, protect local courts from local elites. When media freedom and civil society are too weak to protect courts from interventions by local elites, the independence of courts can be protected by life tenure and financial independence. However, this strategy can be undermined by an authoritarian regime's dependence on the electoral support that can be mobilized by local political and economic leaders (Wang 2020), complicating the vulnerability of the judiciary even further.

Third, in the new illiberal democracies, where electoral competition is very much part of political life, autocratic rulers fear losing power because of the relatively greater risks of being out of office. So there are good reasons why autocrats might want to secure the independence of the courts and why the political insurance thesis is applicable to non-democracies. First, autocrats control economic resources more than in democracies and look to independent courts to protect their property rights when they lose office. Second, autocracies create administrative arrangements to increase their security and do not want these to be used against them, should the opposition gains power electorally. Third, an independent judiciary should provide greater personal security for autocrats who lose office and who might otherwise risk imprisonment, exile or even execution. Fourth, electorally competitive autocracies create higher levels of uncertainty than democracies which independent courts can ameliorate. Consequently, in autocracies 'electoral competition, when present, should incentivise incumbents to respect courts more than they would otherwise' (Epperly 2017: 280).

The logic of the insurance theory therefore applies equally to the new illiberal democracies because the elections which provide autocrats with a modicum of legitimacy make them vulnerable to loss of governmental power. An independent judiciary offers the same benefits as in full democracies, but since autocrats face higher potential costs of losing power than democrats, especially if measured in terms of the personal punishment of former leaders, electoral competition has even greater salience in autocracies than democracies: 'the logic of the existing insurance model, predicated as it is on intertemporal uncertainty and electoral competition, should have not only great salience in the autocratic context, but greater salience than in the democratic. In other words, competition matters, but it matters far more in non-democratic regimes' (Epperly 2019: 11).

Then there is the question of why some states with strong electoral competition have relatively low levels of judicial independence. Governments may come to power through competitive elections which satisfy the necessary democratic criteria of freedom and fairness and then proceed to use their legislative majorities, control of the media and suppression of civil society to change the constitution and bring the judiciary under executive control. Poland and Slovakia are cases in point.

Cases of weak judicial independence despite competitive elections reveal the presence of factors other than executive control and interference which may explain perceptions of the independence of the judiciary. For example, Madagascar (see Figure 5.4) combines free and fair elections with a relatively low level of judicial independence, but while the judiciary has shown greater independence in recent years, the judicial system is marred by corruption, a factor which may enter into the calculations of those expressing views about the judiciary. The Philippines' transition from authoritarian rule in 1986 includes successful and credible elections, yet judicial independence is judged to be weak. However, this is also explained in part by corruption, which favours political and economic elites, rather than by executive power over the judiciary.

Peru's established democratic political institutions include competitive elections allowing peaceful transfers of power. Yet its judicial independence is less than expected, possibly reflecting the fact that the judiciary is perceived as one of the most corrupt institutions in the country, rather than subordination to the executive. In Paraguay, where elections are generally competitive, with opposition parties having a realistic chance of gaining power, despite the dominance of the Colorado

Party, the judiciary is formally independent, but 'money launderers, drug traffickers, and corrupt politicians have co-opted local judicial authorities. . . . Constitutional guarantees of due process are poorly upheld, largely due to corruption that permeates the judicial system'. Ecuador's rating for judicial independence may reflect the era of President Correa when the National Court of Justice and the Constitutional Court faced attacks on their autonomy. Since 2017 the courts have increased their independence under President Moreno's administration, and elections to the National Assembly have resulted in a legislature acting with growing independence and transparency (Freedom House 2020). These cases from Africa, Asia and Latin America suggest that weak judicial independence despite competitive elections reflects the presence of factors such as corruption which undermine the independence of the courts, despite their formal independence in relation to both executive and legislative branches of government.

Political competition, and the alternation of political parties in power, may not be sufficient in all cases to ensure judicial independence that goes beyond the formal autonomy prescribed by constitutional and statutory rules. For judges to behave independently they need to have the requisite attitudes about judicial roles. How else can the cases of 'assertive' decision-making under relatively authoritarian political conditions, or docility despite political freedoms and electoral competition, be explained? In Chile, for example, judges declined to adopt an assertive attitude towards the executive despite the vigorous competitive politics of the pre-Pinochet era. In Tanzania, in contrast, the judiciary developed a new legal culture despite the political context of single-party rule. Such behavioural independence of judges is founded on 'a professional conception of, and commitment to, their role as guarantors of fundamental legal principles' induced by professional education and socialization. Such principles crucially include the duty of judges to protect human rights (Hilbink 2012: 590).

If politicians are to be concerned about the electoral consequences of political interference in judicial appointments, careers and decision-making, it follows that elections must be free and fair. Reforms may be needed to reinforce these aspects of democratic politics. Free elections demand freedom of speech, freedom of association, electoral choice between competing sets of leaders and policies, and freedom to participate as voter, campaigner or candidate, with any restrictions based solely on rational grounds, such as age or mental status, and not on discrimination against legitimate opposition or social groups defined by religion, caste or gender. The media has to be free to advocate and criticize, and not be overwhelmed by government monopolies of election coverage, as in Russia. Holding the executive electorally accountable for undermining judicial independence and the rule of law also requires the electorate to be informed about the costs of political interference in the judicial process. Voters need to be aware that their rights are in jeopardy when the proper relationship between executive and judiciary is abandoned.

Fair elections also require rules and procedures that guarantee elections at regular intervals, restrictions on incumbents from extending their own terms of office, professional electoral administration free from partisan manipulation, a secret ballot, a properly organized count, prompt declaration of results and the prevention of gerrymandering. Judicial independence can be strengthened by reforms designed to guarantee the integrity of the electoral process. Judges can then be relied upon to make fair judgements in accordance with the law on these aspects of the electoral system, if called upon to do so.

Civil society

There is a further political logic, which suggests judicial independence needs to be supported by public opinion and civil society. This support will be found among different sections of society, including those which have a vested interest in the redistribution of wealth to which the judiciary may be ideologically opposed. This is because there will be stronger preferences for the protection provided by judicial independence against the illegal acquisition of wealth and power by politicians and their cronies. Sections of the public benefiting from state interventions with redistributive objectives are also likely to prefer this to be achieved within the rule of law.

Public opinion may thus support judicial independence, despite autonomy being given to judges whose own ideological inclinations affect public policy in ways that go against some sectional interests. In some political cultures, all sections of society prefer the judiciary to be independent, judging the benefits of this to outweigh the costs of not being able to direct the judiciary to favour particular interests. In others, the relative costs and benefits of judicial independence are weighed differently. Nevertheless, a vibrant civil society, supported by social media, can be expected to act as a deterrent to political interference in the judiciary.

As with all aspects of the democratic process, accountability for deviation from judicial independence requires the development of civil society and its constituent organizations, especially those active as watchdogs, advocates and pressure groups within the field of law and order. Such organizations empower those whose interests are harmed by political interference in the judiciary and increase the electoral costs to those who violate the rule of law. In Nigeria, for example, the National Bar Association has been an effective watchdog without which political interference in the judiciary would be even greater than it is.

Romania's Society for Justice shows what can be done by civil society under conditions unfavourable to judicial independence. SoJust was set up in 2005 by a group of like-minded judges, prosecutors, lawyers and other members of the judiciary with the aim of reforming 'not only the magistracy, but of other legal professions as well and of the legal education system, for the purpose of improving the quality of justice' (SoJust 2006: 4). It has paved the way for co-operation between the judicial authorities and non-governmental organizations advocating judicial reform. It has led to co-operation and dialogue between the Superior Council of the Magistracy and NGOs active in the field of judicial reform. Similar dialogue between the state and civil society on judicial reform has also occurred in Bulgaria (Roos 2010).

It is thus significant for judicial independence that the authoritarianism that has engulfed many transitional states in recent years has targeted civil society, with democratic political parties, human rights organizations, women's groups, trade unions, and groups that monitor corruption, legal reform and human rights abuses all coming under pressure. In Poland the government created its own civil society body – the Polish National Foundation – which it controls and used to organize a smear campaign against the judiciary in 2017, prior to its assault on judicial independence. Control of the courts is important when the major weapon against civil society is prosecutions which drain the resources of critical organizations (Ploska 2020).

Judicial independence can also benefit from the influence of legal professionals on civil society. While the history of authoritarianism shows that a subservient judiciary can suit the interests of the legal profession, once a democratic regime is in place the judiciary will have a vested interest in a system which values their expertise, a quality not valued when the judiciary is politically subordinate. The actions which can be taken by the judiciary to underpin its own autonomy include encouraging, through more efficient court procedures, appeals against biased decisions taken in lower-level courts. Senior members of the judiciary can also influence public opinion and opinion-leaders on the benefits of autonomy, including promoting 'legal literacy', or the educating of people in the law and legal procedures. They can develop jurisprudence in the direction of judicial review in order to demonstrate to the public their independence from politics. They can call on international organizations (governmental and non-governmental) to support law reform (including assistance to court administration).

For example, in Poland the judiciary itself has been at the forefront of resistance to the destruction of the rule of law, publishing opinions in social media on draft legislation and the condition of the judiciary in general, organizing public demonstrations in association with other NGOs, and staging mock trials 'in order to ensure that the protests are heard not only in Poland but also abroad' (Gersdorf and Pilich 2020: 348). In 2021 a number of Polish judges, together with the Congress of Civic Democratic Movements, and the former civil rights ombudsman, organized a touring roadshow to inform the public about the damage to the rule of law caused by the Law and Justice party's campaign to 'reform' Poland's courts. This has created, among other changes, a 'disciplinary chamber' of the Supreme Court with the power to lift judges' immunity from prosecution, leaving judges at risk of disciplinary offences for issuing rulings against the government. The EU has declared the restructuring as contrary to judicial independence and the rule of law (*The Guardian* 2021).

International organizations have had a further role, in laying down basic principles to ensure the independence of the judiciary, governing such things as the need for objective criteria when selecting and permanently placing judges, the assignment of administrative tasks to the relevant judicial bodies, transparent procedures, a competent independent body to carry out any advisory functions needed, and disciplinary functions so that when these are not assigned to judicial bodies, they are entrusted to agents of special competence under the control of a superior judicial organ. The Basic Principles on the Independence of the Judiciary adopted at the Seventy Nations Congress on the Prevention of Crime and the Treatment of Offenders in 1985 are an example, as are the recommendations of the Ministers' Committee of the Council of Europe 1994.

International courts and advisory bodies are now found in most regions of the world. They are gradually developing a universalistic jurisprudence derived from accepted perceptions of human rights and the rule of law. The European Court of Human Rights has developed case law to embed and enforce the principles contained in the European Convention into domestic judicial procedures, including the guarantee of impartial and independent tribunals. The court's jurisprudence is permeated by the principles of the rule of law, constitutional democracy and political equality (Spano 2018). The Court of Justice of the European Union reviews domestic rules on the composition of courts, and the appointment, tenure and dismissal of judges, in order to ensure compliance with judicial independence and the rule of law generally (Marques 2021). The Council of Europe's Commission for Democracy through Law provides advice from an authoritative group of constitutional and legal experts to individual states on constitutional amendments, the interpretation of existing constitutions, and the application of constitutional principles by constitutional courts. The commission's work is informed by the 'common heritage' proclaimed in the statute of the Council of Europe: respect for fundamental rights, democracy and the rule of law. The opinions carry great weight because of 'the desire on the part of the country requesting constitutional guidance to be seen as a proper member of the international community of democracies committed to the rule of law and fundamental rights' (De Visser 2015: 991). The commission's assistance extends well beyond its original Western European remit to countries in Eastern Europe, Central Asia, the Middle East, Latin America and Africa, including Kyrgyzstan, Tunisia, Egypt, Morocco, Mexico, Peru and Mozambique. Non-European members of the commission now include senior jurists from Morocco, Algeria, Chile, Peru, Brazil, Mexico, Korea and Kyrgyzstan, representing growing international acceptance of the universal principles of the rule of law and human rights.

This development of an international jurisprudence is further represented by international courts in the Americas and Africa. The American Convention on Human Rights empowered two bodies to enforce those rights: the Inter-American Commission and the Inter-American Court of Human Rights. In its resolution of disputes and advisory jurisdiction, the court has applied the principles of legal certainty, procedural equality, non-discrimination, democracy and the universality of human rights (Pasqualucci 2002). The court's jurisprudence is based on the rule of law principles contained in the American Convention on Human Rights, including 'the right to a hearing, with due guarantees and within a reasonable time, by a competent, independent, and impartial tribunal, previously established by law'. Similarly, the African Court on Human and Peoples' Rights provides both legally binding judicial decisions and advisory opinions on any legal matter relating to human rights, developing a human rights jurisprudence consistent with that of other international courts (Ssenyonjo 2018). Only the Asia Pacific region has so far failed to establish an international court; however, the terms of reference of the ASEAN Intergovernmental Commission on Human Rights of 2009 include promoting and protecting human rights and fundamental freedoms; and adherence to the rule of law, good governance, and the principles of democracy and constitutional government.

There are inevitably problems of enforcement for these international judicial bodies, but their judgements, rulings, opinions and decisions carry sufficient influence for them to make a major contribution to awareness within civil society of fundamental principles of human rights and the rule of law.

Transparency in the way a judiciary manages its caseload helps parliamentarians and civil society to scrutinize the judiciary effectively. In Latin America, a number of innovations are being tried in the hope that greater public awareness of the justice system will reduce arbitrary and corrupt decision-making and increase civil society's support for a judiciary which is free from the influence of powerful economic and political interests. Judiciaries have been required to publicize information on financial allocations and expenditure (Mexico), the personal assets of judges (Argentina), judicial management indicators (Costa Rica), sentencing (Mexico) and Supreme Court rulings (Argentina). The information is made available through judicial websites, judicial council reports, annual statistical series and weekly gazettes. Brazil has a radio station devoted to the judicial system, administered by the Supreme Federal Court (Herrero and López 2010).

Resources devoted to legal education among the public generally, and not just professionals, as well as consciousness-raising, perhaps with the help of legal watchdogs, can also help public opinion to support judicial independence. A number of countries, often with technical assistance funded by international development agencies such as the World Bank, have introduced schemes to improve people's understanding of the law and judicial process. These are often aimed at the poor and other historically disadvantaged groups, including women. They seek to expand 'legal literacy', focusing on people's awareness of their basic rights with reference to employment and education, the availability of legal aid, gender discrimination within the justice system, and public education on the law as it affects women. For example, the Women's Justice Initiative is working to improve the lives of indigenous Guatemalan women and girls through legal empowerment, combining legal literacy courses, information on human rights, and legal support in defence of women's economic rights to property titles, land, alimony, and child support (WJP 2021). The corollary to such efforts are policies to increase awareness within the judiciary itself of the need for equal access to justice for the poor and other vulnerable groups. Initiatives in the field of legal literacy have usually been associated with policies to strengthen the judiciary's capacity to extend justice to those hitherto marginalized or excluded.

In some countries it is possible for civil society to become directly involved in the administration of justice through amicus curiae, a procedure which allows a third party, usually a legal expert, to petition the court for permission to file a brief which draws the court's attention to what the third party regards as aspects of the case which the court might overlook. An amicus curiae provides factual information, legal expertise and the unintended consequences for groups not party to the suit. It can attract the attention of public opinion, strengthen the institutional legitimacy of courts, and remind the state it is under scrutiny (Van den Eynde 2013).

For example, in 2004 the Supreme Court of Argentina's Resolution 28/2004 declared it appropriate 'that in the pending cases before its court and in which matters of institutional import or public interest are examined, intervention should be authorized as Friends of the Court, to third parties that have a recognized competence on the issue examined and demonstrate an unequivocal interest in the final resolution of the case'. The amicus curiae brief 'generates an obvious space for citizen participation, whether through NGOs, professional associations, or academic institutions. In addition, the opening up of the legal discussions (that usually take place inside courtrooms, behind closed doors) to the presentation of "external" arguments contributes decisively to increasing the transparency of judicial work' (Herrero and López 2010: 31, 32).

A free press is another important weapon in the struggle for judicial independence and the rule of law. However, the decline in press freedom in all regions of the world continues. In Hungary and Serbia critical journalism has been eradicated by consolidating media ownership in the hands of government allies so that the major outlets support the government and smear its opponents. In Russia, pressure on independent media has grown since 2011, through draconian laws, and control of leading news outlets and the internet. In Bolivia financial pressure, arbitrary arrests, and impunity for violence against journalists foster a climate of self-censorship. Media ownership in Brazil is concentrated in the hands of big businesses linked to the political class. The confidentiality of journalists' sources is hard to protect, and many investigative reporters have been subjected to abusive judicial proceedings. While freedom of the press was a major achievement of Tunisia's 2011 revolution, since 2019 this freedom has come under pressure from far-right parliamentarians; violence against journalists and media outlets is increasing, and the political climate for the media and journalists has worsened significantly. Journalists in South Africa are harassed and subjected to intimidation campaigns if they report on some aspects of the ruling African National Congress, government finances, the redistribution of land, or corruption. Some state governors in Nigeria have persecuted the media with impunity (RSF 2021).

It is also the case that 'free' mass media are often controlled by powerful vested interests with little concern for the rule of law. The judiciary is itself often used to suppress media freedoms as was seen in Chapter 3. Reform of the media may need to be linked to judicial reform, though this is a political problem which can only be solved by the power of liberal politicians. For these to obtain power they have to have the backing of pro-democratic public opinion. This is problematic for a number of new democracies. Globally, satisfaction with democracy has fallen, and dissatisfaction risen, over the past quarter of a century, but with considerable variations between regions. Some new democracies have recorded their highest-ever levels of democratic dissatisfaction, including Brazil, Mexico, South Africa and Colombia. In Latin America and sub-Saharan Africa the decline in satisfaction has been acute. In Northeast Asia, there are no clear positive or negative trends, while in Southeast Asia and Eastern Europe satisfaction with democracy has been rising in recent years (Foa et al. 2020). Consequently, reforms to provide support for democratic processes and political pluralism, among the benefits of which will be greater judicial independence, cannot be guaranteed.

Legislative scrutiny

An independent judiciary is further supported by legislative institutions capable of forcing members of the executive to explain and justify the use made of the judicial powers entrusted to them by constitutions and statutes. Lack of transparency, preventing scrutiny of executive action, especially appointments to supreme and constitutional courts, has frequently been associated with political interference in judicial decision-making. Executive power, especially disproportionate in new democracies, needs to be balanced by a legislative capacity to exercise effective oversight and accountability.

To perform this function of oversight and scrutiny legislatures need to be constituted on the basis of three principles. The first is that the rights of opposition groups within the legislature should be fully respected. In the Czech Republic this has been enshrined in the Constitution, Article 6 of which says, 'Minorities shall be protected by the majority in decision-making'. Respect for the parliamentary opposition is not just a question of ensuring that opposition MPs are not terrorized with the violence and intimidation that has come to disfigure Zimbabwean government. It also requires rules and procedures which recognize the legitimate role of opposition in all legislative business, including holding parliamentary offices, submitting bills and amendments, and questioning ministers.

Second, parliamentary scrutiny of judicial policy formation and implementation must be effective. This presupposes freedom of information to ensure that the actions and decisions of law-makers are in the open. Accountability is denied by 'state furtiveness' (Dunn 1999: 239). Many transitional states have Freedom of Information laws, such as the Philippines Code of Conduct for State Employees, Thailand's Official Information Act and South Korea's Act on Disclosure of Information by Public Agencies. At least a dozen countries in Asia have adopted such laws. Since 1989, 13 Central and East European countries have adopted FOI laws, sometimes after significant agitation by NGOs, as in Bulgaria, Romania and Slovakia. In Latin America legislation has been passed in six countries and is under consideration in a dozen more. South Africa enacted its legislation in 2001 and Nigeria, Ghana and Kenya followed soon after.

However, the right to information is constantly under pressure by governments that fear transparency. For example, in 2020 a legislative amendment in Romania reduced the state's obligation to provide public information by making those requesting information liable to cover the financial costs, and allowing the authorities to deny information requests because of the volume required, or by alleging the request was malicious in intent. The Covid pandemic has also been used by many governments as a reason to obstruct freedom of information by allowing public officials to decide whether to respond to FOI requests, refuse to respond to questions that are not related to the pandemic' and delay responding until after a state of emergency has been lifted. Alternatively, public bodies simply ignore their legal duty to provide information (Balkan Insight 2020).

Third, oversight of the executive branch requires effective parliamentary scrutiny committees specializing in policy areas (including the system of justice), government agencies (such as ministries of justice) and processes of accountability (such as audit and budgeting). Effective committees are supported by professional staff, a research capacity, libraries, information technology and links with policy research institutes. While the rule of law and separation of powers exclude parliamentary committees from intervening in judicial reviews or trials, defects in the administration of justice revealed by specific cases are legitimate subjects for parliamentary investigation. It follows that committee reports should not interfere with trials that have been or are about to be initiated. 'If such reports must comment on existing judicial decisions in individual cases, they must do so with proper respect and should refrain from expressing any criticism in terms that would amount to a revision of decisions made' (CCEJ 2015: 15).

These conditions are relatively easy to specify as norms of political accountability for the management of the judiciary. It is more difficult for them to be guaranteed in practice. Developments in executive-legislative relations have tended to undermine the capacity of legislatures to provide this precondition of judicial independence. These include the many sources of executive power which create an imbalance between the powers of executive and legislature: the threat of dissolution, control of the legislative timetable, the domination of government business in the work of legislatures, and the exclusion of certain policy areas from parliamentary oversight. In post-authoritarian states executive dominance has been further entrenched by weak democratic traditions, political corruption and clientelism that bypass legislative authority, electoral change reducing the size of the legislature (Hungary), and the militarization of politics. Populism has polarized electoral support, made politics a zero-sum game and weakened legislatures which are designed for deliberation, conflict resolution and accountability. Partisan control of elected representatives has allowed governments to increase their power over the judiciary, as in Bangladesh. The capacity of legislatures to hold governments to account for their policies towards the judiciary has thus been severely compromised (Khmelko et al. 2020). Parliamentary majorities may willingly support their leaders in government, even when judicial independence is being compromised.

Hungary provides evidence of this. Since 2010 the ruling Fidesz party has used its two-thirds majority in parliament to change the judicial system in ways which have convinced the international community, as represented by the European Union, the European Parliament, the Council of Europe, and the governments of the USA and Germany, that the regime has moved away from the rule of law. A new Constitution, five constitutional amendments and numerous new laws have politicized appointments to the National Judicial Council, the constitutional court and the office of chief prosecutor. The administration of justice has also been politicized under powers given to the president of the NJO, a Fidesz-appointed office holder, to transfer cases, notably including some involving members of the political opposition, to courts in areas known to be Fidesz party strongholds, a system that violates the principle of the lawful judge. The Constitutional Court's powers of judicial review have also been reduced. Only repeated criticisms from the Council of Europe have restrained the use of a substantial parliamentary majority to further undermine the rule of law. However, these assaults on the rule of law clearly impress the electorate less than the government's other achievements, since in the 2014 general election the Fidesz party won 44.87 per cent of the vote and 133 (66.8 per cent) of the 199 seats in parliament, though it should be noted that election observers from the Organization for Security and Co-operation in Europe found that biased media coverage and new campaign rules put opposition parties at a serious disadvantage (*The Guardian* 2010; *The Economist* 2013).

The problem of executive dominance is greater under presidential executives. In Latin America accountability has failed to develop under what has been called 'delegative' democracy. Presidentialism means that presidents govern as they think fit. There is practically no 'vertical' accountability in the sense of answerability and electoral sanctions (O'Donnell 1994). Elsewhere, however, there may be more scope for scrutiny and accountability when legislatures and executives are separately elected. For example, empirical studies of legislatures in the new democracies of Central and Eastern Europe suggest that 'the independent political activity and influence of legislatures is greater in presidential systems than parliamentary systems' (Olson and Norton 1996: 7).

Scrutiny of the executive may be given added impetus under coalition governments because transparency enables chief executives to monitor their coalition allies, thus ensuring adherence to government policy by ministers from different political parties. Consequently 'the value that leaders place on monitoring mechanisms increases with the number of parties holding cabinet portfolios' (Michener 2015: 77–78). Evidence in support of this hypothesis has been found in the adoption of freedom of information laws in Latin America and other reforms to strengthen governmental transparency.

Court security

The restraint which the democratic political process places on executive interference in the judiciary should also go some way towards protecting judges and other lawyers against the different forms of intimidation which have occurred in some post-authoritarian states. Political accountability through the ballot box needs to be backed up by a civil society which includes active and vigilant groups of lawyers capable of exposing instances of intimidation and harassment, and demanding that perpetrators are brought to justice and judges made secure from assault and intimidation. For example, legal organizations in the Philippines, including the Integrated Bar of the Philippines and the National Union of People's Lawyers, have mobilized pressure on the government and the courts to put an end to the surge in deadly threats against judges and lawyers, in which at least 61 lawyers, judges and prosecutors were killed between 2016 and 2021 (Amnesty International 2021).

An impediment to reform here is that court security in many new democracies is weak. Judicial institutions are often denied equal treatment with the legislative and executive branches in terms of personal security. Judges and prosecutors frequently complain about the lack of attention paid to their demands regarding personal safety. Denying the judiciary adequate and appropriate security arrangements 'not only further deepens the gap between the judicial, executive and legislative branches of power but also weakens the confidence that the law-seeking public has in the judiciary' (OSCE 2010: 4). Attempts to improve court security include the Ukraine, where there have been many occasions when trials have been violently interrupted, judges attacked and witnesses intimidated. A Court Security Service (CSS) was established in 2018, with EU support, as part of a wider project involving the installation of fire and safety equipment (such as cameras and access controls), staff safety training, the separation of public and staff entrances, and the provision of scanners for the detection of explosives, weapons and other dangerous materials (ICJ 2020). The CSS is accountable to the High Council of Justice and is managed by the State Judicial Administration of Ukraine.

Foreign pressure may help to prevent intimidation by naming and shaming the authorities that need to take more vigorous action to protect the judiciary. In 2017 the United Nations Human Rights Council condemned the increasingly frequent threats, intimidation, violence and reprisals against judges and called upon all states to guarantee the independence of judges by protecting them, their families and professional associates against all forms of violence, threat, retaliation, intimidation and harassment resulting from the discharge of their functions, to condemn such acts and to bring perpetrators to justice (UNHRC 2017).

The assassination in 2011 of a Brazilian judge known for taking a stand against criminal gangs, death squads and corrupt police officers led the United Nations' Rapporteur to criticize the 'pervasive and serious problem regarding the protection of judges in Brazil'. However, there has to be concerted effort, coupled with sanctions (such as withholding development assistance or membership of an international body) before foreign intervention is likely to be effective. The number of calls for better security for judges and their courts far exceeds the actions being taken to provide the necessary resources.

It is also possible for intimidation to be criminalized so that any person who causes, or threatens to cause, injury to a judicial officer can be prosecuted. Intimidating or threatening a witness or juror constitutes perverting the course of justice, a criminal offence usually carrying a significant maximum sentence that in some cases is life imprisonment. In Georgia in 2013 an amendment was made to the Criminal Code making it a criminal instead of an administrative offence to put pressure on judges at a trial.

Reforms to prevent the intimidation of individual judges when exercising their professional duties need to combine terms of employment with accountability. First the law needs to secure a judge's status, terms of office, independence, security, adequate remuneration, conditions of service, pensions and age of retirement. Second, the accountability of judges should follow clear procedures, objective legal criteria, established standards of professional conduct, a clear distinction between disciplinary, civil and criminal liability, and prescribed sanctions: 'Accountability mechanisms should protect judges from any kind of threat, harassment, pressure or interference, regardless of the source, and impose adequate penalties on those who attempt to interfere with the free and independent exercise of the judicial profession' (UN 2020).

Judicial review

The judiciary's power to review the decisions of governments falls into two categories: reviewing the constitutionality of policy and therefore mainly legislation; and reviewing the legality of administration. Constitutional review can be undertaken either by the ordinary courts (generally in common law jurisdictions) or by specialist constitutional courts established during the transition from authoritarianism to democracy: '[I]n the early 21st century world, a well-developed system of constitutional review is now generally accepted as an essential or desirable feature of a liberal constitutional democracy' Chan 2013: 7).

What can be done to protect judicial review against a government which seeks to limit accountability to the courts? First, dedicated constitutional courts need to be protected against prohibitive amendments to the constitution. Constitutional courts have been chosen mainly but not exclusively in civil law jurisdictions because the structure, culture and procedures of the ordinary courts are deemed inappropriate for judging whether statutes are constitutionally valid, or because the absence of precedent as a doctrine (*stare decisis*) can lead to conflicting constitutional rulings when courts are not obliged to honour judicial precedent. Constitutional review by the ordinary courts is problematic, as the case of the Philippines shows.

Here the Constitutional Commission has been forced to elaborate on the meaning of 'political questions' since the Constitution is imprecise on how far the Supreme Court's duty to settle controversies involving rights and abuse of discretion extends to the constitutionality of legislation. The judiciary has to distinguish between 'truly political questions' and controversies which are not truly political questions. Truly political questions are deemed beyond judicial review, even though the Constitution specifies that the Supreme Court can review, revise, reverse, modify or affirm on appeal all cases in which the constitutionality or validity of any treaty, international or executive agreement, law, presidential decree, proclamation, order, instruction, ordinance or regulation is in question. Review of legislation by a constitutional court, on the other hand, would seem to allow a clearer distinction to be drawn between decisions which are claimed to be in conflict with the constitution and decisions which are in conflict with the law.

Second, judicial review of administrative legality, whether undertaken by the ordinary courts or specialist administrative courts, can be protected by statutory specifications of the grounds for review, as in South Africa. Here judicial review is protected by both the Constitution, which entitles all citizens to administrative action that is lawful, reasonable and procedurally fair, and the Promotion of Administrative Justice Act. This statute specifies the grounds for judicial review in great detail. There may be judicial review if the administrative action was by an unauthorized official, was taken under an unauthorized delegation of power, was reasonably suspected of bias, was procedurally unfair or was materially influenced by an error of law. Judicial review is protected by empowering the courts to judge whether administrative action has been taken for a reason authorized by statute, and not for an ulterior purpose or motive; whether it has taken irrelevant considerations into account, or excluded relevant considerations; and whether the administrative decision reflects unauthorized or unwarranted dictates of another person or body, bad faith, arbitrariness or caprice. Administrative action should not contravene the law or constitution, should be authorized by an empowering provision and should be rationally connected to the purpose for which it was taken. A remedy may also be sought if the administrative action taken is so unreasonable that no reasonable person could have so exercised the power or performed the function. A review of a failure to act may be sought if it constitutes non-compliance with a mandatory procedure prescribed by an empowering provision. It is hard to think of a more comprehensive set of prescriptions to protect the citizen when in dispute with the state. In addition, giving constitutional backing to a *right* to legality in administration enables the courts to review actions that escape judicial review under the act (Henrico 2018). The significance of a rights-based approach to administrative review will be examined further in Chapter 8.

Third, civil jurisdictions may choose to create a separate system of administrative law with specialist courts to ensure that public administration is in compliance with law. In Poland, for example, there are 14 administrative courts of first instance at *voivodship* (province) level and a Supreme Administrative Court to hear cassation appeals against the decisions of lower-level courts. Administrative courts can only revoke, annul or uphold the administrative action appealed against. They cannot replace it with a new administrative decision. The Supreme Administrative Court has three specialist chambers, for finance, commerce and general administration. The Financial Chamber supervises the courts of first instance in matters of taxation; the Commercial Chamber specializes in economic matters such as banking, insurance and prices; and the General Administrative Chamber deals with internal affairs, especially cases arising from land use planning and local government.

Cases typically arise from objections to administrative orders, enforcement proceedings, and the enactments of local governments and territorial agencies of central government. Jurisdictional disputes between local governments and between local authorities and central government administrative agencies are also resolved by administrative courts. So extensive is the jurisdiction of the administrative courts that it has been argued that the balance has moved too far in favour of the courts. However, it has never been suggested that the number of acts subject to review should be limited, since it is generally accepted that a broad power of judicial review is compatible with the legal protection required by a democracy.

A notable achievement of Poland's system has been to develop a coherent, consistent and predictable body of administrative law through Supreme Administrative Court resolutions which clarify the law when it has been the source of conflict between the administrative courts, thus ending doubts about the jurisdiction of the courts. Administrative law has become simplified, more accurate, fairer and more efficient, with shorter proceedings (Skoczylas and Swora 2007).

Protecting judicial review from attempts by governments to reduce its scope through constitutional amendments or judicial 'reform' requires the preservation of judicial independence in general and the integrity of constitutional courts in particular. Judicial review can be given constitutional endorsement and statutory specification of what constitutes administrative legality, clarifying the rights of citizens and the duties of public officials. But it has to be recognized that in democracies the constitutional and statutory foundations of judicial review are ultimately a political issue, reflecting judgements about the electoral consequences of using legislative majorities to restrict the courts' powers to hold legislatures and administrative bodies to account. A government's attitude to judicial review will therefore depend upon its current concerns about its policy in an area on which the courts might be called upon to adjudicate.

Exceptional courts

Democratic reforms affecting the judiciary frequently include the abolition of exceptional courts. This generally refers to the use of military tribunals in civilian cases and is sometimes accompanied by the creation of exceptional courts in the form of alternative methods of dispute resolution. In Libya the constitutional declaration of 2011 explicitly prohibits the establishment of exceptional courts in order to protect judicial independence. Article 127 of Morocco's 2011 Constitution also prohibits the establishment of exceptional courts. The constitution of Yemen prohibits the creation of exceptional courts 'under any conditions'. The new Bolivian Constitution stipulates that the Common Law does not acknowledge any type of exceptional court. Military law may only judge military crimes. Article 83 of the Constitution of Georgia specifies that justice is implemented by the common courts. The creation of emergency or exceptional courts is not allowed. Military courts may only be created under war conditions and then only within the system of common courts.

Yet it has proved very difficult to exclude the use of exceptional courts in practice. The independence of the judiciary in Egypt has been compromised by the continued existence of military courts which have exclusive competence to determine whether a given case falls within their jurisdiction and which are unsupervised by civilian courts even though thousands of Egyptian civilians have been tried in them. Tunisians continue to be referred to exceptional courts, including a former presidential advisor brought before a military court. In the Yemen specialized courts exist for the prosecution of media offences in order to silence Yemen's few remaining independent media (EHRN 2012; Freedom House 2012a).

While it is generally accepted that exceptional courts are incompatible with the rule of law, a number of countries have been willing to create them in a bid to improved access to justice, ease court congestion and accelerate the resolution of legal conflict. It is also recognized that providing accessible and affordable dispute-resolution mechanisms can strengthen social stability. Special tribunals and small claims courts can dispense justice cheaply and quickly but in ways which nevertheless preserve the rules of natural justice. Such tribunals can be particularly effective in resolving disputes between the citizen and public authorities, as well as between private litigants such as employers and employees or landlords and tenants.

There are some types of dispute where special courts are thought necessary if justice is to be administered humanely. Juvenile courts fall into this category. In 1985 the United Nations adopted the 'Beijing Rules' for the administration of juvenile justice to provide guidance to governments on the protection of children's rights and respect for their needs through the development of a separate and specialized system of juvenile justice. These rules prescribe that juvenile offenders should be dealt with by a competent court, tribunal, board or council according to the principles of a fair and just trial. An emphasis is placed on the discretion needed at all stages of the process – investigation, prosecution and adjudication – to ensure that the varying special needs of juveniles and the variety of measures available are fully considered. Proceedings should be guided by the best interests of the juvenile. Basic procedural safeguards such as the presumption of innocence, and the right to be notified of the charges, to remain silent, to counsel, to the presence of a parent or guardian, to confront and cross-examine witnesses, and to appeal to a higher authority, should all be guaranteed at all stages of the proceedings.

In 1989 the United Nations' Convention on the Rights of the Child further reiterated that, whenever appropriate and desirable, measures should be sought for dealing with children without resorting to judicial proceedings, providing that human rights and legal safeguards are fully respected. Romania has taken a lead here among the new, post-authoritarian democracies, setting up juvenile courts under amendments to the penal code in 2006 to ensure that the special needs of children are met when they come into conflict with the law. The system aims to separate juveniles from the formal system of juvenile law, use imprisonment as a last resort and emphasize rehabilitation.

However, it can still prove politically difficult for such procedures to incorporate the rules of natural justice if the professionals involved are not given special training, if rights can still be violated in police custody or if children are not kept separate from adult offenders at all stages of the judicial process – problems which still confront juvenile justice in Romania.

Exceptional courts may also be regarded as useful reforms when they take the form of alternative dispute resolution mechanisms. Alternative dispute resolution seeks to offer quicker, cheaper and socially acceptable justice through the use of less formal mechanisms than the regular courts. This encompasses a wide range of institutions, both modern and traditional, formal and informal, including arbitration clauses in contracts (as in Malaysia), informal village *jirgas* (councils) in Afghanistan and Pakistan, local courts in Zambia, community courts in Mozambique, community leaders in Ecuador elected by indigenous communities, and street committees in Brazil.

'Legal pluralism', or the coexistence of state and customary law and legal institutions in the same area of law, is advocated by reformers as a means of promoting the rule of law (Gebeye 2017). For example, the United Nations Development Programme supports informal justice systems in so far as they are more accessible than formal mechanisms; have the potential to provide quick, relatively inexpensive and culturally relevant remedies; and strengthen human rights, the rule of law and access to justice (UNDP 2012). Informal justice can be provided by customary social structures, religious authorities, local administrative authorities, specially constituted state customary courts, and community forums for conflict resolution and mediation.

For example, the *shalish* in Bangladesh is an informal method of dispute resolution used for family and land disputes, preferred to the 'corruption, delay, indifference and physical distance of the courts' (Golub 1993: 19). Corruption in the formal judiciary also drives citizens to community-based methods of dispute resolution in Afghanistan. Formal courts may be concentrated in urban areas, neglecting access to justice for rural communities, whereas traditional and customary courts are practically and culturally accessible, and may be seen by local people as having greater legitimacy (ICJ 2017). In Africa, many governments have incorporated customary laws and institutions into the national judicial framework, in the process transforming customary and informal ways of administering justice in order to bring them into line with human rights and constitutional principles. This has meant that 'the foundations which sustain the customary system have been significantly undermined, and the social system within which customary law operates has been greatly transformed', possibly limiting the contribution which customary law can make to the socio-legal development of local communities (Tchoukou 2020: 269).

The risk with some traditional dispute resolution procedures is that they lack essential qualities required by the rule of law (Swenson 2018). For example, the *shalish* of rural Bangladesh are biased against women and the poor, consisting as they do exclusively of male village leaders. They lack credibility for a number of other reasons: the influence on them of patron-client relations; the involvement of Muslim clerics with an inadequate understanding of the law; the general ignorance of the law of their members combined with harmful interpretations; corruption; and the deliberate misinterpretation of the law in favour of local elites such as landowners. Elsewhere, village courts have been responsible for issuing verdicts that target the innocent (especially women), favour the rich, and demand honour killings and even rape, as in Pakistan's *jirgas*. The procedures used in customary and religious justice institutions may breach fundamental human rights to a fair trial and dispense cruel, harsh and disproportionate corporal punishment, especially against girls and women, as in Afghanistan (Singh 2015).

Traditional, village, religious or informal courts also vary in the extent to which they are officially sanctioned, convene regularly rather than ad hoc, apply codified law rather than unwritten customary law, or seek consensus rather than issue rule-based verdicts. But in many cases they fail to meet the standards required by the rule of law. 'Their norms and processes often are not transparent; are not publicly promulgated; are not independently adjudicated; and are not legally certain' (Tamanaha 2015: 14). They may be rooted in patriarchal systems and 'reinforce harmful gender stereotypes and cultural assumptions that are inherently likely to discriminate against women and children and therefore negatively impact upon their rights'. They can be inconsistent with the right to a competent, independent and impartial tribunal established by law (ICJ 2017).

Despite this, advocates of such traditional institutions claim they provide 'substantive' justice because adjudication is 'oriented towards achieving outcomes that are perceived as right. . . . The decision-makers aim to achieve a consensus or reconciliation of the parties by coming to an outcome that people find acceptable or right' (Tamanaha 2015: 15). This reification of the 'community' poses some awkward questions for justice: what if what the community sees as right is manifestly not right or just; who in the community, which is likely to be far from socially or economically homogenous, decides what is right? Such problems become apparent when gender issues come before traditional institutions. The fact that there is agreement among the community's dominant males that women should have a lower status does not make it 'right'. The 'substantive' justice offered by these institutions begins to look like a reinforcement of customary injustices from which there can be no escape, except through the precepts of the rule of law, and in particular the rules of natural justice. Alternative dispute resolution devices 'should not be understood as a way to drain citizens from national justice . . . but to provide them with an instrument aimed to diversify and enrich the offer of justice' (Esplugues 2015: 7).

It is also important, when examining legal pluralism, to avoid the pitfall of assuming that traditional practices must be given equal status to formal law and legal procedures. Non-Western conceptions of the rule of law may offer 'a more accurate picture of the norms that – actually – govern a community's life' (Zumbansen 2018: 62), but this does not mean that they provide people with the protection afforded by the global conception of the rule of law. This may be a contested concept but not to the extent that it can be judged inferior to a system of dispute resolution that is manifestly unjust though compatible with local traditions, religion and customs. The fact that the rule of law may have been disseminated by colonial rule, imperial expansion, economic development, technical assistance, post-conflict settlement or global democratic discourse does not in itself place alternative conceptions on an equal footing with it.

Understanding the huge range and variety of traditional, customary and indigenous forms of law is essential for socio-legal studies and for deciding whether indigenous practices are fit for purpose as measured by international human rights standards. It still, however, leaves open the question of which conception of law best serves the interests of justice for those for whom legal pluralism is so often recommended, namely the poor.

Nevertheless, the involvement of non-governmental, community organizations in the legal system can improve justice, provided court members and litigants can be given training, legal advice and advocacy. Corruption and patron-client influences can also be discouraged, and the implementation of decisions can be monitored (Benda-Beckman 2001). So it may be possible for the formal judicial system to regulate traditional and religious bodies so that they adhere to standards of procedure demanded by human rights and natural justice (Kotter 2015). Alternatively, simple non-enforcement of legal provisions may overcome conflict between legal systems, as shown by the systematic non-enforcement of certain Sharia criminal laws in Nigeria, Pakistan, Sudan, Egypt, Libya and parts of Indonesia because these conflict with the customary laws of non-Muslim minorities or the universal standards demanded by society generally or by international organizations (Sabrow 2020).

Alternative dispute resolution can also take the form of mediation where the parties to a case select an impartial third party to make a binding decision, having presented evidence and testimony, as with Thailand's out-of-court mediation for financial disputes (Michel 2011). In 2003 Indonesia's Supreme Court introduced mediation which was annexed to the regular courts in order to provide procedures that were faster, simpler and cheaper than those provided by the conventional courts. However, this uniform system resulted in outcomes culturally unacceptable to some ethnic groups and suggests a need for mediation which is more diverse and sensitive to local traditions and languages (Syukur and Bagshaw 2018).

Mediation is becoming more widespread among new democracies. It is applied to disputes in many areas and has been successful in the areas of family, labour, commercial, employment, administrative and criminal law (ECEJ 2010). Mediation may be initiated on the basis of a mutual agreement among the parties, the content of which must be approved by the relevant court, as in Hungary. This formal agreement guides the conduct of the mediation.

Mediation is also designed to provide an efficient and cost-effective alternative to litigation and to lighten the workload of the ordinary courts, as in Romania where mediation has had a legislative framework since 2006. Mediation is supervised, coordinated and managed by a Mediation Council, which is an autonomous legal body charged with protecting the public interest in this facet of the judicial process. To qualify as a professional mediator requires a university degree, three-year work experience, good health, a good reputation with no criminal convictions and completion of a training programme. Mediation can be sought in disputes relating to civil, criminal, family and other fields of law, including consumer disputes. However, matters relating to human rights cannot be the subject of mediation. Recourse to mediation is voluntary, and litigants are free to seek other means of dispute resolution at any stage. It is generally felt that it is particularly important for mediation to remain voluntary in criminal cases.

Despite its apparent advantages, mediation is not always as popular as might be expected. This is explained in, for example, Romania by a lack of awareness and understanding of the scheme by both the judiciary and the public, the cost of a service supposed to be affordable, and an absence of communication between the courts and the mediation service. Overcoming these constraints entails a cultural change so that crime is seen in a different light: 'policymakers, the judiciary, legal and non-legal professionals and the general public have to start viewing crime more as a harm done to the victim and not to the state' (Szabo 2015: 412). There have been similar problems in Albania where a lack of an institutional tradition of mediation, inadequate funding, and limited awareness of the possibility of resolving disputes through mediation have meant that the number of cases referred to mediation is smaller than expected. This is despite the potential scope of mediation including disputes in the fields of civil, commercial, labour, family, intellectual property and consumer rights laws, as well as disputes with public administration bodies, and some provisions under the Code of Criminal Procedure and Juvenile Criminal Justice Code (Koça 2020). A lack of public awareness also partly explains the limited popularity of mediation in Lithuania. Another obstacle is the excessive workload of judges, suggesting that there is a need to involve lay mediators in the process of mediation when connected to the courts. Polish experience indicates the importance of properly qualified and trained mediators if they are to be used in place of judges (Tvaronavičienė et al. 2021).

Mediation can be provided in different ways, including the appointment of crime prevention and conflict mediation volunteers, as in Nicaragua which has 3,000 people working as part of a judicial facilitator project, preventing many cases from going to trial. These judicial facilitators have reduced delays in the justice system, reduced the number of cases going to court by as much as 75 per cent in some years, increased access to justice and reduced levels of crime. They have contributed to the anti-poverty strategy since the services of judicial facilitators are free of charge. The scheme has been extended to Paraguay, Panama, Guatemala, Argentina, Honduras and Costa Rica. The volunteers receive training from a legal literacy programme and can seek advice on legal issues from municipal judges whenever necessary.

There has been a good deal of discussion about whether mediation should be made a compulsory part of the judicial system. At present it is voluntary in most countries. It is likely to remain a voluntary process since it is unlikely to achieve the desired results if litigants are forced to use it. However, it is regarded as desirable for judges to encourage parties to use mediation in suitable cases. In Romania, for example, judges are obliged in certain cases to inform parties of the possibility and advantages of opting for mediation. In some cases, financial incentives can be offered to parties who choose mediation or other alternative dispute resolution proceedings; for example, court fees can be refunded to the plaintiff if mediation during a pending court case is successful. It is also compulsory for anyone intending to go to court in specific areas of law to obtain information about mediation.

Mediation is generally conducted by specially trained and accredited mediators who are not judges. To receive accreditation from Romania's Mediation Council, mediators have to be graduates, though not necessarily in law, and have to undergo a minimum of 80 hours of training, at least 75 per cent of which must provide practical experience, such as role-playing. Mediators have a duty to be impartial and neutral and are under an obligation to refuse a case if anything compromises their independence. They must ensure that the process of mediation respects the freedom, dignity and private lives of the parties. Mediators are also bound by confidentiality, which extends to all information or documents submitted to the mediation process (Ciuca and Gavrila 2012).

The evidence on the value of mediation is not conclusive. Public opinion in Poland, for example, does not show widespread support for the idea that mediation is an effective tool for settling disputes. The general public and the parties to a dispute often have insufficient information about the aims and processes of mediation. Again, if the parties are not willing to find common ground it is unlikely that mediation will work. It is also sometimes felt that mediation needs to be supported by legal aid to reduce costs to the parties involved. Also, a decision by a court may be preferred because it is based on clear legal principles and open to public scrutiny. There may need to be a cultural change in society before people accept that mediation can be effective, more timely and cheaper for the resolution of some types of disputes.

This would seem to be the case in Indonesia, where mediation seeks to provide a method of settling cases involving youth offenders which not only is faster, cheaper and procedurally simpler than the formal system of criminal justice but also offers a more appropriate restorative justice for dealing with juveniles. The innovation has encountered numerous cultural obstacles, notably hostility on the part of Indonesian judges, police, prosecutors and public opinion which favours a prison sentence for any criminal offence and presumes its absence to result from bribery. A lack of laws and regulations supporting mediation has led to misunderstanding of its aims among legal officers trapped in a legalistic paradigm (Syukur and Bagshaw 2015).

Another alternative to the ordinary courts is arbitration where the parties to a case select an impartial third party to make a binding decision, having presented evidence and testimony. Arbitration is most commonly used for the resolution of commercial disputes. The organization of arbitration varies considerably from one country to another. Croatia and Hungary have permanent arbitration tribunals attached to commercial chambers. In Slovenia arbitration is provided by associations of lawyers. In Latvia the Ministry of Justice can authorize the establishment of a permanent arbitration court. Arbitration is generally regulated by special arbitration laws, but in Bulgaria and Romania it forms part of the codes of civil procedure (ECEJ 2010).

Enforcing judgements

As we saw in Chapter 2, fundamental principles are at stake if judicial decisions are not enforced. Effective enforcement of a binding judicial decision is fundamental to the rule of law. This applies particularly to administrative law:

> [I]n a state governed by the Rule of Law, public entities are above all bound to respect judicial decisions, and to implement them in a rapid way 'ex officio'. The very idea of a state body refusing to obey a court decision undermines the concept of primacy of the law.
>
> (CCEJ 2010: para. 31)

Assuming that the decisions to be enforced are fair, having been arrived at by independent and impartial application of the law, it follows that enforcement should be supported by judicial powers and resources. Judges should be allowed to hear appeals against failure to initiate enforcement, delays and abuse of enforcement procedures. The funds required for enforcement should be available. The judiciary has a fundamental role to play in enforcement because '[i]f the rule of law is to be maintained and litigants' trust in the judicial system is to be ensured, enforcement activities must be proportionate, fair and effective' (CCEJ 2010: para. 25). In all such respects the views of the Consultative Council of European Judges have global relevance.

Reforms to ensure the proper enforcement of court decisions have been mainly targeted at finance, personnel and accountability. There needs to be a budget adequate enough to ensure the rapid and procedurally correct enforcement of court judgements. Enforcement can be expensive when legally qualified executors are in short supply and provided by the private sector, as in Romania (ABA 2002).

The personnel requirement is for an effective bailiff service. States vary in how they organize this. In Albania, Bulgaria, Russia and Ukraine enforcement agents are civil servants working for a court or administrative agency. Elsewhere, including Hungary, Poland and Romania, enforcement officers are employed by private firms. Some states, for example the Czech Republic, employ a mix of public and private executors. This allows the authorities to evaluate their respective levels of efficiency.

The consensus of opinion seems to be that enforcement personnel need to have a representative association which can maintain control over standards of recruitment and performance. This can lead to problems when the executors are part of the private sector. In 2012 the Romanian National Association of Judicial Executors was fined by the Competition Council for infringing national competition law by setting excessive membership fees and enforcement expenses.

Accountability for the non-enforcement of court judgements requires reforms which make it easier to establish which officials are responsible for execution and to provide compensation for those adversely affected by non-compliance with the courts. Awareness of the problem and those responsible needs to be raised by civil society organizations and parliamentarians. Accountability is thus very much a political issue. In 2011 the Russian Duma passed a law providing compensation when judgements are not executed within a reasonable time. This has been seen as primarily a measure to appease the European Court of Human Rights which hears large numbers of appeals from Russian citizens who have had court decisions ignored by the authorities, and one which will have little impact on the real problem (Freedom House 2012b).

In some countries the matter has been taken further by the criminalization of non-enforcement of judgements. For example, in Ukraine, which has taken the criminalization of non-enforcement further than many other countries (Mytnynk et al. 2020), Article 382 of the Criminal Code makes wilful failure of an official to comply with a sentence, judgement, ruling or order of a court punishable by a fine or up to three-year imprisonment. Officials who occupy responsible positions, or cause significant damage to 'legally protected rights and freedoms of citizens, state and public interests', are liable to imprisonment for three to eight years. However, the compliance rate remains low, perhaps because it is often difficult to prove intentional non-enforcement of a judgement.

Administrative changes, though important for the litigants concerned, do not address the problem of governments which ignore the decisions of constitutional and administrative review courts. This remains a political matter, dependent on the effectiveness of executive accountability to legislative authority. Nevertheless, the execution of court decisions is, under Article 6 of the European Convention of Human Rights, an indicator of fair administration of justice. It requires enforcement agents to safeguard fundamental rights and individual freedoms while applying enforcement proceedings, perhaps supported by criminal law. To this end the European Commission for the Efficiency of Justice, set up by the Committee of Ministers of the Council of Europe in 2002, has issued a set of 'Standards on Execution' by which to judge the quality of enforcement in any judicial system (ECEJ 2010).

When the credibility of the system of justice can be undermined by the non-enforcement of judgements, which remains a problem in a number of new democracies, reform becomes a democratic necessity: 'Members of the public who have placed their trust in the judicial system should obtain satisfaction, not only on paper but also in practice. To ensure full and prompt execution of court decisions is one of the hallmarks of a democratic society' (Hammarberg 2009).

* * *

A wide range of reforms have been designed to deal with problems arising from political interference in the judiciary, the intimidation of judges and other lawyers, limitations on judicial review, the use of exceptional courts, and the non-enforcement of judgements. Conventional constitutional and legal safeguards protect the judiciary with immunity from political manipulation. However, electoral competition is arguably the most important prerequisite of judicial independence. Politicians need to be concerned about the electoral consequences of political interference in judicial appointments, careers and decision-making. For this there have to be free and fair elections at regular intervals. The relationship between electoral competition and judicial independence in post-authoritarian states in Europe, Latin America, Asia and Africa is far from straightforward, however. Public opinion and civil society are also relevant to the political accountability which is necessary if judicial independence is to be protected. In addition, civil society can become directly involved in the administration of justice.

Judicial independence requires parliamentarians and civil society to exercise effective scrutiny of the judiciary. The judiciary must therefore be managed in a way that is transparent. Legislative institutions must be empowered to require members of the executive to explain and justify the use made of the powers over the judiciary entrusted to them by statute and the constitution. This essential accountability is constrained under contemporary political conditions in many new democracies.

Reforms have also been concerned with protecting judges and other lawyers against different forms of intimidation and improving the security of the courts. Reforms to ensure that the judicial process is free from interference by vested state interests have included the abolition of exceptional courts. Different forms of alternative dispute resolution, entailing the use of less formal mechanisms than the regular courts, have been tried in order to provide quicker, cheaper and more socially acceptable justice. This 'legal pluralism' is found to present its own obstacles to judicial independence and the rule of law. Reforms seeking to ensure the proper enforcement of court decisions have had to address the need for money, personnel and accountability.

There remain to be considered reforms which address obstacles to independent judicial decision-making that arise from within the judiciary itself, as distinct from those that are imposed from other parts of the political system. These are obstacles caused by the inability of courts to provide impartial adjudication – problems of judicial capacity and biased proceedings – and by the behaviour of individual judges who are either biased in their attitudes towards defendants and litigants or corrupt.

Note

1 Scores for electoral competition are based on the Economist Intelligence Unit's category of 'electoral process and pluralism', measured on a 0-to-10 scale. See EIU 2021: 59–60. Scores for judicial independence are taken from the World Economic Forum's *Global Competitiveness Report 2019* response to the survey question, 'In your country, how independent is the judicial system from influences of the government, individuals, or companies?', where 1 = not independent at all and 7 = entirely independent.

References

ABA (2002), *Judicial Reform Index for Romania*, Washington: American Bar Association.

Amnesty International (2021), *Philippines: Surge in Killings of Lawyers and Judges Shows Justice System "In Deadly Danger"*, www.amnesty.org/en/latest/news/2021/03/philippines-surge-killings-lawyers/

Balkan Insight (2020), *Central and Eastern Europe Freedom of Information Rights "Postponed"*, Belgrade: Balkan Investigative Reporting Network.

Benda-Beckman, F. von (2001), 'Legal pluralism and social justice in economic and political development', *IDS Bulletin*, vol. 32, no. 1.

CCEJ (2010), *The Role of Judges in the Enforcement of Judicial Decisions*, Opinion No. 13, Strasbourg: Consultative Council of European Judges.

CCEJ (2015), *The Position of the Judiciary and Its Relation With the Other Powers of State in a Modern Democracy*, Opinion No. 18, Strasbourg: Consultative Council of European Judges.

Chan, A. H. Y. (2013), 'The global expansion of constitutional judicial review: some historical and comparative perspectives', University of Hong Kong Faculty of Law Research Paper No. 2013/001.

Ciuca, A.-E. and C.-A. Gavrila (2012), 'Romania' in G. De Palo and M. B. Trevor (eds.), *EU Mediation: Law and Practice*, Oxford: Oxford University Press.

De Visser, M. (2015), 'A critical assessment of the role of the Venice Commission in processes of domestic constitutional reform', *American Journal of Comparative Law*, vol. 63, no. 4.

Dunn, J. (1999), 'Situating democratic political accountability' in A. Przeworski, S. C. Stokes and B. Manin (eds.), *Democracy, Accountability and Representation*, Cambridge: Cambridge University Press.

ECEJ (2010), *European Judicial Systems: Efficiency and Quality of Justice*, Strasbourg: Council of Europe, European Commission for the Efficiency of Justice.

The Economist (2013), 'Black sheep in the crimson dome: Viktor Orban is once again accused of dismantling the rule of law in Hungary', 8 June, London: The Economist.

EHRN (2012), *The Reform of Judiciaries in the Wake of the Arab Spring*, Copenhagen: Euro-Mediterranean Human Rights Network.

EIU (2021), *Democracy Index 2020: In Sickness and in Health?*, London: Economist Intelligence Unit.

Epperly, B. (2017), 'Political competition and de facto judicial independence in non-democracies', *European Journal of Political Research*, vol. 56, no. 2.

Epperly, B. (2019), *The Political Foundations of Judicial Independence in Dictatorship and Democracy*, Oxford: Oxford Scholarship Online.

Esplugues, C. (2015), 'General report: new developments in civil and commercial mediation: global comparative perspectives' in C. Esplugues and L. Marquis (eds.) *New Developments in Civil and Commercial Mediation*, London: Springer.

European Commission (2015), *Report From the Commission to the European Parliament and Council on Progress in Bulgaria Under the Co-operation and Verification Mechanism*, Brussels: European Commission.

Foa, R.S., A. Klassen, M. Slade, A. Rand and R. Collins (2020), *The Global Satisfaction With Democracy Report 2020*, Cambridge: Centre for the Future of Democracy.

Freedom House (2005), *Nations in Transit 2005: Czech Republic*, New York: Freedom House.

Freedom House (2012a), *Countries at the Crossroads, 2012: Tunisia*, New York: Freedom House.

Freedom House (2012b), *Nations in Transit 2012: Russia*, New York: Freedom House.

Freedom House (2020), *Countries and Territories*, https://freedomhouse.org/countries/freedom-world/scores

Gebeye, B. A. (2017), 'Decoding legal pluralism in Africa', *The Journal of Legal Pluralism and Unofficial Law*, vol. 49, no. 2.

Gersdorf, M. and M. Pilich (2020), 'Judges and representatives of the people: a Polish perspective', *European Constitutional Law Review*, vol. 16, no. 3.

Golub, S. (1993), 'Evaluation of Asia Foundation Legal Service/Human Rights programming in Bangladesh', mimeo, Washington, DC: The Asia Foundation.

The Guardian (2010), 'Hungarian election: Viktor Orbán wins second term as Jobbik support soars', 6 April, London: The Guardian.

The Guardian (2021), 'Last stop for democracy: on tour with Poland's rebel judges', 20 September, London: The Guardian.

Hammarberg, T. (2009), 'Flawed enforcement of court decisions undermines the trust in state justice', Strasbourg: Council of Europe Human Rights Commission, www.coe.int/t/commissioner/Viewpoints/090831_en.asp

Henrico, R. (2018), 'Subverting the promotion of administrative justice act in judicial review: the cause of much uncertainty in South African administrative law', *Journal of South African Law*, vol. 2018, no. 2.

Herrero, A. and G. López (2010), *Access to Information and Transparency in the Judiciary: A Guide to Good Practices From Latin America*, Governance Working Paper, Washington: World Bank Institute.

Hilbink, L. (2012), 'The origins of positive judicial independence', *World Politics*, vol. 64, no. 4.

Hipper, A. M. (2015), *Beyond the Rhetorics of Compliance: Judicial Reform in Romania*, Heidelberg: Springer.

ICJ (2017), *2017 Geneva Forum of Judges & Lawyers: Traditional and Customary Justice Systems*, Geneva: International Commission of Jurists, www.icj.org/gf2017/

ICJ (2020), *Between the Rock and the Anvil: Lawyers Under Attack in Ukraine*, ICJ Mission Report April 2020, Geneva: International Commission of Jurists.

Khmelko, I., R. Stapenhurst and M. L. Mezey (eds.) (2020), *Legislative Decline in the 21st Century: A Comparative Perspective*, New York: Routledge.

Koça, M. (2020), *Mediation in Albania: Problems and Challenges for the Future*, Berlin: Berlin Centre for Integrative Mediation, www.balkanmediation.org/2020/12/markelian-koca-mediation-in-albania-problems-and-challenges-for-the-future/

Kotter, M. (2015), 'Non-state justice institutions: a matter of fact and a matter of legislation' in M. Kotter, T. J. Roder and G. F. Schuppert (eds.), *Non-State Justice Institutions and the Law: Decision-Making at the Interface of Tradition, Religion and the State*, Basingstoke: Palgrave Macmillan.

Leiras, M., G. Tuñón and A. Giraudy (2015), 'Who wants an independent court? Political competition and supreme court autonomy in the Argentine provinces (1984–2008)', *The Journal of Politics*, vol. 77, no. 1.

Marques, F. (2021), 'Rule of law, national judges and the Court of Justice of the European Union: let's keep it juridical', *European Law Journal*, https://doi.org/10.1111/eulj.12386

Michel, J. (2011), *Alternative Dispute Resolution and the Rule of Law in International Development Cooperation*, Justice & Development Working Paper Series 12, Washington, DC: World Bank.

Michener, G. (2015), 'How cabinet size and legislative control shape the strength of transparency laws', *Governance: An International Journal of Policy, Administration, and Institutions*, vol. 28, no. 1.

Mytnynk, A., D. I. Syrota, T. M. Slobodianyk, V. V. Loktionova and O. V. Pleskun (2020), 'Ensuring enforcement of judgements through the prism of reforming criminal provisions', *International Journal of Criminology and Sociology*, vol. 9, 735–747.

O'Donnell, G. O. (1994), 'Delegative democracy', *Journal of Democracy*, vol. 5, no. 1.

Olson, D. M. and P. Norton (1996), 'Legislatures in democratic transition' in D. M. Olson and P. Norton (eds.), *The New Parliaments of Central and Eastern Europe*, London: Frank Cass.

OSCE (2010), *Intimidation of the Judiciary: Security of Judges and Prosecutors*, Vienna: Organization for Security and Co-operation in Europe.

Pasqualucci, J. M. (2002), 'Advisory practice of the Inter-American Court of Human Rights: contributing to the evolution of international human rights law', *Stanford Journal of International Law*, vol. 38, no. 2.

Piana, D. (2009), 'The power knocks at the courts' back door: two waves of post-communist judicial reforms', *Comparative Political Studies*, vol. 42, no. 6.

Ploska, A. (2020), 'Shrinking space for civil society: a case study of Poland', *European Public Law*, vol. 26, no. 4.

Ramseyer, J. M. (1994), 'The puzzling (in)dependence of courts: a comparative approach', *Journal of Legal Studies*, vol. 23, no. 2.

Roos, S. R. (2010), 'Watchdog and co-operation partner', *Development and Co-operation*, vol. 37, no. 3.
RSF (2021), *2021 World Press Freedom Index*, Paris: Reporters Without Frontiers, https://rsf.org/en/ranking
Sabrow, S. (2020), 'Non-enforcement as a tool of mediation in pluralistic societies', *The Journal of Legal Pluralism and Unofficial Law*, vol. 52, no. 2.
Salzberger, E. M. (1993), 'A positive analysis of the doctrine of separation of powers, or: why do we have an independent judiciary?', *International Review of Law and Economics*, vol. 13, no. 4.
Singh, D. (2015), 'Explaining varieties of corruption in the Afghan justice sector', *Journal of Intervention and State-building*, vol. 9, no. 2.
Skoczylas, A. and M. Swora (2007), 'Administrative judiciary in Poland in search for fairness and efficiency: an overview', *Transylvanian Review of Administrative Sciences*, vol. 19, 116–125.
SoJust (2006), *The Justice System in Romania*, Bucharest: Society for Justice.
Spano, R. (2018), 'The future of the ECHR: subsidiarity, process-based review and the rule of law', *Human Rights Law Review*, vol. 18, no. 3.
Ssenyonjo, M. (2018), 'Responding to human rights violations in Africa: assessing the role of the African Commission and Court on Human and Peoples' Rights (1987–2018)', *International Human Rights Law Review*, vol. 7, no. 1.
Swenson, G. (2018), 'Legal pluralism in theory and practice', *International Studies Review*, vol. 20, no. 3.
Syukur, F. A. and D. M. Bagshaw (2015), 'Victim-offender mediation with youth offenders in Indonesia', *Conflict Resolution Quarterly*, vol. 32, no. 4.
Syukur, F. A. and D. M. Bagshaw (2018), 'Indonesia: the role of traditional, indigenous Musyawarah Mufakat process of mediation' in S. P. Stobbe (ed.), *Conflict Resolution in Asia: Mediation and Other Cultural Models*, Lanham: Lexington Books.
Szabo, A. (2015), 'Restorative justice in a climate of liberal changes: the case of Romania', *Restorative Justice*, vol. 3, no. 3, 405–413.
Tamanaha, B. Z. (2015), 'A bifurcated theory of law in hybrid societies' in M. Kotter, T. J. Roder and G. F. Schuppert (eds.), *Non-State Justice Institutions and the Law: Decision-Making at the Interface of Tradition, Religion and the State*, Basingstoke: Palgrave Macmillan.
Tchoukou, J. Y. A. (2020), 'A conceptual framework for regulating customary law within pluralistic African states: reassessing justice sector reforms for reconciling legal traditions', *Global Journal of Comparative Law*, vol. 9, no. 2.
Tvaronavičienė, A., N. Kaminskienė, I. Žemaitaitytė and M. Cudowska (2021), 'Towards more sustainable dispute resolution in courts: empirical study on challenges of the court-connected mediation in Lithuania', *Entrepreneurship and Sustainability*, vol. 8, no. 3.
UN (2020), *Report of the Special Rapporteur on the Independence of Judges and Lawyers, Diego García-Sayán*, A/75/172, New York: United Nations, https://undocs.org/A/75/172.
UNDP (2012), *Informal Justice Systems: Charting a Course for Human Rights-Based Engagement*, New York: United Nations Development Programme.
UNHRC (2017), *Resolution Adopted by the Human Rights Council on 22 June 2017*, New York: United Nations Human Rights Council.
Van den Eynde, L. (2013), 'An empirical look at the amicus curiae practice of human rights NGOs before the European Court of Human Rights', *Netherlands Quarterly of Human Rights*, vol. 31, no. 3.
Wang, Y. (2020), 'The more authoritarian, the more judicial independence? The paradox of court reforms in China and Russia', *Journal of Constitutional Law*, vol. 22, no. 2.

WEF (2020), *Global Competitiveness Report 2019*, Geneva: World Economic Forum.

Wetzel, A. and J. Orbie (2015), *The Substance of EU Democracy Promotion: Concepts and Cases*, Basingstoke: Palgrave Macmillan.

Widner, J. (1999), 'Building judicial independence in common law Africa' in A. Schedler, L. Diamond and M. Plattner (eds.), *The Self-Restraining State: Power and Accountability in New Democracies*, London: Lynne Rienner.

WJP (2021), 'Improving Maya women's access to justice in rural Guatemala', Washington: World Justice Project, https://worldjusticeproject.org/world-justice-challenge-2021/improving-maya-womens-access-justice-rural-guatemala

Yadav, V. and B. Mukherjee (2014), *Democracy, Electoral Systems, and Judicial Empowerment in Developing Countries*, Ann Arbor: University of Michigan Press.

Zumbansen, P. (2018), 'The rule of law, legal pluralism, and challenges to a Western-centric view: some very preliminary observations' in C. May and A. Winchester (eds.), *Handbook on the Rule of Law*, Cheltenham: Edward Elgar.

6 Reforming judicial behaviour

Introduction

Reforms aimed at the way members of the judiciary function range from the design of measures to evaluate performance, with the aim of improving the quality of judicial decision-making, to procedures calculated to eradicate corruption. Training programmes are widely used to reorient judges and prosecutors towards values implicit in systems of justice under democratic regimes. Judicial bias has been tackled by purges of judges believed to be too closely associated with the *ancien regime*, appellate procedures and codes of conduct.

This chapter deals first with reforms aimed at modernizing the working environment so that the individual judge can render impartial decisions. Information technology has a part to play, but the risks to justice need to be recognized. Defence against judicial bias has been sought in jury trials, raising questions about their cultural acceptability. Three other areas of concern have been addressed by reformers: the need for translation and interpretation facilities so that nobody is denied a fair trial because they do not speak or understand the language used throughout the judicial process; the need for information about basic legal rights; and assistance when encountering legal procedures. We then look at attempts to change the behaviour of judges more directly and the issues raised by the use of performance indicators, training, lustration, constraints on a judge's political activities and measures to eradicate corruption.

Judicial capacity

Judicial capacity-building has involved the modernization of judicial institutions, especially courts. Here the main emphasis has been on the value of information technology to the reform of judicial systems, the development of viable performance indicators to measure the efficiency of courts and individual judges, and the resources needed to support the judicial system.

The modernization of judicial facilities has relied heavily on computerization to increase efficiency in the processing of cases and so reduce the delays which plague the legal process in many new democracies. Information technology has been upgraded with new computer equipment, modern case management software,

DOI: 10.4324/9781003334613-7

websites for information sharing, and area networks to connect district and higher-level courts (Anderson and Gray 2007). Information technology is being exploited in case and file management, the development of templates in the formulation of judicial decisions, the provision of online access to law and jurisprudence databases, electronic filing, and exchange of electronic legal documents. It has developed improved communication between the courts and litigants and made the user's access to the courts easier (CEPEJ 2014).

For example, in Ukraine's administrative courts, information support is provided by a unified state register of court decisions, an automated system of court documentation, and a Judicial Information and Telecommunication System which registers documents coming to court, determines which judge will consider each case, exchanges documents between a court and the participants in the case, and arranges videoconferencing where appropriate (Shkuta 2020). Well-designed judicial websites can in theory increase openness and participation in the judicial system, though in practice they tend to concentrate on providing information and transparency rather than citizen participation or interaction with websites. The emphasis is likely to be on internal judicial management rather than obtaining feedback from citizens, as found in Mexico (Sandoval-Almazan and Gil-Garcia 2018).

New technology, especially audio- and videoconferencing equipment and online procedural documents, can prove effective in dealing with a backlog of cases, as for example in Latvia. In Brazil, a US$ 2.3 billion investment in new technologies between 2009 and 2015, including equipment, software, digitization, electronic portals, databases and online registries, has had a positive effect on the ability of courts to deal with over 80 million pending cases that had accumulated by 2016 (Gomes et al. 2018). Information technology allows the creation of integrated case management systems and unified statistical systems for the monitoring of cases and enables the overall efficiency of the judicial system and the productivity of judicial officials to be monitored, as in Croatia. Technological improvements to databases and registers can bring down the average duration of legal proceedings, as in Estonia (Freedom House 2015b).

Information technology also offers new opportunities for improving access to justice. Information about court procedures, case-law, the costs of proceedings and alternative methods of dispute resolution can be widely disseminated. Court proceedings can be initiated electronically (e-filing). The management of files and cases can be rationalized and made more transparent. Cases can be distributed between courts more objectively. IT is thus

> [a] means to improve the administration of justice, to facilitate the user's access to the courts and to reinforce the safeguards laid down in Article 6 of the European Convention on Human Rights: access to justice, impartiality, independence of the judge, fairness and reasonable duration of proceedings.
>
> (CCEJ 2011: para. 5)

This is how IT should ideally be used. It is, however, increasingly recognized that IT poses risks to justice if it compromises the procedural rights of litigants to a fair hearing. There is a concern that the introduction of IT into court administration might 'compromise the human and symbolic faces of justice. If justice is perceived by the users as purely technical, without its real and fundamental function, it risks being dehumanized. . . . IT must not prevent judges from applying the law in an independent manner and with impartiality' (CCEJ 2011: para. 6). In Russia, the development of information technology in the judiciary has led to the creation of online courts, easier access to court decisions, the ability to track the progress of a case, the payment of court fees, remote participation in court hearings, and public familiarization with court practices, but not without creating concerns that fundamental elements of the judicial system and principles of justice might be put at risk (Rostovschikov et al. 2019). Traditional forms of information and assistance are particularly important for vulnerable litigants. Consequently, reformers argue that judges should be involved in the introduction of IT systems so that judicial procedures, independence and impartiality are not compromised by technological imperatives (CCEJ 2011: paras. 6, 8).

A further risk is that information and communication technology may not be equally accessible. Access to the internet may be unevenly distributed between areas and socio-economic groups. Levels of funding and skills may vary. Consequently, reformers may decide to focus resources on making courts and offices more physically accessible, rather than on new technology, as in parts of Mexico (Sandoval-Almazan and Gil-Garcia 2018).

Modernization has involved other innovations to reduce delays in judgements, including processing small claims by correspondence, settling uncontested divorces by notaries, and tightening rules to reduce absentee rates of litigants due to illness, as in Latvia. Here additional judges have been appointed or transferred from less busy to busier courts. However, budgetary problems remain, including poor rates of remuneration for administrative personnel, which have led to calls for strike action. In Estonia, extra support staff have been employed, and in Poland, small claims can be submitted, and judgements delivered, via the internet or e-courts. In 2011 in Lublin, where the first e-court facility was established, over a million cases were resolved in this way. Efficiency can be enhanced by simplified procedures in straightforward or non-disputed cases, leaving judges with more time to devote to more serious cases. Such procedures include judgement without a hearing, hearings in the judge's office and accelerated procedures. They have been applied to enforcement procedures (in Hungary), labour disputes (in Azerbaijan), commercial disputes (in Russia) and minor criminal offences, as in the Czech Republic (CEPEJ 2014). The publication of gazettes, statutes, court decisions and procedural rules has also been given priority. Attempts have been made, though with little success, to strengthen court administration, reduce delays and improve case management in Bangladesh by the introduction of management information systems and office automation in the civil courts.

Much emphasis has been placed on the development of performance indicators to enable the efficiency of courts to be assessed. Responsibility for evaluating the performances of courts and setting targets normally rests with the judiciary, though the scope of annual evaluations varies from country to country. For example, the judiciaries in Armenia and Georgia monitor incoming cases, the number of decisions, the volume of postponed cases and the length of proceedings. However, Georgia is more active than Armenia in measuring backlogs, analysing waiting times during court procedures, and defining performance indicators. Georgia has also established quality standards for the courts (Council of Europe 2013). Other quantitative information includes the frequency and causes of adjournments, and the incidence and success of appeals. Indicators are also increasingly used to assess the performance of individual judges. These are discussed later in the chapter.

When performance indicators are used to compare countries they can have an effect on a government's investment in the judiciary and on pressure for reform from public opinion (Garoupa and Ginsburg 2015). However, there is a risk that the enforcement of quantitative indicators of performance on the judiciary might put qualitative dimensions of justice at risk, as when pursuit of faster case disposition leads to departures from the rules of natural justice. Improving judicial efficiency (perhaps measured by reduced costs) does not necessarily threaten the judicial system's ability to meet the demands of justice, but it is none the less important to recognize that there is no inevitable correlation between judicial performance and the quality of justice: '[E]fficacy can be achieved even by a highly inefficient system devoting excessive resources to the judiciary. At the same time, an efficient yet undersized judiciary can turn out to be ineffective when trying to meet the current requirements of justice' (Marciano et al. 2019: 85). Hence the importance of recognizing that indicators of efficiency and of effectiveness measure different dimensions of judicial performance.

Modernization is also expensive, which makes the idea of reducing the number of courts attractive. However, this can run counter to constitutional requirements, as was found in Albania when an attempt was made to deal with the problem of inefficiency in the judiciary by reducing the number of district courts and judges. While the Constitution guaranteed the continuous employment of judges, the reform required the number of judges to be reduced. The increased workloads also reduced efficiency and increased costs so that the modernization of court infrastructure – courtrooms, archives and equipment – could not be afforded (EC 2020).

It is generally accepted that judicial independence will be difficult to sustain if the judiciary is starved of resources. According to the Basic Principles on the Independence of the Judiciary adopted by the United Nations in 1985, 'it is the duty of each Member State to provide adequate resources to enable the judiciary to properly perform its functions'. In addition to supporting the proper day-to-day functioning of the judiciary, increasing its capacity will obviously demand, at least in the short term, additional public expenditure. But ensuring adequate funding for the judiciary has been a recurring problem in new democracies.

One method of guaranteeing resources for the judiciary so that it can perform its functions in an independent way is to make constant the judiciary's share of the state budget. This was tried in El Salvador, where financial dependence on the executive had been a contributory factor in the politicization of the judiciary. In 1991 it was enacted that the judiciary's share of the national budget should increase from 2 per cent to 6 per cent by 1996, with 4 per cent to finance the judiciary and 2 per cent to fund the offices of the Attorney General, the State Counsel and the Procurator for the Defense of Human Rights (Dodson and Jackson 2001). However, budgetary guarantees provided no protection against attacks from the legislature on the independence of the judiciary, disciplinary action against judges who made decisions unfavourable to the executive, or a lack of impartiality in the selection of Supreme Court justices.

Unbiased proceedings

The constitutional and statutory provisions needed to secure the right to a fair trial have been put in place in most new democracies, specifying human rights, fundamental freedoms and judicial independence. Constitutional reforms have also formally increased the independence of courts. Efforts to change criminal procedures from inquisitorial or quasi-inquisitorial to accusatorial have been made in a number of Latin American countries (Argentina, Bolivia, Chile, Colombia, Costa Rica, Ecuador, El Salvador, Guatemala, Honduras, Paraguay and Venezuela) because of the latter's association with greater fairness. However, the reforms which exist on paper have not always been applied in practice, largely because of the persistence of legal cultures inherited from the previous (authoritarian) regimes.

A procedural reform which has gained considerable support among transitional democracies is trial by jury. In many countries of Central and Eastern Europe, Central and South America, Southeast Asia and Africa, lay participation in the administration of justice has become 'a symbol of democratic ideals . . . perceived to effectively elevate ordinary citizens into the position of self-governance, and in fact become an avenue to secure direct, participatory democratic reforms' (Fukurai et al. 2011: 1), though some countries in which jury trials have been associated with the consolidation of democracy have yet to implement them (e.g. Thailand, Taiwan and the Philippines). The 1995 Constitution of Kazakhstan stipulates that 'criminal procedure shall be carried out with the participation of jurors'. In 2012 legislation was presented to the Ukrainian parliament to introduce trial by jury, a right long provided for in the Constitution. Introducing jury trials has also been part of recent legal reforms of the criminal law in Georgia, where the aim is to establish a system based on the adversarial trial principle. South Korea introduced citizen participation in the judiciary in 2008. In 2013 the Argentinian province of Buenos Aires made trial by jury possible for offences punishable with at least fifteen-year imprisonment.

The idea that citizens rather than magistrates should sit in judgement of their peers is widely regarded as an essential part of democratic governance. This form of participation in the system of justice, though ideally shielded from political considerations, aims to strengthen public confidence in, and support for, democracy. Thus, in South Korea lay participation in judicial decision-making is seen as a way of reinforcing 'the democratic legitimacy of the judicial process. . . . Korea's adoption of the jury system was mainly driven by participatory democratic concerns' (Lee 2009: 180). The jury system represents a democratic contrast to the authoritarianism of 1961 to 1987 under which the courts were often used as a political weapon. To a large extent the Korean reform reflects American influences because it was believed that a jury system modelled on the American would reinforce a democratic political culture by making the judicial system more transparent and thus comprehensible to the public.

The introduction of jury trials in the Republic of Georgia was also designed to demonstrate to the international community that Georgia is fully embracing democratic governance. In a country in which hitherto 99 per cent of criminal cases ended in conviction, damaging public confidence in the independence of the judiciary, a major appeal of jury trials was the possibility they hold out of providing a fair trial through an independent process. Although constitutional provision for jury trials was provided by amendments to the Constitution of the Republic of Georgia in 2004, it was not until a new criminal code came into effect in 2010 that trial by jury became part of the criminal justice system.

The relationship between democracy and confidence in the judicial system was also a factor behind the introduction of jury trials in Ukraine: 'Lay citizen participation in the judicial system is vital generally, and it is even more important in a fledgling democracy seeking to rid itself of corruption and instill trust in the work of its government and the rule of law' (Sheyn 2010: 689). The reintroduction of jury trials in Russia in 1993 was also intended to demonstrate the regime's commitment to the rule of law and democratic reform (Plotkin 1994).

Support for jury trials has also been motivated by distrust in aspects of the formal judiciary and professional judges, especially political interference, corruption, inefficiency (leading to long delays) and incompetence (leading to miscarriages of justice). For example, in Argentina the jury system was seen as a response to widespread distrust of courts characterized by delay and lack of transparency. In Georgia the involvement of jurors was expected to enhance the independence of the judiciary, strengthen the fairness of trials, provide more rapid and effective justice, reduce corruption and build trust in the judiciary. It was hoped that the introduction of trial by jury in Russia would give the criminal courts greater legitimacy (Ivkovic et al. 2021).

There are subtle variations in the way that the concept of trial by jury has been applied in different countries, but some commonalities are evident. First, defendants are usually allowed to choose whether to opt for trial by jury. In Georgia, for example, trial by jury is optional in that if both defence and prosecution agree, the case can be heard before a judge. Defendants in criminal cases in Russia are given a choice between trial by a 12-person jury and a hearing before a judge, if the crimes of which they stand accused are punishable by long-term or life imprisonment.

Second, where the constitutional legitimacy of juries is contested (the Korean Constitution only specifies a right to trial by judges), the reformers have only allowed jury verdicts to be advisory during the early years of the experiment.

However, Korean judges must explain publicly any disagreement with the jury, and written final judgements must include the jury's verdict. Elements of the German lay assessor system have also been incorporated. A jury unable to reach a unanimous verdict must hear the judge's opinion, following which a simple majority verdict is rendered. Jurors also participate in sentencing by submitting their opinion to the presiding judge. This is widely believed to put pressure on judges to accept the jury's decision, especially since a study of all jury trials held during the first three years of the new procedure found that judges and juries agreed on over 90 per cent of verdicts (Lee 2009). However, given the rules governing unanimous and majority verdicts, it is likely that judges still have a good deal of influence on juries.

Third, jury trials have been limited to the most serious crimes, such as murder and rape, not least because of resourcing problems. Initially in Georgia the innovation was limited to cases of aggravated murder, but in 2013 the procedure was extended to other serious crimes such as manslaughter.

Fourth, there are rules governing eligibility and disqualification. In Korea, these are the same as for judges and other public officials. In Georgia there are extensive disqualifications designed to ensure independence and impartiality, and lawyers for both prosecution and defence can challenge individuals on a shortlist of potential jurors. It is hoped that since jurors are not dependent on the state, do not act alone but as members of a group, and have little to lose in exercising their own judgement, they will be better than judges at resisting unlawful pressure from the government.

Finally, misgivings have often been expressed about the compatibility of the local culture with judicial procedures involving juries. The Georgian case vividly illustrates the challenges faced by reformers when attempting to introduce new procedures into an inhospitable cultural context. Alien common law adversarial or accusatorial procedures had to be superimposed upon the civil law inquisitorial tradition. Judges are required to act as impartial referees, ensuring that due process and the principles of natural justice are observed, rather than leading an investigation into the guilt or innocence of the accused by supervising the gathering of evidence and questioning witnesses (TI Georgia 2010). Because it was also believed that Georgian culture makes it difficult for conflicting interests to reach a consensus, majority verdicts are allowed if after three hours of deliberation a jury fails to reach a unanimous verdict. The jury's decision is final and, in the case of acquittal, cannot be appealed against.

Juries then have to achieve independence and impartiality in the context of extensive kinship networks covering a small population. It may prove difficult to protect jurors from pressures exercised by those supporting the parties to a case, especially given the existence of 'thieves-in-law' who traditionally have provided protection to disputants with little faith in the legal system. It is also difficult to limit jurors' attention solely to the evidence presented in court in the face of aggressive coverage by both print and broadcast media with a reputation for publishing their own judgements before evidence has been presented in court.

Trial by jury has also to be accommodated by a culture which doubts the ability of lay adjudicators to assess the evidence presented to them correctly. It is recognized in Georgia that there will need to be an extensive educational campaign among the public in general and jurors in particular if they are to understand the new procedures. Judges, prosecutors and attorneys will have to be trained in the rules of adversarial decision-making, especially in cases of violence against women, when a gender-sensitive approach will have to find a foothold in an aggressively patriarchal culture, in which cases of sexual violence have traditionally been dealt with privately between families, usually to the disadvantage of the victim.

The existence of widespread distrust of government in Georgian political culture has raised concerns that an implausibly high rate of convictions might be replaced by an equally improbable rate of acquittals, regardless of the evidence presented in court. This possibility is made greater by the power given to juries to refuse under some circumstances to apply a law under which the defendant is technically guilty, on the grounds that it is inappropriate to bring a case under that particular law.

Russia's legal culture also throws up obstacles to trial by jury, including a lack of confidence in the presumption of innocence, or in the ability of laypeople to understand complex legal proceedings, especially when educated and employed people find it easy to avoid jury duty, leaving it to people who are open to manipulation through intimidation and corruption. This has influenced the rate of acquittal following jury trials. Although rates of acquittal by juries have averaged only around 20 per cent, this compares with a conviction rate of nearly 100 per cent before jury trials were reintroduced, and with an acquittal rate of 2.4 per cent in criminal courts overall, making Russian juries nine times more likely to acquit defendants than judges sitting alone (The Economist 2009). However, between a quarter and half of jury acquittals are overturned on appeal to the Supreme Court, compared to less than 10 per cent of convictions.

As jury trials expanded geographically across Russia, the number of cases heard before juries declined until they constituted only 0.05 per cent of all criminal cases. Non-jury trials were eventually reverted to for all cases except murder. In 2008 an amendment to the Criminal Procedure Code, upheld following an application to the Constitutional Court, abolished jury trials for crimes designated as terrorism. This was prompted by what law-makers saw as an excessive number of acquittals and guilty verdicts granting 'mercy' which prevent sentences being handed down that exceed two-thirds of the maximum allowed. One conclusion of the Constitutional Court was that it was impossible in terrorism cases to find unbiased jurors, thus making the right to trial by jury conditional upon the right to a fair trial. In this the Russian Court was influenced by the European Court of Human Rights which has consistently ruled that the absence of trial by jury does not necessarily violate the right to a fair trial. By implication, and with significance beyond the limits of anti-terrorism laws, the right to a fair trial might actually be compromised by a jury whose independence and impartiality cannot be guaranteed (Davis and Tyulkina 2014).

Despite such obstacles, jury trials can heighten awareness of the rule of law, improve understanding of the importance of evidence in court proceedings and modify the role of judges (Lee 2010). If the high level of agreement between judges and jurors is a sign that jurors are competent in making judgements, this could lead to juries being given greater powers in the form of binding, rather than advisory, decisions (Kim et al. 2013). In Korea the system is under review by the Supreme Court's Committee for Citizens' Participation in the Judicial System. In Georgia, jury trials provide no cause to fear that society is unable to furnish courts with jurors who have the necessary understanding of law and justice. And there is evidence that the introduction of jury trials in a limited range of criminal cases has significantly increased public trust in the judiciary (Freedom House 2012).

Experience of juries as part of judicial reform has revealed the need for legal training to include the use of lay participation in criminal justice. The diligence of jurors has generally been well received by the judiciary, though concerns have been expressed about the capacity of lay participants to understand and apply the law, arrive at fair decisions, articulate reasoned verdicts and provide efficient (i.e. cost-effective) justice. The Russian experiment with juries has been particularly badly affected by lack of support in the judiciary for lay participation, showing that 'to survive, juries need not only a legal procedure that allows them to thrive, but also a legal culture that supports lay participation' (Ivkovic et al. 2021: 18). A jury system is unlikely to have the support of a judiciary that is managed so as to do the bidding of the political executive. Once again, we are reminded of the importance of judicial independence to judicial reform.

Both public trust and judicial independence are likely to suffer setbacks when a system of lay participation in criminal justice is designed to assist executive control of the judiciary. The 'mixed court' system in Kazakhstan, where a judge and ten lay assessors decide on both verdict and sentence, was chosen specifically to prevent jurors from finding defendants innocent when the government favours conviction. This system constitutes much less of a threat to the dominant role of the judge than Anglo-American trial by jury. The deliberations of the judge and assessors are conducted in secret so that the defence cannot monitor whether the assessors have been misled, manipulated or intimidated by the judge, and assessors have no one to whom they can complain about a judge's misconduct. The number of cases heard by mixed courts is small because information about the right to such a hearing is regularly withheld from the accused, and charges can be downgraded by the prosecution to evade trial by mixed courts. There have been serious violations of the law in the selection of lay assessors, and rules of evidence have been interpreted by trial judges in favour of the prosecution. Political crimes are excluded from the system, as are cases relating to freedom of speech and the press. Consequently, lay adjudication 'has not yet succeeded in achieving its primary tasks including providing the defendants with a more independent and impartial tribunal than a bench trial and increasing public confidence in the criminal justice system' (Kovalev and Suleymenova 2010: 276).

Language, information and assistance

In societies where there are ethnic minorities that might struggle with the language in which court proceedings are conducted, a fair hearing might depend upon the availability of court interpreters. This entitlement is enshrined under Article 6 of the European Convention on Human Rights, which specifies the right of everyone charged with a criminal offence to be informed promptly, in a familiar language and in detail, of the nature and cause of the accusation and to have the free assistance of an interpreter if the accused cannot understand or speak the language used in court. The United Nations Office of the High Commissioner for Human Rights, citing the International Covenant on Civil and Political Rights and the International Convention on the Elimination of All Forms of Racial Discrimination, stipulates that

> [f]ree interpretation should be available in criminal proceedings if an accused member of a linguistic minority does not understand the language of proceedings, as well as free translation of the court documents necessary for his or her defense, preferably in their own language.

Essential documents should be translated without cost to the defendant. Court proceedings, civil or criminal, and other judicial or quasi-judicial hearings should be conducted in a minority language if the concentration and the number of speakers make this practicable (UN 2017: 29).

It is obvious that if a language that is not understood by one of the parties is used in court the right to a fair trial or fair proceedings is jeopardized. This is particularly important in criminal cases. Anyone charged with a criminal offence should be informed, in a language which he or she understands, of the nature and cause of the accusation, the reasons for arrest or detention, and the nature and cause of any charge brought. There is no shortage of advice available to reformers on how to disseminate information, organize interpreters, exploit information technology, legally enforce the right and provide for appeal against a lack of interpretation or its quality. However, the language right is not always recognized because of insufficient financial resources, qualified interpreters or public awareness.

Reforms designed to provide courts with interpreters include the University Diploma in Legal Translation and Interpreting established by South Africa's Department of Justice in collaboration with a number of universities; and the use of Italian or Hungarian in Slovenian courts in areas where these minorities are sufficiently numerous and concentrated.

Reforms designed to improve knowledge of legal rights and how to use that knowledge effectively in the judicial system, including customary courts and administrative tribunals, have been dubbed 'legal empowerment' or giving people, especially the poor, the ability to understand and use the law. A broad definition of legal empowerment encompasses rights to property, employment protection (labour rights) and enterprise (business rights), whereas empowering people to use the justice system entails enabling people to access it by improving their knowledge of the system, providing legal services, and making legal entitlements practical, enforceable and meaningful. The reform of court proceedings draws on legal empowerment in relation to access to justice rather than attempts to increase people's power to influence law-making. Empowerment thus takes the form of legal aid, the deployment of paralegals and legal literacy programmes.

Legislation in a number of post-authoritarian states in Eastern and Central Europe has provided a statutory basis for the constitutional guarantees of the rights to counsel and legal aid, such as Lithuania's Law on State Guaranteed Legal Aid and Slovakia's Legal Aid Act. The legislation has been designed to expand the types of cases open to legal aid and provide a better legal aid service. However, these reforms have not always been successful in expanding aid beyond mandatory defence, clarifying rules of eligibility, providing guarantees of legal representation in civil cases, and improving the management of the legal aid system. The criteria for eligibility are often vague and ambiguous, appointment procedures lack transparency, and the quality of legal representation is poor. Management is often divided between the Ministry of Justice, bar associations and the courts, leading to inefficiency (PILNET 2003).

An alternative to legal aid is a system of paralegals, or local volunteers, usually trained by non-governmental organizations to provide a link between legal professionals and local communities, to give legal advice and support on legal processes and options for pursuing remedies, and to mediate in some disputes. Such services enable people 'to conceive of themselves as bearers of rights, as agents capable of action' (Maru and Gauri 2018: 2).

What is often a voluntary activity can be given state support, as in Tanzania's Legal Aid Act of 2017, which established a regulatory framework and statutory recognition for paralegals. A Legal Services Facility provides financial support. The statutory duties of paralegals include educational programmes on legal questions, assistance with obtaining legal documents, advice on alternative dispute procedures, and help in dealings with the courts, though, as is the case generally, paralegals do not have the authority to represent litigants, despite recommendations on legal assistance issued by the United Nations.

Community paralegals have also been given statutory recognition in Afghanistan, Indonesia, Kenya, Malawi, Moldova, Nigeria, Sierra Leone and Uganda. The Bangladesh Rural Advancement Committee has over 6,000 paralegals working in legal aid clinics. Legal Aid South Africa (LASA) is the country's largest employer of paralegals. Its 185 paralegals work from 64 justice centres and 55 satellite offices. In the Philippines a large number of NGOs train and deploy paralegals specializing in agrarian reform, rural development, environmental problems, and human rights in relation to politics, land, labour, indigenous people, women and children. Indonesia's community-based paralegals have to work alongside traditional dispute resolution mechanisms but receive legal advice from community lawyers for complex cases (WJP 2016). Their impact 'does not lie so much in improving the access to the formal legal system, but rather in countering the impact of power imbalances between disputing parties on the outcome of processes of grievance and dispute handling' (Berenschot and Rinaldi 2018: 161). Paralegals in Kenya also tend to specialize on specific topics or groups such as sex workers, minorities, women's rights, terminal illness and customary land claims. There are over 30 organizations providing paralegal services across the country under the Paralegal Support Network which provides training material, campaigns on behalf of paralegals, and works with the Kenya Law Reform Commission on the establishment of small claims courts. However, most paralegals are recruited, trained and deployed by community groups which are heavily dependent on aid donors.

The first problem encountered by paralegals, which need to be addressed by reformers, is that, unlike in Tanzania, they do not generally have an official status and structure of regulations, partly because there is no internationally accepted definition of paralegal. They also lack recognition within the legal professional lawyers. Second, the authority of paralegals is likely to clash with the power of established community leaders who often have a judicial role, especially in pluralistic systems of justice. Programmes to give paralegals some official status rarely consider those aspects of local power relations which obstruct access to justice. Paralegals 'must be able to facilitate access to justice, if necessary, by challenging local power relations; but they cannot rely on the established authority that comes from being a community leader, precisely because of their relatively weak embeddedness in local power bases' (Dancer 2018: 61). Paralegals need rigorous training, supervision, and support if their work is to be of consistent quality. There is also a risk of abuse if paralegals use their knowledge and status to take advantage of others. Funding from donors and aid agencies can be inadequate and unreliable. Reformers need to consider the potential for the state to roll local initiatives out nationally with stable funding.

In addition to the education in law and court procedures that can be provided by paralegals, law reform may include legal literacy programmes to provide people, especially vulnerable groups, with increased knowledge of national and local laws, legal rights, and ways to seek redress through the courts. Legal education also aims to develop skills, change attitudes and build confidence. It deploys a range of techniques, including the provision of information via documents, electronic media, and teaching programmes led by professional lawyers including judges (Grimes 2018).

As with paralegals, civil society organizations are likely to have a role in legal literacy. Alternatively, they may be part of the training of lawyers, as in Street Law courses. An example is the Prague Street Law programme founded in 2009 to provide legal education to laypersons as part of the professional development of law students. Street Law team members are usually graduates of Street Law courses working predominantly on a voluntary basis. Legal literacy work has included legal workshops for Roma children, and seminars and workshops in day care centres, community centres and libraries, focusing on topics of importance to elderly people (such as the laws on inheritance, consumer protection, family, patient's rights, domestic violence and privacy). Mock trials have been conducted. Seminars have been arranged for prison inmates about to be released, focusing primarily on debt and loss of property. Workshops have been run for children in care homes, and special law courses provided for teachers, covering civil law, public law and human rights. The programme has benefited from a large team of volunteer Street Law graduates who are encouraged to design their own projects and make an input into the design of the whole programme (Urban and Friedel 2019).

Despite shortcomings, these empowerment initiatives have generally had positive impacts on people's knowledge of the law, their willingness to use the courts, their acquisition of a remedy or entitlement, their perceptions of fairness, and levels of satisfaction with the resolution of their case (Goodwin and Maru 2017). As such, they contribute to making a fair trial a matter of routine.

Efficient judges

Reforms which seek to reinforce the independence of individual judges rely heavily on the development of objective, non-political methods of evaluating individual performance. International pressure has played a part here. For example, the regular evaluation of judges and prosecutors has been insisted upon by the EU in its accession negotiations, particularly in the case of Serbia (European Commission 2014a). Extensive reliance has also been placed on training programmes for judicial personnel, especially judges, court officials and prosecutors.

A growing number of new democracies have defined quality standards for their courts, including Estonia which, since 2012, has developed standards for court management and proceedings. Performance indicators are usually negotiated between the courts and either the judicial council or ministry of justice, but best practice is felt to require the judiciary rather than the executive to set targets for individual judges, as in Poland, in order to avoid compromising judicial independence.

A wide variety of indicators has been developed. The commonest relate to the length of court proceedings, the number of closed and pending cases, backlogs, and indicators measuring the productivity of judges and court staff. But numerous others have been devised, including the length of administrative proceedings, the number of adjourned cases, and the number of cases handled by individual judges. In countries where judicial inefficiency constitutes a violation of human rights and has damaged trust in the judiciary, as for example in Latvia, performance evaluation is also aimed at improving the quality and timing of sentencing (Freedom House 2015c). Management information systems are increasingly being used to analyse backlogs, delays and length of proceedings (CEPEJ 2014).

Data relating to the efficiency with which cases are processed are often gathered together with information on the quality of a judge's decision-making and his or her professional conduct, bearing in mind that performance evaluation is aimed not only at increasing the efficiency of the courts but also at improving the judge's professional performance and increasing public trust in the judiciary. Evaluations can also be made of a judge's legal knowledge, efficiency and personal qualities such as respect for ethical standards, requiring the collection of data on a random selection of decisions, the number of cases handled, decisions made by superior courts and training, as is done in Lithuania (Wittrup 2006). Career advancement can be determined by objective evaluations covering such criteria as the quality of a judge's opinion writing and the number of cases processed by each judge (as in Romania). It is also possible to devise qualitative and quantitative criteria to be used in assessment at key stages of the judge's career. These include reviews of cases and observations of hearings, as in Hungary (Open Society Institute 2002).

Evaluating the quality of judicial decisions presents some difficult problems. In theory it is clear that high-quality decisions are the result of 'a correct application of legal rules, of a fair proceeding and a proper factual evaluation, as well as being effectively enforceable'. Good judicial decisions are intelligible, clearly reasoned in accessible language and *properly* reasoned, that is, 'consistent, clear, unambiguous and not contradictory', and include 'an examination of the factual and legal issues lying at the heart of the dispute' (CCEJ 2008: paras. 31, 36, 42). A judiciary needs a reputation for high-quality decision-making that is authoritative, impartial and independent if it is to gain legitimacy in the eyes of the legal community and the public generally (Garoupa and Ginsburg 2015).

In practice, however, the quality of a judge's decisions is affected by a range of factors in addition to the character of the individual judge: the quality of legislation, the adequacy of resources, the quality of legal training, the judge's professionalism, court procedures and case management. Any system of evaluation needs to recognize this complexity and be designed so as not to interfere with the independence of individual judges or the judiciary as a whole (CCEJ 2008). This is of particular concern in the Czech Republic where the consensus is that the Ministry of Justice 'should not measure the "quality" of judicial reasoning, as this might constitute interference with judicial independence' (Kühn 2018: 177). If judicial indicators mean that judicial activity is monitored, measured and regulated objectively, and not 'punished or rewarded according to the substantive content of their sentences, as sanctions or rewards based on substantive judgment or ideological perspectives', then judicial independence can be preserved, as Brazilian experience has shown (Fortes 2015: 40).

Designing performance measures in the judiciary thus requires considerable sensitivity. The objectives of the judiciary which is to be evaluated are often defined too subjectively for the purposes of measurement. 'Who is to say what is "just", after all? What level of cost is "acceptable"? Because of the variety and subjectivity of goals, designing performance indicators to assess the "performance" of the legal system as a whole is both methodologically tricky and politically sensitive' (World Bank 2016). Outputs (e.g. training courses completed) are easier to measure and therefore to assess objectively than outcomes (e.g. the quality of decisions handed down) which can be affected by many factors other than those which are purely judicial. For example, it is difficult enough to measure whether the poor's access to justice has been improved, but even more difficult to say with confidence that improvement is the result of a change in judicial behaviour. Broad objectives such as giving the poor greater access to justice 'are affected by many social, cultural, economic, and political factors, and the marginal impact of a reform program – even a thoroughly successful reform program – may be hard to detect, no matter how accurate the indicators for the broad systemic goal' (World Bank 2016).

Other problems with the use of quantitative measures of judicial efficiency, such as the number of cases received and disposed of, include the difficulty of reflecting in the statistics factors such as the complexity of the cases dealt with, the location of different courts, and the availability of support staff. There is thus a risk that

> the incentives that a numerical system creates for reducing delays may in fact lower the quality of adjudication; when not complemented by qualitative criteria, purely quantitative evaluation encourages judges to focus on completing cases quickly rather than deciding them well. This is especially true where sanctions attach to negative evaluations.
>
> (Open Society Institute 2002: 37)

A managerial approach to judicial decision-making may compromise the fairness of a judicial hearing. Performance indicators become 'an intrusion of neo-liberal, managerial executive-driven thinking and policies into a part of the body politic that more than anything else is based on the idea that everyone should get a fair and thorough hearing, by a dispassionate and meticulous judge' (Bohlander 2021: 146–147).

Where possible, transitional states have supported quantitative measures with qualitative criteria, defined to take into account the complexities of court procedures and other intervening factors. Qualitative data, being derived from surveys or expert evaluations, are subjective and perhaps affected by biased vested interests. However, mixing quantitative and qualitative data, for example statistics on trial durations and surveys of users which ask for judgements about court efficiency, can produce useful information, whether or not they provide conflicting results. Examples of how quantitative measures can be mixed with qualitative are found in Romania, where success is measured by a smaller case backlog, speedier court proceedings and the affordability of litigation, as well as the fairness of adjudication; improvements in the public image of the judiciary; and the enhancement of competence, professionalism and integrity among judges and court staff (World Bank 2012).

Nevertheless, objective evaluation sometimes proves elusive. A number of post-authoritarian states have still to define coherent and objective criteria for evaluating judges' performance, and there is often a lack of transparency when judges are found unsatisfactory or in need of disciplinary action. For example, judges may be disciplined for professional incompetence but without objective criteria for measuring 'incompetence', as in Romania. If performance indicators are to include the quality of a judge's reasoning, it 'cannot be separated from the institutional and social background of the judicial activity. Workload, political pressure, organizational interests, social expectations and other circumstances permanently influence the adjudication and thus, the quality of judicial reasoning' (Bencze and Ng 2018: 22). Performance measures also rely on the collection of data that is expensive in both time and money. Poorer democracies may have difficulty finding the necessary resources for a full evaluation regime.

Performance evaluation also attracts hostility from members of the judiciary who tend to regard it as open to political manipulation and thus a potential threat to judicial independence. When an Act on Courts and Judges was passed in the Czech Republic in 2002, introducing periodic evaluations of judges' performance, it was struck down by the Constitutional Court on the grounds that the powers conferred on the Ministry of Justice, court presidents and a new evaluation council would give the executive branch excessive influence over the judiciary, violating the separation of powers and judicial independence. The court also ruled that judges should only be dismissed after disciplinary proceedings for specific violations of responsibility and not as a result of routine performance evaluation.

Training for judges has been an important component of legal reform in democratizing countries, based on the principle that democracies require judicial training to reinforce judicial independence as well as convey legal concepts: '[T]he need for training of magistrates lies in the constitutional framework of modern democracies in view of the fundamental role that judges play, namely of resolving conflicts and enforcing the law, functions that must be carried out with complete independence and impartiality in order to ensure the effectiveness of judicial systems' (Lazzari 2019: 209).

The priority given to judicial training varies greatly between countries, and resources for training are likely to be vulnerable when governments give higher priority to other policy objectives. For example, the budget for judicial education and training decreased in the Ukraine by 87 per cent between 2008 and 2010 due to the allocation of state spending to other policy areas.

In order to protect the independence of judges, it is generally accepted that the authority responsible for supervising training should be independent of both executive and legislature. For example, the High School of Justice in Georgia is managed by an Independent Council consisting of six members, none of whom is from the executive branch, and chaired by the Chairman of the Supreme Court. Training may be provided by bodies outside the judiciary such as university faculties of law. However, the political executive is often represented on the managing bodies of training institutes. For example, the Judicial School in Armenia is managed by a governing board on which sits one representative from the Ministry of Justice.

The delivery of training also raises concerns about judicial independence. For example, when the Czech Republic's Act on Courts and Judges of 2002 created a new Judicial Academy, the Constitutional Court struck down the monopoly for judicial training given to the academy on the grounds that it ran counter to the independence of the judiciary and the separation of powers. Following amendment, the academy was established and began work in September 2002.

Different training programmes emphasize different aspects of the judge's role. Some concentrate on building capacity for effective and efficient administration of justice, as with Ghana's Judicial Training Institute. The most significant development is the introduction of human rights awareness into training courses, often with assistance from aid donors. For example, in 2012 the International Bar Association carried out judicial human rights training in Tunisia, as part of a larger project which aims to train the majority of Tunisian judges on human rights and on judging in a democratic society.

This distinctive feature of judicial training in democratizing countries includes material on the rights and obligations enshrined in the new constitutions. Emphasis is sometimes placed on gender issues, as in Bangladesh, where training aims to raise the level of gender sensitivity within the legal profession. Elsewhere the emphasis has been on human rights and humanitarian law, including Indonesia's two-year human rights and conflict prevention training programme for judges, prosecutors, police, prison officials and National Human Rights Commission investigators. In Georgia the High School of Justice provides training in a variety of human rights topics, including international legal norms on human rights protection, and the responsibilities of the Georgian state under international legal instruments. In Bosnia and Herzegovina judicial training includes a module on human rights, and seminars on the protection of human rights and freedoms, the Law on Prohibition of Discrimination, and gender equality. However, training for judges, lawyers and court staff on issues relating to women and minorities is by no means as extensive as it needs to be (UNDP 2013).

Whether judicial training is having the desired results is very hard to say, since so far there is a great paucity of evidence on whether training has improved access to justice, fairness, efficiency and cost-effectiveness (Armytage 2015). But in general, efficiency reforms need not threaten the quality of justice, as shown by the case of Bulgaria where measures such as performance targets, output monitoring, training and productivity incentives have improved the quality of judicial decision-making (Dimitrova-Grajzla et al. 2016).

Unbiased judges

One way to control judicial bias is to purge courts of judges believed to have ideological sympathies for the *ancien regime*. This happened in most of the post-communist states of Eastern Europe through the process of 'lustration'. Lustration is usually excused by reference to three arguments: the prophylactic (compelling holders of public office in new democracies to disclose their past), the blackmail argument (protecting officials against blackmail for their previous associations) and the public empowerment argument (making new institutions transparent, thereby restoring trust in them) (Venice Commission 2014; Horne 2017).

Lustration affects the judiciary by barring judges of the former regime from holding judicial office within the new system of law. For example, Poland's

Lustration Act of 2007 required judges, lawyers and court enforcement officers to submit affidavits declaring whether they had cooperated with the state security organs of the Polish People's Republic any time between 1944 and 1990. Non-submission meant exclusion from public life for ten years. Between 400,000 and 700,000 people were affected. Libya's Political Isolation Law prohibits officials close to the Gaddafi regime from taking public office. This includes members of the judiciary.

There is obviously a risk that such laws will be motivated more by revenge than by the need for an independent judiciary, that they violate human rights, and that, when the rules are introduced long after the political transition, they threaten the independence of the judiciary. Lustration 'imposes the legal order of the new regime on actions undertaken in a different legal setting under different forms of state coercion' (Issacharoff 2011: 1006). It can be used to disadvantage legitimate opponents of the current government. In Poland the Constitutional Court had to rule that the lustration laws were not to be used as an instrument to punish political opposition. Many other post-communist lustration laws have been struck down by constitutional courts, usually on the grounds that they violate the rule of law by being retroactive and discriminatory (Iancu 2010).

Since lustration can have far-reaching and damaging consequences for the individuals affected, international standards have been devised to protect human rights and the rule of law. It is argued that lustration procedures should be proportionate, judicial and constitutional. They should not be used for political punishment, retribution or revenge, and should only apply to offences under the *ancien regime*. Current party affiliation or ideological position should not be grounds for lustration. Four criteria need to be applied to test whether lustration procedures are acceptable in a state governed by the rule of law: guilt must be proven in each individual case; the right of defence, the presumption of innocence and the right to appeal to a court must be guaranteed; the functions and aims of lustration (the protection of the new democracy) have to be clearly distinguished from those of the criminal law (punishing people proved guilty); and lustration has to meet strict time limits in both the period of its enforcement and the period to be screened (Venice Commission 2014).

These standards explain why the attempt by the Ukrainian government in 2014 to purge the politically subservient judiciary installed under the Yanukovych presidency attracted international condemnation. While there is much evidence that the judiciary had violated civil and political rights under the previous regime, there was scepticism about the appropriateness of lustration as a policy to deal with this problem (Popova 2014). International objections focused on the failure of the Law on the Restoration of Trust in the Judiciary to observe acceptable judicial standards. The list of positions to be lustrated contains some which posed no significant danger to human rights or democracy. Officials can be dismissed based on collective responsibility rather than individual guilt, thus contravening the presumption of innocence. The process is in the hands of the Ministry of Justice rather than an independent body and does not guarantee a fair trial, thus violating the principle that the lustration of judges should only be carried out 'with full respect of the constitutional provisions guaranteeing their independence, and only the High Council of Justice should be responsible for any dismissal of a judge' (Venice Commission 2014). In 2019 the European Court of Human Rights found that the rights of five Ukrainians had been violated when they were dismissed from their posts under the lustration law.

Lustration may also have to rely on unreliable documents from the earlier regime. It risks labelling former public officials with undeserved reputations. It may 'backfire' by encouraging subservience and damaging judicial independence if judges fear retribution following rulings which go against government policy. It may also reduce the supply of scarce professional skills. There is often no alternative to keeping existing judges in their posts. As the International Legal Assistance Consortium pointed out in the case of Libya, on the one hand the Libyan judiciary's subservience to the regime makes it difficult to imagine many existing judges legitimately serving a democratic Libya. On the other hand, 'total lustration, similar to the de-Baathification steps taken in Iraq, could leave the judicial system with no experienced judges and prosecutors, while creating a cadre of former regime loyalists embittered by their loss of professional standing and income' (ILAC 2011: 12).

At first sight it might seem that a purge of the judiciary is needed to ensure that democracy is supported by judicial independence rather than weakened by bias in favour of the previous power-holders and their successors. However, the institutionalization of judicial independence may require stability rather than disruption, making the gradual removal of authoritarian remnants the preferred option, as in Chile in 1993, when three justices were impeached by the Chamber of Deputies for supporting the transfer of an important human rights case to a military tribunal. For the judiciary to be fully institutionalized as an independent branch of government it may also be better to remove judges for specific infringements of the constitution or common jurisprudence rather than because of a general association with a particular regime. There should be 'precise cause' for the removal of judges if there is not to be a long delay in the institutionalization of judicial independence and thus the rule of law (Larkins 1996: 623).

This principle is especially important in restraining governments from using lustration, not to protect democracy against remnants of the *ancien regime*, but to punish members of an earlier government, as in the case of Ukraine in 2014 (Goshovska et al. 2020). The Venice Commission found it difficult to justify lustration measures so many years after the end of the Soviet regime, stating that 'the enactment of a democratic constitution in Ukraine requires cogent reasons justifying the specific threat for democracy which former communists pose nowadays'. Applying lustration measures to the recent past ultimately amounts 'to questioning the actual functioning of the constitutional and legal framework of Ukraine as a democratic state governed by the rule of law' (Venice Commission 2014: 21).

Within the judicial system itself, the initial response to judicial bias is to resort to a system of appeals. Most court decisions are subject to review by an appeals court. For example, in Hungary local courts are the courts of first instance jurisdiction, from which appeals may be submitted to the county courts (and the Municipal

Court of Budapest), which function mainly as appellate courts. Eight regional courts of appeal hear appeals against decisions of both local and county courts. Most cases heard at regional level may be contested by appeal to the Supreme Court. A by-product of the number of levels in the judicial hierarchy has been a reduction in the time taken to complete the passage of cases through the courts. Legal challenges to administrative decisions are heard by specialized tribunals of the Regional Courts, from which appeals can be made to the Supreme Administrative Court.

One of the grounds for appeal is that a judge is biased. This was claimed when members of a feminist Russian punk band on trial for performing a stunt against Vladimir Putin in Moscow's main cathedral sought (unsuccessfully) to have the judge dismissed on the grounds that she was politically biased. Three members of the band were convicted of hooliganism, and their appeal to Moscow City Court resulted in the original verdict being upheld for two of them, with the third freed on probation with a suspended sentence.

It is also possible to require judges to declare personal interests in a case before standing down. Litigants who fear that a judge will be biased against them may lodge a request that the judge recuse themselves. Paragraph 2 of Article 5 in Romania's 2004 Law on the Judge and the Prosecutor specifies a judge's duty when there is a conflict of interest:

> Judges and prosecutors are obliged to refrain from any activity related to the act of justice if they suppose the existence of a conflict between their interests and the public interest of accomplishing justice or of protecting the general interests of society, unless the conflict of interests has been brought in writing to the cognisance of the leading board of the court or prosecutor's office and it was deemed that the existence of the conflict of interests does not affect the unbiased fulfilment of working duties.

Since requests for recusal may be motivated by dissatisfaction with the court's ruling or other vexatious causes, higher courts have had to clarify the conditions under which fear of bias is justified. In South Africa the Constitutional Court has ruled that 'the prior associations of a judge cannot form the basis of a reasonable apprehension of bias unless the *subject matter* of the litigation arises from such association'. While it is right to test whether a litigant's apprehension of bias is reasonable, this has to be balanced by a presumption of impartiality in favour of judicial officers. Recusal should not, if judicial independence is to be preserved, encourage parties to seek disqualification in the hope that another judge will be more likely to find in their favour (Siyo and Mubangizi 2015). In addition, any financial interest must be in the actual outcome of the proceedings before a complaint that a judge's financial interests will cause bias can be upheld.

Judges can also be prohibited from holding other public offices or being members of political organizations, as in Hungary, though this does not guarantee absolute impartiality. Most new democracies have signed up to international agreements or national codes of conduct stipulating the rules demanded by an independent judiciary. In the former category are found the Bangalore principles which only exclude overt political activity by implication. They specify what a judge may do: write, lecture, teach and participate in activities concerning the law, the legal system, the administration of justice or related matters; appear at a public hearing on legal matters; serve as a member of an official body if such membership is consistent with judicial impartiality and political neutrality; and join associations representing the interests of judges. In contrast, the Latin America Code of Judicial Ethics states that judicial independence implies that a judge is ethically prohibited from participating in any party-political activity. Individual judges are required under the Czech Law on Courts and Judges of 1991 to refrain from any actions which might 'threaten the trust in independent, impartial and fair judicial decision-making', but they are not banned from political activity or membership of political parties (except Constitutional Courts justices). Freedom of association in the Czech Republic allows judges, like other professionals, to form associations to represent their interests.

National codes of conduct or judicial ethics vary greatly in their scope and in the way they specify the restrictions. Two examples will suffice as illustrations. The Judicial Service Code of Conduct and Ethics of Kenya prohibits a judicial officer from editing a newspaper, publishing anything which may be reasonably regarded as of a political nature or being interviewed on questions of public policy. Judicial officers cannot stand for election to the national assembly or a local authority or hold any political office. Political views must not be expressed publicly, and family, social and political relationships should not be allowed to influence conduct or judgement.

The Armenian code similarly prohibits family, social or political ties from influencing judicial conduct and decisions. Judges must be independent from all parties to a case, including political parties, trade unions, religious bodies, the mass media and governmental bodies. A judge must be independent from political, economic and social relations. Outside the court, no judge may be a leader or member of any political party, make public speeches in favour of any political party or a candidate for political office, express opinions for or against any political party or candidate, or organize fundraising.

Such rules express values entirely consistent with an independent judiciary and the rule of law. They also add to the information available on how the system of justice is supposed to work: 'The introduction of a code of conduct can serve as a kind of customer charter that informs court users of the kind of conduct and professionalism they should expect from the judiciary' (TI 2007a: 2). But they will never eliminate the influence of a judge's own social, and therefore political, values on his or her decisions. Otherwise, why would the appointment of judges to courts that can review the constitutionality or legality of legislation be given such priority by presidents and prime ministers?

There is also evidence that codes of conduct need to be couched in strong and explicit 'high obligation' language rather than vague guidance, to remove uncertainty and ensure judges give full weight to the code's prescriptions. Judicial independence and public confidence are both served by such unambiguous content. However, codes also need to be supported where necessary (in Cambodia, for example) by statutes insulating the judiciary from the other branches of government (Lee 2015).

Honest judges

Since the judiciary is itself intrinsic to the eradication of corruption generally, the existence of judicial corruption raises exceptionally difficult problems, not least that of preventing the control of corruption from becoming a new form of political interference. Removing judicial officers on charges of corruption, and replacing them with appointees approved by the executive, can affect judicial independence, as the case of Kenya shows (TI 2007b).

Judicial corruption in new democracies has been tackled on two broad fronts. First, there is the socio-political approach, which involves a new relationship between civil society and the judiciary. As far as civil society is concerned, this requires the development of organizations capable of rigorous scrutiny and monitoring of the judiciary. Complementing this on the part of the judiciary are reforms designed to make it more difficult to hide corruption by making the judicial process more transparent and so opening it up to public scrutiny. The second type of reform changes the institutional environment within which the judiciary functions by making corruption more dangerous and costly for those who seek to benefit from it.

It is now generally accepted that no anti-corruption strategy will succeed unless it is linked to measures to strengthen the ability of civil society to challenge corruption (Gillespie and Okruhlik 1991). This means increasing society's opposition to and awareness of corruption through education, public vigilance and the scrutiny of judicial behaviour. Organizations within civil society, especially associations of lawyers but also human rights groups, raise public awareness of corruption and lobby for new laws and institutions. Romania's Society for Justice, local chapters of Transparency International, Ghana's Forum for Governance and Justice, and Nigeria's Zero Corruption Coalition are important examples. Civic associations and community groups identify where in the judiciary corruption is located and lobby for appropriate counter-measures to be taken. The United Nations has experimented, through its Office on Drugs and Crime, with national committees to coordinate the implementation of reforms with members drawn from the Ministry of Justice, the judiciary, prosecutors, the police, the prisons service, the Bar, NGOs, academics and private practice.

Before any strategy to deal with corruption is likely to be effective, it has to be backed by strong political will on the part of a leadership that is motivated to devise reforms that are technically and politically feasible, adopt credible sanctions and allocate significant resources, including expertise, to the campaign. Political will is clearly problematic if, as is alleged, Nigerian legislators had to be bribed to pass an anti-corruption law (*Guardian* 2004: 16). It is only likely to be forthcoming if there is sufficient effective political demand within society to convince politicians that it is in their interest to eradicate corruption. Civil society groups can help build political demand by collecting and disseminating information about the experiences which individuals, businesses and households have of judicial corruption and by mobilizing activists to expose it. The eradication of corruption becomes yet another reason for increasing political participation within civil society.

The media make a particularly important contribution to scrutiny by civil society, though, as was shown in Chapter 5, press freedom has declined in recent years in many new democracies, increasing the difficulties for the media in exposing corruption. In the private sector, corporations and industrial organizations can oblige their members to refrain from bribery, forming 'islands of integrity' where members sign up to anti-bribery pacts.

Monitoring by civil society has to be matched by changes within the judiciary which make judicial processes more transparent and visible because a 'lack of transparency in administrative processes within the judiciary can provide opportunities for undue influence and bribery and dent public confidence in the institution as a whole' (TI 2007a: 1). Publicizing records of complaints, case files and other performance measures, as in Brazil, make the assessment of judicial performance more visible. Judicial proceedings must be open rather than closed, unless justice demands that hearings be held *in camera*. Systematic monitoring, wide publicity for delays in hearing cases, training which emphasizes judicial professionalism and well-drafted laws which make it clear when judicial discretion is being abused, all contribute to the eradication of judicial corruption (UNDP 1997; Heywood 1997). The Judicial School of Ecuador conducts training courses based on the Bangalore Principles of Judicial Conduct and the United Nations Convention against Corruption. Training in judicial ethics aims to clarify concepts and identify potential obstacles to an honest judiciary such as social media and scepticism about the justice system's legitimacy (Sanchez 2021).

Published reasoned decisions, and information on how the courts work, litigants' rights and the appeals process, make it even more difficult to conceal corruption. The publication of judicial decisions is a particularly important weapon against judicial corruption and can 'expose corrupt judges who are unable to justify their rulings by reasoned opinions, while protecting judges whose reasoning demonstrates that they have properly applied the law to the facts in a case'. The publication of judicial opinions in the form of verbatim transcripts enables the public to detect impropriety and inaccuracy in judicial rulings (Pepys 2007: 9).

Democratic political competition can make it harder for corruption to be hidden since political opponents have strong incentives to expose it among their competitors for legislative and executive office at all levels of government. Making corruption costly for political elites also strengthens professionalism among investigators, judges and prosecutors, as in Taiwan where it is now 'more likely that corrupt behaviour will be discovered . . . and much harder to exert illicit influence over an investigation or a trial' (Goebel 2016: 136). In fact, all reforms, which strengthen professionalism within the judiciary, including recruitment on merit, high standards of entry, training, as well as codes of professional ethics, help eradicate corruption: 'Professionalism is a key means of enhancing institutional identity for the judiciary, and of building a culture that is averse to corruption . . . a professional judicial environment activates an important check on judicial corruption, since judges will tend to measure themselves against the high standards of the profession as a whole' (TI 2007a: 4).

It may also be necessary to restrict judicial immunity to the protection of judges against malicious or frivolous actions for damages by disgruntled litigants, and not extend it to corruption and other forms of judicial misconduct as it has been in some new democracies such as Albania and El Salvador, where judicial immunity 'operates on a near-absolute basis to shield judges from legal protection for acts committed in violation of the law' (Lothian 2003: 18). Pressure from the European Union prompted Albania to introduce legislation amending the rules governing the legal immunity of judges and prosecutors. Albania's constitutional reforms of 2016, aimed mainly at the prevention of judicial corruption, retained immunity for Constitutional Court judges 'except where the judge acts based upon personal interests or malice', making it possible to investigate judges for corruption (Albert et al. 2017). Limiting the immunity of judges suspected of corruption is one of the reforms designed to combat corruption in Ukraine (Jaroszewicz and Zochowski 2015).

The second type of anti-corruption reform changes the institutional context. An institutional structure to tackle judicial corruption takes the form of stronger legal rules prohibiting corruption and regulating judicial behaviour. While isolated cases of corruption can be treated as ordinary crimes, systemic corruption requires institutional reforms which allocate powers to investigate allegations to judicial inspection units and ombudsmen, and which make it easier to monitor judicial performance through management information systems, citizen consultations and support to non-governmental organizations specializing in anti-corruption work (Hammergren 2000). Anti-corruption laws need to specify clearly the nature of the offence, the penalties incurred, and their relationship to the size and type of bribery. Specific anti-corruption rules can be accompanied by a more general commitment to make all laws and regulations clear and explicit. Rules and codes of conduct can be formulated governing the disclosure of assets from non-governmental sources and conflicts of interest. For example, in Kenya section 26 (1) of the Public Officer Ethics Act of 2003 requires every public officer to submit an annual declaration of the income, assets and liabilities of him- or herself, spouse and dependent children under the age of eighteen years to the Judicial Commission. Laws designed to make corruption more dangerous for judicial officials include prohibitions on the receipt of remuneration from parties to a dispute. Under the 2016 reforms in Albania the personal assets and background of all judges are investigated before appointment, to disqualify any whose backgrounds raise doubts about their integrity or support for transparency and the public interest (Albert et al. 2017). In 2020 the European Commission reported that the vetting process had rendered 'concrete and tangible results', with more than 62 per cent of the vetting dossiers processed resulting in dismissals or resignations (EC 2020).

Anti-corruption laws can be monitored for the level of enforcement by scrutiny of the proportion of allegations that have been investigated, the proportion of investigations that have led to prosecutions' and how many prosecutions have led to convictions. Unfortunately, the monitoring of the implementation of anti-corruption strategies 'is often weak, formalistic, or non-existent' (Hussmann et al. 2009: 16). Anti-corruption legislation includes freedom of information laws, which can be extended to judicial decisions; and statutory protection for 'whistle-blowers' to prevent the harassment, intimidation and sanctioning of staff who call attention to corruption within the judiciary.

Independent anti-corruption agencies are a familiar part of anti-corruption strategies with many models from which lessons may be learnt and applied to judicial corruption. Evidence from Hong Kong and Singapore indicates that to be effective anti-corruption agencies need to receive strong, long-term support by political leaders, be empowered to act independently of the police and political executive, be endowed with broad mandates, and be allowed to target 'high' corruption. Parliamentary oversight and judicial review of agency work are also essential. An anti-corruption commission, to which the judiciary's governing body can report suspected corruption, depoliticizes the process to some extent by making investigation and prosecution the responsibility of a special agency rather than a ministry within the government.

Effective agencies combine investigation and prosecution with public education and prevention (Quah 1995; Doig 1995; Doig and Riley 1998; Skidmore 1996). Preventive work includes policy advice, training, managerial reforms, educational campaigns and openness to complaints from the public. Making anti-corruption agencies answerable to parliament, and guaranteeing the prosecution of staff suspected of corruption, make it more difficult for agencies themselves to succumb to corruption. Guarding the guardians is an essential element of anti-corruption work (Quah 2002).

Publicity is another vital part of the work of anti-corruption agencies, and there is much that can be done: information on anti-corruption measures in all official languages, online information about the activities of anti-corruption agencies, and training for journalists and editors by local Transparency International chapters (as in Estonia). Research findings on corruption can be disseminated by NGOs, and cases of corruption can be widely reported in the media (as in Georgia), underlining the importance of a strong civil society and media to anti-corruption work (Freedom House 2015a). Other measures advocated by pressure groups and aid agencies to prevent corruption include 'asset declarations', appointment on merit, the publication of court judgements, public scrutiny of court records, and the random assignment of cases. In Indonesia, e-court technology has been introduced into the Supreme Court administration, allowing the online submission of court documents to minimize the interaction of court officials with litigants and so avoid the potential for judicial corruption. However, the innovation has encountered a lack of technical understanding by court staff and a lack of public awareness of the system (Susanto 2020).

To complement the work of anti-corruption agencies a number of new democracies, including Slovakia, Croatia, Ghana and Indonesia, have created specialized courts and other judicial institutions. Some have been established as independent courts with equivalent status to other senior courts, such as Slovakia's Specialised

Criminal Court, and others as divisions of the high court, such as Ghana's Financial and Economic Crimes Court. Some are permanent, while others convene ad hoc when a criminal prosecution has been initiated. Their effectiveness appears to depend upon proceedings being transparent so that any interference with the court's independence becomes immediately apparent and upon adequate technical and financial resources. Other judicial institutions include Indonesia's Corruption Eradication Commission and Albania's High Justice Inspector.

Success has been variable. While Slovakia's court is equipped with the necessary resources and trained personnel for cases to be conducted reasonably quickly (EC 2014b), Uganda's Anti-Corruption Division has been under-staffed and under-resourced financially and technically (Carson 2015). Indonesia's Corruption Eradication Commission significantly reduced the time needed to complete cases, as well as the cost of the system and the period of uncertainty for defendants (Partohap and Pradiptyo 2015), until it becomes subjected to political control, reducing the number of investigations and protecting powerful figures in politically sensitive cases (Mulholland 2021). Pakistan's Accountability Courts have been tainted by politically motivated prosecutions. In 2020 Albania's opposition parties claimed the newly appointed High Inspector of Justice was too close to the governing party to be politically independent (Erebara 2020).

There is a shortage of evidence with which to assess the effect of anti-corruption courts on corruption in the judiciary itself, as distinct from within government generally, but it may be significant that the Risk & Compliance Portal believes there is still a high risk of encountering corruption in the Croatian judiciary; that systemic corruption weakens judicial independence in Uganda; and that the Indonesian courts remain plagued by corruption (Freedom House 2021).

The motivation to act corruptly on the part of judicial officers can be reduced by strengthening formal incentives against corruption such as improvements to officials' salaries and informal incentives such as career opportunities and reputations, all of which increase the relative benefits of probity and costs of corruption.

As we saw in Chapter 4, it is widely believed that low levels of remuneration increase the likelihood of corruption within the judiciary and that a cleaner judiciary can be had by raising judicial salaries as a disincentive to accept bribes. 'Judicial salaries that are too low to attract qualified legal personnel or retain them, and that do not enable judges and court staff to support their families in a secure environment, mean that judges are more susceptible to corruption' (TI 2007a: 5). In response to such reasoning, in 1997 Romania increased judges' salaries. In 2013 Indonesian judges were given a substantial salary increase in an attempt to curb corruption and became among the highest paid in Asia. Salaries have been raised for low-paid judges in Kyrgyzstan in order to create a cleaner judiciary after the justice system came under criticism from the European Union and the United Nations for corruption. In 2012 Zimbabwe's most senior judge demanded better pay for the police, prosecutors, magistrates and judges as under-funding had led to corruption in the judiciary, especially at its lower levels.

While it is generally accepted that low salaries for judicial personnel make the job of controlling corruption harder, the coexistence of adequate remuneration and corruption suggests that a reasonable salary is a necessary but not sufficient condition for an honest judiciary (Langseth and Stolpe 2001). In addition, increased wages could prove very expensive for poor countries and certainly cannot be the sole measure against corruption. Furthermore, higher wages might lead to demands for higher bribes because of the higher cost of losing one's job if caught out (Tanzi 1998).

There is little hard evidence of successful measures to combat judicial corruption. Most effort is directed at freeing appointments and dismissals from political manipulation. This confuses corruption with nepotism, cronyism and patronage. It cannot be assumed that an independent judiciary will be incorruptible. However, it is fairly safe to assume that corruption becomes more difficult if there is greater transparency in the assignment of cases, the publication of judgements, and the administration of the courts.

The politics of judicial reform

Judicial reform is not a straightforward technical activity, even with international support. It is a highly political process. Comparison of attempts to reform legal systems in new democracies has revealed three types of obstacle to reform. The first is indeed more managerial than political and relates to shortages of financial, technological and human resources. However, additional resources cannot alone guarantee judicial reforms beneficial to judicial independence. The main obstacles to law reform in support of judicial independence and the rule of law are political. The effects of additional investment in the judicial system are qualified by the other two obstacles: cultural values and entrenched political interests.

The cultural values which bear directly upon attitudes towards the judicial system, as distinct from broader cultural perceptions, include the attitudes of a country's legal profession towards legal education and training; public preferences for the suppression of crime regardless of the consequences for human rights of illegal acts by the police and penal institutions; public distrust of judicial institutions because of their former associations with authoritarianism; and 'entrenched ideological resistance to the separation of legal professionals from state control' (Trebilcock and Daniels 2008). The knowledge of the world which judges bring to bear in court is inevitably culturally constrained. Whether there is much scope in transitional states for broadening judges' understanding of other cultures, by the use of social science evidence in court in order to provide testimonies and opinion from anthropological and sociological experts, remains to be seen (Sagiv 2015).

In order that laws and constitutions can be rewritten, judges and bureaucrats retrained, and institutions restructured, elites have to be motivated to accept the ensuing constraints on their behaviour, such as refraining from interfering in judicial decision-making. This is underlined by evidence that judicial reform is a source of judicial instability, providing opportunities for partisan manipulation of the judiciary's composition, especially in supreme and constitutional courts (Pérez-Liñán and Castagnola 2016).

Institutional change in the judiciary involves bargaining between political actors who wish to design rules and institutions that will be responsive to their political interests. If the reform process is dominated by a single political party, the reforms will create a judiciary responsive to an executive or legislature under the control of a dominant party. If, however, there is intense party competition, reform is more likely to protect judicial independence (Bumin 2015). Thus, political reform may have to precede judicial reform. Without political reform, judicial reform may be left in the hands of authoritarian elites, leading to a worsening of judicial independence and undermining, rather than strengthening, the rule of law (Mendelski 2016). Reforms will fall short of addressing fundamental concerns about judicial professionalism and independence if judicial appointments are driven by political and ideological factors, as in Croatia (Freedom House 2015b).

The problem is to know how to create incentives for political leaders to respect the rule of law. Making their decisions transparent is obviously crucial, as is permitting appeals to the judiciary against what are perceived to be illegal decisions by politicians and bureaucrats. An active civil society, including a free press, is a further requirement. Together with regular and free elections, these conditions make it clear to politicians that they risk losing office if they try to place themselves above the law. Incentives to support the rule of law are thus derived ultimately from transparency and accountability in politics. So the internal political will to reform is crucially important. However, breaking down entrenched political interests and developing new kinds of political leaders needed for effective judicial reform are difficult and long-term remedies (Carothers 1998). Judicial reform affects the distribution of power between state institutions (the executive, legislative and judicial branches of government) and between social strata. It requires changes in cultural values and norms, as well as long-term improvements in institutional capacity. It may need the support of international judicial bodies committed to guaranteeing the independence of domestic judges, such as the Court of Justice of the European Union and the European Court of Human Rights (Jelić and Kapetanakis 2021). All this means that gradual and incremental changes are more likely to have lasting beneficial effects than interventions designed to produce quick results (Biebesheimer and Payne 2001; Faundez 1997).

Political opposition to reform comes from a wide range of entrenched interests: corrupt politicians and officials, politicians wishing to exert control over judicial decisions, and groups with vested interests in militarized police or politicized prosecutors. Group interests in the *status quo* go beyond legal professionals and political elites to include business interests and other powerful economic groups. For example, wealthy people in Bangladesh who were heavily in debt to the state banks used their political clout to ensure that a new enforcement procedure was fatally flawed. In the Ukraine judicial reform is vulnerable to parliamentary groups who draft imprecisely worded laws which as a consequence do not threaten the interests of their patrons (Stewart 2016). In Bosnia politicians have shown little interest in judicial reform, especially when it might reduce their influence within the judiciary and thereby 'jeopardize their positions' (Hrle 2016: 77). Reform of the judiciary may not suit the ruling elite when it uses the courts to persecute opposition activists. The implementation of reforms can fall victim to political interests when they are used as a means of installing politically loyal judges, as claimed by human rights activists in Kyrgyzstan.

Judicial reform takes the form of a political settlement which aims to achieve 'an institutional outcome in which the distribution of privileges and benefits is consistent with the power of prevailing social groups' (Desai et al. 2014: 244). Reforms based on a poor understanding of political conditions, and ignorance of how existing judicial arrangements serve the interests of specific economic, political and professional groups, are likely to fail. Reformers thus need sound information about the interests of powerful groups.

Since judicial independence is not always regarded as a top priority by key social groups, there may well be resistance to legal reform in political cultures in which patronage, clientelism, predatory rule and circumventions of the law are institutionalized, and when judges and politicians fear that past corruption will be disclosed and punished. Interest groups may have stronger incentives to push for social and economic reforms than to agitate for the protection of judicial independence. Civil society groups cannot be guaranteed to support reform since they are often more involved in partisan and ideological conflict and competition with each other and with state institutions. Public demand has rarely initiated reform, public dissatisfaction with the judicial system has never directed the course of reform, and the involvement of the public in reform efforts has been minimal.

Lawyers themselves may be neither sufficiently powerful nor motivated to promote judicial independence. Judges may find it difficult to resist the influence of powerful economic and political interests, including their own class or corporate values and preferences. Judges play a part in judicial reform as members of informal judicial networks based on ideology, political interests, social class, kinship, professional relationships within the judiciary, cultural identity, religion and patron–client obligations. Such connections 'reflect different types of intrapersonal dynamics, such as individual benefits, ideational affinities, identity, authority, loyalty and reciprocity' (Dressel et al. 2018: 576). The power of judicial networks depends on size of membership, resources, leadership and level of judicial hierarchy of which they are a part. Judicial networks may be loyal to the executive, giving them protection against discipline for misbehaviour, as in Ukraine, where lobbying and resistance by collectives of judges on the appointment of court presidents, lustration and the evaluation of judges 'generated intra-judicial conflict and enabled or obstructed these judicial reforms' (Trochev 2018: 676). Such conflict within judicial networks has also been observed in Taiwan, where the legal profession, previously united in defiance of authoritarian control, became divided under democracy over judicial reform to transform the judiciary's infrastructure and protect human rights. Different sections of the judiciary – lawyers, judges and prosecutors – had different policies on judicial accountability and restructuring of the criminal appeals system, showing that 'as the legal complex enters a democratic system, internal differences surface quickly, and conflicts become concrete' (Hsu 2021: 279).

Legislators have stronger incentives to by-pass the judiciary than to support its independence, and governments may feel that the judiciary is blocking policies arrived at democratically and usurping the power of parliament. Changes in political leadership can reduce levels of political support for reform, as has happened in Bangladesh. Often the resources and presence of foreign aid donors have had to substitute for political will (raising questions about how lasting the reforms will be). The new Bulgarian Cabinet promised a new strategy of judicial reform in 2014 among doubts about its willingness to challenge the status quo.

Because of the powerful political interests at stake, and despite assistance from donors, legal systems have not been reformed enough in many transitional countries to fulfil the requirements of judicial independence and the rule of law. For example, in Russia judges and court officials still receive poor salaries and inadequate education and training. Consequently, incompetence among judges and prosecutors, and corruption (especially in the provinces and ethnic republics) persist. There is conflict between laws or judicial procedures on the one hand and the Constitution or the new Criminal-Procedural Code on the other. Undue influence is exerted by government authorities over court decisions, all leading to 'the deeply cynical view of the legal system held by millions of Russians' (Aron 2002: 10).

Reform is further politicized when barriers to justice are caused by poverty. Access to justice then becomes a social and political problem that can only be solved by a willing government. It is up to society to hold political leaders accountable for their failures to address poverty and inequality. Most of the measures required to remove barriers to justice for the poor – affordable legal representation, stronger anti-discrimination legislation, responsible policing, stronger rights for women and other disadvantaged groups, wider dissemination of legal information, and more accessible procedures – depend upon government action supported by civil society through bar associations, legal advocacy and monitoring, trade unions, and educational institutions (UNDP 2004).

The trend towards authoritarianism in transitional states has meant that changes to the judiciary have been in pursuit of political control over the judiciary by the executive, rather than stronger judicial independence and democratization. In 2016 the Albanian parliament approved a number of reforms designed to strengthen the independence of the judiciary, but implementation has been slow, despite their importance in the country's bid to join the EU. Changes to the judiciary in Poland in 2017 increased executive control and politicization rather than independence. Bulgaria's judiciary, which has benefited from reforms required by EU membership, is still subject to politicization. Since taking office in 2019, the president of Argentina has initiated 'reforms' which diminish judicial independence, including increasing the number of federal courts in Buenos Aires and creating new tribunals, allowing the president and Peronist-controlled Senate to appoint many new judges, and reducing the influence of the Supreme Court. Overall, less progress has been made in judicial reform in transitional democracies than in any other area of institutional development (Beers 2016).

* * *

This chapter examined reforms which address problems of judicial capacity, biased proceedings, biased judges and corruption. These are the obstacles to independent judicial decision-making that arise from within the judiciary itself, rather than other parts of the political system. Judicial capacity-building requires the design of politically neutral methods of evaluating performance by objective criteria, free from unwarranted external political influence. Capacity-building also includes the modernization of judicial institutions, especially courts, to increase efficiency in the processing of cases and to reduce the delays which feed public dissatisfaction with the judiciary. Training for judicial personnel, especially judges, court officials and public prosecutors, also features among law reforms designed to strengthen judicial capacity.

Biased proceedings violate the right to a fair trial. The major areas of concern in transitional states are the need for information about basic legal rights and the ability of people brought before the courts to understand the proceedings. Trial by jury is widely regarded as contributing to public confidence in the justice system as well as support for democracy itself. However, experience of jury trials varies greatly from one post-authoritarian country to another, generating conflicting views on this method of participatory justice.

A controversial method of dealing with judicial bias carrying over from the pre-democratic regime is 'lustration'. Many risks are associated with this policy. The method for dealing with bias on the part of individual judges that is most consistent with the rule of law is a system of appeals. However, it is possible to require judges to declare personal interests in a case before standing down or to be prohibited from holding other public offices or being members of political organizations. National codes of conduct or judicial ethics also assist in ensuring judges act and decide fairly.

Judicial corruption raises exceptionally difficult problems because the judiciary is intrinsic to the eradication of corruption generally. The prevention of corruption can also be an opportunity for political interference. Anti-corruption measures fall into two broad categories: first, the socio-political, requiring civil society to scrutinize and monitor the judiciary, and the judiciary to be transparent and open to public scrutiny. Improving the transparency of the judicial process rests on the publication of performance measures, explicit anti-corruption rules, the monitoring of anti-corruption strategies, freedom of information laws, independent anti-corruption agencies and stronger incentives for judges to behave honestly and professionally. The second type of reform is institutional, which changes the environment within which the judiciary functions to make corruption more dangerous and costly for those who seek to benefit from it. However, judicial reform is ultimately a political rather than a technical process because it affects the distribution of power between state institutions (the executive, legislative and judicial branches of government) and between political interests and social strata.

Many of the reforms enacted during the transition from authoritarianism have changed the organizational management of the judiciary in order to make the judiciary independent of other government powers. Although there have been certain features adopted by many transitional constitutions, especially the appointment of judicial councils with powers of judicial management, the organizational structures adopted for the judiciaries of transitional democracies are highly varied. While not every judiciary is sui generis, it is not easy to distinguish self-contained models of judicial administration among which all judicial systems can be allocated, as the next chapter shows.

References

Albert, R., J. Z. Benvindo, K. Rado and F. Zhilla (2017), 'Constitutional reform in Brazil: lessons from Albania?', Boston College Law School Legal Studies Research Paper No. 453.

Anderson, J. H. and C. W. Gray (2007), *Transforming Judicial Systems in Europe and Central Asia*, Washington: World Bank.

Armytage, L. (2015), 'Educating judges: where to from here?', *Journal of Dispute Resolution*, vol. 2015, no. 1.

Aron, L. (2002), 'Russia reinvents the rule of law', *AEI Russian Outlook*, Spring.

Beers, D. J. (2016), 'Judicial reform in comparative perspective: assessing the prospects for Ukraine' in H. E. Hale and R. W. Orttung (eds.), *Beyond the Euromaidan: Comparative Perspectives on Advancing Reform in Ukraine*, Stanford: Stanford University Press.

Bencze, M. and G. Y. Ng (2018), 'Measuring the unmeasurable?' in M. Bencze and G. Y. Ng (eds.), *How to Measure the Quality of Judicial Reasoning*, Cham: Springer.

Berenschot, W. and T. Rinaldi (2018), 'Paralegalism in Indonesia: balancing relationships in the shadow of the law' in V. Maru and V. Gauri (eds.), *Community Paralegals and the Pursuit of Justice*, Cambridge: Cambridge University Press.

Biebesheimer, C. and J. M. Payne (2001), *IDB Experience in Justice Reform: Lessons Learned and Elements for Policy Formation*, Washington: Inter-American Development Bank, 2000.

Bohlander, M. (2021), 'Commodification of justice: a personal view on managerial performance indicators in the judicial context' in S. Shetreet, H. Chodosh and H. Eric (eds.), *Challenged Justice: In Pursuit of Judicial Independence*, Leiden: Brill and Nijhoff.

Bumin, K. M. (2015), 'Determinants of judicial institutionalization: a study of the post-communist constitutional courts', *Journal of Power, Politics & Governance*, vol. 3, no. 1.

Carothers, T. (1998), 'The rule of law revival', *Foreign Affairs*, vol. 77, no. 2.

Carson, L. (2015), 'Institutional specialisation in the battle against corruption: Uganda's anti-corruption court' in *The Public Sphere: 2015 LSE Africa Summit*, London: London School of Economics.

CCEJ (2008), *Opinion No. 11 (2008) of the Consultative Council of European Judges to the Attention of the Committee of Ministers of the Council of Europe on the Quality of Judicial Decisions*, Strasbourg: Consultative Council of European Judges.

CCEJ (2011), *Justice and Information Technologies (IT)*, Opinion No. 14, Strasbourg: CCJE.

CEPEJ (2014), *European Judicial Systems: Efficiency and Quality of Justice*, Strasbourg: European Commission for the Efficiency of Justice.

Council of Europe (2013), *Enhancing Judicial Reform in the Eastern Partnership Countries*, Working Group on Efficient Judicial Systems, Directorate General of Human Rights and Rule of Law, Strasbourg: Council of Europe.

Dancer, H. (2018), 'Power and rights in the community: paralegals as leaders in women's legal empowerment in Tanzania', *Feminist Legal Studies*, vol. 26, no. 1.

Davis, F. and S. Tyulkina (2014), 'Terrorism and trial by jury in Russia', *Vienna Journal of International Constitutional Law*, vol. 8, no. 1.

Desai, D., R. Wagner and M. Woolcock (2014), 'The missing middle: reconfiguring rule of law reform as if politics and process mattered', *Hague Journal on the Rule of Law*, vol. 6, no. 2.

Dimitrova-Grajzla, V., P. Grajzlb, A. Slavovd and K. Zajoe (2016), 'Courts in a transition economy: case disposition and the quantity-quality trade-off in Bulgaria', *Economic Systems*, vol. 40, no. 1.
Dodson, J. M. and D. W. Jackson (2001), 'Judicial independence and instability in Central America' in P. H. Russell and D. M. O'Brien (eds.), *Judicial Independence in the Age of Democracy*, Charlottesville: University Press of Virginia.
Doig, A. (1995), 'Good government and sustainable anti-corruption strategies: a role for independent anti-corruption agencies?', *Public Administration and Development*, vol. 15, no. 2.
Doig, A. and Riley, S. (1998), 'Corruption and anti-corruption strategies: issues and case studies from developing countries' in UNDP/OECD Development Centre, *Corruption and Integrity Improvement Initiatives in Developing Countries*, New York: UNDP.
Dressel, B., R. Sanchez-Urribarri and A. Stroh (2018), 'Courts and informal networks: towards a relational perspective on judicial politics outside Western democracies', *International Political Science Review*, vol. 39, no. 5.
EC (2014a), *Serbia Progress Report*, Brussels: European Commission.
EC (2014b), *Slovakia Annex to the EU Anti-Corruption Report*, Annex 25, 3 March, Brussels: European Commission.
EC (2020), *Albania 2020 Report*, Commission Staff Working Document 354, Brussels: European Commission.
Erebara, G. (2020), 'Albania opposition claims new justice inspector is "PM's servant"', *Balkan Insight*, 21 January.
Faundez, J. (1997), 'Legal technical assistance' in J. Faundez (ed.), *Good Government and Law: Legal and Institutional Reform in Developing Countries*, London: Macmillan.
Fortes, P. R. B. (2015), 'How legal indicators influence a justice system and judicial behaviour: The Brazilian National Council of Justice and justice in numbers', *The Journal of Legal Pluralism and Unofficial Law*, vol. 47, no. 1.
Freedom House (2012), *Nations in Transit 2012: Georgia*, New York: Freedom House.
Freedom House (2015a), *Nations in Transit 2015*, New York: Freedom House.
Freedom House (2015b), *Nations in Transit 2015: Croatia*, New York: Freedom House.
Freedom House (2015c), *Nations in Transit 2015: Latvia*, New York: Freedom House.
Freedom House (2021), *Freedom in the World 2021, Countries and Territories*, New York: Freedom House, https://freedomhouse.org/countries/freedom-world/scores
Fukurai, H. et al. (2011), 'Introduction to the special issue: the future of lay adjudication and theorizing today's resurgence of civic, legal participatory systems in East and Central Asia', *International Journal of Law, Crime and Justice*, vol. 38, no. 4.
Garoupa, N. and T. Ginsburg (2015), *Judicial Reputation: A Comparative Theory*, Chicago: University of Chicago Press.
Gillespie, K. and Okruhlik, G. (1991), 'The political dimensions of corruption cleanups: A framework for analysis', *Comparative Politics*, vol. 24, no. 1.
Goebel, C. (2016), 'Taiwan's fight against corruption', *Journal of Democracy*, vol. 27, no. 1.
Gomes, A. O., S. T. Alves and J. T. Silva (2018), 'Effects of investment in information and communication technologies on productivity of courts in Brazil', *Government Information Quarterly*, vol. 35, no. 3.
Goodwin, L. and V. Maru (2017), 'What do we know about legal empowerment? Mapping the evidence', *Hague Journal on the Rule of Law*, vol. 9, no. 1.
Goshovska, V., V. Goshovskyi and L. Dubchak (2020), 'The implementation of state policy of power cleaning in the conditions of political transformation: experience of Ukraine

and countries of Central and Eastern Europe', *European Journal of Sustainable Development*, vol. 9, no. 2.

Grimes, R. (2018), 'Evaluating legal literacy programmes: aims, challenges, models and a call to action', *International Journal of Public Legal Education*, vol. 2, no. 1.

Guardian (2004), 'Nigeria launches anti-graft campaign', 24 January.

Hammergren, L. (2000), *The Multilateral Development Banks and Judicial Corruption*, Washington: The World Bank.

Heywood, P. (1997), 'Political corruption: problems and perspectives', *Political Studies*, vol. 45, no. 3.

Horne, C. M. (2017), 'Transitional justice: vetting and lustration' in C. Lawther, L. Moffett and D. Jacobs (eds.), *Research Handbook on Transitional Justice*, Cheltenham: Edward Elgar.

Hrle, M. S. (2016), 'Building the rule of law: judicial reform in Bosnia and Herzegovina' in S. Keil and V. Perry (eds.), *State-Building and Democratization in Bosnia and Herzegovina*, Abingdon: Routledge.

Hsu, C.-f. (2021), 'The legal complex fractured: legal professional coalition and collision in Taiwan's judicial reform', *Law and Policy*, vol. 43, no. 3.

Hussmann, K., H. Hechler and M. Peñailillo (2009), *Institutional Arrangements for Corruption Prevention: Considerations for the Implementation of the United Nations Convention against Corruption, Article 6*, Anti-Corruption Resource Centre, Bergen: Chr. Michelsen Institute.

Iancu, B. (2010), 'Post-accession constitutionalism with a human face: judicial reform and lustration in Romania', *European Constitutional Law Review*, vol. 6, no. 1.

ILAC (2011), *Report of the Pre-Assessment Mission, Libya*, Stockholm: International Legal Assistance Consortium.

Issacharoff, S. (2011), 'Constitutional courts and democratic hedging', *The Georgetown Law Journal*, vol. 99, no. 4.

Ivkovic, K. et al. (2021), 'Introduction' in K. Ivkovic, S. S. Diamond, V. P. Hans and N. S. Marder (eds.), *Juris, Lay Judges and Mixed Courts: A Global Perspective*, Cambridge: Cambridge University Press.

Jaroszewicz, M. and P. Zochowski (2015), 'Combating corruption in Ukraine: The beginning of a long march', OSW (Centre for Eastern Studies) Commentary, No. 170.

Jelić, I. and D. Kapetanakis (2021), 'European judicial supervision of the rule of law: the protection of the independence of national judges by the CJEU and the ECtHR', *Hague Journal on the Rule of Law*, vol. 13, no. 1.

Kim, S. et al. (2013), 'Judge-jury agreement in criminal cases: the first three years of the Korean jury system', *Journal of Empirical Legal Studies*, vol. 10, no. 1.

Kovalev, N. and G. Suleymenova (2010), 'New Kazakhstani quasi-jury system: challenges, trends and reforms', *International Journal of Law, Crime and Justice*, vol. 38, no. 4.

Kühn, Z. (2018), 'The quality of justice and of judicial reasoning in the Czech Republic' in M. Bencze and G. Y. Ng (eds.), *How to Measure the Quality of Judicial Reasoning*, Cham: Springer.

Langseth, P. and O. Stolpe (2001), *Strengthening Judicial Integrity Against Corruption*, Vienna: United Nations Centre for International Crime Prevention.

Larkins, C. M. (1996), 'Judicial independence and democratization: a theoretical and conceptual analysis', *American Journal of Comparative Law*, vol. 44, no. 4.

Lazzari, J. (2019), 'For an effective training of magistrates', *University of Bologna Law Review*, vol. 4, no. 1.

Lee, J.-H. (2009), 'Getting citizens involved: civil participation in judicial decision-making in Korea', *East Asian Law Review*, vol. 4, no. 2.

Lee, J.-H. (2010), 'Korean jury trial: has the new system brought about changes?', *Asian-Pacific Law & Policy Journal*, vol. 12, no. 1.

Lee, T. (2015), 'Rebuilding judicial ethics and Independence: a comparative analysis of the Cambodian Code of Ethics for Judges and Prosecutors', *Georgetown Journal of Legal Ethics*, vol. 28, no. 3.

Lothian, T. (2003), *The FUSADES Strategy for El Salvador: Priority Areas for Judicial Reform and the Problem of Corruption*, San Salvador: FUSADES.

Marciano, A., A. Melcarne and G. B. Ramello (2019), 'The economic importance of judicial institutions, their performance and the proper way to measure them', *Journal of Institutional Economics*, vol. 15, no. 1.

Maru, V. and V. Gauri (2018), 'Paralegals in comparative perspective: what have we learned across these six countries?' in V. Maru and V. Gauri (eds.), *Community Paralegals and the Pursuit of Justice*, Cambridge: Cambridge University Press.

Mendelski, M. (2016), 'The EU's rule of law promotion in central and eastern Europe: where and why does it fail, and what can be done about it?', Global Rule of Law Exchange Papers, London: Bingham Centre for the Rule of Law.

Mulholland, J. (2021), 'Indonesia's corruption eradication commission in dire straits', *East Asia Forum*, vol. 13, no. 1.

Open Society Institute (2002), *Monitoring the EU Accession Process: Judicial Capacity*, New York: Open Society Foundations.

Partohap, T. H. and R. Pradiptyo (2015), 'Who cares of anti-corruption agency? An assessment of court decisions for corruption cases in Indonesia using proportional hazard model', SSRN: http://ssrn.com/abstract=2593384

Pepys, M. N. (2007), 'Corruption within the judiciary: causes and remedies' in *Transparency International, Global Corruption Report 2007, Corruption in Judicial Systems*, Cambridge: Cambridge University Press.

Pérez-Liñán, A. and A. Castagnola (2016), 'Judicial instability and endogenous constitutional change: lessons from Latin America', *British Journal of Political Science*, vol. 46, no. 2.

PILNET (2003), *Access to Justice in Central and Eastern and Central Europe*, Budapest: Public Interest Law Initiative; London: Interights; Sofia: Bulgarian Helsinki Committee; Warsaw: Polish Helsinki Committee for Human Rights.

Plotkin, S. R. (1994), 'The jury trial in Russia', *Tulane Journal of International and Comparative Law*, vol. 2, no. 1.

Popova, M (2014), 'Ukraine's legal problems: why Kiev's plans to purge the judiciary will backfire', *Foreign Affairs*, vol. 93, no. 2.

Quah, J. S. T. (1995), 'Controlling corruption in city states: a comparative study of Hong Kong and Singapore', *Crime, Law and Social Change*, vol. 22, no. 3.

Quah, J. S. T. (2002), 'Responses to corruption in Asian societies' in A. J. Heidenheimer and M. Johnston (eds.), *Political Corruption: Concepts and Contexts*, New Brunswick, NJ: Transaction Publishers.

Rostovschikov, I. V., I. A. Aleshkova and O. K. Molokaeva (2019), 'Judiciary power and information society: new approaches and opportunities' in E. G. Popkova (ed.), *Ubiquitous Computing and the Internet of Things: Prerequisites for the Development of ICT*, Cham: Springer.

Sagiv, M. (2015), 'Cultural bias in judicial decision making', *Boston College Journal of Law and Social Policy*, vol. 35, no. 2.

Sanchez, M. C. M. (2021), 'Training judges in judicial ethics and conduct against corruption: a priority for judiciaries', United Nations Office on Drugs and Crime, www.unodc.org/dohadeclaration/en/news/2021/08

Sandoval-Almazan, R. and J. R. Gil-Garcia (2018), 'Understanding e-justice and open justice through the assessment of judicial websites: toward a conceptual framework', *Social Science Computer Review*, vol. 38, no. 3.
Sheyn, E. R. (2010), 'A foothold for real democracy in Eastern Europe: how instituting jury trials in Ukraine can bring about meaningful governmental and juridical reforms and can help spread these reforms across Eastern Europe', *Vanderbilt Journal of Transnational Law*, vol. 43, 649.
Shkuta, O. O. (2020), 'Scientific and theoretical foundations of information support for administrative legal proceedings in Ukraine' in V. M. Halunko et al. (eds.), *Jurisprudence and Fundamentals of Legal Behaviour in Modern Civil Society*, Lviv: Liha Press Publishers.
Siyo, L. and J. C. Mubangizi (2015), 'The independence of South African judges: a constitutional and legislative perspective', *Potchefstroom Electronic Law Journal*, vol. 18, no. 4.
Skidmore, M. J. (1996), 'Promise and peril in combating corruption: Hong Kong's ICAC', *Annals of the American Academy of Political Science*, No. 547.
Stewart, S. (2016), 'The rule of law in contemporary Ukraine: widespread elite failure puts reforms at risk', SWP Comments 10/2016, Berlin: German Institute for International and Security Affairs, http://nbn-resolving.de/urn:nbn:de:0168-ssoar-464314
Susanto, E. M. (2020), 'E-court as the efforts of pressing the potential of corruption', *Yustisia*, vol. 9, no. 1.
Tanzi, V. (1998), 'Corruption around the world: Causes, consequences, scope and cures', *IMF Staff Papers*, vol. 45, no. 4.
The Economist (2009), *The Jury Is Out*, London: The Economist Newspaper Ltd.
TI (2007a), *Combating Corruption in Judicial Systems*, Berlin: Transparency International.
TI (2007b), "Radical surgery" in Kenya's judiciary' in *Transparency International, Global Corruption Report 2007: Corruption in Judicial Systems*, Cambridge: Cambridge University Press.
TI Georgia (2010), *Refreshing Georgia's Courts: Trial by Jury: More Democracy or a Face-lift for the Judiciary?*, Tbilisi: Transparency International.
Trebilcock, M. J. and R. J. Daniels (2008), *Rule of Law Reform and Development: Charting the Fragile Path of Progress*, Cheltenham: Edward Elgar.
Trochev, A. (2018), 'Patronal politics, judicial networks and collective judicial autonomy in post-Soviet Ukraine', *International Political Science Review*, vol. 39, no. 5.
UN (2017), *Language Rights of Linguistic Minorities*, Geneva: Office of the High Commissioner for Human Rights.
UNDP (1997), *Corruption and Good Governance*, Discussion Paper No. 3, New York: United Nations Development Programme.
UNDP (2004), *Access to Justice*, New York: United Nations Development Programme.
UNDP (2013), *Strengthening Judicial Integrity Through Enhanced Access to Justice*, New York: United Nations Development Programme Regional Centre for Europe and the CIS.
Urban, M. and T. Friedel (2019), 'Ten years of Prague street law: lessons to learn from our first decade', *International Journal of Clinical Legal Education*, vol. 26, no. 3.
Venice Commission (2014), *Interim Opinion on the Law on Government Cleansing (Lustration Law) of Ukraine*, Opinion no. 788/2014, Strasbourg: European Commission for Democracy Through Law.
Wittrup, J. (2006), 'Analysis of the system for measuring and monitoring judicial performance in Romania', www.csm1909.ro/csm/linkuri/14_02_2011__39242_ro.pdf

WJP (2016), *Judicial Corruption Monitoring in Indonesia through Legal Clinics*, Washington: World Justice Project.
World Bank (2012), *Initiatives in Justice Reform 1992–2012*, Washington: World Bank.
World Bank (2016), 'Performance measures topic brief', www.worldbank.org/WBSITE/EXTERNAL/TOPICS/EXTLAWJUSTINST.

7 Managing the judiciary

Introduction

The management of the judiciary raises complex questions about the role of different institutions and how their involvement can be made compatible with judicial independence and the rule of law. The underlying problem is that some involvement of politicians in managing the judicial branch of government is unavoidable. Senior judges have to be appointed and expenditure on the judiciary – its personnel, buildings and supporting facilities – approved. The judicial branch cannot be totally isolated from the other branches of government. So a crucial constitutional question is how legislative or executive involvement can be made compatible with judicial independence.

The transition from authoritarianism to democracy has produced highly variable models of judicial administration. This is despite the fact that all constitutions aim to make the judiciary politically independent. One approach is to think of management as arranged along a continuum. At one end is judicial self-management where the management of the judiciary is dominated by a separate body of lawyers chosen from a group elected by their peers, and entrusted with the appointment, promotion, relocation and disciplining of judges, and the management of the judicial branch. The Romanian Superior Council of the Magistracy (SCM) is one example and the Hungarian National Council of Justice another. At the other end of the continuum power to administer the judiciary is assigned to the executive branch of government. The Czech Republic comes close to this position.

However, the picture is complicated by the varying degrees of responsibility allocated to the executive, and the involvement of the legislative branch, meaning that it is necessary to examine the part played by each of the constitutional branches in order to identify any threats that might emerge to judicial independence. Every judiciary is unique in the form and extent of involvement by the executive, legislature and judiciary, meaning that no system can be placed at the extremities of the continuum. In the judiciaries of transitional states there is mixed responsibility for their management: '[A] number of models for the governance of the magistracy can be used, and the new democracies have available to them a number of alternatives. In fact, this explains the variety of solutions actually chosen' (Bartole 1998: 9).

This chapter examines the management of the judiciary through judicial councils, their composition and powers. It asks how the funding of the judiciary can be

DOI: 10.4324/9781003334613-8

made compatible with judicial independence. The risks attendant upon judicial self-management are explored. The executive model of management is examined to see whether this poses a threat to judicial independence. The management of the judiciary is never concentrated in a single institution, so it is necessary to ask what role other parts of the state, especially legislatures, play and how far this involvement can be made compatible with judicial independence.

Judicial self-management

The delegation of administrative powers to the judiciary itself has been a common reaction to concerns about political interference in the judicial process. Examples include Poland's National Judicial Council, established in 1989 and empowered to make binding recommendations on judicial appointments to the president; and Argentina's Council of Magistrates, one of the constitutional reforms of 1994. Indonesia's Judicial Commission was established by a constitutional amendment in 2001. Latvia created a judicial council (the High Council of Justice) in 2010. It has encouraged judicial officers to take new initiatives and innovations to speed up the judicial process such as processing small claims by correspondence and using notaries to settle uncontested divorces.

Judicial councils are seen as a solution to the lack of independence of the judiciary from ministries of justice. This is reflected in the declaration of the European Network of Councils for the Judiciary (ENCJ) that the protection of judicial independence needs a properly functioning council 'to consider and determine or to make recommendations to government on all matters relevant to judicial remuneration and conditions. It is the essential task of the ENCJ and all Councils for the Judiciary to maintain and strengthen the independence of the Judiciary, especially when it is threatened' (ENCJ 2013: 2). The ENCJ has produced guidance on the principles which should govern the status, composition, structure, competencies, duties, funding and accountability of judicial councils in order to ensure their independence, effectiveness and efficiency (ENCJ 2021).

For example, judicial independence in Romania was a major cause of concern as membership of the European Union approached. In 2003, a joint committee of the Romanian and European parliaments expressed concerns about 'protests from legal circles regarding undue political pressure on judges and prosecutors and interference by the executive in the justice system' (EU-Romania Joint Parliamentary Committee 2003: 4). The committee identified a need for improvements in the transparency of judicial recruitment and selection, procedures for the dismissal and disciplining of judges, and the training of magistrates, clerks and other legal professionals. In 2004 the Romanian Superior Council of the Magistracy was restructured in order to secure its independence from the executive branch.

Judicial self-management is designed to combine autonomy from the executive with a degree of accountability through the members who are not judges.

Management by judicial council should leave judges independent, immovable and legally protected from improper influences. Arbitrary decision-making about how the judiciary is managed becomes more difficult, and impartiality is strengthened. Cases will be distributed randomly, again protecting the integrity of judges and the fairness of trials.

The composition of judicial councils varies greatly from one country to another. Membership is generally defined to ensure the independence of the judiciary from the other branches of government, but it is nevertheless common to find both executive and legislature represented to some degree. For example, the Romanian Council has 14 members chosen by parliament from a list of 45 elected by their peers, two elected by the Romanian Senate from among experienced lawyers from civil society organizations, and three are ex officio: the minister of justice, the general prosecutor and the president of the High Court. In contrast, Brazil's National Council of Justice has no ex officio members, being composed of nine judges, two public prosecutors (one federal, one state), two lawyers appointed by the Federal Council of the Brazilian Bar Association, and two citizens of 'notable juridical learning and spotless reputation', one appointed by the Chamber of Deputies and the other appointed by the Federal Senate. South Africa's Judicial Service Commission has only three judges among its 23 members. The others are advocates, attorneys, members of the National Assembly, a teacher of law, four members of the National Council of Provinces, the minister of justice and four persons designated by the president after consulting the leaders of all the parties in the National Assembly. It was originally intended that Tunisia's Supreme Judicial Council would be appointed by the head of state, but this was changed so that a majority of the members will be elected by the judges themselves, thereby, it is hoped, preserving judicial independence.

Judicial self-management always involves collaboration with other branches of government. For example, in Bulgaria the chairs of the Supreme Court of Cassation (the country's final court of appeal) and Supreme Administrative Court, as well as the chief prosecutor are appointed and dismissed by the president, albeit on a motion from the Supreme Judicial Council. The Albanian Ministry of Justice provides an inspection service in parallel to that carried out by the High Council of Justice, and the Minister sits on the HCJ with the power to initiate, though not vote on, disciplinary proceedings against judges. In Romania the Superior Council of the Magistracy is elected for a term of four years by the Chamber of Deputies and the Senate in joint session. The Romanian minister of justice presides over council meetings but without voting rights. In Lithuania, the majority of members of the Council of Courts are representatives of judges, but the nine ex-officio members include representatives of the president and chairman of parliament, the ministers of Justice and Finance, and the chairs of parliament's legal and budget committees. In Georgia the chairman and other Supreme Court judges are appointed for a term of ten years by a majority vote in parliament, upon nomination by the president. The Constitutional Court judges are selected by all branches of government, with the president, parliament and Supreme Court each appointing three judges. No judiciary is entirely self-governing.

It is generally felt to be right that the membership of judicial councils should be drawn from all parts of the judiciary. However, this diverse membership can produce conflicts of interest. Judicial councils can become arenas for internal power struggles, as between judges and prosecutors in Romania's SCM, with politicians becoming heavily involved (Freedom House 2015b). Councils may become dominated by the heads of the courts that they are meant to supervise. Holding dual offices was upheld by the Romanian Constitutional Court, enabling control of the SCM to be concentrated in the hands of senior, conservative judges. A council's membership may include groups subordinate to the Ministry of Justice, such as the prosecutors on the SCM. Consequently, a formal transfer of power over the appointment of judges from the Ministry to the Council 'risks making little actual change in practice' (Freedom House 2004: 14; EU Commission 2006).

The powers delegated to judicial councils also vary a great deal, ranging from appointments to the bench to administrative responsibility for the entire judiciary, including in the Hungarian case the submission of budget proposals to the government and accountability for expenditure. Powers sometimes extend to the whole judiciary and sometimes only to lower courts. Nigeria's National Judicial Council only supervises federal courts. The Romanian Superior Council of the Magistracy is charged with the tasks of defending the impartiality and independence of the judiciary, and protecting its professional reputation by ensuring that legislation affecting the judiciary is consistent with its professional and ethical standards (e.g. in 2006 it proposed amendments to the legislation on the disciplining of judges).

The powers of judicial councils may extend to the appointment, promotion, rotation, periodic evaluation, and dismissal of judges, investigators, and prosecutors; and the resolution of disciplinary matters. A council may have the responsibility of proposing a draft budget for the judiciary to the legislature, initiating organizational changes within national judicial institutions, and managing the property and other assets of judicial institutions, as in Bulgaria where, before the Constitutional amendment of 2015, these were functions of the Ministry of Justice (Library of Congress 2015). Some have advisory roles in policy-making for judicial reform. Tunisia's Supreme Judicial Council can advise law-makers on any reforms that concern the judiciary. A council may be empowered to change its own procedures in the interest of judicial independence by, for example, introducing new rules to prevent council members from voting on disciplinary matters affecting their own court or by adopting more objective criteria for the promotion of judges.

In addition, the different political environments in which councils operate lead to different degrees of importance being attached to independence and accountability. The legal environment – whether based on civil or common law traditions – is a further variable (Autheman and Elena 2004). Legal origin also varies, with some councils enshrined in the constitution while the composition and powers of others are defined in ordinary legislation. This distinction appears to be significant for judicial independence, whether or not councils are a response to demands for accountability or for stronger independence. Those owing their origins to ordinary statute appear to be more vulnerable to political interference than those which are 'constitutionalized' (Garoupa and Ginsburg 2015). Such variation in composition, powers and constitutional status makes it very difficult to identify patterns of causal relationships between the existence of councils and the performance of the judiciary.

Funding the judiciary

Self-governing bodies also have varying levels of involvement in funding decisions for the judiciary. It is generally accepted as a matter of principle that the funding of the judiciary should not be determined by political considerations and that neither the executive nor the legislature should use budgets to exert pressure on the judiciary. This may be taken to imply that the involvement of self-governing judicial bodies in both the drafting of budgets and negotiations with government and parliament 'is a pre-requisite to ensuring judicial institutional independence' (Council of Europe 2011: 30). Consequently, it is widely accepted that self-managing bodies should have a role in state budgeting for the judiciary. A key factor in judicial management is the way the budget for the judiciary is formulated. How courts are funded has implications for both judicial independence and the right to fair proceedings conducted within a reasonable time frame.

The challenge for new democracies here is to turn what is unavoidably a political process into one that is a-political. On the one hand, funding for the judiciary is part of the state's overall budgetary process which entails negotiations between the ministries of justice and finance, and the presentation of a budget to the legislature by the executive. The level of funding for the courts is inevitably a political decision. On the other hand, the politics involved must somehow avoid compromising judicial independence. Ideally the funding of courts should not be subject to political fluctuations. The separation of powers demands that 'neither the executive nor the legislative authorities are able to exert any pressure on the judiciary when setting its budget. Decisions on the allocation of funds to the courts must be taken with the strictest respect for judicial independence' (CCJE 2001: para. 5).

Different solutions to the problem of securing adequate funding while preserving judicial independence have been tried. All involve the judiciary itself to some extent. One method is to allow the Supreme Court to present the Ministry of Finance with a proposed budget, as in Slovenia. However, the influence exercised here by the Supreme Court is largely informal and arises from its detailed knowledge of the financial needs of different courts. The process has not protected the judiciary from austerity measures – including a reduction of funding of 7.5 per cent in 2013 – which threaten reforms designed to increase efficiency in the judicial system and reduce a backlog of cases regarded as unacceptably large, objectives which are both relevant to judicial independence.

Alternatively, the Constitution may specify a fixed percentage of the national budget to be allocated to the judiciary: for example, no less than 4 per cent of the General Budget of the Republic in Nicaragua and no less than 3 per cent of current revenues in Honduras. Countries also vary in terms of who provides the judiciary's budget, how the budget is negotiated and by whom, whether parts of the judicial budget are hypothecated, and how the judiciary is held accountable for its management of the budget (Rosselli 2020).

Judges may be given the right to take part in negotiations over the national budget in both executive and legislature, as in Russia. Here the chairpersons of the three high courts, and the Council of Russian Judges, participate in the drafting of the budget for the judiciary by the cabinet. Following any disagreement, the judiciary's figures have to be appended to the draft budget when it is presented to the federal parliament. Under the Law of the Russian Federation on the Judicial System the judiciary is entitled to be represented in the chambers of the Russian Federal Assembly when the federal budget is being discussed. The budget for the judiciary cannot be reduced without the consent of the All-Russia Congress of Judges or the Council of Judges, a right which has been upheld by the Constitutional Court in defence of judicial independence and constitutional rights (Popova 2012; Trochev 2008).

However, judicial councils have generally been allocated weak financial responsibilities. For example, in Armenia the judiciary's budget is drafted by the Ministry of Justice, and though approval is sought from the Council of Presidents of Courts, the Justice Council has no influence in the budgetary process. Georgia's Council of Justice approves a draft budget prepared by the Department of Common Courts, though 'the participation of the self-governing bodies of the judiciary in the later stages is curtailed considerably'. In a number of new democracies the judiciary has no formal role in the negotiations conducted by the Ministry of Justice to agree a budget for the judicial system. Croatia and Ukraine fall into this category. The Council of Europe found that in the East European countries it had investigated 'the judicial self-governing bodies are rather limited in terms of their capacity to present the budgetary needs of the judiciary to their governments and parliaments' and that the role of judicial self-governing bodies in the management of allocated funds should be enhanced to ensure that 'parliamentary adoption of budgets requires parliament to obtain the views of the judiciary' (Popova 2012: 33, 36).

Although there is no strong evidence that the greater the participation of the judiciary in the budgetary process, the more adequate the funding will be, current thinking nevertheless advocates procedures allowing the views of the judiciary to form part of the parliamentary procedure for adopting the state budget. Examples include allowing judicial councils, where they exist, to coordinate the courts' requests for funding and advise parliament or its relevant committee on the needs of the judiciary for material resources and staff. Transferring the right to present parliament with the budget for the judiciary from the Ministry of Justice to the Supreme Court can also enhance the judiciary's financial independence.

Risks of self-management

It has become clear that there are risks in seeking judicial independence through self-management. First, the constraints on behaviour consistent with autonomy (political connections and other behaviour that might cast doubts on their impartiality) are aimed at the judiciary, rather than the politicians who might seek to subvert their autonomy. This is because of the prevalence in post-authoritarian countries of justices who served the previous regime and whose decisions had been one way in which judicial independence had been compromised. In Romania, for example, a judge or prosecutor has to be a senior magistrate before being eligible for election to the SCM, and this, for a while, made it a conservative body, with some senior members closely associated with communist repression, and who in the past 'had yielded their independence to political or other interests' (OECD 2005: 23). In the longer term, restructuring the management of the judiciary may not be enough to end the habit of political interference that is strongly embedded in political and judicial cultures. It is significant in the case of European transitional countries that the European Court of Human Rights and the European Union have provided more pressures for the reform of judicial councils than domestic political forces (Freedom House 2005b). There is no conclusive evidence that assigning managerial functions to a judicial council has increased either the quality or the independence of the judiciary (Garoupa and Ginsburg 2015; Ortiz 2017).

Second, elections to judicial councils may become entangled with partisan conflict. Elections to Romania's SCM have occasionally come under political pressures which have deterred some magistrates from standing against more senior judges and prosecutors whose candidatures have received official support. Judicial councils only provide a convincing representation of the separation of powers when it becomes electorally damaging for an incumbent government to deploy these kinds of pressures.

Third, the delegation of judicial administration to councils of judges and magistrates raises concerns about the corporate strength of the judiciary, especially if there is a close political relationship between the executive and some members of the judiciary based on ideological identities and political interests. In Romania the SCM has become a body representative of the top management of the judiciary and 'a defender of corporate interests rather than a reformer and controller' (OECD 2005: 15). It has hired most of its staff from the Ministry of Justice. The independence of the SCM has not been matched with transparency and accountability, leading to political attacks on the judiciary, media scandals, conflicts between judges and prosecutors within the SCM, and a lack of public confidence. Consequently, the Romanian model of judicial self-government has not been sufficient to protect 'the true independence of the judiciary against repeated assaults from the political sphere' (Selejan-Guțan 2018: 1739)

The corporate influence of the judiciary can also slow down the pace of judicial reform because judicial self-management makes it more difficult for external influences to be brought to bear, as shown by the case of Indonesia. Furthermore, the corporate autonomy of the judiciary may serve to protected judges whose behaviour has been shown to be reprehensible, make the judiciary overly bureaucratic and secretive, and compromise the ability of a council to guarantee the judiciary's independence. Where the judiciary has an important share of management responsibilities there is also the risk that its elitist and conservative social background may bias its advice and recommendations (Vyas 1992: 142). Management by judicial councils has not always led to greater efficiency, transparency and justice and probably requires the development of a stronger culture of justice than is found in many transitional states (Bobek and Kosar 2015).

Fourth, if a council tries to act as a check on the corporate strength of the judiciary, self-management may face opposition from within the judiciary itself. The creation of Brazil's National Council of Justice in 2005 encountered considerable opposition from a judiciary that was used to handling disciplinary matters internally. The Brazilian Judges' Association claimed the Council was unconstitutional. Reform had been motivated by the feeling that the corporate power of the judiciary was too great when investigating and disciplining justices for wrongdoing such as corruption, selling verdicts or diverting public funds to local masonic lodges. It was also very difficult to register complaints against the way judges managed the judicial process. Despite the fact that the Council is dominated by judges and prosecutors, with only two lawyers appointed by the bar association, and two from academia, one appointed by the Chamber of Deputies and the other by the Federal Senate, and is presided over by the Chief Justice of the Federal Supreme Court, some sections of the judiciary still considered the Council to represent excessive intervention in the control of judicial behaviour. The Council had been quick to block nepotism in the judiciary by requiring the relatives of judges to leave judicial office and by prohibiting relatives from selling goods or services to courts within the jurisdiction of family members (OECD 2012).

The Latvian judiciary's opposition to the creation of a judicial council included a number of Supreme Court justices who argued that giving senior judges the task of evaluating the performance of junior colleagues would inhibit the latter from acting freely, rather than in fear of repercussions from higher levels in the judiciary.

In a number of countries a minority of judges – 3 per cent in Poland, 15 per cent in Bulgaria, for example – feel that self-government has failed to achieve its main objective, namely protect judicial independence. This does not appear to be related to the strength of judicial councils. In Bulgaria a powerful council attracts distrust among a section of the judiciary, while in Slovakia and Poland the judicial councils are relatively weak yet not thought to have endangered judicial independence. Romania, Lithuania and Slovenia have powerful councils but low levels of concern about judicial independence. Concerns about judicial independence are highest where the judiciary is tainted by corruption, and it is thought that powerful judicial councils have prevented other branches of government, as well as the judiciary itself, from conducting effective anti-corruption campaigns. However, it is also acknowledged that weak councils are unlikely to be able to prevent incursions into judicial independence by the executive branch, as in Poland (Ortiz 2017).

The executive model of management

Towards the other end of the management continuum the power to administer the judiciary is largely assigned to the executive branch, perhaps counterbalanced by the recognition of special personal rights granted to individual judges. Judges are appointed by the executive, for example by the president after recommendations from the minister of justice, as in the Czech Republic. The presidents and vice presidents of supreme courts will be appointed by the heads of state, perhaps with their appointments requiring no further governmental endorsement. Ministers of justice will appoint the presidents and vice presidents of high, regional and district courts. Whether judges continue beyond the end of their tenure will be at the discretion of the executive (OSI 2001).

Although a constitution will invariably enshrine the rule of law and judicial independence, in practice in the executive model there is little separation of executive and judicial powers. A constitution may distinguish judicial from legislative and executive power, but the judiciary will not necessarily be recognized as a separate branch of government (OSI 2001). However, judges may be given individual rights, for example, to consent to transfers to a higher, lower or different court. Disciplinary measures against judges may fall under the jurisdiction of special judicial organs (Bartole 1998). Nevertheless, overall, the responsibilities entrusted to ministries of justice for the administration of the judiciary under the executive model often appear to limit the independence of judicial decision-making.

Unlike Romania, the Czech judiciary has no formal structure of self-management. The political will to provide a clearer separation of powers has been lacking in parliament, reflecting public dissatisfaction with the legal system, a dissatisfaction largely based on unreasonable expectations of the judiciary's ability to solve social and economic problems (misperceptions that are fed by the media). The inability of the judiciary to adjudicate without undue delay is another source of hostility. Inadequate levels of funding have adversely affected court efficiency and productivity. There has been a long history of inadequate staff, premises and information technology. Consequently, hearings have taken inordinate lengths of time to be completed, so much so that the Republic has lost numerous cases in the European Court of Human Rights over the length of court proceedings. The lack of public support for a measure of self-administration by the judiciary because of its inefficiency means that reforms which might ensure greater independence can be resisted, as was the case with the proposal in 2000 to create a Supreme Judicial Council similar to that in Romania.

Failure to create an independent administrative agency for the judiciary leaves Estonia as a further example of the executive model. The courts are formally administered by the Ministry of Justice. Judges of first and second instance courts are appointed to office for life by the president of the Republic. Presidents of first and second instance courts are appointed by the minister of justice, following approval by the Council for the Administration of Courts, an advisory body. The ministry is responsible for the courts' budgets, accounting, IT, housing and the training of clerks but is expected to refrain from interfering in the administration of justice. The Ministry of Justice collects statistics and prepares reports on the functioning of courts. The ministry's overall control over the budget and the budgetary process, and its right to re-allocate funding during the budgetary year, is perceived by some as posing a threat to judicial independence (Council of Europe 2013).

When the political executive is dominant in the management of the judiciary the Ministry of Justice will monitor the performance of courts; distribute caseload; supervise judges' behaviour; determine the need for new judicial offices; maintain court records, archives and statistics; and have responsibility for training. The allocation and control of court budgets, premises and other assets will also be managed by the ministry. Ministerial discretion in deciding on the appointment and transfer of judges creates incentives for judges to make decisions that are in the executive's interests.

In the Czech Republic, for example, the influence of the Ministry of Justice over the administration of the courts and the careers of judges (including appointment, transfer, promotion and, in so far as court presidents act of representatives of the ministry, discipline), the selection of court presidents, and the use of judges as high-ranking officials in the ministry (such as deputy ministers) are widely believed to threaten judicial independence. In 2003 the president nominated two senior political figures to the Constitutional Court, one a deputy prime minister, the other minister for defence. In the following year the president openly and directly attacked the Supreme Court for annulling, because of campaign violations, an election for a Senate seat won by a party-political colleague of the president, raising concerns that the growing power of the president's party could upset the separation of powers. These events led respected constitutional experts to claim that the independence of the courts had seriously declined (Freedom House 2005a). In 2014 the government introduced legislation to strengthen the minister of justice's power over the public prosecution service.

However, the Czech case shows that a lack of judicial self-management does not inevitably mean a loss of judicial independence. The powers of the Ministry of Justice undoubtedly create opportunities for undue influence, but these opportunities are rarely taken in practice. A detailed report on the Czech judicial system by the Open Society Institute concluded that 'judges are generally not subject to undue pressure through the supervision of their decisions or through the assignment of cases' (OSI 2001: 143). In 2005, the Economist Intelligence Unit found the judiciary to be 'independent in law and in practice', although noting that the nomination of judges by the Ministry of Justice leaves some scope for political interference (*Economist* 2005: 3). It was found that 'there is more talk about the potential for abuse . . . than about cases of overt meddling, which remain relatively rare' (Freedom House 2005a: 16). The Constitutional Court has rejected government proposals which in its view threatened the separation of powers and the independence of the judiciary. An important example was an attempt to provide the Ministry of Justice with the power temporarily to allocate and transfer judges without their consent in order to ensure 'an orderly course of justice'. Estonia has also had few problems of political interference in the judiciary, and the judiciary is widely regarded as independent.

Despite the absence of a judicial council, a measure of judicial self-government has protected the independence of the Czech judiciary from the executive. This has taken the form of managerial powers delegated to court presidents. Court presidents have eroded the minister of justice's influence but enlarged their own powers over recruitment, discipline, promotions, case assignment, the reassignment of judges among the panels and the selection of judges for the grand chambers of the most senior courts. Ministers of Justice are further dependent on court presidents for information relevant to policy-making in the absence of judicial statistics, performance evaluations and the judgements of lower courts. The Constitutional Court has declared it unconstitutional, and contrary to the separation of powers and the independence of the judiciary, for the executive to exercise powers of dismissal over presidents and vice presidents of courts. This security of tenure could only be modified by the Czech government establishing term limits. Judges are thus protected against threats to independence from the executive and legislature but vulnerable to dependence upon court presidents.

> The Czech court presidents are thus both protectors of judicial independence and simultaneously a threat to it. More specifically, while court presidents have generally managed to gain independence from the Ministry of Justice and increase judicial autonomy, some have also misused their newly-accrued powers against rank-and-file judges with the intent of keeping them compliant and loyal.
>
> (Kosar 2017: 97–98)

The powers of court presidents can be abused if left unchecked.

Court presidents also enjoy significant powers in Hungary, Poland, Bulgaria, Romania, Slovakia and Croatia, all of which have judicial councils. Concern about the independence of individual judges, as distinct from the independence of the judiciary from political interference, has attracted the attention of international bodies such as the European Court of Human Rights. These cases show that judicial independence is not just a matter of freedom from political interference by the executive.

Judicial independence under the executive model may be partly explained by the fact that management of the judiciary is rarely exclusive to the executive branch. While the appointment of judges may be in the hands of the executive, candidates for judicial office often undergo a selection procedure in which representatives of the judiciary play a large role. Customary practices can develop under which the executive defers to court presidents on the assignment, transfer and promotion of judges.

It appears that shared responsibility for the management of the judiciary is universal. A special institution of judges provided by law may be empowered to submit recommendations to the executive concerning the appointment, promotion, transfer or dismissal of judges (as in Lithuania). The function of such bodies may be strictly advisory or they may make binding recommendations. Measures regarding the careers of judges may be entrusted to top executive and legislative authorities, with judges elected by parliament based on proposals of the government, as in Slovakia. Alternatively, Supreme Court justices may be empowered to nominate candidates to succeed them or for positions in lower courts (as in Chile), leaving the executive to select from the list of nominees. Selection and appointment procedures may be led by the judiciary, with a Supreme Court guaranteeing due process, thus protecting the judiciary from improper influences, as in Estonia. Appointments may be based on explicit professional criteria. Budgets can be prepared in consultation with court presidents and may be reviewed during the year only with good reason and following consultations. The scope for variation in relations between executive and judiciary is large.

The role of legislatures

Although some post-communist European parliaments disempowered themselves when it came to deciding on the management of the judiciary (Parau 2013), others acquired significant powers.

The legislatures of new democracies are involved in the management of the judiciary in a range of different ways, but especially in the organs of judicial self-government. In Romania, the Superior Council of the Magistracy is elected for a term of four years by the Chamber of Deputies and Senate in joint session. In Slovakia, the National Council has a role in managing the careers of judges elected by parliament based on proposals from the government. In Lithuania, the nine ex-officio members of the Council of Courts include representatives of the chairman of parliament and the chairs of parliament's legal and budget committees. The parliament of Georgia nominates candidates for the High Council of Justice. The Armenian National Assembly appoints two members of the Justice Council.

Other forms of legislative involvement in the judiciary include the selection of six members to sit on the Judicial Service Commission by the South African National Assembly. The National Assembly may also call for a judge to be removed, by a resolution supported by a two-thirds majority, if found by the Judicial Service Commission to be incapable, grossly incompetent, or guilty of gross misconduct. Judicial reforms in Malaysia since 2018 have included the creation of a parliamentary select committee on major public service appointments, to determine key appointments to four commissions, including the chairmen and members of the JAC. Many states involve the legislature in the appointment of judges, usually in a mixed selection process that allows different branches of government to nominate or appoint judges to specific courts (Tiede 2020).

Legislative involvement in the management of the judiciary falls into three main categories: consultative, endorsement or election. The consultative role entails the legislature advising whoever has the power of appointment. For example, in South Africa the President appoints the Chief Justice, Deputy Chief Justice and judges of the Constitutional Court after consulting the leaders of parties represented in the National Assembly.

In some states legislative endorsement of nominees from an official of the executive or judicial branches is required. For example, Estonian Supreme Court justices are appointed by parliament from among the Chief Justice's nominees. Judges of the Lithuanian Supreme Court and court of appeal are appointed following parliamentary approval of presidential nominations. Georgian Supreme Court judges are appointed by a majority vote in parliament, following nomination by the President. The 11 members of the Hungarian Constitutional Court are elected by two-thirds majority in the National Assembly on the nomination of the President. The Brazilian Federal Senate approves the President's nominations for the Supreme Federal Tribunal. Candidate justices of the Indonesian Supreme Court are proposed by the Judicial Commission for parliamentary approval but subsequently appointed by the President.

The direct selection of justices by the legislature is everywhere reserved for constitutional courts. The accepted opinion is that involvement in appointments to the ordinary courts risks the politicization of judicial appointments. The selection of ordinary judges should be based on merit, defined by qualifications, integrity, ability and efficiency. Elections by parliament could lead to political considerations overriding objective criteria. The Venice Commission observed that

> the parliament is undoubtedly much more engrossed in political games and the appointments of judges could result in political bargaining in the parliament in which every member of Parliament coming from one district or another will want to have his or her own judge.
>
> (Venice Commission 2007: 3)

Latvia is unusual in granting power of confirmation of all judicial appointments to the unicameral parliament.

However, with constitutional courts a degree of politicization is recognized as inevitable, but it is also assumed that the independence of the court will be shielded from political influences once the appointment procedure is over, that competent and experienced judges will be recruited, that the court and its administration of justice will be balanced and legitimate, and that, in federal constitutions, different regional groups will be represented (Venice Commission 1997).

The role of parliament is obviously greatest when members of the constitutional court are chosen by the legislature itself. This is found in a small number of transitional states. Georgian Constitutional Court judges are selected by all branches of government: the President, parliament and Supreme Court each appointing three. The Lithuanian parliament (Seimas) appoints justices of the Constitutional Court from candidates submitted by the President, the president of the Seimas and the president of the Supreme Court. Judges of the Armenian Constitutional Court are elected by the National Assembly on a three-fifths majority. Three of the nine justices are nominated by the President, three by the government and three by the General Assembly of Judges. The National Assembly also elects each judge of the Court of Cassation from a list of three candidates presented by the Supreme Judicial Council, again by a three-fifths majority. Successful candidates are appointed by the President. The chairperson of the Court of Cassation is nominated by the Supreme Judicial Council and elected by the National Assembly by a simple majority vote. In Belarus six of the 12 judges of the Constitutional Court are elected by the Council of the Republic, and six are appointed by the President. The Latvian legislature confirms the appointment of judges to the Constitutional Court by a majority of the votes of not fewer than 51 of its 100 members.

In principle, such involvement of parliament in judicial management should offer numerous benefits. Transparency is increased by the openness of parliament's proceedings, which may include oversight of the Ministry of Justice and its financial and administrative functions. For example, in 2010 the Romanian Chamber of Deputies held its hearings on its appointment of a member of the Constitutional Court in public. In Latin America, a lack of vigorous legislative scrutiny of Supreme Court appointments has made it easier for the executive to abuse its powers of appointment. Where the role of legislatures in appointments has been strengthened, the transparency of the process has been noticeably increased (Domingo 1999). Giving different institutions the right to nominate members of a constitutional court should also improve the quality of deliberation and decision, thus making final rulings more acceptable to the wider public (Tiede 2020).

Or do judges respond to the interests of their selectors, rather than decide independently and impartially? If the legislature is involved in the selection of constitutional court justices, will justices be more reluctant to strike down legislation as unconstitutional? The surprising answer on the limited evidence available is that judges' propensity to strike down laws is affected by the institution that selects them. A comparison of decisions by the Chilean and Colombian constitutional courts found that the legislative appointees on the Chilean Tribunal were 15 per cent more likely to strike down laws than justices appointed by the Supreme Court. In the Chilean case, judges selected by the President and legislature were grouped together. Their decisions were found to reflect the approach to constitutional decision-making of the different institutions selecting them. 'Judges live up to the expectations of their selectors in deciding the constitutionality of laws due to an understanding of the selecting institution's mission and role in government.' The political logic assumed here is that elected institutions (the president and legislature)

> will tend to choose judges that are more willing to consider political factors in their decisions and play an active role in the policy-making process, much the way that elected politicians do when enacting laws. This may result in judges selected by elected institutions who are more willing to strike down laws as unconstitutional.
>
> (Tiede 2020: 1120, 1095)

This is a significant conclusion for reformers seeking to strengthen the impartiality of constitutional courts, especially since judges selected by parliament might be expected to defer to the legislature's law-making power, and be reluctant to find laws unconstitutional. It suggests that the greater the legislature's role in selecting constitutional court judges, the more likely the justices will strike down legislation as unconstitutional.

Yet in three of the countries where members of the constitutional court are chosen by the legislature – Georgia, Armenia and Belarus – the court is subject to executive interference. In Georgia it comes under excessive pressure from government bodies. The Armenian constitutional amendments in 2019 removed three

Constitutional Court justices who had served 12 years and replaced them by a legislative process that politicized the selection. In Belarus all courts are subservient to the President. The Constitutional Court of the Republic of Lithuania has strongly protected fundamental rights and effectively arbitrated in disputes between different branches government, but in comparison with the powers conferred on the constitutional courts of other Eastern and Central European states, the competence of the Lithuanian Constitutional Court is relatively narrow (Pūraitė-Andrikienė 2019). Only in Latvia is it clear that judgements of the Constitutional Court reveal respect for the legislature's power and that the legislature takes into consideration findings that result from constitutional review. The court has circumscribed the legislature's discretion in various fields, including family life, education, criminal policy and health care, proving it to be 'an independent judicial institution that handed down objective and fair judgments' (Ziemele et al. 2020: 517). It is thus difficult to show the effects in these cases of direct legislative involvement in constitutional court appointments.

When parliaments operate according to strict party discipline, involvement in the management of the judiciary may only serve to reinforce the power of the executive if the president is drawn from the party or ruling coalition with a majority in parliament. The Albanian Constitutional and High Courts have been accused of political bias as a consequence of the ruling party in parliament having the two-thirds majority needed to consent to presidential appointments. In Nicaragua, executive control of the National Assembly enables politically loyal magistrates to be appointed to the Supreme Court of Justice which then appoints judges to the lower courts. Political clientelism persists despite rules requiring personnel to be recruited, promoted and disciplined solely on merit.

The potential effect on judicial independence of party dominance is further illustrated by the Hungarian parliament's enactment in 2011 of Acts on the Legal Status and Remuneration of Judges and the Organisation and Administration of Courts. These empower parliament to elect by a two-thirds majority the president of the NJO – the Judicial Council's bureaucracy – for a nine-year period, following the expression of opinions on the nominees by the council. The president of the NJO exercises considerable discretionary powers, including the selection of judges and other senior judicial officers, control of the organization of the judiciary and many powers previously exercised by the Council. Amendments to this legislation were passed following critical recommendations from the EU's Venice Commission which found that the original changes contradicted 'European standards for the organisation of the judiciary, especially its independence' and were also 'problematic as concerns the right to a fair trial under Article 6 of the European Convention on Human Rights' (Venice Commission 2012a: para. 120). While these amendments strengthened the accountability of the NJO's president and transferred some powers back to the council, the Venice Commission, following a review of the amendments, remained concerned that 'the powers of the President of the NJO remain very extensive to be wielded by a single person and their effective supervision remains difficult' (Venice Commission 2012b: para. 88).

A particular problem is that the dominant party in Hungary's parliament, the centre-right Fidesz Party, has been inclined to use its dominance to place its supporters in positions which are supposed to be politically neutral, including the wife of a senior party member as president of the NJO. Hungary established a strong National Council of Judges soon after the new democratic regime was brought in. Most of the powers of the Ministry of Justice were delegated to it, and the council quickly became recognized as an independent body on which judges were well represented and which protected judicial independence. Yet the NCJ's bureaucracy dealt with most of the council's business on a day-to-day basis, including transferring judges and assigning cases to specific courts, powers which might compromise the right to a fair trial. The Venice Commission found the system of transferring cases to be inconsistent with 'the principle of the lawful judge, which is essential to the rule of law' (Venice Commission 2012b: para. 92). Strengthening the role of this organization and its president pushed Hungary towards the executive model of judicial management.

Parliamentary decision-making is invariably highly partisan. Decisions affecting the management of the judiciary are easily drawn into party conflicts between government and opposition, again raising concerns about judicial independence. While it may seem obvious that the legislature should be given a role in the ratification of judicial appointments and other critical career decisions, there can be no guarantee that such formalities will negate the effect on parliamentary scrutiny of party discipline and the support that this gives to executives with powerful majorities in the legislature. In Eastern Europe generally, parliamentary appointments to judicial councils have been 'even more politically motivated than the appointments made by the Ministry of Justice' (Bobek 2008: 120). The incursion of party politics into judicial management becomes particularly damaging to the independence of the judiciary when it is called upon to rule on the legality of electoral procedures in response to challenges by MPs to the decisions of electoral commissions.

The corollary of this is that parliamentary opposition, mobilized against partisan nominations to the judiciary, may disrupt judicial administration. In 2011 the boycott of parliament by the opposition in Albania jeopardized the normal functioning of the High Council of Justice and led to the rejection by parliament's law committee of most of the candidates proposed by the President to fill vacancies in the Constitutional and High Courts. In 2014 conflict between executive and legislature over appointments to the Supreme and Constitutional Courts led to prolonged vacancies and promotions on political rather than professional criteria, including whether judges were felt to be more or less likely to rule against parliamentarians in corruption cases (Freedom House 2015a).

Thus, parliamentary conflict can politicize processes which ought to reflect professional merit rather than party allegiance. In Guatemala, where the political parties in Congress can nominate judges according to the number of seats they hold, the nomination of justices to the Supreme Court and Constitutional Court has become highly politicized, especially when some magistrates are known to be sympathetic to prosecution for human rights violations under the old regime. The consequences of parliamentary involvement inevitably raise questions about the suitability of the legislature's nominees. The appointment of presidential and parliamentary nominees to the High Council of Justice in Georgia has also encountered the problem of ensuring that such appointees have appropriate qualifications and ethical standards, rather than just being actively involved in party politics. The presence of members elected by the Ukrainian parliament on the High Council of Justice of Ukraine has also prompted questions about political influence and suitable qualifications (Council of Europe 2011).

* * *

Two highly generalized models have been distinguished – self-management and executive management – in order to provide a broad context in which to clarify the role in judicial management of other branches of government, and assesses each model's compatibility with judicial independence. There are risks attendant upon the delegation of administrative powers to the judiciary itself, through judicial councils, yet the executive model does not necessarily threaten independence. Though the executive model assigns power to administer the judiciary to the executive branch, there are usually varying levels of involvement from other institutions, including members of the judiciary itself. There is much sharing of responsibility for the management of the judiciary. Some legislatures have significant powers, for example over judicial appointments. However, the theoretical benefits of legislative involvement are often negated by the partisan nature of parliamentary decision-making, which draws the management of the judiciary into party conflicts. Strict party discipline within a legislature can reinforce the power of the executive in relation to the judiciary by politicizing managerial processes which ought to reflect professional merit rather than party allegiance.

While concerns about political interference in the judiciary persist, in some transitional states the autonomy granted to the judiciary in post-authoritarian constitutions raises the possibility that the legitimate authority of governments and parliaments will be usurped. The growing involvement of the judiciary in disputes about the constitutional powers of governments, the interpretation of statutes and the application of precedents has contributed to a sense that increasingly the judiciary is making the law rather than just administering it. Such is the power given to courts that judicial review has been considered premature in transitions to democracy because it creates the impression of an unelected and elitist body challenging the will of the people as enunciated by their elected representatives through legislation. This in turn has led to calls for the judiciary to be made more accountable. The expansion of judicial activism and power is the subject of the next chapter.

References

Autheman, V. and S. Elena (2004), *Global Best Practices: Judicial Councils: Lessons Learned From Europe and Latin America*, IFES Rule of Law White Paper, Washington, DC: International Foundation for Electoral Systems.

Bartole, S. (1998), 'Alternative models of judicial independence: organizing the judiciary in Central and Eastern Europe', *East European Constitutional Review*, vol. 7, no. 1.
Bobek, M. (2008), 'The fortress of judicial independence and the mental transitions of the Central European judiciaries', *European Public Law*, vol. 14, no. 1.
Bobek, M. and D. Kosar (2015), '"Euro-products" and institutional reform in central and eastern Europe: a critical study in judicial councils' in M. Bobek (ed.), *Central European Judges under the European Influence: The Transformative Power of the EU Revisited*, Oxford: Hart Publishing.
CCJE (2001), 'Opinion no. 2 (2001) of the Consultative Council of European Judges (CCJE) for the attention of the Committee of Ministers of the Council of Europe on the funding and management of courts with reference to the efficiency of the judiciary and to Article 6 of the European Convention on Human Rights', Strasbourg: Consultative Council of European Judges.
Council of Europe (2011), *Judicial Self-Governing Bodies*, Strasbourg: Council of Europe.
Council of Europe (2013), *Corruption Prevention in Respect of Members of Parliament, Judges and Prosecutors: Evaluation Report, Estonia*, Strasbourg: Council of Europe.
Domingo, P. (1999), 'Judicial independence and judicial reform in Latin America' in A. Schedler et al. (eds.), *The Self-Restraining State: Power and Accountability in New Democracies*, London: Lynne Rienner.
Economist (2005), 'Country briefing: Czech Republic, political forces', www.economist.com/countries/CzechRepublic/profile
ENCJ (2013), 'Sofia declaration on judicial independence and accountability', Declaration of the General Assembly held in Sofia, June, European Network of Councils for the Judiciary, Brussels.
ENCJ (2021), *Compendium on Councils for the Judiciary*, Brussels: European Network of Councils for the Judiciary.
EU Commission (2006), *Monitoring Report on the State of Preparedness for EU Membership of Bulgaria and Romania*, Brussels: Commission of the European Communities.
EU-Romania Joint Parliamentary Committee (2003), *Declaration and Recommendations*, Brussels: European Parliament and Parliament of Romania.
Freedom House (2004), *Nations in Transit 2004: Romania*, New York: Freedom House.
Freedom House (2005a), *Nations in Transit 2005: Czech Republic*, New York: Freedom House.
Freedom House (2005b), *Nations in Transit 2005: Romania*, New York: Freedom House.
Freedom House (2015a), *Nations in Transit 2015: Albania*, New York: Freedom House.
Freedom House (2015b), *Nations in Transit 2015: Romania*, New York: Freedom House.
Garoupa, N. and T. Ginsburg (2015), *Judicial Reputation: A Comparative Theory*, Chicago: University of Chicago Press.
Kosar, D. (2017), 'Politics of judicial independence and judicial accountability in Czechia: bargaining in the shadow of the law between Court Presidents and the Ministry of Justice', *European Constitutional Law Review*, vol. 13, no. 1.
Library of Congress (2015), 'Bulgaria: constitutional amendment provides for judicial reform', *Global Legal Monitor*, 30 December.
OECD (2005), *Romania: Elements of the Public Integrity System*, Paris: Organization for Economic Co-operation and Development.
OECD (2012), *Integrity Review of Brazil: Managing Risk for a Cleaner Public Service*, OECD Public Governance Review, Paris: Organization for Economic Co-operation and Development.
Ortiz, P. J. C. (2017), 'Councils of the judiciary and judges' perception of respect to their independence in Europe', *Hague Journal on the Rule of Law*, vol. 9, no. 2.

OSI (2001), *Monitoring the EU Accession Process: Judicial Independence in the Czech Republic*, Brussels: Open Society Institute.

Parau, C. E. (2013), 'The dormancy of parliaments: the invisible cause of judiciary empowerment in central and eastern Europe', *Journal of Representative Democracy*, vol. 40, no. 3.

Popova, M. (2012), *Politicized Justice in Emerging Democracies: A Study of Courts in Russia and Ukraine*, Cambridge: Cambridge University Press.

Pūraitė-Andrikienė, D. (2019), 'The legal force of conclusions by the Lithuanian Constitutional Court and the issue of their (non-) finality: has the time come to amend the Constitution?', *Review of Central and East European Law*, vol. 44, 232–268.

Rosselli, A. (2020), 'Judicial independence and the budget: a taxonomy of judicial budgeting mechanisms', *Indiana Journal of Constitutional Design*, vol. 5, no. 1.

Selejan-Guțan, B. (2018), 'Romania: perils of a "Perfect Euro-Model" of judicial council', *German Law Journal*, vol. 19, no. 7.

Tiede, L. B. (2020), 'Mixed judicial selection and constitutional review', *Comparative Political Studies*, vol. 53, no. 7.

Trochev, A. (2008), *Judging Russia: The Role of the Constitutional Court in Russian Politics, 1990–2006*, Cambridge: Cambridge University Press.

Venice Commission (1997), *The Composition of Constitutional Courts*, Strasbourg: European Commission for Democracy Through Law.

Venice Commission (2007), *Judicial Appointments*, Opinion No. 403/2006, Strasbourg: European Commission for Democracy Through Law.

Venice Commission (2012a), *Opinion on Act CLXII of 2011 on the Legal Status and Remuneration of Judges and Act CLXI of 2011 on the Organisation and Administration of Courts of Hungary*, Venice: European Commission for Democracy Through Law.

Venice Commission (2012b) *Opinion on the Cardinal Acts on the Judiciary That Were Amended Following the Adoption of Opinion CDL-AD (2012) on Hungary*, Venice: European Commission for Democracy Through Law.

Vyas, Y. (1992), 'The independence of the judiciary: a Third World perspective', *Third World Legal Studies*, vol. 11, no. 1.

Ziemele, I., A. Spale and L. Jurcēna (2020), 'The constitutional court of the Republic of Latvia' in A. von Bogdandy, P. Huber and C. Grabenwarter (eds.), *The Max Planck Handbooks in European Public Law. Volume III: Constitutional Adjudication: Institutions*, Oxford: Oxford Scholarship Online.

8 Judicial activism

Introduction

The creation of constitutional courts and the empowerment of ordinary courts to exercise judicial review of administrative action have formed parts of the process of democratic transition in most post-authoritarian states. Judges have become more active in the political process as a consequence. 'Activism' here does not carry with it any judgement about appropriate levels of judicial involvement. It refers to responsibilities placed upon judiciaries arising from the rights bestowed on citizens by post-authoritarian constitutions. It does not pre-judge whether judicial activism usurps the legitimate authority of elected legislatures or political executives.

This chapter examines the powers given to judiciaries to review legislation and administrative decisions. These are distinguished first as abstract constitutional review, under which the courts interpret the rules of the constitution itself. Next, attempts by governments to amend constitutions call for judicial interpretations, drawing the courts into politics. The following section shows how the courts can be asked to rule on the legality of policy decisions under constitutional provisions which make all areas of public policy open to judicial review. Then there is the question of how the courts test the constitutionality of the political process itself, affecting civil society, elections, parliamentary business, and the composition of the executive. Finally, there is judicial review of administrative action to ensure that those who administer the law keep within it, a basic principle of the rule of law. The final section examines how governmental leaders have fought back against the expansion and politicization of judicial interventionism and in so doing pose a threat to judicial independence.

Judicial power

While the methods and intensity of judicial interventionism vary from country to country, the 'third wave' of democratization has on the whole seen a global expansion of judicial power (Tate and Vallinder 1995; Gloppen et al. 2010), partly because politicians overseeing the drafting of constitutions had an incentive to restrain executive powers which they might lose through the democratic process.

DOI: 10.4324/9781003334613-9

Judicial power extends far beyond the scrutiny of administrative decisions to include guaranteeing human rights, testing the constitutionality of statutes, applying the justices' own constitutional principles, and managing inter-governmental relations, especially in federal systems of government. Much of this is backed up by international bodies such as the European Court of Human Rights, the International Court of Justice, the Council of Europe, the United Nations' Office of the High Commissioner for Human Rights and the Court of Justice of the European Union (Lachmayer 2020).

The addition of a bill of rights to the constitutions of some post-authoritarian regimes was in part seen as protection against a lack of popular commitment to democratic values (Yowell 2020), a precaution that turned out to be prescient in the case of the illiberal democracies. Judicial involvement in policy-making has been encouraged by the acceptance of basic freedoms, usually expressed in terms of fundamental human rights, on which even democratically elected governments should not encroach (Guarnieri 2003). The development of constitutional review was also a response to political pressure from groups excluded from effective political participation, as in Colombia, where weak mechanisms of political representation and the high risks of political activism created the 'temptation to substitute judicial for political action' (Uprimy 2004: 44; Ginsburg 2003).

Other factors have combined to encourage judicial activism and incursions by the judiciary into public policy-making. The process of democratic consolidation itself created space for the courts to expand their influence. Democratic competition meant the fragmentation of political power, rather than its concentration as in authoritarian regimes, encouraging judicial review of legislative and administrative action. Post-authoritarian Philippines, South Korea, Thailand, Taiwan and Indonesia are typical in showing that 'as it becomes more difficult to produce legislation, courts have more policy space in which to insert themselves into policymaking without fear of legislative correction or discipline by other political actors' (Ginsburg 2009: 7).

Democratization also means that civil society and the media have more opportunities to demand and support judicial interventions to strengthen government accountability. The new constitutional regimes also offer more freedom to challenge state authorities without fear of reprisal. Conversely, as the Singapore case shows, the absence of a participatory political culture in which there is access to relevant information, opportunities for public consultation, and awareness of individual rights, has severely constrained the courts in providing judicial review of executive action. Consequently, the Singapore judiciary 'has not articulated any express policies or conceptualized theory of judicial review' and is rarely asked to review executive action (Lin 2009: 295, 302).

Interventionism has also been in part a response to the growth of executive power, leading to more challenges to legislative and executive actions. It has even been suggested that, as a consequence of growing judicial restraint on the other two constitutional powers, 'for parties in litigation, and for society as a whole, the court process provides a kind of alternative democratic arena, where arguments between sections of the public and the powers of the state are exchanged and questions of general concern are debated' (CCEJ 2015: para. 1). Where this growing executive power has shown authoritarian tendencies, it has drawn the judiciary further into politics, increasing the caseloads of the courts, notably in Russia (Trochev 2016).

The expansion of constitutional and administrative review by the judiciary is inevitably controversial politically. When judges are called upon to decide whether executive and administrative decisions are lawful, there is always the risk that they will substitute their own interpretation of a law's intention for that of the legislators. When judicial review extends to constitutional matters, such as whether a legislature has jurisdiction over a particular subject, or is entitled to pursue political objectives through legislation, judicial independence enters a potential minefield. Both constitutional and ordinary courts are brought into the policy-making process, creating scope for independent judges to make decisions contrary to the intentions of democratically constituted legislatures.

The problem becomes particularly acute if a constitutional court can initiate legislation, as in Russia, or can consider petitions proposing the annulment of statutes as unconstitutional, a power available to minority party MPs in the Czech Republic seeking to overturn the majority party's decisions. Constitutional review thus becomes a continuation of political conflict, particularly over social policy. When there has been no clear government majority, governing parties have used petitions as a way of getting round opposition in the legislature. For example, the Czech Senate has used petitions to compensate for its constitutionally weak position in the legislative process (Kopeček and Petrov 2016).

Judicial activism reflects the way the courts use the opportunities provided by the cases brought before them to become involved in policy-making. The expansion of formal judicial authority into constitutional review cases can have an even greater effect than ideologically inspired changes in the composition of the court on the politicization of the judicial process, as in Brazil's Supreme Federal Tribunal between 1999 and 2004, where greater judicial activism provided incentives for judges to bring ideological preferences to bear (Desposato et al. 2015).

Abstract constitutional review

Constitutional courts are a common feature of governance in new democracies, especially in Europe, Africa and the Middle East (Sweet 2012). The largest grouping of states that have created constitutional courts are the new democracies of Central and Eastern Europe. Elsewhere constitutional courts are found in countries with the civil law system, including Indonesia, South Korea, Thailand and Taiwan. Most common law countries have not established constitutional courts, charging the Supreme Court with the review of constitutionality. The exception is South Africa, though here the courts are required to consider international law (Chang and Yeh 2012). Constitutional and supreme courts have been at the centre of the controversy surrounding the powers of the judiciary during democratic consolidation. The first of these concerns abstract judicial review.

Normally, judicial activism on constitutional matters sees constitutional or supreme courts ruling on the constitutionality of actions by other branches of government, including attempts to amend the country's constitution. But occasionally the judiciary has been empowered to amend the very rules which define the powers of executive, legislature and judiciary. This redefinition of constitutional rules results from 'abstract' constitutional review. Abstract review is a specialized form of judicial review in that it allows a complaint about the constitutionality of a legislative act (statutes and regulations made under them) to be filed by a person without having an individual interest in a specific case or act of law enforcement. When enshrined in the constitution, as it is in some Central and Eastern European countries, constitutional courts have the power to interpret the constitution without being prompted by a specific appeal against a piece of legislation.

Thus with abstract review the judges do not have to consider the application of a contested law to a specific or 'concrete' case. They are free to judge whether the legislature has adhered to the principles of the constitution, and whether a statute is compatible with the constitution, without anyone having brought a specific complaint to the court about the statute's implementation. In such cases the courts seek to resolve political disputes on their own initiative, frequently prompting conflict with the legislature and the sections of civil society which they represent. In this way the primary responsibility of constitutional courts 'is to interpret the constitution, not to adjudicate cases . . . their constitutions mandate judicial activism' (Howard 2001: 100). Abstract review creates the impression that the judiciary is acting in a legislative capacity, calling into question its political independence and legitimacy.

Consequently, in response some constitutional rulings have been ignored by the executive, and the jurisdictions of constitutional courts have been revised. The most striking case was that of Hungary, the only former Eastern bloc country that did not adopt a new constitution immediately following the end of the communist regime, but which eventually enacted a new Fundamental Law in 2011. This still gave the Constitutional Court the power to test, at the proposal of a judge, any legal regulation applied in a particular case for conformity with the Fundamental Law. This is in addition to the more conventional powers to examine the conformity of adopted Acts to the Fundamental Law. The court can also review legal regulations and court rulings following complaints from members of the public or proposals from specific interested parties, including the government, one-fourth of the members of parliament, the President of the Curia, the Supreme Prosecutor, and the Commissioner for Fundamental Rights. But even then, the Constitutional Court may review or annul a legal regulation not submitted to it for a review, though only if its substance is closely related to a legal regulation that has already been submitted to it. However, in comparison with the previous Constitution, the new Fundamental Law still makes it more difficult for the court to review laws in the abstract for their compliance with the constitution. In Hungary as elsewhere 'changes of constitutional jurisprudence have been brought about by the unquestionable authoritarian tendencies building up a so-called "illiberal democracy", declining all institutional counterbalances against the executive power' (Szente and Gárdos-Orosz 2018: 106).

Even 'abstract' reviews of legal norms have to be initiated by some agency. It is rare for a constitution to allow any individual to claim public interest through *actio popularis* or the right of any member of a community to take legal action in vindication of a public interest. The Hungarian Constitutional Court was originally empowered in this way, but the Fundamental Law of 2011 disallowed individuals from initiating abstract review, restricting the right to specific state organizations. In Poland, the Constitutional Tribunal can review legal provisions without reference to a particular case in which the provisions were applied, and the Constitution specifies the entities that are authorized to initiate abstract review. These include the First President of the Supreme Court, the President of the Chief Administrative Court, the Public Prosecutor-General, the President of the Republic, the Prime Minister, groups of deputies and senators, the Commissioner for Citizens' Rights, local authorities, trade unions, employers' organizations and religious bodies, provided that the subject of the review relates to their activities. In Bulgaria the Constitutional Court cannot be approached directly by the citizen. They have to make indirect constitutional complaints by applying to either the national Ombudsman or the Supreme Bar Council to initiate a case in defence of constitutionally protected human rights allegedly infringed by an act of parliament (Belov and Tsekov 2020).

It is not the norm for a constitutional court to be empowered to initiate a review *sua sponte*, or on its own motion, though it is undoubtedly this power that is a major source of concern about the separation of legislative and judicial power so important in democratic governance. Such was the response to the demand in 2010 from Pakistan's Supreme Court for a constitutional amendment to increase the court's control of judicial appointments to the superior courts at the expense of the legislature. The resulting 19th amendment was regarded by some observers as usurping parliament's right to amend the constitution only by a two-thirds majority, a rule designed to require support within parliament extending beyond the governing party (Khan 2013). However, the petitions to the Supreme Court challenging certain provisions of the 18th amendment, particularly the formation of the judicial commission for the appointment of judges in the superior courts, represented a body of opinion worried that the 18th amendment retained many provisions introduced by the former military ruler Pervez Musharraf. The fact that the National Assembly amended the Constitution twice in one year without political conflict may be seen as a sign of Pakistan's strengthening democracy, but it is understandable that some might be anxious that the judiciary should appear to be the dominant branch of government.

The Czech Constitutional Court has also on several occasions redefined basic principles of Czech constitutional law by 'purposive interpretation', thus expanding the scope of constitutional rules, filling gaps in Czech law and prescribing how parliament should approach a specific policy problem (Malír and Ondrejková 2020).

Abstract constitutional review undoubtedly provides effective protection for human rights (Brovko et al. 2021). However, there are risks that abstract review in response to *actio popularis* can overburden the courts with abusive complaints. This consideration has led the Venice Commission to advise member states of the EU to allow only victims of violations to have the right to raise a constitutional complaint before a court (Venice Commission 2021). Experience of the Bulgarian

Constitutional Court's power of abstract interpretation shows that, while enhancing the protection of human rights, the interpretation of the constitution can produce unclear and indeterminate legal rules. This is problematic for the rule of law because it denies citizens certain knowledge of the legal consequences of their actions, thus violating the principles of legal certainty and legal predictability (Belov and Tsekov 2020).

Constitutional amendment

The rules governing constitutional amendment are usually spelt out in the constitution, providing essential guidance to the court when deciding whether a proposed amendment can be deemed consistent with it. Such rules occasionally cover the replacement of the constitution (general amendment) as well as proposed amendments which will need to be judged as to whether they are consistent with the current constitution (partial amendment). In the case of the latter, constitutional courts find themselves having to adjudicate when a sovereign democratic legislature has decided that the existing constitution is obsolete. They may also have to judge whether a constitutional amendment is so foreign to the original provisions that it is tantamount to replacing them. To help with this, the Constitutional Court of Colombia developed a doctrine of constitutional substitution to protect the Constitution against replacement by a sequence of amendments.

The more controversial the proposals for amendment, the more constitutional courts become involved in politics, opening up debate on how far the courts can defend the constitution against the legitimate right of the legislature to amend it. The idea that a constitutional amendment could be found unconstitutional immediately raises democratic concerns.

> It seems contrary to the very idea of a constitution – which ought to reflect the views and wishes of those bound by it – that there could be enforceable limits to what the people may do acting through their representatives when they amend their constitution in perfect conformity with the entrenched procedures for constitutional change.
>
> (Albert 2017: 8)

When constitutional amendments are invalidated by the courts on the grounds that a government is trying to usurp power, violate human rights or threaten another constitutional principle, democrats are likely to object that the judiciary is blocking the will of the people as expressed through legislative enactment. Judicial review here involves the judiciary in the conflict between sections of the population and their elected representatives who support amendment and those who oppose it. An example is found in the history of constitutional provision for emergency powers in Korea, where substantial sections of the population opposed legislation that declared rules to be beyond judicial oversight (Seong-Hak Kim 2015).

Although it has become widely accepted in post-authoritarian states that there should be limitations on the legislature's amendment powers, widening the judicial review of constitutional amendments considerably, no satisfactory doctrine has emerged to reconcile the conflicting powers of legislatures and judiciaries. The courts become special political actors whose legitimacy derives not from democratic election but from a reputation for neutral, independent and apolitical decisions. This conflict became acute when the Colombian Constitutional Court ruled in 2003 that Congress cannot replace the Constitution but only amend it (Cajas-Sarria 2017). The legitimacy of the courts is at risk when all there is for the justices to call on are their own political strategies, ideologies, political preferences and values.

Among the most controversial issues demanding the attention of constitutional courts have been attempts to extend the terms of office of key political executives. Even in countries lacking a tradition of constitutional review, such as Malawi and Zambia, the courts have intervened in political conflicts, displaying 'a striking tendency to render decisions that have challenged the interests of elected power-holders', especially when attempts have been made to change the constitution to give incumbent presidents extended or unlimited terms of office (Vondoepp 2005: 276; Guarnieri 2003). In 2021 the Court of Appeal in Kenya continued in this tradition by upholding a High Court decision that a constitutional amendment process initiated by the President violated the Constitution, which only allows parliament or popular initiative to initiate amendments. However, African courts still face executives whose powers vis-à-vis the judiciary have 'called into question the prospects for sustaining the democratic transition' (Fombad 2020: 65).

The independence of the courts can quickly be called into question when they themselves support, through somewhat creative interpretations, attempts to prolong the power of the incumbent executive, as in Nicaragua where amendments to the Constitution passed in 2013 by the National Assembly, in which the President's party held 63 of the 92 seats, removed presidential term limits. This had been preceded by a ruling from the Constitutional Chamber of the Supreme Court of Justice in 2009 authorizing presidential re-election following a petition from a number of elected officials, including President Ortega, arguing that the electoral prohibition found in Articles 147 and 178 contradicted the constitutional principle of unconditional equality before the law and equality of the political right to participate in the political affairs of the country. The court reasoned that the application of the constitutional provisions prohibiting re-election of certain officials constituted unequal treatment since the only constitution grounds for limiting re-election are age, criminal conviction or civil interdiction. The court also claimed that the articles restricting re-election were not part of the original Constitution but had been added by amendment, violating the constitutional guarantee of sovereignty. Not surprisingly the judiciary in Nicaragua is widely thought to lack independence from political influence.

In 2013 Bolivia's Constitutional Tribunal also ruled that the president could run for a third term in the 2014 elections, despite amendments to the Constitution in 2009 which specified that presidents should only serve two consecutive terms. The Tribunal ruled that the two-term constitutional rule did not apply retroactively to President Morales' first term, which had taken place before the new constitution came into effect, meaning that the 2014 elections would legally count as Morales's first re-election. Critics said the ruling showed that the court was controlled by the government, especially since only one re-election had been allowed under the previous constitution.

Judicial review of constitutional amendments by special constitutional courts thus poses fundamental questions concerning democratic government: who should prevail when a legislature seeks to amend the constitution or even replace it with a new one? Can an appeal to the principles of the old constitution by the judiciary satisfy those seeking what are perceived to be essential reforms? How far should the current political majority be constrained by a past generation or a judicial elite? (Doyle 2017). When an authoritarian government backed by a legislative majority seeks to limit the rights of individuals and groups, to which values apart from their own can judges refer in defence of human rights?

One option is for the constitutional court to refer to a constitutional preamble or Bill of Rights, endorsing democratic values, social justice and fundamental human rights, which can be used to test the quality of proposed constitutional amendments. An example is the preamble to the Constitution of the Philippines, which perceives the constitution as establishing a government which, in order to build a just and humane society, promotes the common good, conserves and develops the people's patrimony, and 'secures *to ourselves and our posterity* (emphasis added) the blessings of independence and democracy under the rule of law and a regime of truth, justice, freedom, love, equality, and peace'. Whether these principles and values are accepted for all posterity, and therefore indefinitely available to the courts for use as constitutional standards, is ultimately a question to be answered through political dialogue and competition.

Alternatively, national judiciaries may turn to guidance and rulings from international jurisprudence. Indeed some, such as South Africa's, are required to consider international law. International covenants such as the European Convention on Human Rights, their interpretation by courts such as the European Court of Human Rights, dialogues between national and international jurists, and the decisions of international courts, all offer guidance to jurists on constitutional courts dealing with intractable problems of constitutional amendment (Rosenfeld and Sajo 2012). The strength of internationalization varies from region to region with the European Union at the stronger end of the continuum and the Association of Southeast Asian Nations at the other, exemplified by instructions to the Malaysian Court to interpret the constitution 'domestically'. The constitutional courts of South Korea and Taiwan have also been criticized for neglecting to apply international human rights treaties to domestic cases.

In fact, there is no region where constitutional courts seek guidance from foreign or international law to the extent which might be expected, though the new constitutional courts in Europe, such as those of Hungry and Romania, make more references to foreign decisions than the long-established national courts. The judicial dialogues that do take place are generally confined within regions, and trans-regional influence is only between courts in the same legal family of civil or common law. The Supreme Court of Argentina seldom refers to foreign cases in its decisions, despite a constitutional requirement that international human rights should be considered when laws are being enacted. The common law courts of the Philippines and Malaysia have been more open to foreign influence than the constitutional courts of South Korea and Taiwan. However, it is expected that reference to foreign or international law by constitutional courts in new democracies is likely to increase (Chang and Yeh 2012).

Testing the constitutionality of public policy

Judicial review of constitutionality in democratizing countries draws the courts into many public policy disputes, even when these have been resolved through the legislative process. This has been encouraged by the protection afforded to human rights in the new constitutions.

Policy areas have included abortion and taxation in Poland, capital punishment and regulation of the tobacco market in Hungary, and access to telecommunications data and civil procedure in the courts (Romania). Judicial interventions have affected government austerity measures including cuts in civil service pay (Lithuania), education (Indonesia), housing (South Africa), workers' rights (Egypt) and health care (Argentina), all as a consequence of mobilization by civil society organizations in support of social and economic rights.

The Brazilian judiciary has been drawn into policy-making on labour conditions, fiscal reforms, wages, taxation, social security, privatization and other aspects of economic policy, once again causing concern about the power of an unelected branch of government. Since 1988 the judiciary has been involved in 'practically all significant reforms encompassing Brazil's social economic and political spheres' (Sadek and Cavalcanti 2003: 223; February 2007; Gauri and Brinks 2008; Roux 2004; Santiso 2004). In 2021 Mexico's Supreme Court struck down sections of the country's health legislation, which prohibited the consumption and home cultivation of marijuana, as unconstitutional, on the unusual grounds that the law violated the human right to the free development of one's personality. Malawi's constitutional court, the Malawi Supreme Court of Appeal, is empowered to make 'any orders that are necessary and appropriate' to secure the enjoyment of rights. Among its many cases it has been asked to rule on the mandatory nature of the death penalty, the power of police officers to arrest anyone found to be loitering and charge them with the offence of being a rogue and vagabond, and conditions in Malawi's prisons (Nkhata 2020).

In Pakistan, Chief Justice Chaudhry revived *suo moto* powers in order to maximize his influence over a range of public policy areas, including national security, the extension of rights to the transgender community, government contracts, privatization, taxation and the price of basic foodstuffs. *Suo moto* refers to the decision of a court to take action on its own motion, rather than at the request of an affected party, or a judge's order made without a request by any party to the case. Pakistan's *suo moto* cases allowed the Supreme Court 'to interact directly with the public and be seen as a responsive actor in a country that is sorely lacking them' (Garoupa and Ginsburg 2015: 39).

The role of constitutional courts as guardians of human rights, prescribed in post-authoritarian constitutions, has in many states, especially in post-communist

Europe, taken precedence over adjudication on the constitutional powers of different branches or (in federations) territorial levels of government. So, in Central and Eastern Europe, 'rights adjudication from the very beginning was at the centre of constitutional courts' activities and clearly outweighed decisions on competences' (Sadurski 2009: 501; Nolan et al. 2007).

Sometimes this has been achieved despite attempts by parliaments and presidents to undermine the independence of the courts through powers over judicial appointments, dismissals and court procedures, as in Ukraine where the 1996 Constitution protects an extraordinary range of social, economic and cultural rights: to work, safe and healthy labour conditions, a minimum wage, rest, form and join trade unions, strike, social security, and a standard of living sufficient to provide adequate nutrition, clothing and housing. Other articles protect the right to housing, health, medical care, medical insurance and education. Freedom of literary, artistic, scientific and technical activities is included, as well as the protection of family, childhood, motherhood and fatherhood. The court has retained sufficient independence so that '[a]fter more than two decades of functioning, the Court developed impressive doctrine and case law to protect economic, social and cultural rights enshrined in the Constitution of Ukraine and international human rights treaties' (Sheliazhenko 2020: 95).

As was shown in Chapter 1, the new constitutions of Third Wave democracies often accepted the human rights dimension of the rule of law, enshrining extensive positive rights in constitutional documents. This has made it difficult in some cases to think of an area of public policy that is not potentially judicialized. These 'positive' rights impose duties on governments to provide material benefits to citizens, and their interpretation by the courts inevitably obliges judges to make judgements about public policy, leading sceptics to ask why it should be thought that judges 'have a better insight than any other intelligent citizen into the correct interpretation of freedom of speech, gender equality, or a right to education' (Sadurski 2009: 518). One of the reasons why judicial activism has led to demands for stronger accountability on the part of the judiciary is that a sub-set of 'intelligent citizens' comprises democratically elected representatives, responsible and accountable for designing public policy.

The existence of justiciable rights has serious implications for the separation of powers, since social and economic policies normally thought to be the legitimate preserve of executives and legislatures are exposed to review by judges. There are two major concerns here: that judges do not have the legitimacy to intervene in the implementation of economic, social and cultural rights; and that judges have neither the professional nor institutional capacity to intervene in conflicts over such rights.

As regards the legitimacy argument – that public policy should be left to democratically elected politicians – it is difficult to see how the courts can be excluded when public policy implementation takes place through law. There is no clear boundary between the 'political' and the 'legal'. The root of the problem lies in the expansion of rights from protection against the incursions of others (sometimes referred to as 'rights of forbearance') to include policies for the provision of goods and services claimed as necessary for people to achieve some desired end. Social and economic demands and aims, however justifiable and desirable, are inevitably in competition with demands from other sections of society with conflicting interests. In democracies, the outcomes of such conflicts require negotiations and compromises. Rights, on the other hand, are non-negotiable and inalienable. An ideal is something to aim at; a right is something that can and must be respected now. If a constitution accepts that the language of 'rights' is applicable to social and economic objectives and ideals, then inevitably the courts will be required to determine when such rights have been violated.

Since rights imply correlative duties, judges also have to identify who the duty-holders are. Duties are more obvious in the case of 'negative' rights where the duty is not to take actions that infringe the rights of other citizens. With social and economic rights, only politicians can be instructed by judges on their duties concerning policy and spending choices. Judges will also be called upon to specify the level below which a right is denied and a case for redress could be made. Here judges will have to rely on statistics on such matters as infant mortality, life expectancy, school enrolments and other 'basic needs' in order to provide evidence of rights denials, again drawing them into disputes over public spending priorities.

In the light of these problems, it seems optimistic to assume, as does the International Commission of Jurists, that '[i]f the law provides for rights or benefits, and the administration fails to deliver them, judicial enforcement of rights could be seen as a means to reinforce the democratic decision of the legislature, rather than as an invasion in the political sphere' (International Commission of Jurists 2008: 80). If the interpretation of a Constitutional or Supreme Court differs from that of a democratically elected legislature over whether a satisfactory level or type of health care or educational provision has been achieved, how can the supremacy of the judges' interpretation be deemed more democratic? How can the determination of legislative omissions arising from judgements on concrete policy decisions avoid becoming attacks on the competence of legislatures?

The International Commission of Jurists finds the solution in a comparison with judicial review of administrative action: 'Judges ordinarily assess governments' compliance by measuring this against constitutional or statutory standards, such as reasonableness, adequateness, proportionality, equality/non-discrimination or non-retrogression' (ICJ 2008: 81). However, this comparison fails to explain how judges remain aloof from politics when determining the content of public policy on the basis of criteria relating to social and economic rights, such as whether a class of people excluded by legislators from a particular public benefit should have the benefit extended to them. In 1998 the Constitutional Court of Colombia tried to explain the distinction by arguing that it was not acting to replace the public authorities liable for a failure to provide for the vaccination of children, but rather it was ordering the state to fulfil its duties where it was clear that failure to act violated a fundamental constitutional right.

The only way round such a debatable distinction is to limit the role of judicial review to ensuring that *some* level or type of provision is made by government in the areas of public policy covered by economic and social rights. Whatever the solution found by a particular system of judicial review, no one would deny that when a constitution specifies political goals in terms of rights, with numerous means by which such goals might be judged to have been achieved, there will need to be collaboration between the judiciary and the other branches of government, 'and probably some deference by the judiciary'. The hope is that new democracies will be able to rely on the traditional reticence of pro-democratic judges towards the review of matters considered to be 'political': 'Although the extent of this reluctance varies, judges tend to be reticent about adopting decisions that imply reviewing budgetary allocations, or which imply the design or implementation of public policies, group or goal priorities, in the absence of a firm legal basis to do so' (ICJ 2008: 85).

Turning to the argument that the professional and institutional capacities of the judiciary are inadequate for resolving conflicts arising from social and economic policy-making, much of the debate seems to miss the point at issue, which is whether judges might usurp the legitimate roles in a democracy of legislatures and executives. Litigation over rights may not necessarily be more complex than property, criminal or commercial law, but the capacity of judges to *understand* the issues does not itself justify their *determination* of them. No doubt judges are just as capable of forming views on political issues as the journalists, business executives, lawyers and trade unionists from whose ranks many legislators are drawn. Judges' educational and professional achievements probably mean they are better qualified than many other citizens to engage in political debates around policy-making. But their level of understanding does not justify a power to overrule elected representatives. The professional capacity of judges does not of itself justify the enforcement of social and economic rights by courts of law.

Consequently, arguments about the institutional capacity of the judiciary tend to focus on the enforceability of the courts' decisions, the adequacy of the judicial hearing for resolving disputes over public policy, and the suitability of procedures designed to hear individual grievances for the resolution of collective claims. One way of solving such problems may be to devise new procedures based on those already available for class actions and which extend locus standi to officials such as ombudsmen so that they can represent collective complaints. The International Commission of Jurists, for example, is optimistic that 'developments in this field today are promising'. With economic, social and cultural rights as well as civil and political rights, 'the effect of purely *individual* cases may also lead political authorities to take general measures that can benefit *groups* of persons, beyond the individual interest of the plaintiff or petitioner' (ICJ 2008: 97).

Two cases heard by the South African Constitutional Court illustrate how governments may be challenged for both their actions and omissions. Benefits under the Social Assistance Act were restricted to South African citizens. In 2004 this was alleged by a group of Mozambicans with permanent resident status in South Africa to discriminate against them unfairly and to be in breach of their constitutional rights. Despite the government's claim that the inclusion of non-citizen permanent residents was unaffordable, the court found the relevant provisions of the act unconstitutional and in breach of Section 9 (3) of the Constitution's Bill of Rights which provides that '[t]he state may not unfairly discriminate directly or indirectly against anyone on one or more grounds, including race, gender, sex, pregnancy, marital status, ethnic or social origin, colour, sexual orientation, age, disability, religion, conscience, belief, culture, language and birth', and Section 27 (1) which gives everyone 'the right to have access to health care services, including reproductive health care'.

Failure to act became the basis for a case brought in 2002 by the Treatment Action Campaign launched by a group of NGOs advocating better prevention and treatment for sufferers from HIV/AIDS. The campaign sought an order from the High Court directing the state to make the anti-retroviral drug Nevirapine, shown by both the World Health Organization and South Africa's Medicines Control Council to prevent mother-to-child transmission of HIV, available at all public health childbirth facilities. The High Court granted the order, which was upheld on appeal to the Constitutional Court, on the grounds that the state's refusal to make the drug more widely available, and as part of a comprehensive plan to deal with the problem of mother-to-child transmission, breached the rights of mothers and newborn babies to health care under Section 27 (1). The court heard the scientific evidence and rejected the state's concerns about the drug's safety and effectiveness. It directed the state to make Nevirapine available at all facilities where needed and to implement a comprehensive prevention plan (ICJ 2008).

Control by the judiciary of the state's legislative omissions is one of the most controversial aspects of judicial review of government policy or more precisely of a government's refusal to accept what some sections of society regard as requiring public provision and governmental intervention. Such review is especially controversial since it empowers the courts to judge what can be afforded by the state, as in Section 27 (2) of South Africa's Constitution which requires the state to 'take reasonable legislative and other measures, within its available resources, to achieve the progressive realization of each of these rights'. In similar vein, the Constitutional Courts of Colombia, Brazil and Venezuela have ordered social security agencies to provide medicines and treatment, and the Brazilian Federal Supreme Court has found that the constitutional right to education obliges the state to provide day care and kindergartens for children under six years of age.

Various tests or standards have been developed by the courts to ensure that governments at least meet their core or minimum obligations, including asking whether powers have been exercised in a way that is 'reasonable', 'adequate' or 'proportionate'. A test of 'reasonableness' has enabled the South African Constitutional Court to deal effectively with objections to the judiciary imposing obligations on governments, regardless of administrative or financial constraints. This involves asking whether government policy was as comprehensive and well coordinated as it could be, whether there was an appropriate division of political and expert authority in its formulation, whether it is sufficiently balanced and flexible, whether it includes all significant segments of society and takes into account those persons most in need, and whether all reasonable steps have been taken to advance a particular social right (Christiansen 2007).

In all regions of the world the post-authoritarian constitutions have been notable for the power given to judges to test the conformity of legislation to the protection extended to human rights in the constitution. Equally, in all regions the extent and effectiveness of judicial activism vary greatly. In Eastern and Central Europe, 'one of the most striking features of the transitions in the post-communist region has been the spectacular growth in the role and prominence of constitutional courts' (Bumin 2017: 67). Many have become vigorous in controlling legislation in the interest of individual rights and democratic consolidation. However, the effectiveness of constitutional courts varies across the region as does the frequency with which legislation is struck down with some being very activist and others relatively restrained.

In the Middle East and North Africa constitutional review has been 'one of the most significant trends following the Arab Spring'. Responding to demands for states based on the rule of law and the protection of rights, and constitutions which reflect international standards, constitutional review bodies became 'a fundamental element of the new constitutional frameworks' (Biagi 2021: 161, 167). However, in the majority of cases deference is shown to the political executive.

Following the third wave of democratization in Latin America, supreme and constitutional courts became a key political institution, expanding and creating fundamental rights, so that now '[t]he frequency with which Latin American courts assert their power is unprecedented, often pushing judges into the political wilderness. Indeed, some rulings champion highly controversial rights and have huge budgetary implications, sending shock waves across these new democracies' (Gonzalez-Ocantos 2021). Yet at the same time and on many occasions the courts have failed to guarantee basic human rights and have had their independence curtailed by the executive and legislative branches (Sieder 2020).

Constitutional reviews in Asia, as in other regions, have varied in their levels of judicial activism with the Taiwanese, South Korean and Indonesian the most successful in support of constitutional justice (Jones 2015; Chen 2018).

In Africa the power assigned to the courts to protect human rights through constitutional review is 'one of the most remarkable aspects of Africa's transition from authoritarianism to constitutional democracy' (Fombad 2020: 17). Constitutional protection of human rights through judicial review has been especially successful in South Africa and Kenya, where the courts have advanced equality despite prevailing prejudices. However, elsewhere in sub-Saharan Africa the judiciary struggles to uphold constitutionalism and human rights, especially in Uganda, Zimbabwe, Zambia and Tanzania. Judicial activism has also been used to sustain authoritarian tendencies. Yet domestic and international pressures are likely to lead to more convergence: '[M]any countries in Africa are currently in or will soon be in a watershed moment for constitutional reform since the conclusion of the situations they currently face are likely to be mediated through constitutional change' (Kibet and Fombad 2017: 365).

The levels of success achieved by the courts exercising judicial review under new democratic constitutions, though varied, have nonetheless attracted hostility from two diametrically opposed sources. One consists of the new authoritarians who have responded by executive suppression of the judiciary and the other of democratic theorists, alarmed at the spectacle of judges striking down laws made by democratically elected legislatures following prescribed democratic procedures. Later sections of this chapter attend to the backlash against judicial activism and the problem posed for democratic theory by judges who defend the rights enshrined in constitutions by defying the country's elected representatives.

Testing the constitutionality of the political process

Judicial review of constitutional provisions draws the judiciary into disputes going far beyond the content of public policy to affect all stages of the political process and the rules of the political game. Earlier in this chapter reference was made to the role of constitutional courts when attempts have been made to extend the terms of office of key political executives. In addition, judges have had to adjudicate on the political activities of civil society organizations, rule on the legality of referenda and elections, and intervene in disputes over parliamentary procedure. The 'judicialization' of politics has found judges to be 'increasingly willing to regulate the conduct of political activity itself – whether practiced in or around legislatures, agencies, or the electorate – by constructing and enforcing standards of acceptable behaviour for interest groups, political parties, and both elected and appointed officials' (Ferejohn 2002: 41). In South Korea, for example, the Constitutional Court's involvement in the political process during the presidency of Roh Moo Hyun from 2002 to 2007 meant that 'virtually every political conflict between pro-Roh political forces and anti-Roh forces ended up in the docket of the Constitutional Court at some point' (Kim 2009: 7). In 2014 the Bulgarian Constitutional Court was called on to intervene in a power struggle between the President and parliament when a group of MPs challenged the constitutionality of the President's appointment of members of the Central Electoral Commission (Freedom House 2015).

First, the judiciary plays a part in negotiating the political demands emanating from civil society by drawing attention to policy issues, especially those affecting human rights. The courts can increase the visibility and legitimacy of organized interests, thereby endowing them with valuable political assets. For example, in South Africa the campaign referred to earlier to secure the right to HIV/AIDS treatment in the face of a reluctant government found a partner in the Constitutional Court (Forbath 2011). This relationship strengthened the political will of the Treatment Action Campaign and gave encouragement to its supporters within government.

In Eastern Europe judicial review has focused attention on issues 'which may otherwise not have received public scrutiny' (Skach 2006: 67), especially since a good deal of media attention is usually given to constitutional courts' decisions.

Some Eastern European courts have been authorized to rule on policies advocated by an exceptionally wide range of civil interests, including pressure groups and even individual citizens, as well as on their own initiative.

Judicial activism in Nigeria has included the formation of alliances with NGOs and trade unions in support of human rights: 'NGOs have been an important factor in ensuring that activist judges have, in their own quiet jurisprudential way, continued to offer conceptual and practical resistance to governmental excesses and abuses' (Okafor 2006: 155). Rulings on socio-economic rights by Argentina's Supreme Court have been reinforced by oversight mechanisms which have monitored responses to judicial decisions through follow-up committees, public hearings and information requests from civil society bodies, thus creating 'collaborative oversight arenas' for collaboration between judges, elected representatives and civil society. These 'arenas' resulted in the dissemination of information, the exchange of information about public policy, and greater impact from the court's rulings; 'via the creation of collaborative oversight arenas, courts can become facilitators, or focal points, that actors in society can use to coordinate and generate change' (Botero 2018: 170).

The history of the Indonesian Constitutional Court between 2003 and 2013 provides a further example of how sections of society that lack representation in the legislature can be given the means to influence public policy and challenge the government, first by submitting petitions setting the court's agenda and second by enlarging the justices' understanding of the policy implications of their decisions through briefings, oral arguments and hearings. Civil society organizations bring the majority of social and economic rights cases to the court, often resulting in controversial decisions and expanding the range of constitutional questions addressed. The petitions submitted by civil society organizations are regularly cited in the justices' written decisions. The court has made it easier for civil society to challenge legislation by abolishing filing fees, and allowing 'standing', even when the petitioners have suffered no specific harm. Judicial activism supported by civil society increases participation in policy-making, especially among otherwise excluded groups, by allowing them 'to circumvent the democratic accountability deficit plaguing Indonesia's elected institutions through the Constitutional Court' (Nardi 2018: 271).

Civil society initiatives pursued through the courts become a significant part of the democratic process under illiberal governments which have used their legislative majorities to exclude sections of society from representation in parliament. The relationship between the courts and civil society is also reciprocal, since support from civil society can help the courts protect their independence; and civil society initiatives can increase the role of the courts as guardians of the constitution. The more the judiciary integrates itself with civil society, through networks of judges and contacts with organized interests, NGOs and community groups, the better the judiciary can defend itself against political interference (Arato 2019; Heyl 2019).

Second, judicial oversight can be brought to bear on political parties. In Poland, the Constitutional Tribunal can be called on to ascertain whether the programmes and activities of a political party comply with the Constitution. The Romanian

Constitutional Court can decide on objections to the constitutionality of a political party. In 2002 the Czech Constitutional Court cancelled statutory amendments adopted by the Chamber of Deputies designed to cut public financing for small political parties, a move by the court designed to protect access to public financing by smaller parties and thus ensure equality of opportunities for all parties and movements. The Federal Supreme Court of Brazil, acting in support of the political and civic rights enshrined in the Constitution of 1988, has ruled on the defection of elected deputies from their political party in order to preserve the legitimacy of the electoral process, guarantee the proportional electoral system, and ensure that elected representatives observe the policies under which they and their party ran for office. The court has also ruled on party coalitions, the protection of small minority parties, and campaign and financing, thus ensuring 'the integrity of the political and electoral process' (Lima 2020: 200).

Third, referenda and elections have been subject to judicial interventions. The Constitutional Court of Ukraine ruled in 2013 that the National Referendum Law of 2012 was consistent with the Constitution, despite arguments that the law allowed matters to be settled by referenda that were specifically prohibited by the constitution from being decided in this way, such as presidential term limits and constitutional amendment. The new law also makes it possible to circumvent the constitutional requirement that a two-thirds majority in parliament should support any constitutional amendment. The political impartiality of the court was consequently called into question. In 2014 constitutional courts ruled on regulations governing municipal elections (Hungary) and the reinstatement of party activists on the electoral register (Lithuania).

Asian courts have been called upon to defend democracy against attempts by politicians to redesign rules on voting, electoral boundaries, apportionments and electoral administration in order to prolong their hold on power. The courts have performed their supervisory role under both dominant party systems and frequent electoral turnovers. They have ruled on voting arrangements for prisoners and citizens living abroad (Malaysia); the population size of electoral districts and the number of votes an elector may cast in National Assembly elections (South Korea); the allocation of votes in the second round of voting, the timing of legislative and presidential elections, and the proportion of votes needed to secure a seat in the national legislature (Indonesia); and in Taiwan, the use of libel suits by rival politicians and the validity of election results (Yap 2016).

Disputes over election results frequently involve the courts in key decisions about the constitutional legitimacy of governments. The Kenyan Supreme Court's confirmation of the presidential election result in 2013, and its acceptance by opposition groups, was widely seen as reflecting a significant step forward for Kenyan democracy in which the judiciary had played a major part. The court's ruling was accepted as independent and free from political pressure, encouraging public confidence in not only the rule of law but also the electoral process. This was especially welcome, given the violence that had marred the previous general election. In 2017 the court declared the presidential election invalid, null and void on the grounds that it had not been conducted according to the Constitution. Later in the year the court was able to uphold the result. On both occasions the court attracted virulent opposition from the losing side yet 'played an important part in checking and balancing political interests and thus helped to moderate the "winner-takes-all" dynamics of politics' (Kanyingaa and Odoteb 2019: 249).

A very different outcome followed the decision of Egypt's Supreme Constitutional Court to order the Islamist-dominated parliament to be dissolved on the grounds that, since a third of the legislature was elected illegally, the entire chamber was illegal. The law governing parliamentary elections had been found unconstitutional by a lower court because it breached the principle of equality by allowing political party members to contest a third of the seats reserved for independents. Since the Constitutional Court's judges were appointed by the ousted President Mubarak, the decision led to accusations by the successful parliamentary parties that the court was acting on behalf of the army. It thus contributed to the subsequent political instability in the country and the demise of constitutional democracy.

Fourth, the judiciary may be called on to adjudicate on the conduct of parliamentary business. For example, in the Philippines the Supreme Court declared unconstitutional an attempt by a group of Congressmen to impeach the Chief Justice, and the High Court dismissed a petition to disqualify a presidential candidate, while in 2012 Romania's Constitutional Court validated the impeachment by parliament of the president. In the same year Hungary's Constitutional Court ruled that the governing coalition in parliament must follow the appropriate legal procedure when passing laws and could not avoid judicial review of legislation by altering the Constitution without a formal amendment procedure. In 2013 the Bulgarian Constitutional Court confirmed a member of parliament's right to take his seat despite having been head of the State Agency for National Security for a short period. Article 72 of the Constitution prohibits membership of parliament by someone who occupies a position of ineligibility or incompatibility. The court controversially found that at the time of the application by 96 parliamentarians to have the member ruled not to be an MP, he did not fail the test of incompatibility because he was not then head of the agency.

In 2014 the Ugandan Constitutional Court found that parliamentary rules of procedure had been flouted. Having been petitioned by a group of MPs, academics, journalists and human rights activists, the court struck down the Anti-Homosexuality Act, ruling that the bill had been passed when the House had been inquorate. The justices found the speaker had acted illegally in not ascertaining whether there was a quorum, even though at least three MPs had alerted her to the possibility. It upheld that

> the act of the 9th Parliament in enacting the Anti-Homosexuality Bill into law without quorum is inconsistent with articles 88, 94 of the Constitution and Rule 23 of the Parliamentary Rules of Procedure. We come to a conclusion that she (Ms Kadaga) acted illegally and failure to obey the law makes the Act null and void.
>
> (*Saturday Monitor* 2014)

South Africa shows how far judicial review of parliamentary business can be taken when backed by a democratic constitution. The court has become increasingly active in judging the constitutionality of both the legislative process and the National Assembly's rules governing the conduct of its business. This has included demands for the establishment of rules where previously none existed. The court has ruled on whether floor-crossing was consistent with multiparty democracy, the rule of law or the political rights contained in the Constitution; on parliament's obligation to facilitate public involvement in law-making; on the individual rights of MPs to introduce bills or schedule a motion of no-confidence in the president; on the National Assembly's constitutional obligation to hold the president accountable; on the speaker's power to call for a secret ballot on a motion of no-confidence in the president; and on the failure of the assembly to fulfil its constitutional obligation to create a special process for impeachment. To many, this level of activism breached the separation of powers between judiciary and legislature. However, it was also argued that the rulings strengthened the separation of powers between executive and legislature at a time when the executive was systematically abusing its dominant party status. The rulings of the South African Court could be justified as consistent with not only the separation of powers but also the rule of law, both enshrined in the Constitution.

> Where abuse of dominant position results instead in the weaponization of the legislature to help create impunity and resist accountability – especially for criminal violations by party leaders – the rule of law and separation of powers come together to justify judicial intervention to bolster the ability of a parliamentary legislature to fulfil its distinctive function.
>
> (Gardbaum 2019: 17)

Hungary's Constitutional Court was petitioned about a large number of procedural irregularities in the legislative process between 2010 and 2019, following the election of the illiberal Fidesz-KDNP coalition government. The irregularities included deficiencies in the preparation of legislative proposals such as a lack of preliminary consultation or impact assessment; a lack of time for parliamentary debate; abuse of 'exceptional and urgent' procedures; unjustified use of an extraordinary parliamentary session; violation of standing orders; voting irregularities, including failure to use the qualified majority rule; and irregular exercise of the president's power of veto. However, although these violations of the legislative process constituted infringements of the rule of law, most of the petitions were found inadmissible or rejected by the Constitutional Court, which 'remained very deferential to the political branches' (Kazai 2021: 21).

Finally, judicial activism has tested the legitimacy of political executives, as when courts in Latin America have subjected members of governments to judicial investigation, trial and conviction (Guarnieri 2003). The Thai Constitution enables the Constitutional Court to ban people from holding political office on the recommendation of the Counter-Corruption Commission. In May 2014 the court ruled that the prime minister and nine cabinet ministers had acted illegally in reassigning a senior security council official, thus removing him from office, in a decision widely seen as a political act by a hostile judiciary acting on behalf of Thailand's urban middle class. The court argued that the PM had abused her constitutional powers by interfering in the transfer of a permanent government official, even though the removal of a military official from a civil service post is well within the PM's jurisdiction. The court also found the transfer to have been made 'too hastily', indicating a 'hidden intention' that was 'not in the national interest'. This was the third time since 2006 that a prime minister representing the political movement founded by the prime minister's brother had been removed by order of the courts. The movement has won every election since 2001, and the 2014 decision caused further political disturbances, eventually leading to yet another military coup.

In 2012 the Chief Justice of Pakistan disqualified the country's prime minister from office, arguing that, having been convicted of contempt for refusing to comply with a Supreme Court order, the PM was automatically disqualified to be a member of parliament and head of the government. The court was criticized for moving the system of government closer to a 'judicial dictatorship'. A backlash within the political elite followed, calmed only by the retirement of the Chief Justice at the end of 2013.

The judiciary has also been used to prosecute a large number for former political executives in new democracies when they leave office, including the former Philippines President Arroyo, President Portillo of Guatemala, Hungary's Prime Minister Orban, South Korea's President Roh Moo Hyun and Malawian President Muluzi. It is clear that political capital can be acquired for an incumbent government by prosecuting a predecessor. It can demonstrate a commitment to accountability and the rule of law. However, the fact that investigation and prosecution are more likely when the judicial system is less independent suggests other motives such as consolidating the position of a government with a weak political base, deflecting the blame for poor economic management, escaping the influence of a former patron, or continuing intra-party factional conflict (Bahry and Kim 2021).

Judicial review of administrative action

In addition to an expanding role for the judiciary resulting from their duty to interpret constitutions and the domestic impact of international conventions, especially those pertaining to human rights, legislation has been passed in most transitional states empowering the courts to review administrative decisions such as Taiwan's Administrative Procedure Act. Laws which have been found to be compatible with the constitution are thus subject to further review when they come to be applied in practice. Judicial review may be sought if it is thought that an administrative agency has acted beyond the powers given to it by statute. Here the complaint is that a state agency – government ministry, local authority or other public body – is *ultra vires*. In addition, judicial review usually extends to judging whether executive powers of a quasi-judicial nature have been exercised according to the rules of natural justice. Depending on the country concerned, *ultra vires* in common law jurisdictions encompasses excess of powers, procedural errors, abuse of power (or decisions taken in bad faith), unreasonableness, irrelevance, improper purpose, arbitrariness, capriciousness and neglect of legitimate expectation.

In civil law jurisdictions, where there are usually mixtures of specialized administrative courts and ordinary civil courts for the purpose of judicial review, the principles applied to test the legality of administrative acts vary considerably. In Brazil, for example, Article 37 of the Constitution stipulates that 'governmental entities and entities owned by the Government in any of the powers of the Union, the states, the Federal District and the Municipalities shall obey the principles of lawfulness, impersonality, morality, publicity, and efficiency'. In Ukraine administrative acts may be reviewed to determine legality, the competence of the agency concerned, the effect on the citizen's rights, and the implications for the 'normal functioning of society and state' (Fenton 2010: 487). The administrative courts of Lithuania consider complaints about the lawfulness of actions performed by administrative entities, the legality of refusal to act within the remit of their competence, delay, and compensation for material and moral damage inflicted on a person or organization by unlawful acts or omissions. Article 9 of Thailand's Act on the Establishment of an Administrative Court and Administrative Court Procedure, 1999, gives the court the power to decide whether an administrative agency has acted without or beyond the scope of its powers and duties; in a manner inconsistent with the law or the form, process or procedure required; in bad faith; with unfair discrimination; causing excessive burden on the public; with undue exercise of discretion; with neglect of duty; or with unreasonable delay. It has the power to grant remedies, revoke by-laws and administrative regulations, order the performance of a duty, and prevent the performance of an illegal act (Leyland 2009). The application of all such principles affects the policy intentions of governments as administrative action seeks to give concrete form to statutory powers which are often defined very broadly and in abstract terms. The Supreme Administrative Court of the Czech Republic has ruled against the arbitrary exercise of discretion by the minister of finance in support of transparency in the management of state property, freedom of information, and emergency social security benefit to ensure basic living conditions (Supreme Administrative Court 2011).

Some systems of administrative law, including those of the Czech Republic and Chile, have expanded the concept of reasonableness to encompass 'proportionality' in order to determine whether the grounds for limiting the citizen's freedoms are proportionate to the protection given those freedoms in the constitution. This entails a move away from the formalist interpretation of statutes to a judgement as to whether fundamental rights have been limited by administrative action only to the extent necessary in the public interest. The principle of proportionality requires administrative authorities to use the least intrusive means consistent with the administration's objectives. Interference with individual rights should be as restrained as possible. When applied by the courts, the proportionality test uses the criteria of suitability, necessity and the relative importance of the conflicting interests. 'Suitability' determines whether the administrative act will achieve its objective. 'Necessity' asks whether a less-intrusive measure could achieve the same objective. 'Relative importance' balances the conflicting interests against each other. If the administrative action is found not to be proportionate, it is invalid and must be revoked or changed by the administration, or quashed by the administrative court. Through proportionality, administrative action is judged by its impact on human rights (Janderova 2019; Cuevas 2017).

A number of legal systems provide procedural guarantees that have evolved into a right to good administration. A rights-based approach to administrative review is based on the principle that human dignity requires fair treatment by the state's public bodies. Procedural fairness requires respect for procedural rights. 'This is a requirement and component of the underlying principle of rule of law: the fundamental premise of this tenet is that the exercise of the public power is legitimate only if it is exerted according to and within the limits of the law' (Szente 2017: 12).

For example, according to Article 22 of the Basic Law of Hungary, '[e]veryone shall have the right to have his or her affairs handled impartially, fairly and within a reasonable time by the authorities. This right involves the obligation of such authorities to attach reasoning to their decisions'. The constitutional importance of the right to good administration is also reflected in the Hungarian Code of Administrative Court Procedure of 2017. It is obligatory to annul an administrative act if the courts cannot remedy an infringement caused by the violation of rules of administrative procedure, though any procedural defect must have a relevant effect on the case. Proper administrative procedures protect the rights and interests of those affected by administrative action, and it is for the courts to decide which procedural rules are to be regarded as relevant to the right to good administration (Rozsnyai 2019). The right to good administration is further fleshed out by confirmation of the rights to be a party in administrative procedures, to appeal, to administrative decision within a prescribed time, to access to relevant documents, to counsel, to be heard, and to adequate justification. Major achievements in Hungarian administrative law include the application to administrative proceedings of the concept of legal certainty (central to the rule of law) and the principle of a fair trial by an independent and impartial court established by law (Gárdos-Orosz and Temesi 2017). The right to a fair trial is also fundamental to administrative jurisprudence in Poland (Lemanska 2017).

A right to good public administration has also been created in South Africa. Under section 33 of the Constitution, everyone has the right to administrative action that is lawful, reasonable and procedurally fair. When other rights are adversely affected by administrative action written reasons must be given. The Constitution further requires this right to be embodied in legislation which provides for the review of administrative action by a court or tribunal and imposes a duty on the state to provide an efficient administration. The legislation should create statutory procedures and mechanisms which make the realization of the right a reality. This constitutional directive was enacted by the Promotion of Administrative Justice Act 2000, which provides recourse to constitutional standards of administrative justice when administrative action threatens individual rights. Other constitutional and statutory provisions, such as those on the Human

Rights Commission, access to information and access to the courts, 'facilitate the enforcement of the right to just administrative action, and they confirm the robustness of South African law in guaranteeing administrative justice as human right' (Omidere 2021: 135).

Despite the importance for the rule of law of judicial review, problems for governance can occur by the power which judicial review of administration places in the hands of judges. First, the values of judges may conflict with those of politicians as to what is in the public interest. Judges are drawn into politics by shaping social and economic developments through rulings on the *merits* of decisions (e.g. the economic viability of an infrastructure project). Furthermore, judges, in controlling the executive branch, claim a legitimacy equal to that of elected representatives, 'developing a parallel channel of accountability' (James 1996: 627), evading 'ouster' clauses in statutes and publicly criticizing ministers' broad discretionary powers. Judicial decisions can also have the effect of entrenching the role of pressure groups in public policy-making by such means as extending the duty to consult or abandoning the locus standi rule. However, such powers, irritating though they may be to ministers and civil servants, are not incompatible with democratic government.

Second, judicial review of administrative action can create a certain amount of uncertainty about public policy. Litigation is inevitably sporadic, yet it is from this that judges develop common law as applied to administrative decisions. Judges may also be inconsistent in their approach to public policy or the administrative process (e.g. what judges count as 'unreasonable' can vary greatly). Decision-making in the administration may be inhibited in anticipation of judicial challenge if judicial intervention creates a legalistic and defensive ethos in policy implementation. Administrators may also feel that the expectations of judges require a model of rationality in decision-making that is hard (if not impossible) to emulate in practice. Or agencies may be obliged to carry out functions for which they may not have the resources. Judicial review also affects administrative practice by prescribing procedural consistency if a 'legitimate expectation' has been created.

When there is an independent judiciary, these drawbacks need not threaten the consolidation of democracy. Judges are likely to be more concerned with the procedural qualities of executive decisions than with their substantive content, especially when those decisions have a quasi-judicial quality themselves. Judicial review 'controls' administration not in the sense of determining individual decisions but in the sense of directing administrators to do their legal duty as laid down in law. It limits the scope of discretion only by enforcing procedural preconditions, if any; and ensuring powers are exercised by the correct body (guarding against improper delegation). The courts do not dictate the results of the exercise of discretion, only that the decision is within the permissible range of an authority's power.

Furthermore, legislatures can also (and regularly do) nullify judicial decisions which cause administrative difficulties by passing laws which have retrospective effect. The extent to which the judiciary can correct things thus depends on the wishes of those who are to be corrected. Neither will civil servants necessarily be overly inhibited by judicial review, mainly because the principles of administrative law developed by the courts are often insufficiently precise to offer clear guidance. Very few of the often small number of cases coming before the courts raise principles of general application.

Judicial review tends to concentrate on a narrow range of administrative activity and only covers an infinitesimal percentage of the millions of decisions taken daily by public authorities. Even when the scope of judicial review is extended it will not necessarily have a direct marked effect on administrative practice. For example, the rules of 'natural justice' leave administrators considerable discretion in deciding when they should be applied and what procedures would be regarded as complying with them. And while judges may see their role as 'curbing' or 'controlling' the state through judicial review of administrative action, the *availability* of judicial review may actually legitimize public administration.

Executive suppression of judicial independence

Having been drawn into political conflicts through their responsibilities for constitutional and administrative review, judges in new democracies have inevitably become the focus of political conflict, even though, as we have seen, the courts have often been deferential towards the legislature or ruled in support of authoritarian measures initiated by the executive branch. Comparative studies of both old and new democracies confirm that '[a]s courts, especially the higher courts, become more activist and autonomous in their decision making by upholding challenges to the activities of the other branches of government and by dealing with hotly contested issues of public law, they attract much more political attention and criticism' (Russell 2001: 301). The role of courts in policy-making, the constraints on democratic politics of constitutional law, and the influence of international jurists resulting from membership of international organizations, conventions and covenants have produced a backlash: '[I]t is precisely in reprisal for such domination of legal and judicial elites that contemporary populism, neo-authoritarianism, democratic backsliding or retrogression of liberal constitutionalism has emerged or resurged' (Chang 2019: 455).

Consequently, as was shown in Chapter 3, judges have often found themselves exposed to extreme forms of partisan pressure and hostility from those whose political ambitions have been thwarted by the courts, including personal threats to individual judges, accusations of corruption, blockades of courthouses, suspension and dismissal from office, and forced resignation. In some Latin American countries the expansion of judicial power has been so controversial that it has brought about the suspension of constitutional courts and the executive suppression of judicial independence. In Chile the Constitutional Court has been reluctant to use its power to pronounce on the constitutionality of legislation for fear that intervention in the context of Chilean politics puts independence at risk (Couso 2004).

In post-communist Europe the courts have been 'subject to various pressures from the political power; the instruments of pressure ranging from banal trade-offs with courts' and judicial logistics and remuneration, removal of judges from office and misuse of the law for their persecution, to threats to personal and physical wellbeing, as well as physical abuse *per se*' (Mazmanyan 2009: 73). In the populist authoritarian post-communist states, such as Hungary and Poland, the constitutional courts have been targeted for defying the will of the people which the populist government claims to represent. A wide range of techniques has been deployed to tame the courts so that they support the government's ideological agenda. Jurisdictions have been reduced to limit a court's competence to review legislation in a particular policy area (financial laws and constitutional amendments in the case of the Hungarian Constitutional Court). In order to retain the judiciary as a legitimizing institution and as a weapon against political opposition, illiberal governments have politicized the constitutional court through court packing, changes to appointment procedures and revised rules of court procedure (such as the order in which cases can be decided, the size of the quorum, the size of the majority required to quash a statute, and not publishing decisions). These techniques are frequently accompanied by attacks on the courts in the public utterances of political leaders, reducing 'the court's long-term ability to defend itself and to defend liberal democratic values' (Petrov 2021: 12).

Fear of repercussions following judicial review of highly controversial political decisions has led some courts to abstain from judgement: '"[A]bstentionism" is in fact often their only way out when they are caught between their primary responsibilities, imposed by constitutions on the one hand and considerations of personal well-being on the other' (Mazmanyan 2009: 75). The need to appease those with political power has sometimes meant compromising on the merits of the case, thereby sacrificing the court's legitimacy in the eyes of the public. One response from legal scholars has been to advocate removing the issues posing the greatest danger to the independence of the judiciary, such as the validity of elections, referenda and impeachment proceedings, from the jurisdiction of the courts.

However, this dramatic, risk-averse solution would rob the new democracy of the contribution which an independent, pro-democracy and rights-protecting judiciary can make to the development of a strong democratic political culture. For example, in Slovakia, where the Constitutional Court has been effective in controlling authoritarian tendencies, and where justices have been drawn from a westernized, pro-democratic elite, the public popularity of the court is high (Schwartz 1999). By defending basic constitutional and judicial principles in its confrontations with the political executive and its supporters in the legislature, the judiciary can attract support in the wider community and contribute to the development of a democratic political culture in which judicial independence has a central role: 'A constitutional court that spends its "institutional capacity" intelligently not only can survive these confrontations but also can come out of them with a stronger popular base for the judiciary's independence'

(Russell 2001: 305). A number of countries, including Estonia, Indonesia and Chile, have legislated against abstention in judicial decision-making.

Judges may also choose to render judicial review politically less confrontational by judicial deferral, where a decision which finds legislation constitutionally invalid is suspended. This device, successfully tried in transitional states including South Africa, Colombia and Indonesia gives governments a chance to modify public policy in the light of a constitutional court's reasoning. The effect can be to reduce doubts about the democratic legitimacy of judicial review, enabling the courts to 'increase the acceptance and effectiveness of their jurisprudence in conditions of judicial and democratic fragility' (Dixon and Issacharoff 2016: 728).

In fact, judges have a number of strategies at their disposal with which to defend themselves against political interference in the judicial process or attempts to reduce the power of the judiciary overall, even under the least auspicious circumstances, such as the resurgent authoritarianism of many regimes. Courts may be able to retain a degree of independence by providing governments with information about divisions within political elites. Such information helps the government stay in power. Courts which defy attempts to bring them under control are also less costly sources of opposition to government policies than a free media, free elections, well-organized political parties or local governments controlled by opposition parties (Garoupa and Karakas 2021).

Judicial empowerment can also be sought by actions to strengthen the legitimacy of the judiciary in the eyes of the public, such as embedding democratic values, rule of law norms and constitutionalism in judgements. In South Korea, a 'supermajority' of six justices out of nine is required for the Constitutional Court to rule a law unconstitutional. This unusual voting requirement was designed to limit the court's review power. However, this has had the effect of extending the influence of the court through the signals which the court gives to lower courts, political groups and the general public about the substance of its jurisprudence in different divisive and controversial policy areas. As a consequence the court's authority and democratic legitimacy have grown stronger 'by alleviating concerns that some of the most important and controversial matters facing the country would hinge on a single swing vote and by muting accusations of "judicial activism" on the Court' (Hong 2019: 179).

The courts can also protect themselves by disseminating information drawing attention to defects in the political process such as corruption, electoral irregularities or the non-enforcement of judgements, thereby increasing the transparency of politics and the accountability of politicians. In 2021 Polish judges, threatened with disciplinary offences for rulings which the government found unhelpful, took the Constitution 'on tour' in over 80 towns, warning the public about the governing party's campaign to undermine the judiciary's independence and the rule of law (see Chapter 5). In addition, allies can be forged in civil society and the media by judgements which indicate how similar cases might fare in the future or a willingness to entertain challenges to government policy or political strategy. Judges can engage in advocacy through their representative associations such as law societies to defend judicial independence or promote reform. Senior judges can provide leadership in negotiations with the executive over relationships between the two branches of government (Ellett 2013). Some transitional judiciaries provide useful guidance for their colleagues in other countries as to what they themselves can do to protect their independence.

Judicial activism and democracy

Entrusting the judiciary with the constitution and the rights enshrined in it would seem an obvious way to protect society against arbitrary government. Yet the more judges are asked to adjudicate on conflicts between legislation and the constitution, the greater the concern that the powers of elected representatives are being usurped. One view is that in a democracy legislation is preferable to judicial review in settling disagreements about rights. Judges are no better than politicians at deciding what health, education or welfare policy should be, and their socio-economic backgrounds might bias them towards a privileged minority. In a political, rather than legal, view of the constitution, the decisions of democratically elected politicians should not be overturned by the courts. 'For political constitutionalists, a healthy democratic system is one in which political conflicts are solved by political means and in which judicial actors defer to the democratically-elected legislature when it comes to the decisions on the general rules that regulate society' (Castillo-Ortiz 2019: 54).

Constitutional courts, notably in Eastern Europe, have been especially accused of 'enacting' constitutional rules, changing existing legislation, identifying legislative omissions, and changing the procedures for judicial review. They have deferred their own rulings, thereby altering the date at which laws become effective. In protecting the wording, spirit and values expressed in the constitution, constitutional courts have been found to *creatively* interpret the law (Florczak-Wator 2020).

A contrasting view finds the judiciary indispensable for protecting minorities against the 'tyranny of the majority', the supremacy of the constitution over ordinary legislation, and the individual rights and freedoms enshrined in those constitutions. The introduction of judicially enforceable rights into constitutions turned the judiciary into a political force that has to be included in the negotiations between political interests (Petrov 2021). Empowering the courts to rule on whether due process has been observed in the administration of executive powers can have consequences beneficial to democracy. Judicial review, though generally costly and slow, provides opportunities for grievances to be redressed and justice to be done in matters of great relevance to people's livelihoods and welfare. Procedural resolutions by the courts, requiring governments to reconsider their policy options in the manner prescribed by law, can be helpful in defusing political crises, prompting political dialogue and consultation, as shown by litigation on Taiwan's highway tolls, nuclear installations and national health insurance (Yeh 2009).

When subjected to closer examination, constitutional courts in new democracies appear to be carrying out the roles demanded of them by the constitution, rather than usurping the powers of democratic legislatures by making laws themselves. Rulings confirming the unconstitutionality of legislative acts are not law-making; and rulings about omissions invite the legislature to remedy the situation in line with the constitution. Giving advice to parliament when issuing explanations of rulings may or may not influence future legislation, but it does not amount to a legislative act itself. It is not clear how protecting the identity of the Constitution, in the Slovak case identified as the rule of law and independence of the judiciary, or in the Czech case as including international treaties protecting human rights, means that constitutional courts 'thus place themselves de facto above the Constituent bodies' (Florczak-Wator 2020: 250).

It transpires that in many new democracies few provisions of the constitution are subject to examination by the constitutional court. And while the courts may adapt the constitution to changing social conditions, it still remains for parliament to decide whether to accept such changes, endorse them or reject them. Creative interpretations of constitutions tend to develop individual rights and freedoms on the basis of constitutional principles. Constitutional courts do not have the power to create new legislation. They regularly defer ruling on unconstitutional laws, giving parliament time to amend it. Often the court will rule a new statute to be partially unconstitutional, under the conviction that 'moderation is required with respect to interference with the parliament's legislative powers' (Florczak-Wator 2020: 258). Court rulings may contain directives, guidelines and recommendations for the legislature, but these are not binding. If this constitutes 'interference' in law-making, it is no more so than the pressure from powerful vested interests, which is far less impartial than the recommendations of the courts.

Judicial activism is too diverse a phenomenon to allow sweeping conclusions about constraints on democratic legislatures, leading to proposals to contextualize the abstract debate 'paying attention to *particular* effects, produced by *particular* institutions in *particular* socio-historical circumstances' (Jovanović 2015: 80). In the case of Central and Eastern Europe, constitutional adjudication has been shown to be more diverse than assumed in terms of types of judicial ruling and strength of constraint on legislatures. Different courts make variable use of rulings on legislative omissions, procedural unconstitutionality, constitutional requirements, the timing for rulings to take effect, remedies, dissenting opinions, the scope of annulments, and the type of prescription determined by the court. The general pattern which does emerge, however, is that constitutional courts exercise slight constraints over parliaments and observe self-restraint and moderation rather than undermine democracy. For example, the Czech Constitutional Court, though renowned for the scope of its judicial review, nevertheless leaves the legislature 'considerable room for manoeuvre'

(Sipulova 2019: 33). The Hungarian Court also 'did not constrain the legislature very heavily' (Pocza et al. 2019: 121). Even at the height of its power, the Slovak Court 'never became a third legislator' (Lastic and Steuer 2019: 244). Accusations that the courts have usurped democracy are not supported by the evidence.

> Consequently, the general argument of the political actors of those countries, which states that courts intruded into the field of politics and illegitimately constrained the democratically elected legislatures, seems to be inadequate and should be considered rather as a fictitious narrative which aims to underpin the political intentions of the dominant actors.
>
> (Pocza 2019: 2)

In the post-authoritarian states of Central and Eastern Europe judiciaries have had more to fear from illiberal democracies and the authoritarian tendencies of populist governments than elected legislatures have had to fear from judicial review. For example, the Polish Constitutional Tribunal was originally very powerful and authoritative, partly because of a lack of leadership in the fragmented parliament, but once the populist Law and Justice party gained control it curbed the power of judges and rendered them harmless by politicization. Hungary's Fidesz party under Prime Minister Viktor Orbán has 'packed' the Constitutional Court. Authoritarians in other regions have followed suit. Representative examples include Azerbaijan, where the authoritarian regime of Ilham Aliyev brings trumped-up cases against opposition figures and critics before politically subservient courts. In Bangladesh the Awami League government has politicized the judiciary. Thailand's military-dominated government has used the Constitutional Court to dissolve political parties and overthrow elected officials. The Zimbabwe, the African National Union–Patriotic Front (ZANU-PF) government has eroded the judiciary's independence through pressure on the courts to endorse executive actions and protect ZANU-PF's interests. Politicization of the judiciary has greatly increased under Presidents Chávez and Maduro of Venezuela.

The problem of legislature versus judiciary in matters falling under constitutional review arises mainly from the inclusion of social and economic benefits within the category of 'rights'. A democratic, representative legislature would seem to be superior to the courts in deciding on the allocation of resources to social and economic objectives and the role of the state in this process. The value of the judiciary lies in the protection which it can and should give to civil and political rights, if only because when governments interfere with basic political freedoms that are firmly established, it can only be to damage enjoyment of them. The role of the courts is to guard against such infringement. If legislation seeks to modify our right to, say, freedom of speech, in order to protect people against libel, it is useful to have the judiciary decide whether this infringement leaves our freedom otherwise unaffected.

However, governments may feel they have a mandate to curtail other freedoms such as freedom of association with, say, trade union legislation. Are the courts best placed to judge when the law has been pushed too far? Judges are political animals and have their own ideological and even party preferences. What the constitutions of new democracies have done is draw the judiciary ever further into policy-making, thereby creating powerful incentives for majoritarian governments to interfere in the judicial process and for judges to allow their political values to affect their judgements. Nevertheless, the politicization of the judiciary is more often the result of executive interference rather than an exercise of power by a judicial elite. For example, judicial activism in post-communist Europe has not meant 'a real transfer of political decision-making from the representative branches to the courts . . . judicial involvement in politics is more often than not a by-product of political pressure or manipulation of constitutional law and of the constitutional judiciary' (Mazmanyan 2015: 217–218).

In theory, the solution is robust political competition that punishes electorally the party whose government encroaches upon judicial independence. But what if, having 'packed' the Supreme Court with political supporters, the government legislates to disadvantage the opposition by gerrymandering or other forms of electoral manipulation? What protection can a politicized judiciary offer democracy then? Post-authoritarian history offers no reassuring answer to this question. The judiciary may seem like the last bastion of democracy when governments in transitional states develop authoritarian tendencies. Where democracy has not been consolidated, judicial empowerment and the judicialization of politics create 'an illuminating paradox: while judicialization is conventionally treated as a counter-democratic practice, in non-consolidated democracies it clearly signals success of democratization' (Mazmanyan 2015: 201).

Because judicial review of legislation and administration can appear to represent an unelected and elitist body challenging and overriding the will of the people as enunciated by their elected representatives, it may be thought that the empowerment of judges in the transition to democracy is premature. It is something that should await democratic consolidation. Because of the occasional backlash against judicial 'interference' in policy-making it might be argued that 'a consolidated democracy constitutes a necessary condition for the proper introduction of judicial review' (Couso 2004: 89), rather than judicial review being required before democracy can be consolidated. However, it is not clear how a democracy can be judged to be consolidated before the courts are able to protect human rights and prevent illegal administration through judicial review. A regime can hardly be presented as democratic in the absence of these essential components of the rule of law.

* * *

Post-authoritarian constitutions have endowed the judiciary with exceptional powers, encouraging and facilitating 'judicial activism'. The judiciary is drawn into the definition of constitutional rules, the amendment of constitutions, challenges to the legality of policy decisions, adjudicating on the constitutionality of the political process, and judicial review of administrative action. In some jurisdictions judicial review of administrative decisions and procedures has evolved into a right to good administration. Judicial activism has drawn judges into political conflicts and attracted hostility from sections of society whose interests are adversely affected by judicial interpretations of legislative and administrative actions and from governments, especially those attempting to deviate from democratic constitutional norms.

The power granted to the judiciary to adjudicate in disputes about the constitutional powers of governments, the interpretation of statutes and the application of precedents has prompted accusations that the legitimate authority of democratic legislatures is being usurped. Judges then appear to be making the law, rather than just administering it. Constitutional endorsement of the human rights dimension of the rule of law, enshrining extensive positive social and economic rights in constitutions, has inevitably involved interpretation by the courts and obliged justices to make judgements about public policy.

It is easy to understand demands for greater accountability of judiciaries wielding such extensive powers of review, even when it is difficult to see how such accountability can be made compatible with the preservation of judicial independence. Devising ways to make judges accountable becomes additionally significant when we consider other aspects of judicial autonomy in democratizing countries. The following chapter examines the seemingly self-contradictory concept of 'judicial accountability'.

References

Albert, R. (2017), 'The state of the art in constitutional amendment' in R. Albert, X. Contiades and A. Fotiadou (eds.), *The Foundations and Traditions of Constitutional Amendment*, Oxford: Hart Publishing.

Arato, A. (2019), 'Populism, constitutional courts, and civil society' in C. Landfried (ed.), *Judicial Power: How Constitutional Courts Affect Political Transformations*, Cambridge: Cambridge University Press.

Bahry, D. and Y. H. Kim (2021), 'Executive turnover and the investigation of former leaders in new democracies', *Political Research Quarterly*, vol. 74, no. 1.

Belov, M. and A. Tsekov (2020), 'The constitutional court of the Republic of Bulgaria as a law-maker' in Monika Florczak-Wator (ed.), *Judicial Law-Making in European Constitutional Courts*, Abingdon: Routledge.

Biagi, F. (2021), 'Constitutional review after the Arab Spring: reforms, challenges and perspectives' in A. Schoeller-Schletter (ed.), *Constitutional Review in the Middle East and North Africa*, Baden-Baden: Nomos.

Botero, S. (2018), 'Judges, litigants, and the politics of rights enforcement in Argentina', *Comparative Politics*, vol. 50, no. 2.

Brovko, N. I., L. P. Medvid, I. Y. Mahnovskyi, V. A. Ahmadov and M. I. Leonenko (2021), 'The role of the constitutional complaint in the legislative process: comparative legal aspect', *Cuestiones Políticas*, vol. 39, no. 69.

Bumin, K. M. (2017), 'Judicial institutionalization and judicial activism of the post-communist constitutional courts', *Journal of Politics and Law*, vol. 10, no. 2.

Cajas-Sarria, M. A. (2017), 'Judicial review of constitutional amendments in Colombia: a political and historical perspective, 1955–2016', *The Theory and Practice of Legislation*, vol. 5, no. 3.

Castillo-Ortiz, P. (2019), 'The illiberal abuse of constitutional courts in Europe', *European Constitutional Law Review*, vol. 15, no. 1.
Chang, W.-C. (2019), 'Back into the political? Rethinking judicial, legal, and transnational constitutionalism', *International Journal of Constitutional Law*, vol. 17, no. 2.
Chang, W.-C. and J.-R. Yeh (2012), 'Internationalization of constitutional law', in M. Rosenfeld and A. Sajó (eds.), *Oxford Handbook of Comparative Constitutional Law*, Oxford: Oxford University Press.
Chen, A. H. Y. (2018), 'Constitutional courts in Asia: Western origins and Asian practice' in A. H. Y. Chen and A. Harding (eds.), *Constitutional Courts in Asia: A Comparative Perspective*, Cambridge: Cambridge University Press.
Christiansen, E. C. (2007), 'Adjudicating non-justiciable rights: socio-economic rights and the South African Constitutional Court', *Columbia Human Rights Law Review*, vol. 38, no. 2.
CCEJ (2015), *The Position of the Judiciary and Its Relation With the Other Powers of State in a Modern Democracy*, Opinion No. 18 (2015), London: Consultative Council of European Judges.
Couso, J. A. (2004), 'The politics of judicial review in Chile in the era of democratic transition, 1990–2002' in S. Gloppen, R. Gargarella and E. Sklaar (eds.), *Democratization and the Judiciary: The Accountability Function of Courts in New Democracies*, London: Frank Cass.
Cuevas, I. C. (2017), 'Reception of the proportionality test by Chilean scholars: a critical analysis' in R. Arnold and J. I. Martínez-Estay (eds.), *Rule of Law, Human Rights and Judicial Control of Power Some Reflections from National and International Law*, Cham: SpringerCastillo.
Desposato, S. W., M. C. Ingram and O. P. Lannes (2015), 'Power, composition, and decision making: the behavioural consequences of institutional reform on Brazil's *Supremo Tribunal Federal*', *Journal of Law, Economics and Organization*, vol. 31, no. 3.
Dixon, R. and S. Issacharoff (2016), 'Living to fight another day: judicial deferral in defense of democracy', *Wisconsin Law Review*, vol. 4, no. 1.
Doyle, O. (2017), 'Constraints on constitutional amendment powers' in R. Albert, X. Contiades and A. Fotiadou (eds.), *The Foundations and Traditions of Constitutional Amendment*, Oxford: Hart Publishing.
Ellett, R. (2013), *Pathways to Judicial Power in Transitional States. Perspectives from African Courts*, Abingdon: Routledge.
February, J. (2007), 'Misappropriations mar South Africa's courts' in *Transparency International, Global Corruption Report 2007: Corruption in Judicial Systems*, Cambridge: Cambridge University Press.
Fenton, H. N. (2010), 'Where too little judicial deference can impair the administrative process: the case of Ukraine' in S. Rose-Ackerman and P. Lindseth (eds.), *Comparative Administrative Law*, Cheltenham: Edward Elgar.
Ferejohn, J. (2002), 'Judicializing politics, politicizing law', *Law and Contemporary Problems*, vol. 65, no. 3.
Florczak-Wator, M. (2020), 'European constitutional courts as law-makers: research synthesis' in M. Florczak-Wator (ed.), *Judicial Law-Making in European Constitutional Courts*, Abingdon: Routledge.
Fombad, C. M. (2020), 'Taming executive authoritarianism in Africa: some reflections on current trends in horizontal and vertical accountability', *Hague Journal on the Rule of Law*, vol. 12, no. 1.

Forbath, W. (2011), 'Cultural transformation, deep institutional reform and ESR practice: South Africa's treatment action campaign' in L. E. White and J. Perelman (eds.), *Stones of Hope: How African Activists Reclaim Human Rights to Challenge Global Poverty*, Stanford: Stanford University Press.

Freedom House (2015), *Nations in Transit 2015: Bulgaria*, New York: Freedom House.

Gardbaum, S. (2019), 'Pushing the boundaries: judicial review of legislative procedures in South Africa', *Constitutional Court Review*, vol. 19, no. 1.

Gárdos-Orosz, F and I. Temesi (2017), 'The principle of effective legal protection in Hungarian administrative law', in Z. Szente and K. Lachmayer (eds.), *The Principle of Effective Legal Protection in Administrative Law: A European Comparison*, Abingdon: Routledge.

Garoupa, N. and T. Ginsburg (2015), *Judicial Reputation. A Comparative Theory*, Chicago: University of Chicago Press.

Garoupa, N. and L. D. Karakas (2021), 'A theory of defiant courts in nondemocratic regimes', *Journal of Legal Studies*, vol. 50, no. 1.

Gauri, V. and Brinks, D. (2008), *Courting Social Justice: Judicial Enforcement of Social and Economic Rights in the Developing World*, Cambridge: Cambridge University Press.

Ginsburg, T. (2003), *Judicial Review in New Democracies: Constitutional Courts in Asian Cases*, Cambridge: Cambridge University Press.

Ginsburg, T. (2009), 'The judicialization of administrative governance: Causes, consequences and limits' in T. Ginsburg and A. H. Y Chen (eds.), *Administrative Law and Governance in Asia: Comparative Perspectives*, London: Routledge.

Gloppen, S., Wilson, B. M., Gargarella, R., Skaar, E. and Kinander, M. (2010), *Courts and Power in Latin America and Africa*, New York: Palgrave Macmillan.

Gonzalez-Ocantos, E. (2021), 'Courts in Latin America' in G. Provost and H. F. Vanden (eds.), *The Oxford Encyclopaedia of Latin American Politics*, New York: Oxford University Press.

Guarnieri, C. (2003), 'Courts as an instrument of horizontal accountability: the case of Latin America' in J. M. Maravall and A. Przeworski (eds.), *Democracy and the Rule of Law*, Cambridge: Cambridge University Press.

Heyl, C. (2019), 'The judiciary and the rule of law in Africa' in N. Cheeseman (ed.), *The Oxford Encyclopaedia of African Politics*, Oxford: Oxford University Press.

Hong, J. S. (2019), 'Signalling the turn: the supermajority requirement and judicial power on the Constitutional Court of Korea', *American Journal of Comparative Law*, vol. 67, no. 1.

Howard, A. E. D. (2001), 'Judicial independence in post-communist central and eastern Europe' in P. H. Russell and D. M O'Brien (eds.), *Judicial Independence in the Age of Democracy*, Charlottesville: University Press of Virginia.

ICJ (2008), *Courts and the Legal Enforcement of Economic, Social and Cultural Rights: Comparative Experiences of Justiciability*, Human Rights and Rule of Law Series No. 2, Geneva: International Commission of Jurists.

James, S. (1996), 'The political and administrative consequences of judicial review', *Public Administration*, vol. 74, no. 4.

Janderova, J. (2019), 'Impact of the rule of law as fundamental public governance principle on administrative law interpretation in the Czech Republic', *Central European Public Administration Review*, vol. 17, no. 2.

Jones, B. C. (2015), 'Assessing the constitutionality of legislation: constitutional review in Taiwan's legislative Yuan', *Asia Pacific Law Review*, vol. 23, no. 2.

Jovanović, M. (2015), 'On the abstract case against constitutional review', in M. Jovanović (ed.), *Constitutional Review and Democracy*, Utrecht: Eleven Publishing International.
Kanyingaa, K. and C. Odoteb (2019), 'Judicialisation of politics and Kenya's 2017 elections', *Journal of Eastern African Studies*, vol. 13, no. 2.
Kazai, V. Z. (2021), 'The misuse of the legislative process as part of the illiberal toolkit: The case of Hungary', *The Theory and Practice of Legislation*, https://doi.org/10.1080/20508840.2021.1942366
Khan, M. S. (2013), 'Ambiguous ambitions', *Development and Co-Operation*, vol. 40, no. 12.
Kibet, E. and C. Fombad (2017), 'Transformative constitutionalism and the adjudication of constitutional rights in Africa', *African Human Rights Law Journal*, vol. 17, no. 2.
Kim, J. (2009), 'Government reform, judicialization, and the development of public law in the Republic of Korea' in T. Ginsburg and A. H. Y. Chen (eds.), *Administrative Law and Governance in Asia: Comparative Perspectives*, London: Routledge.
Kopeček, L. and J. Petrov (2016), 'From parliament to courtroom: judicial review of legislation as a political tool in the Czech Republic', *East European Politics and Societies*, vol. 30, no. 1.
Lachmayer, K. (2020), 'Disempowering courts: the interrelationship between courts and politics in contemporary legal orders or the manifold ways of attacking judicial independence' in M. Belov (ed.), *Courts, Politics and Constitutional Law*, Abingdon: Routledge.
Lastic, E. and M. Steuer (2019), 'The Slovak Constitutional Court: the third legislator' in K. Pocza (ed.), *Constitutional Politics and the Judiciary: Decision-Making in Central and Eastern Europe*, Abingdon: Routledge.
Lemanska, J. (2017), 'The principle of effective legal protection in Polish administrative law' in Z. Szente and K. Lachmayer (eds.), *The Principle of Effective Legal Protection in Administrative Law: A European Comparison*, Abingdon: Routledge.
Leyland, P. (2009), 'The emergence of administrative justice in Thailand under the 1977 Constitution' in T. Ginsburg and A. H. Y. Chen (eds.), *Administrative Law and Governance in Asia: Comparative Perspectives*, London: Routledge.
Lima, F. (2020), 'Protecting political rights or interfering in the political arena?', *Humanities and Rights Global Network Journal*, vol. 2, no. 2.
Lin, J. (2009), 'The judicialization of governance: the case of Singapore' in T. Ginsburg and A. H. Y. Chen (eds.), *Administrative Law and Governance in Asia: Comparative Perspectives*, London: Routledge.
Malír, J. and J. Ondrejková (2020), 'Law-making activity of the Czech Constitutional Court' in Monika Florczak-Wator (ed.), *Judicial Law-Making in European Constitutional Courts*, Abingdon: Routledge.
Mazmanyan, A. (2009), 'Should constitutional courts adjudicate political disputes? The perspectives of democratization in Soviet successor states', *Review of Central and East European Law*, vol. 34, no. 1.
Mazmanyan, A. (2015), 'Judicialization of politics: the post-Soviet way', *International Journal of Comparative Law*, vol. 13, no. 1.
Nardi, D. J. (2018), 'Can NGOs change the constitution? Civil society and the Indonesian Constitutional Court', *Contemporary Southeast Asia*, vol. 40, no. 2.
Nkhata, J. M. (2020). 'The High Court of Malawi as a constitutional court: constitutional adjudication the Malawian way', *Law, Democracy and Development*, vol. 24, no. 1.
Nolan, A., B. Porter and M. Langford (2007), *The Justiciability of Social and Economic Rights: An Updated Appraisal*, Centre for Human Rights and Global Justice Working Paper No. 15, New York.

Okafor, O. C. (2006), *Legitimizing Human Rights NGOs: Lessons from Nigeria*, Trenton, NJ: Africa World Press.

Omidere, K. (2021), 'Administrative justice as human right: a perspective from South Africa', *International Journal of Law and Society*, vol. 4, no. 2.

Petrov, J. (2021), '(De-)judicialization of politics in the era of populism: lessons from Central and Eastern Europe', *The International Journal of Human Rights*, DOI: 10.1080/13642987.2021.1931138

Pocza, K. (2019), 'Introduction' in K. Pocza (ed.), *Constitutional Politics and the Judiciary: Decision-Making in Central and Eastern Europe*, Abingdon: Routledge.

Pocza, K., G. Dobos and A. Gyulai (2019), 'The Hungarian Constitutional Court: a constructive partner in constitutional dialogue' in K. Pocza (ed.), *Constitutional Politics and the Judiciary: Decision-Making in Central and Eastern Europe*, Abingdon: Routledge.

Rosenfeld, M. and A. Sajó (2012), 'Introduction' in M. Rosenfeld and A. Sajó (eds.), *Oxford Handbook of Comparative Constitutional Law*, Oxford: Oxford University Press.

Rozsnyai, K. F. (2019), 'Current tendencies of judicial review as reflected in the new Hungarian Code of Administrative Court Procedure', *Central European Public Administration Review*, vol. 17, no. 1.

Roux, T. (2004), 'Legitimating transformation: political resource allocation in the South African Constitutional Court' in S. Gloppen, R. Gargarella and E. Sklaar (eds.), *Democratization and the Judiciary: The Accountability Function of Courts in New Democracies*, London: Frank Cass.

Russell, P. H. (2001), 'Conclusion: judicial independence in comparative perspective' in P. H. Russell and D. M. O'Brien (eds.), *Judicial Independence in the Age of Democracy: Critical Perspectives From Around the World*, Charlottesville: University Press of Virginia.

Sadek, M. T. and R. B. Cavalcanti (2003), 'The new Brazilian Public Prosecution: an agent of accountability' in S. Mainwaring and C. Welna (eds.), *Democratic Accountability in Latin America*, Oxford: Oxford University Press.

Sadurski, W. (2009), 'Judicial review in Central and Eastern Europe: rationales or rationalization?', *Israel Law Review*, vol. 42, no. 3.

Santiso, C. (2004), 'Economic reform and judicial governance in Brazil: balancing independence with accountability' in S. Gloppen, R. Gargarella and E. Sklaar (eds.), *Democratization and the Judiciary: The Accountability Function of Courts in New Democracies*, London: Frank Cass.

Saturday Monitor, Uganda (2014), 'Court quashes anti-gays law', 2 August, www.monitor,co.ug

Schwartz, H. (1999), 'Surprising success: the new Eastern European constitutional courts' in A. Schedler, L. Diamond and M. F. Plattner (eds.), *The Self-Restraining State: Power and Accountability in New Democracies*, London: Lynne Rienner.

Seong-Hak Kim, M. (2015), 'Travails of judges: courts and constitutional authoritarianism in South Korea', *American Journal of Comparative Law*, vol. 63, no. 3.

Sheliazhenko, Y. (2020), 'Against the odds: protection of economic, social, and cultural rights by the Constitutional Court of Ukraine', *Constitutional Review*, vol. 6, no. 1.

Sieder, R. (2020), 'The juridification of politics', in M.-C. Foblets, M. Goodale, M. Sapignoli, and O. Zenker (eds.), *The Oxford Handbook of Law and Anthropology*, Oxford: Oxford University Press.

Sipulova, K. (2019), 'The Czech Constitutional Court: far away from political influence' in K. Pocza (ed.), *Constitutional Politics and the Judiciary: Decision-Making in Central and Eastern Europe*, Abingdon: Routledge.

Skach, S. (2006), 'Rethinking judicial review: shaping the toleration of difference?' in A. Czarnota, M. Krygier and W. Sadurski (eds.), *Rethinking the Rule of Law after Communism*, Budapest: Central European Press.

Supreme Administrative Court (2011), *Decision of the Supreme Administrative Court of the Czech Republic*, 14 December, file no. 6, www.nssoud.cz/artlist/135

Sweet, A. S. (2012), 'Constitutional courts' in M. Rosenfeld and A. Sajó (eds.), *Oxford Handbook of Comparative Constitutional Law*, Oxford: Oxford University Press.

Szente, Z. (2017), 'Conceptualising the principle of effective legal protection in administrative law' in Z. Szente and K. Lachmayer (eds.), *The Principle of Effective Legal Protection in Administrative Law: A European Comparison*, Abingdon: Routledge.

Szente, Z. and F. Gárdos-Orosz (2018), 'Judicial deference or political loyalty? The Hungarian Constitutional Court's role in tackling crisis situations' in Z. Szente and F. Gárdos-Orosz (eds.), *New Challenges to Constitutional Adjudication in Europe*, Abingdon: Routledge.

Tate, N. and T. Vallinder (1995), *The Global Expansion of Judicial Power*, New York: New York University Press.

Trochev, A. (2016), 'Legitimacy, accountability and discretion of the Russian courts' in M. Brusis, J. Ahrend and M. S. Wessel (eds.), *Politics and Legitimacy in Post-Soviet Eurasia*, Basingstoke: Palgrave Macmillan.

Uprimy, R. (2004), 'The Constitutional Court and control of presidential extraordinary powers in Colombia' in S. Gloppen, R. Gargarella and E. Sklaar (eds.), *Democratization and the Judiciary: The Accountability Function of Courts in New Democracies*, London: Frank Cass.

Venice Commission (2021), *Revised Report on Individual Access to Constitutional Justice*, Opinion No. 1004/2020, Strasbourg: European Commission for Democracy Through Law.

Vondoepp, P. (2005), 'The problem of judicial control in Africa's neopatrimonial democracies: Malawi and Zambia', *Political Science Quarterly*, vol. 120, no. 2.

Yap, P. J. (2016), 'Courts and elections in Asia' in P. J. Yap (ed.), *Judicial Review of Elections in Asia*, Abingdon: Routledge.

Yeh, J. (2009), 'Democracy-driven transformation to regulatory state: The case of Taiwan' in T. Ginsburg and A. H. Y. Chen (eds.), *Administrative Law and Governance in Asia: Comparative Perspectives*, London: Routledge.

Yowell, P. (2020), 'The negative legislator: on Kelsen's idea of a constitutional court' in M. Belov (ed.), *Courts, Politics and Constitutional Law*, Abingdon: Routledge.

9 Judicial accountability

Introduction

One factor affecting the constitutional structuring of relationships between the judiciary and other branches of government is the fear that judges might, through constitutional review, interpretation of statute or application of precedent, make law rather than just apply it to specific cases. Concern that judicial activism is usurping the legitimate authority of elected legislatures has generated demands for the judiciary to be made more accountable. This raises the key question of how such accountability can be designed so that it is compatible with the preservation of judicial independence. 'This potential for conflict with cherished ideals of judicial impartiality has led to a sensitivity to, and hesitancy to embrace, accountability and responsibility. Judicial accountability evokes mixed reactions, ranging from ambivalence to suspicion and even outright hostility' (McIntyre 2019: 229).

The main root of the accountability problem, if problem it is, is the independence guaranteed to the judiciary in the constitutions of post-authoritarian states, the extensive powers of constitutional and administrative review bestowed by the constitution and the law, and the self-managing powers delegated to judicial councils to protect the judiciary against political interference. But accountability has also been sought as a cure for the problems which undermine the courts' responsibility to provide fair and impartial adjudication: corruption, political bias, inefficiency and inaccessibility. In this chapter we note why demands for judicial accountability have arisen before discussing the difficulties associated with the concept of accountability when applied to the judiciary. The remaining sections apply the concept to the judiciary's role in policy-making, self-management, corruption, bias, ineffectiveness and impeded access to justice. The final section argues that transparency is the key to all aspects of judicial accountability.

Demands for judicial accountability

The presence in most transitional countries of one or more of the controversial developments mentioned in previous chapters has prompted calls for judicial independence to be counter-balanced by accountability. In 2014 the United Nations' Special Rapporteur on the independence of judges and lawyers observed that the

DOI: 10.4324/9781003334613-10

issue of judicial accountability was receiving widespread attention in different parts of the world by governments, institutions, human rights defenders, civil society and international organizations, 'all of which have been increasingly calling for concrete action to address the issue of judicial accountability' (United Nations 2014: para. 20).

Accountability is especially high on the agenda of international bodies concerned with systems of justice. For example, the International Commission of Jurists organized two conferences on judicial accountability in 2015 in which judges and lawyers from a number of transitional states took part, including Kenya, Tunisia, Zimbabwe, Columbia, Guatemala, Uruguay and Myanmar, to discuss mechanisms and procedures for holding judges to account for involvement in violations of human rights, judicial corruption and similar judicial misconduct. Accountability is also receiving attention in individual countries, such as Uganda, where the first annual judges' conference was held in 2016 on 'promoting the rule of law in Uganda through judicial accountability and excellence'.

Policy intervention by the judiciary has been the leading cause of demands that the judiciary should somehow be held accountable. In policy-making, the tension between independence and accountability has been noted in Eastern Europe and Central Asia where 'as judiciaries have gained independence, their ability to ensure accountability has not kept pace'. The extent of policy intervention by the judiciary has meant 'reform-minded ministers of justice want to push for greater accountability, but independence has taken away most of their levers of influence' (Anderson and Gray 2007: 333, 334). Throughout Latin America, Africa, Eastern Europe and Asia there is evidence of 'growing emphasis on the fact that judicial independence can exist only where the judiciary is responsible and accountable for its operations and decisions' (Gramckow 2005: 112). The extent to which the Brazilian judiciary 'has been forced to render its opinion over public policy and governmental decisions' has raised concerns about judicial accountability (albeit among groups sensing a threat to their vested interests) (Sadek and Cavalcanti 2003: 223).

Self-management of the judiciary has also given rise to calls for accountability. As was shown earlier, judicial councils have been created to strengthen the independence of judges whose appointment, promotion and discipline might otherwise fall prey to political manipulation. They have also been credited with making a contribution to judicial accountability by acting as a managerial intermediary between the public and the judges, allowing 'a wide number of stakeholders to participate in discussions of judicial governance' (Garoupa and Ginsburg 2015: 139). But self-administration has raised concerns about accountability for the efficient and effective use of resources and conduct of business, which can be made more difficult if the judiciary is allowed a large degree of self-administration. Judicial councils have often succumbed to political influences, and their independence has sometimes produced new forms of corruption. 'Two lessons, now shaping support to reforms, are that more attention is required to the content (as opposed to the structure) of the targeted functions and that whoever exercises them should also be accountable for their performance' (Hammergren 2000: 14).

Different aspects of self-administration have prompted demands for accountability: the power of judges to discipline their junior colleagues in Albania; a loss of transparency, leading to accusations that judicial appointments and promotions are more dependent on family and other personal connections than on merit, accusations voiced in Hungary; corporate power which increases bureaucracy and secrecy, as in Romania and some Latin American countries (SOJUST 2006; Guarnieri 2003). Problems with Romania's SCM have been noted by international observers, such as the Commission of the European Union, including broken rules on council elections, with some members refusing to stand down at the end of their terms of office and others offering themselves for re-election despite membership being restricted to a single, six-year term; and the appointment by the Senate of an ineligible civil society representative. To whom the SCM should be accountable, however, and in what way, is rarely specified.

The public's conviction that their country's judiciary is corrupt has also prompted demands for accountability. The Policy Framework for Preventing and Eliminating Corruption and Ensuring the Impartiality of the Judicial System, adopted by an expert group convened by the Centre for the Independence of Judges and Lawyers in 2000, linked accountability to eliminating 'the corrosive effect which corruption has on the achievement of impartiality' (CIJL 2001: 128). In 2002 a group of Commonwealth judicial officers, including heads of judiciary, sought to identify strategies, best practices and actions that would achieve the objective of securing the independence, integrity and accountability of judicial officers, and judicial systems free from corruption (Commonwealth Judicial Colloquium 2002). The assumption that accountability is one of the remedies for corruption in the judiciary also pervades Transparency International's 2007 report on corruption in judicial systems: 'Fostering a culture of independence, impartiality and accountability among judges is a vital step towards ensuring the overall integrity of the judiciary. This is particularly the case in countries where there is a lack of accountability in other branches of government' (Transparency International 2007: 7). In Indonesia, the demand for judicial accountability was in large part prompted by incidents of alleged judicial corruption (Roux and Siregar 2016).

Accountability has also been seen as a solution to the problem of judicial bias. International concern about political bias on the part of judges in some countries was represented by the United Nations' Special Rapporteur on the independence of judges and lawyers who noted in 2003 that abuse of judicial independence 'has triggered a public furor through the media, drawing the executive, supported by the public, to seek greater accountability from the judiciary'. Identifying ideological bias in particular as exposing the need for accountability, he concluded that 'judicial independence and judicial accountability must be sufficiently balanced so as to strengthen judicial integrity for effective judicial impartiality' (Cumaraswamy 2003: 5, 9).

The ability of the judiciary to deliver justice can be further undermined by shortcomings in the management of the courts usually because the judiciary is under-resourced, hearings are protracted and the quality of much legal representation is poor. As was shown earlier, judicial inefficiency means a denial of natural justice and basic rights. One solution is again thought to be accountability, which subjects the judiciary to non-legal standards in the management of courts and judicial procedures: '[M]anagerial accountability ensures that the judiciary allocates the resources – in terms of money and of time – in an efficient manner, managing the case-flow in a way that speeds up the judicial proceedings and manages effectively the human resources available' (Piana 2010: 30). The Council of Europe has provided guidance to a number of transitional countries, including Ukraine, to assist with the establishment of an efficient and professional judiciary by means of transparency and accountability. Designing mechanisms of managerial accountability is one of the Council's top priorities in its support for judicial reform in post-communist countries.

The concept of accountability

Having identified the concerns raised by the operation of the judiciary under rules designed to protect its independence, it should be possible to progress to the next stage of the inquiry, which is to answer the question: to whom should the judiciary be accountable? In governance a relationship of accountability entails someone in office having an obligation to explain and justify the way they have used their powers to a group with the authority to demand information, interrogate the office holder, pass judgement and demand change if unsatisfied: '[T]he implementation of judicial accountability mechanisms implies that certain parties can and should exercise power of supervision and control over others' (United Nations 2014: para. 48). Accountability thus has two dimensions: answerability, or the obligation on the part of an agent to provide an account of activities and achievements; and enforcement, or the power of the principal to deploy sanctions when the account is deemed unsatisfactory.

It follows that accountability should ideally be precise about who is answerable, before whom they have to defend their actions, what actions they are accountable for, and the source of the obligation to render accounts and answers (Bovens 2007; Kosar 2016). Unfortunately, those anxious to secure the accountability of judges rarely if ever provide descriptions of these dimensions of accountability.

So far the problem of accountability has been approached by the formulation of principles which should govern how judges and other members of the judiciary should behave, rather than specifying to whom judges should be held accountable and through what rules and relationships. For example, in 2000 a group of African and Asian judges drew up, under the auspices of the United Nations, a set of principles to underpin the core values of independence, impartiality, integrity, equality, propriety and competence that should govern judicial conduct. But these offer guidance to the judiciary, rather than explain 'what an appropriate mechanism for the enforcement of the standards contained therein should look like' (Mayne 2007: 43).

There are three factors explaining this failure to plug the 'accountability gap'. First, an accountable, independent judiciary appears to be a contradiction in terms. How can the judiciary be independent if it has to answer to some higher authority other than the law, an authority which is inevitably to some extent political? It is too simplistic to announce that '[l]ike other branches of government, it must also be accountable to the general public it serves . . . the judiciary must be responsible to the citizens of a country, and civil society actors, including the media and NGOs, must play an enhanced role in demanding judicial accountability' (Transparency International 2007: 7). It could be argued that accountability is not an appropriate concept to use to depict the relationship between the judiciary and other branches of government or civil society. It is not easy to see how the independence of the judiciary can be maintained if judges have to justify their decisions to politicians, whether of the executive or legislative branches, or to the public via the media or NGOs; or be subjected to sanctions if found culpable for going against the policies or political interests of the government or its supporters.

Second, it is much easier to specify how the answerability dimension of accountability works than the enforcement dimension when considering to whom the judiciary is accountable. Indeed, it has been argued that answerability is the only dimension consistent with judicial independence. Accountability can only mean giving reasons for judicial decisions. '"Accountable" does not mean that the judiciary is responsible to or subordinate to another power of the state, because that would betray its constitutional role of being an independent body of people whose function is to decide cases impartially and according to law' (CCJE 2015: para. 20).

Third, we would normally expect the judiciary to hold others accountable, and especially governments and parliaments, through judicial review of administration and constitutional review of legislation. Public authorities in a democracy must defend the legality of their actions through the courts, rather than demand justifications for judicial decisions before imposing sanctions. For this is what accountability means: answerability followed by sanctions if the explanation given is unsatisfactory.

This is why the most commonly understood form of judicial accountability is internal, when judges are held accountable by a system of appeals heard through a hierarchy of courts. When judicial decisions are tested for legality on points of fact or law in higher courts, judges become accountable for any wrong decisions. Both dimensions of accountability are present: explanation and correction. Accountability begins with the reasoned decisions which conclude a hearing. When combined with the scrutiny given by the appellate court, that requirement for full explanation under scrutiny is satisfied. The opportunity given to higher courts to correct or reverse any misapplication of the law which the appellant alleges has been made by the inferior court satisfies the second condition of accountability. Judicial accountability is thus consistent with judicial independence because decisions rather than judges are subject to scrutiny and corrective action. Judicial independence is preserved because review occurs within the judiciary itself. Individual judges are not penalized if their decisions sometimes have to be reversed by a higher court (Dung 2003).

The case of South African Oscar Pistorius, initially convicted of culpable homicide by the Gauteng Division of the High Court, illustrates the principles at issue here. On appeal by the Director of Public Prosecutions, the Supreme Court of Appeal set aside the original conviction on the grounds that it was based on two errors of law concerning legal intention (*dolus eventualis*), replacing it with conviction for murder. Nowhere was it implied that the trial court judge was incompetent or lacking in integrity, only that a particular interpretation of the facts needed to be revised. Indeed the Supreme Court's ruling drew specific attention to this:

> The trial judge conducted the hearing with a degree of dignity and patience that is a credit to the judiciary. The fact that this court has determined that certain mistakes were made should not be seen as an adverse comment upon her competence and ability. The fact is that different judges reach different conclusions and, in the light of an appeal structure, those of the appellate court prevail. But the fact that the appeal has succeeded is not to be regarded as a slight upon the trial judge who is to be congratulated for the manner in which she conducted the proceedings.
>
> (Supreme Court 2015)

Appeals are, however, especially significant when a large proportion of first-instance judges are ill-prepared for their role, and their decisions have to be reversed because of faulty reasoning, though this can mean that second-instance courts become clogged with cases that should have been dealt with in trial courts: '[T]he consequence is that the judiciary is burdened with unnecessary repetitive work – a burden that precludes judges from attending to and focusing their energy on significant appeals that deserve more attention' (Zimmer 2006: 84). So in Brazil, for example, the system of appeals 'permits literally hundreds of appeals and other legal maneuvers that competent and high-priced lawyers can string out for years' (Freedom House 2011: 70). Appeals which exacerbate the problem of length of court proceedings have led to litigation in the European Court of Human Rights. Defendants of high socio-economic status may be given preferential treatment during appeal, such as being released from custody. Appeals can also be used to reverse rulings that go against the government's wishes. Appellate courts in new democracies are vulnerable to all the abuses that threaten the independence of first-instance courts.

Accountability for policy review

When the concept of accountability is applied to the other features of judicial systems which have given cause for concern, the analysis becomes more complex. In the case of judicial activism, the growing involvement of the judiciary in policy matters through court rulings on specific cases may tempt governments to manipulate the judiciary through appointments or illegal pressures. Clearly this way of dealing with controversial policy interventions is incompatible with democratic governance as well as judicial independence. If the courts, in the proper execution of their powers of judicial review, arrive at policy decisions unacceptable to the government of the day then the democratic procedure is to use the legislative process to determine what public policy should be. If politicians are concerned that judges have altered public policy it is better to use the legislative process to clarify and reinstate the government's intentions rather than resort to some mechanism of judicial accountability. This provides a form of accountability from the judiciary to the legislature but one which does not interfere with the independence of the judiciary to implement the law. A change in the law can be introduced without compromising judicial independence by political interference in the proper functioning of the courts.

Constitutional review presents a more complex problem for governments and legislatures since the judiciary is empowered to judge whether the original legislation is constitutional, thus potentially blocking the use of legislation to correct the effect of judicial review on public policy. Here the demand for accountability 'reflects a significant expansion in the constitutional role of the judiciary. The growth of regulation, the welfare state and human rights have led to expanded judicial oversight and review, and therefore a greater (legitimate) demand for accountability to the broader polity' (McIntyre 2019: 231). Hence the temptation to 'pack' constitutional courts with justices who are ideologically in favour of the government's policy objectives. If this is regarded as an abuse of political authority, it is for the electorate to hold those responsible accountable.

Ultimately it is unavoidably a political judgement as to whether judicial interventionism represents a genuine wish to protect the rights of the citizen or political bias on the part of senior justices who identify themselves with particular ideological positions or special interests. This is why public opinion and relevant civil society organizations (e.g. bar associations) can play a part in calling the judiciary to account but only by making the workings of the judiciary transparent so that deviations from justice are clearly evident to pressure groups, the media and society generally. Only complete openness enables an informed judgement to be made about the reasoning behind particular interpretations of the law and the constitution. The more a court is required to justify its decision, the easier it is to see what kind of values judges is bringing to bear on the evidence.

Accountability through self-management

The delegation of managerial responsibilities to a judicial council on which the judiciary is well represented is intended to provide an important accountability relationship, as well as acting as a defence against political interference. Though it is sometimes thought that, in order to avoid political interference, a council should be composed entirely of members of the judiciary, with no political representation permitted, the inclusion of representatives from other appropriate interests is thought to be a way of making judges and prosecutors accountable to the public they serve (United Nations 2014; Garoupa and Ginsburg 2015).

The key attribute of such councils then becomes the balance which is struck between independence and accountability. Too much independence may leave unacceptable judicial behaviour uninvestigated and unsanctioned. Equally, too much intervention in the management of the judiciary by the political members of the council risks political interference in the management of cases and their outcomes. This is why the role of holding individual justices accountable for their conduct is sometimes kept quite separate from that of enabling the government to hold the whole judiciary to account. In Bulgaria, for example, where the Supreme Judicial Council controls appointments, dismissals and other aspects of a judge's career, reforms were needed in 2007 to provide a better balance between independence and accountability in favour of the latter. So the chairs of the Supreme Administrative Court and the Supreme Court of Cassation now have to report directly to parliament on the management of the courts. An inspectorate elected by parliament monitors the performance of magistrates. Members of the Supreme Judicial Council no longer act as judges during their tenure on the council.

Though accountability is associated with judicial self-management, it is by no means clear how judicial councils achieve this. One possible obstacle is that judges are usually in a clear majority on the council. Furthermore, the work of judicial councils is dependent on the judges for information and expertise, and judges have strong incentives to protect the interests of their fellow judges with whom they will have to work following service on the council, unlike the representatives of the other 'stakeholders' (Garoupa and Ginsburg 2015). The idea that accountability can be achieved through council members drawn from outside the judiciary would appear to leave a body responsible for the efficient management of the judiciary accountable to itself.

In addition, the diverse and sometimes conflicting interests of members drawn from outwith the judiciary (e.g. interest groups versus parliamentarians) fragment accountability, with different groups seeking different things from their representatives and with no cohesive identity of interest in the judicial system. Nor is it usually made clear whether the accountability being sought is to hold judges answerable for their interventions in the policy process or for the quality of justice offered by their courts (Garoupa and Ginsburg 2009).

Any sanctions placed at the disposal of judicial councils represent a strong form of accountability. However, this is vulnerable to political manipulation, either by the representatives of government on the council or by senior judges, especially if partisan politics have affected their initial appointment. The danger implicit in judicial councils is that they might not act impartially and a-politically when making appointments to the bench and when disciplining judges whose decision-making has departed from proper judicial standards. However, if judicial councils see their role as ensuring the good management of the judiciary, rather than seeking particular outcomes in cases involving policy or constitutional matters, the executive can then be left accountable for public policy and for ensuring that senior members of the judiciary are appointed and promoted on merit and not through nepotism or partisan connection.

Appointing the members of a judicial council by a transparent selection process helps to provide accountability, though it is difficult to know how such a process should be designed. It is generally agreed that the representatives of the judiciary should be elected by their peers and that membership should be mixed, including some chosen by the legislature. In order to secure transparency best practice recommends that the power of appointment to judicial councils be shared by as many relevant institutions as possible – legislature, executive, professional bodies, law schools, lower-level judges – in order to provide checks and balances when such important bodies are being constituted:

> [N]either election by peers nor appointment by the executive and/or Parliament is likely to entirely insulate the council from external interference, politicization and undue pressures. There are additional ways of building checks into the system such as ensuring that the power to appoint is shared between several authorities who either concur in the appointment of all members or each appoint certain members.
>
> (Autheman and Elena 2004: 10)

With judicial councils, the accountability sought is mainly of a managerial kind. Distancing the management of the judiciary from the political process by delegating powers that would otherwise be exercised by the executive is a familiar way of limiting political involvement in a function of government. If judicial councils are regarded as quasi-autonomous bodies for managing the judiciary it is possible to see how the courts might be held accountable to council members acting as a kind of management board of a hived-off agency. But then the question arises as to whom the council itself is accountable. The answer must be the minister of justice who can then be held accountable in turn to the legislature.

Accountability for corruption

In one sense this is the easiest form of judicial accountability to envisage. A corrupt judge has broken the law and is subject to its sanctions in the same way as any other citizen. If there is a failure to investigate and prosecute cases of corruption within the judiciary, then ultimately it is for parliament to hold the executive to account for its failure to administer the law. Similarly, if the low salaries found in many transitional countries create incentives for corruption (as well as deterring well-qualified lawyers from seeking judicial appointments in preference for the private sector), then governments can be held to account for failure to resource the judiciary properly.

Judges are in fact rarely prosecuted for criminal activities, even when there is a body, such as Nigeria's Economic and Financial Crimes Commission, with powers to, investigate, prosecute and penalize judges for financial and economic crimes including corruption (ICJ 2015). Nevertheless, accountability for corruption might entail removing a judge from office. In such cases justice requires that the procedure adopted, such as an ad hoc tribunal, should guarantee independence and impartiality. This could mean giving a judicial council the right to select the members of the tribunal, rather than the legislature or executive. The inclusion of foreign judges is sometimes recommended in order to help secure impartiality in such cases.

Accountability for bias

Other misconducts, including persistent bias and discrimination, if not dealt with through the appeals procedure, are best dealt with by disciplinary procedures. This raises the question of who should have the power to exercise such discipline. In order to minimize the risk of political interference in the judicial process, discipline is increasingly made a matter for self-managing bodies. However, self-regulation may be regarded as too soft on judicial misconduct, as in the Czech Republic where the system of discipline was reformed in 2008 by requiring the judicial disciplinary board to draw half its members from lawyers who are not judges, selected by the chief state attorney, the chair of the bar association and the deans of law faculties, rather than leave it composed exclusively of judges. An important development of wider significance is that, in order to avoid interfering with judicial independence, disciplinary powers have been used as *ultima ratio* or only when the misconduct is unequivocal. Of equal significance is the publicity given to disciplinary proceedings so that the judiciary can garner public trust by demonstrating its determination to hold its members to account (Friedel and Urban 2016).

An active bar association can further add to professional accountability by ensuring that all lawyers conform to the profession's code of conduct. This may be seen as particularly important when, as in South Africa, the judiciary 'is constitutionally empowered to overturn the decisions of elected representatives' (February 2007: 273). In the 'Basic Principles on the Role of Lawyers' adopted by the United Nations in 1990, professional associations of lawyers are given 'a vital role to play in upholding professional standards and ethics, protecting their members from persecution and improper restrictions and infringements, providing legal services to all in need of them, and cooperating with governmental and other institutions in furthering the ends of justice and public interest'. Together with governments and educational institutions, bar associations ensure that lawyers are aware of human rights and fundamental freedoms recognized by national and international law, as well as having appropriate education and training and awareness of the lawyer's ethical duties (United Nations 1990). Unfortunately, it cannot always be assumed that a bar association will itself be politically impartial.

When judicial bias results from interference by the political executive in judicial appointments and decision-making, accountability again becomes a political matter and dependent upon politicians being held accountable for bringing pressure to bear on judges. Ideological and social bias on the part of judges is usually the result of failure to appoint on the basis of merit alone, a failure for which the executive must ultimately be held accountable. International support may even be sought, as in the Ukraine in 2008, when the Council of Judges reported the President and other leading politicians to the Council of Europe and the Organization for Security and Co-operation in Europe for interfering in the judicial process.

Accountability for ineffectiveness

Failure to administer justice in a timely and effective manner has further mobilized demands for greater accountability. However, again it is important that accountability is only demanded from those responsible for the defects. To the extent that poor management of the judiciary is the responsibility of government under-funding, it is the executive agency responsible for the resources allocated to the judiciary that should be called to account.

The judiciary is inevitably accountable to the Ministry of Justice for the effective use of resources, with the Ministry of Justice in turn held accountable to parliament for the adequacy of those resources. An interesting innovation here is that introduced in Lithuania by the 2002 Law on National Courts Administration, making it illegal to damage the financial, material and technical resources of the courts, unless there has been a worsening of the country's economic and financial situation.

The ineffective administration of justice does not arise solely from inadequate resources. Individual judges may cause undue delays, reveal ignorance of the law or act negligently. When judges are ineffective because of their own deficiencies, those charged with holding them accountable can be assisted by the publication of performance statistics showing how a judge compares with his or her peers. 'Systematic assessment of individual judges' performance in accordance with pre-established standards is a form of individual accountability' (Open Society Institute 2002: 33). This approach to accountability has been endorsed by the Chief Justice of Zimbabwe in response to poor performance in the disposal of cases and delivery of judgements (*The Zimbabwean* 2015).

Under a stronger form of judicial appraisal, the actions of judges causing personal or financial injury in a civil case, or eliciting actions or omissions of a criminal nature, might require compensation or submission to a criminal investigation followed possibly by prosecution, conviction and punishment (United Nations 2014). However, experience in a number of transitional states, including Armenia, Georgia, Moldova and Ukraine, shows a lack of clarity and consistency in the grounds for disciplinary sanctions, their practical application, and the official definition of different types of disciplinary sanctions against judges. Support to rectify such deficiencies may be available from international bodies such as the Council of Europe (European Human Rights Advocacy Centre 2015).

External observers of performance evaluation in the judiciaries of transitional states are agreed that evaluation must not reduce judicial independence and that where sanctions or serious consequences for a judge's career result from evaluation, accountability should be to an independent body or the judiciary itself in the form of court presidents or special commissions, and not the executive (ENCJ 2015). However, if judicial bodies are given the authority to carry out evaluations, judicial independence demands objectivity: '[N]on-controlling mechanisms for making evaluation procedures transparent can help ensure that the judiciary does not lapse into insular or self-serving institutional behaviour' (Open Society Institute 2002: 34). Furthermore, accountability also implies that when the independent body entrusted with evaluation includes representatives of the Ministry of Justice, they are not able to dominate the process.

Ministers of justice can then be held accountable for the decisions which they make to support the judiciary financially and manage it as a governmental responsibility. Such accountability includes the costs of running the courts, their efficiency in handling cases (including the adequacy of facilities such as buildings, libraries and records), the access to justice which they provide (including the costs of litigation and the availability of legal information), the security of judges, their remuneration and other personnel matters relating to courts and their staff, including training. This then allows the executive to be held accountable for whether the management of the judiciary upholds or undermines its independence. It therefore follows that effective parliamentary scrutiny and control over ministerial action are necessary for judicial independence.

Accountability for impeded access to justice

In so far as access to justice is impeded by the cost of bribery, accountability to the law should solve the problem. When access to the courts is restricted by inefficiencies within the judiciary, accountability must be to the Ministry of Justice as the member of the executive responsible for the effective functioning of the judiciary and the person accountable to the legislature and, through it, to the public for failures of this kind. But if caused by poverty, impeded access is a social and political problem that can only be solved by a willing government. It is up to society to hold political leaders accountable for failure to address poverty and inequality. Most of the other measures required to remove barriers to justice also need to be introduced by governments supported by civil society through bar associations, advocacy and monitoring organizations, and educational institutions. In particular, these include affordable legal representation, stronger law enforcement, proper use of police powers, anti-discrimination laws, wider dissemination of legal information, and reform of judicial procedures to make them more accessible, physically as well as socially (Abregu 2001; UNDP 2004).

The problem of anti-poor bias in legal institutions arises from the difficulty of making the judiciary more responsive to the legal needs of the poor. Rather than requiring judicial accountability, correcting anti-poor bias requires reforms that make the judiciary stronger in holding state officials accountable. Improved access to justice is also a function of legal reforms which remove anti-poor bias from statutes, especially statutes which explicitly contradict constitutional provisions protecting human rights and which revise legal procedures which are biased against the poor, including where necessary rules governing the language in which legal proceedings are conducted (Anderson 2003). These reforms are for legislatures to enact and governments to implement, and these are the institutions to be held accountable by civil society for their success or lack of it.

In all this it is important not to confuse accountability with access, as in one study which identified 'the key elements of accountability' as equal access to justice institutions, adequate public information on the procedures and activities of those institutions, and public participation in judicial reform: 'For institutions to deliver justice, and be accountable for the quality of that justice, they must obviously be accessible' (Castillejo 2009: 4). Ensuring that the conditions exist for justice to be accessible is a task that falls mainly to other parts of the government system than the judiciary.

The responsibilities of governments for improving access to justice are further indicated by notions of legal empowerment. Access to justice is included among the aims of reforms to empower the poor as actors in the legal system (Commission on Legal Empowerment of the Poor 2008). Legal empowerment entails strengthening the poor's capacity to secure their rights as citizens, employees and owners of assets such as land. Improved access to justice is one method of protecting human rights. However, legal empowerment is dependent on state policies which provide people with legal identity as well as information about rights and judicial procedures, and which remove legal and administrative barriers to the enjoyment of basic rights, including an adequate number of courts in accessible locations.

It is clear from the concept of empowerment that responsibility for the contribution to be made by the legal system rests with national governments. Laws which confer rights, powers, privileges and immunities are needed if the poor are to be legally empowered, together with judicial reforms so that legal entitlements are enforceable. 'As part of the access to justice effort it is necessary to audit all laws, regulations, procedures, and institutional set-ups. Laws that discriminate against the rights, interests, and livelihoods of the poor need critical evaluation and revision' (Commission on Legal Empowerment of the Poor 2008: 61). Thus, governments, not judiciaries, must be held accountable for failures to reform the law to empower the poor in their encounters with the judiciary.

Elected judges

So far, political accountability as a means of underpinning the rule of law has envisaged the electorate holding to account those in government responsible for the proper functioning of the judiciary. It is rarely thought appropriate to hold judges politically accountable by making them run for office in a system of direct elections. This is because it has been found to be incompatible with judicial independence.

The USA, where a majority of states holds competitive elections for Supreme Court, appellate or trial court judges, was, until recently, the only country to employ this method of accountability. There is little support for its extension to other democracies, mainly because it is seen as constituting a greater threat to judicial independence than appointment by accountable political officials or organs of judicial self-government. A candidate for election is bound to be influenced by the power of local groups and individuals who might become involved in litigation. 'A system that requires judges to win popularity contests to retain office takes democratic accountability to the point of destroying judicial independence' (Russell 2001: 16).

Judicial elections that are partisan reduce independence even more: '[P]artisan-elected judges decide cases in a more clearly partisan fashion . . . dissent less frequently with respect to politically controversial issues . . . side less frequently with challengers to a regulatory status quo . . . are more responsive to politically influential constituencies . . . and inspire less pre-emption from incumbent officials in the other branches' (Hanssen 2004: 717). Since it is now generally accepted that judicial elections in the USA 'have taken on all of the trappings of partisan politics' (Rothman and Schotland 2001: 1369) this type of accountability is unlikely to find favour in democracies concerned about the rule of law.

In 1998 the United Nations Human Rights Committee found that the election of judges in Armenia did not ensure their independence and impartiality. Judicial reform in 1999 replaced election with selection based on examinations and interviews organized by the Ministry of Justice, approval of a list of nominees by the Council of Justice and final approval by the president. A few years later, however, it was noted that 'a disproportionately large set of powers has been vested in the presidency' and that the 'constitutional order has precluded the emergence of a strong and independent judiciary' (Freedom House 2003).

The results of a recent experiment in Bolivia provide few grounds for confidence in this method of judicial selection. Under the new constitution of 2009, Bolivia held elections in 2011 for Supreme Court, Constitutional Tribunal and Agricultural Court judges. Although the intention was to boost public confidence in the judiciary through a 'democratized' system of justice, and ensure the selection of non-political and professionally expert judges, thereby ending party patronage in the judiciary, the opposite occurred. The selection of candidates was highly politicized rather than based on merit. Successful candidates were chosen for their social background and political characteristics rather than professional qualifications. Subsequently, public confidence in the judiciary declined markedly overall (though increased among supporters of the government). Whether the diversification of the judiciary brought about by the elections, with more jurists from minority groups and women, will compensate for continued politicization remains to be seen (Driscoll and Nelson 2015).

Judicial accountability to electorates politicizes the selection process, threatens the right to a fair trial and undermines judicial independence and impartiality. As such it is a serious impediment to the rule of law and inferior to a system of appointment based on merit. Judicial selection by popular election threatens the basic principles on the independence of the judiciary contained in Article 14 of the United Nations' International Covenant on Civil and Political Rights: non-interference, non-discrimination and security of tenure (IBA 2013).

Transparency

Whatever the aim of judicial accountability, transparency would seem to be the key factor. For accountability to be compatible with independence, judicial proceedings have to be based on the principle of openness: not only must justice be done; it must also be seen to be done. Or as the philosopher and jurist Jeremy Bentham put it: 'Publicity is the very soul of justice. It is the keenest spur to exertion, and the surest of all guards against improbity. It keeps the judge himself, while trying, under trial' (Bentham 1843: 316). Judicial transparency rests on information about three types of activity: adjudicative (transcripts, pre- and post-trial documents, trial exhibits, recordings, settlements, opinions and dockets); administrative (including court budgets, personnel, contracts and organizational matters); and personal (including salaries, personal finances and disciplinary matters).

Because external accountability raises serious concerns about judicial independence, the appropriate mechanisms mainly have to do with openness: public hearings, the publication of court decisions, public scrutiny of the judiciary by the media and civil society, annual reports to parliament, and information on the judiciary's website (United Nations 2014: para. 55). Transparency in performance measurement improves perceptions of and trust in the judiciary. Hiding judicial administration and decision-making from public scrutiny, especially the assignment of cases and the conduct of hearings, can protect nepotism, corruption and incompetence.

Rules preventing decision-making from being hidden behind contempt, defamation, libel and sedition laws, especially from the media, also support transparency (Robertson 2007). However, public criticism of judges might be regarded as incompatible with judicial independence. Freedom of speech, a democratic value of equal importance to the principle of judicial independence, is then called into question. Striking the right balance between an independent judiciary and freedom of speech is difficult with different regimes attaching different weights to these fundamental democratic principles. Public criticism of the judgements and even the persons of judges may be tolerated, but seemingly in mature rather than new democracies (Addo 2000).

A number of new democracies have made progress in opening up judicial procedures to public scrutiny. Croatia's constitution provides journalists with a right to judicial information, and the Law on the Right to Access Information of 2003 gives the public the right to seek and receive information from the courts, which are required to place judicial information on an internet database. The Ministry of Justice's 'e-portal' repository of opinions and rulings aims to increase transparency. The Ministry of Justice also runs a website with information about decisions, the courts and the judicial system generally. However, openness is limited by a wide range of exclusions: information on state, military, official, professional or business secrets; publicity that would interfere with the prevention, uncovering or prosecution of criminal offences; the conduct of administrative supervision; the protection of life, health or safety of people or the environment; the implementation of economic or monetary policies; or intellectual property rights.

A right of access to information held by the state may be guaranteed by the constitution, but not extend to the judiciary, as in South Africa. The Promotion of Access to Information Act does not apply to the judicial functions of courts or judicial officers, and law enforcement and legal proceedings are also exempt from the provisions of the statute. Nevertheless, some courts, including the Constitutional Court, the Supreme Court of Appeal and the Cape High Court maintain websites with information on landmark judgements, procedures, proceedings and judges (Susman and Moore 2009).

Under Romania's Free Access to Information Act, persons other than the parties to the litigation can obtain access to documents and transcripts, thus providing for judgements to be public and open. In addition, most court proceedings (including trials, judgements, verdicts and rulings) are open to the public (Voermans 2007). This enabled the activities of corrupt magistrates to be publicly exposed in 2014, an event that was seen as a positive development in the country's judicial system (Freedom House 2015).

If the workings of the judiciary are transparent, the 'answerability' dimension of accountability becomes effective. The public then has the information required to decide how far judicial proceedings are honest, effective and fair. This requires the judiciary to be open about its professional standards, the reasons for decisions and the procedures governing the conduct of hearings. Transparency enables civil society to judge how far interpretations of statutes or constitutions are motivated by political bias rather than the demands of justice and the law. Transparency in the actions of judicial councils enables civil society to be more effective in seeking reform when councils fail to ensure judges are appointed and promoted on merit, courts are accessible, cases are dealt with efficiently, and disciplinary powers are used fairly. Such transparency is particularly important in view of the consensus that the majority of council members should be judges.

Transparency is also beneficial in countries where public perceptions of corruption are unwarranted by actual experience. If public opinion becomes more accurate in its assessment of the judiciary, public trust in the institution will be strengthened.

The greatest benefit of transparency is that it clarifies who is responsible for remedial action in cases of judicial corruption, inefficiency and bias. It follows that transparency is also needed in the way the executive manages its obligations in relation to the judiciary. The recruitment, transfer, discipline and removal of justices, as well as the processing of cases, should be fully exposed to public scrutiny so that whichever part of the executive is responsible for providing the judiciary with resources, and sharing in judicial self-management, can be held accountable to the legislature. Openness and transparency in the appointment and disciplining of judges and prosecutors, the assignment of cases and judicial decision-making are also likely to produce competent and independent judges, reduce bias and corruption, and provide soundly reasoned decisions (Dung 2003: 28).

* * *

Accountability can only be applied to the judiciary with great difficulty. The relationship between the judiciary and other agencies is significantly different from that between other parts of government which stand in an accountability relationship: civil service and ministers; ministers and parliamentarians; and parliamentarians and the electorate. In democracies the strongest form of accountability involving the judiciary sees it holding others to account. In addition, judicial independence demands that the judiciary should not be held accountable for decisions made by others which affect judicial performance. Democratic theory requires the executive branch to pursue its policy objective through the legislative process and not through accountability which becomes an excuse for pressure on, or interference in, the judicial process. In principal-agent terms, judicial self-management appears to require accountability to a separate principal rather than to some members of the agent itself, but it is not clear which external principal is consistent with judicial independence. Accountability for judicial corruption would appear to place the corrupt judge on the same footing as any other criminal, except that to a large extent the judiciary polices itself when it comes to the prosecution of corruption within the judiciary. The biased judge can be held accountable to a disciplinary body, so long as a way is found to create one that is independent of all branches of government. The executive is the most appropriate body to hold accountable for any defects in the performance of the judiciary, and access to it, arising from underinvestment. Accountability is an aspect of judicial independence which requires further consideration, especially in the specific contexts of particular judicial systems.

References

Abregu, M. (2001), 'Barricades or obstacles: the challenges of access to justice' in R. V. Van Puymbroeck (ed.), *Comprehensive Legal and Judicial Development*, Washington, DC: The World Bank.

Addo, M. K. (2000), 'Can the independence of the judiciary withstand criticism? An introduction to the criticism of judges in Europe' in M. K. Addo (ed.), *Freedom of Expression and the Criticism of Judges: A Comparative Study of European Legal Standards*, Aldershot: Ashgate.

Anderson, J. H. and C. W. Gray (2007), 'Transforming judicial systems in Europe and Central Asia' in B. Pleskovic and J. E. Stiglitz (eds.), *Annual World Bank Conference on Economic Development*, Washington: The World Bank.

Anderson, M. R. (2003), *Access to Justice and Legal Process: Making Legal Institutions Responsive to Poor People in LDCs*, IDS Working Paper 178, Brighton: Institute of Development Studies.

Autheman, V. and S. Elena (2004), *Global Best Practices: Judicial Councils: Lessons Learned From Europe and Latin America*, IFES Rule of Law White Paper, Washington DC: International Foundation for Electoral Systems.

Bentham, J. (1843), 'Draught of a new plan for the organization of the judicial establishment in France' in *The Works of Jeremy Bentham*, vol. 4, Edinburgh: Tait.

Bovens, M. (2007), 'Analysing and assessing accountability: a conceptual framework', *European Law Journal*, vol. 13, no. 4.

Castillejo, C. (2009), *Building Accountable Justice in Sierra Leone*, FRIDE Working Paper No. 76, Madrid: Foundation for International Relations and Foreign Dialogue.

CCJE (2015), *The Position of the Judiciary and Its Relation With the Other Powers of State in a Modern Democracy*, Opinion No. 18 (2015), London: Consultative Council of European Judges.

CIJL (2001), 'Strengthening judicial independence: eliminating judicial corruption' in *CIJL Yearbook*, vol. 9, Geneva: Centre for the Independence of Judges and Lawyers, International Commission of Jurists.

Commission on Legal Empowerment of the Poor (2008), *Making the Law Work for Everyone*, New York: United Nations Development Programme.

Commonwealth Judicial Colloquium on Combatting Corruption within the Judiciary (2002), *Limassol Conclusions*, www.cmja.org/downloads/limassolconclusionwithannexe

Cumaraswamy, D. P. (2003), 'Tension between judicial independence and judicial accountability', www.article2.org/mainfile/php/0205/104

Driscoll, A. and M. J. Nelson (2015), 'Judicial selection and the democratization of justice: lessons from the Bolivian judicial elections', *Journal of Law and Courts*, vol. 3, no. 1.

Dung, L. T. (2003), *Judicial Independence in Transitional Countries*, Oslo: UNDP Governance Centre.

ENCJ (2015), *Independence and Accountability of the Judiciary and of the Prosecution, Performance Indicators 2015*, The Hague: European Network of Councils for the Judiciary.

European Human Rights Advocacy Centre (2015), 'Council of Europe launches project to strengthen judicial accountability in Ukraine', ehrac.org.uk/news/council-of-europe-launches-project-to-strengthen-judicial-accountability-in-ukraine/

February, J. (2007), 'Misappropriations mar South Africa's courts' in Transparency International (ed.), *Global Corruption Report 2007: Corruption in Judicial Systems*, Cambridge: Cambridge University Press.

Freedom House (2003), *Nations in Transit 2003: Armenia*, New York: Freedom House, https://freedomhouse.org/report/nations-transit/2003/armenia

Freedom House (2015), *Nations in Transit 2015: Romania*, New York: Freedom House.

Freedom House (2011), *Nations at the Crossroads, 2011: Brazil*, New York: Freedom House.

Friedel, T. and M. Urban (2016), 'What Czech judges can and cannot do? Practice of judicial disciplinary authorities in the Czech Republic: empirical analyses of all disciplinary decisions between 2008 and 2014', *Asian Journal of Legal Education*, vol. 3, no. 1.

Garoupa, N. and T. Ginsburg (2009), 'Guarding the guardians: judicial councils and judicial independence', *American Journal of Comparative Law*, vol. 57, no. 1.

Garoupa, N. and T. Ginsburg (2015), *Judicial Reputation: A Comparative Theory*, Chicago: University of Chicago Press.

Gramckow, H. (2005), 'International trends: strengthening judicial independence and accountability' in T. Peters (ed.), *Future Trends in State Courts*, Williamsburg, VA: National Centre for State Courts.
Guarnieri, C. (2003), 'Courts as an instrument of horizontal accountability: the case of Latin America' in J. M. Maravall and A. Przeworski (eds.), *Democracy and the Rule of Law*, Cambridge: Cambridge University Press.
Hammergren, L. (2000), 'Multilateral development banks and judicial corruption', siteresources.worldbank.org/INTLAWJUSTINST/Resources/THEMULTI.doc
Hanssen, F. A. (2004), 'Is there a politically optimal level of judicial independence?', *American Economic Review*, vol. 94, no. 3.
IBA (2013), *Challenges to the Independence of the Judiciary*, London: International Bar Association, Human Rights Institute.
ICJ (2015), *Judicial Accountability in Developing Countries*, Geneva: International Commission of Jurists.
Kosar, D. (2016), *Perils of Judicial Self-Government in Transitional Societies*, Cambridge: Cambridge University Press.
Mayne, G. (2007), 'Judicial integrity: the accountability gap and the Bangalore Principles' in Transparency International (ed.), *Global Corruption Report 2007: Corruption in Judicial Systems*, Cambridge: Cambridge University Press.
McIntyre, J. (2019), *The Judicial Function. Fundamental Principles of Contemporary Judging*, Singapore: Springer.
Open Society Institute (2002), *Monitoring the EU Accession Process: Judicial Capacity*, Budapest: Open Society Institute.
Piana, D. (2010), *Judicial Accountabilities in New Europe: From Rule of Law to Quality of Justice*, Farnham: Ashgate.
Robertson, G. (2007), 'The media and judicial corruption' in Transparency International (ed.), *Global Corruption Report 2007: Corruption in Judicial Systems*, Cambridge: Cambridge University Press.
Rothman, D. B. and R. A. Schotland (2001), 'What makes judicial elections unique?', *Loyola Law Review*, vol. 34, no. 4.
Roux, T. and F. Siregar (2016), 'Trajectories of curial power: the rise, fall and partial rehabilitation of the Indonesian Constitutional Court', *Australian Journal of Asian Law*, vol. 16, no. 2.
Russell, P. H. (2001), 'Conclusion: judicial independence in comparative perspective' in P. H. Russell and D. M. O'Brien (eds.), *Judicial Independence in the Age of Democracy: Critical Perspectives from Around the World*, Charlottesville: University Press of Virginia.
Sadek, M. T. and R. B. Cavalcanti (2003), 'The new Brazilian Public Prosecution: an agent of accountability' in S. Mainwaring and C. Welna (eds.), *Democratic Accountability in Latin America*, Oxford: Oxford University Press.
SOJUST (2006), *The Justice System in Romania*, Bucharest: Society for Justice.
Supreme Court (2015), *Director of Public Prosecutions, Gauteng v Pistorius* (96/2015) [2015] ZASCA 204, 3 December.
Susman, T. M. and M. S. Moore (2009), *Report on Access to Judicial Information*, New York: Open Society Justice Initiative.
Transparency International (2007), *Combating Corruption in Judicial Systems*, Berlin: Transparency International.
UNDP (2004), *Access to Justice*, New York: United Nations Development Programme.
United Nations (1990), *Basic Principles on the Role of Lawyers*, adopted at the Eighth United Nations Congress on the Prevention of Crime and the Treatment of Offenders,

United Nations, New York, www.ohchr.org/EN/ProfessionalInterest/Pages/RoleOfLawyers.aspx

United Nations (2014), *Report of the Special Rapporteur on the Independence of Judges and Lawyers, Gabriela Knaul*, A/HRC/26/32, New York: United Nations.

Voermans, W. (2007), 'Judicial transparency furthering public accountability for new judiciaries', *Utrecht Law Review*, vol. 3, no. 1.

The Zimbabwean (2015), '2015: a test for judicial accountability', 14 January.

Zimmer, M. B. (2006), 'Judicial independence in Central and East Europe: the institutional context', *Tulsa Journal of Comparative and International Law*, vol. 14, no. 1.

10 Conclusion

The dilemma of judicial independence

Introduction

All the states in Eastern Europe, Latin America, Africa and Asia that form part of the 'third wave' of democratization have been equipped with constitutions which enshrine the principles which enable a state to be built upon the rule of law: judicial independence, the separation of powers, inalienable rights, and judicial review of legislation and public administration. This reflects a conviction on the part of the authors of these constitutions that democracy cannot be consolidated without the rule of law. Yet despite the constitutional significance attached to the rule of law and judicial independence, the history of 'third wave' democracies is to a large extent one of tension between the principle of judicial independence and the determination of political leaders to prolong their power and achieve their policy objectives regardless of the law and the constitution. The impartiality of the judiciary is tested further the more it is involved in actively contributing towards the development of public policy through its review and interpretation of constitutions and statutes. Despite the almost universal commitment to judicial independence enshrined in the new constitutions of post-authoritarian states, judiciaries have been engaged in a constant struggle to preserve their independence. This in part explains why democracy is in decline in so many 'third wave' countries.

This concluding chapter first shows how the judiciary contributed to the demise of the authoritarian state and helped write new democratic constitutions during the transition period. The consolidation of democracy has called on the judiciary to safeguard the rule of law, and protect democratic principles and procedures: political pluralism, universal suffrage, free and fair elections, representative government, accountability, majoritarianism, freedom of association, freedom of speech and judicial review. The judiciary's support for democracy is illustrated by cases from 'third wave' states. The next section explores the political reactions to judicial activism: reforms to strengthen judicial independence (in states attempting to consolidate democracy); 'reforms' designed to undermine independence (in the illiberal democracies and new autocracies); demands for more judicial accountability; and demands for more culturally sensitive systems of justice. Finally, we return to the argument that judiciaries pose a threat to democracy and conclude that justices

DOI: 10.4324/9781003334613-11

are more likely to be found trying to defend the democratic constitution than usurping the democratic process.

The judiciary in transition

The contribution of judiciaries to democratic development began with the transition from the authoritarian regime. Judiciaries have been involved in all stages of the transition to democracy. While it is true that 'judges do not make or unmake revolutions' it needs to be recognized that they do not just 'crystalize and advance ideas that start elsewhere in the processes of government' (Frankel 2018). Even before the creation of new constitutions, the courts often played a part in the demise of the authoritarian regime by constantly exposing its shortcomings when tested against the principles which comprise the rule of law.

For example, in South Africa the courts were sometimes able to call on the principles which gave the white population some of the benefits bestowed by the rule of law in order to provide justice for all:

> [T]he struggle against South Africa's lawlessness was waged, in part, in South Africa's courts, where anti-apartheid lawyers could invoke South Africa's notional liberties to sometimes undercut its actual injustices. Apartheid was not defeated in the courts but in the world of politics, mass mobilization, military force, and international sanctions – but the events in the courts were a part of this story.
>
> (Ellmann 2016: 58)

Lawyers, including judges, were also involved in some of the popular protest movements that led to the fall of autocratic regimes. An example is Tunisia during the Arab Spring of 2010–2012, where protests included a strike by 95 per cent of the country's 8,000 lawyers in January 2011 demanding an end to violence on the part of security forces during acts of civil disobedience. The lawyers' Save the Judiciary movement in Pakistan from 2007 to 2009 also showed how judges and other lawyers were successfully mobilized against the authoritarian and unconstitutional regime of General Musharraf. When the movement was joined by other civil society groups, such as students, women's rights activists, religious groups, unions, and political parties, to form a broad pro-democracy movement, it was able to hasten the end of a dictatorial regime and restore democracy. The movement's tactics included mass meetings at local bar associations led by the Chief Justice of the Supreme Court and other judges, campaigns to illicit support from the USA and UK, a four-day 'march' of protesters from Karachi to Islamabad, and strikes in district and high courts (Ahmed and Stephan 2010; Shafqat 2018). Most senior judges also refused to accept the imposition of emergency rule. The movement's success was partly attributable to the liberalization forced upon Musharraf by the need to increase his regime's domestic legitimacy and respond to external pressures.

The next role for members of the judiciary in transitions was to contribute to the design of new constitutions to replace those of the authoritarian era. Most transitions from authoritarianism were planned during negotiations among existing elites, conducted as the regime disintegrated, leading to 'pacts' between representatives of the old regime and those opposed to it. In a minority of cases authoritarianism was ended by popular protest or revolutionary action with mass movements encountering anti-democratic resistance from established elites (Smith 2013), but revolutionary protest was usually succeeded by negotiations among elites. These elites have included judges involved in the design of new constitutions, notably in Hungary, Indonesia, South Africa and Colombia. As 'skilled, connected, and committed lawyer-politicians' their professional and political commitments, and relationships with political leaders, helped ensure constitutional changes that were widely endowed with legitimacy. For example, in Hungary Lazlo Sólyom, a practising lawyer, professor of law, and legal advisor to civil and environmental movements, participated as a leading negotiator for the Democratic Forum at the roundtable talks held in 1989 to discuss the constitutional amendments passed by parliament to create a multiparty democracy and the agreement between the communist government and opposition parties. He later became Chief Justice of the new Constitutional Court (Dixon 2017: 43).

Once a reformed judiciary had been created according to constitutional principles and specifications it could begin to demonstrate, especially through constitutional courts, that the new regime adhered to the rule of law. This has often been a struggle when the new governments have tried to expand their power unconstitutionally, as the Latin American case shows (Stotzky and Nino 2018). Elsewhere, for example Hungary, the Constitutional Court came to represent the protection of human rights, the rule of law principle of legal certainty, and the morality of the constitution: it 'put the right to human dignity on the top of the hierarchy of fundamental rights and connected it with equality: the right to equal dignity constituted the base of the most important decisions' (Solyom 2003: 153). It is not only the highest-level courts that have been important for the transition to democracy. Proceedings in lower-level courts, dealing with uncontroversial civil and criminal cases, have demonstrated the principle of equality before the law, reinforcing public confidence that the state is built on the rule of law.

Next, the exercise of review powers in the early years of transition has tended to emphasize the democratic principles embodied in the new constitutions, again reinforcing the message that a new democratic regime is in place, to which new governments must defer. Indeed, the constitutions created during transition reflected the democratic aspirations of the population, allowing the courts to reflect in their judgements what the public expected from their governments: '[A]ggressively enforcing constitutional provisions to the detriment of ordinary legislation may be what democratic publics actually prefer and what democratic publics expect democracies to provide' (Scheppele 2005: 26). Unfortunately for democracy, illiberal political parties have responded to this use of judicial power by dismantling judicial independence. For the most part, the courts have lost the battle for democracy.

Finally, the courts, especially constitutional courts, clarified the break with the past by demonstrating how authoritarian practices were incompatible with democracy. Taiwan's Council of Grand Justices is a notable example of a court which revealed 'the disconnection between residual authoritarian statutes and regulations and the Constitution's promise of democracy and limitations on government powers' (McBeath 2004: 70). It defined governmental powers and fundamental rights. Its early decisions enforced the principles of regular elections for legislative office, the independence of political parties and interest groups, the separation of powers, and fundamental rights, especially procedural rights, the rights of labour and women, and civil liberties (freedom of speech and the press, academic freedom, rights to petition, freedom to travel and freedom of religion). In so doing the council reflected elite and popular consensus concerning democratic development.

The judiciary and democracy

The role of the judiciary in democratic consolidation begins with the rule of law, which guards against arbitrary government, guarantees civil and political rights, and holds state officials legally accountable through judicial and constitutional review. It protects individual liberties with legal certainty, independent adjudication and constraints on executive power. It ensures effective citizenship and provides legitimacy to democratic politics. By guaranteeing the legality of the political process the rule of law helps build a consensus in favour of democracy. It keeps all political activities – whether by voters, political parties, organized interests, members of the executive, legislators and public officials – within the law and the constitution. The sanctions which accompany the implementation of public policy are kept consistent with inalienable rights.

The principles of justice which together constitute the rule of law – ubiquity, regularity, consistency, certainty, equality, and due process (or the rules of natural justice) – cannot be realized without an independent judiciary. An independent judiciary is constitutionally recognized as central to this process. Its freedom to act impartially, making decisions based exclusively on the law, free from improper interference by either public or private interests, is fundamental to the rule of law and hence to democratic political development.

Judicial independence then supports democratic consolidation by protecting the democratic political process against political forces which would otherwise seek to subvert it in their own interest. Independent adjudication strengthens trust in democracy by limiting the exercise of power to the conditions laid down by law and the constitution, rather than allowing powerful interests to negate the political equality on which democracy rests. Independent judges prevent politicians from undermining basic political rights. They protect the fundamental attributes of procedural democracy (Saffon and Urbinati 2013).

The first of these is pluralism, which legalizes competition between partisan groups seeking electoral support. Democracy entails a multiparty competition for governmental power. If a political party is unable to register, or is threatened with dissolution, and cannot secure redress in the courts, it is usually because the judiciary is under the control of the government. However, occasionally the courts are able to support a new party against ministerial rejection of an application to register. For example, in 2021 the Malaysian High Court allowed a judicial review of the decision to refuse registration of the Malaysian United Democratic Alliance and ordered the Interior Minister to register the party. In 2012 Zambia's High Court overturned the de-registration of the Movement for Multi-Party Democracy, one of Zambia's oldest political parties and winner in 1991 of the country's first multiparty elections. At the time of de-registration it was the largest opposition group in parliament. De-registration was widely seen as an attempt by the Patriot Front government to intimidate the opposition.

The second requirement of procedural democracy is universal suffrage, which allows no restriction on the right to vote that would constitute discrimination on grounds that would conflict with political equality such as gender, ethnicity, wealth, religion or ownership of property. The principle was applied by the Constitutional Court of Korea in 2007 to the issue of voting rights of Koreans living overseas. The court ruled that

> all citizens, as sovereigns, should enjoy an equal right to vote no matter where they reside, and the state has an obligation to do all that is in its power to realize such an equal right to vote is a constitutional commitment stemming from the principles of popular sovereignty and democracy. . . . On the one hand, the legislative branch, when restricting the people's right to vote, must respect the significance that right holds as a means to realize popular sovereignty and representative democracy in democratic countries. On the other hand, when examining the constitutionality of a law restricting the right to vote, the standard of review must be strict scrutiny.
>
> (quoted in Im and Kim 2014: 7)

Third, democracy requires free and fair elections which conform to rules on the registration of voters, campaigning, the conduct of the ballot and the tabulation of votes cast. In 2020 the High Court of Malawi was required to apply this principle to the 2019 presidential election. Sitting as the constitutional court, it nullified the result, citing 'widespread, systematic and grave' irregularities, including the acceptance by the Electoral Commission of results sheets altered with correctional fluid (in what became known as the Tipp-Ex election), a lack of party monitor and presiding officer signatures on results sheets, the completion of results sheets at the homes of presiding officers, and failure to conduct a thorough audit of complaints before announcing the results. The court found that '[g]iven the gravity of these irregularities, the conduct of the Electoral Commission in managing these elections was severely lacking and demonstrated incompetence for failing in multiple dimensions to follow clearly laid out legal processes'. The government and Malawi Electoral Commission appealed the judgement to the Supreme Court, which upheld the order for a re-run of the presidential election, asserting that the constitutional duty of the Electoral Commission is to conduct elections that are free and fair and that an election can only be free, fair and credible if it fully complies with the dictates of the constitution and applicable electoral laws as well as principles of transparency and accountability. The court found

> the litany of irregularities in the Presidential election revealed by the record of appeal not only serious but also troubling. . . . The level of lack of seriousness and incompetence of the Commissioners poses a serious danger to the conduct of elections and the institution of democracy in this country.
>
> (Supreme Court of Appeal 2020)

The judgements were widely regarded as having strengthened confidence in the integrity and impartiality of the judiciary, particularly in the light of attempts to bribe five of the High Court judges.

Fourth, in the absence of direct democracy, government must be representative, with the elected members of assemblies and parliaments accountable to their electorates which have regular opportunities to assess their performance. Periodic elections are thus essential features of the democratic process. The Constitutional Court of Zimbabwe was required to apply this principle in 2013 when the director of the Centre for Elections and Democracy in Southern Africa filed an application seeking an order directing the president to proclaim the presidential, general and local government elections. Claiming that his constitutional right to have public officials obey the law had been breached by the failure to proclaim the elections, he cited the president, the prime minister, Deputy Prime Minister Mutambara, the leader of the MDC and the attorney-general as respondents. Declaring that the elections should be held no later than 31 July, 2013, the court noted:

> Nowhere in the Constitution is there an excuse to function without anyone of these branches for an extended period of time . . . it is inconceivable that an interpretation that permits or allows for any extended period without one or other arms of State, in this case Parliament, can be sustainable. To exist too long without a Parliament would be tantamount to shredding the Constitution and inviting a state of lawlessness and disorder. . . . When the first respondent failed to fix and proclaim a date for Presidential, Parliamentary and local government elections, as required by s 58(1) of the Constitution, to enable elections to be held on the dissolution of Parliament on 29 June 2013, not only did he violate the applicant's fundamental right as protected by s 18 of the Constitution, he thereby derailed the electoral process. From then onwards, the rule of law as regards the electoral process was no longer extant. It is imperative that the rule of law be restored to the electoral process.
>
> (Constitutional Court 2013)

Fifth, representative government assumes the accountability of the executive to the legislature so that elected representatives can determine whether their decisions have been properly implemented. This is an essential link in the chain of accountability from government to the people. Between 2002 and 2017 the South African Constitutional Court extended its oversight of legislative procedures to a remarkable level, including the 'key function in a parliamentary democracy of holding the executive politically accountable'. In 2016 the court unanimously held that the National Assembly has a constitutional obligation to hold the President accountable and had violated this duty by not ensuring compliance with the public protector's report on impropriety relating to the installation and implementation of security measures by the Department of Public Works at the private residence of President Jacob Zuma (Guardbaum 2019: 2).

The accountability of the executive branch in a democracy is generally thought to require a politically neutral civil service, able to offer advice to ministers based on relevant expertise. The political heads of ministries and departments decide whether or not to follow that advice and answer to the legislature for the consequences. Officials are further isolated from politics by appointment on merit rather than political affiliation. The principle is enshrined in Article 153 of the 1997 Polish Constitution which requires civil servants to operate in order 'to ensure a professional, diligent, impartial and politically neutral discharge of the State's obligations'. The Constitutional Tribunal has upheld the principle on numerous occasions: in 1999 it asserted 'the imperative of political neutrality in the performance of state tasks, especially the neutrality towards interests of political groups and disputes held by these groups or individual politicians'. In 2002 it affirmed the importance to professionalism and reliability of open, objective and competitive recruitment, free from political interference. In 2003 it reiterated that political neutrality and competence depended on recruitment on merit. However, these judgements did not prevent the increasingly illiberal Law and Justice party (PiS) government from abolishing open, competitive recruitment and security of tenure for senior positions in the civil service, thereby politicizing the service at senior levels (Wójcicka 2018). But by then the PiS had

> transformed the CT from an effective, counter-majoritarian device to scrutinise laws for their unconstitutionality, into a powerless institution paralysed by consecutive bills rendering it unable to review new PiS laws, and then into a positive supporter of the enhanced majoritarian powers. . . . In Poland, the Tribunal became a defender and protector of the legislative majority.
>
> (Sadurski 2019: 82)

Next, democracy implies majoritarianism; decisions selecting office-holders and choosing between policy options should be made on the basis of majority vote to reflect the opinions of the greatest number of participants (voters, legislators), while protecting the rights of minorities (especially legislative minorities) to evaluate, criticize, oppose and compete. One way of strengthening minority rights in legislatures is to allow members to initiate abstract judicial review of legislation following the passage of a Bill, 'a powerful weapon for opposition parties' (Vanberg 1998: 300). This procedure was made available under the constitutions of a number of new democracies, including Bulgaria, the Czech Republic, Hungary, Poland and Russia.

Alternatively, the courts might support an individual MP who challenges the constitutional validity of a parliamentary rule, as happened in South Africa in 2012. The Constitutional Court invalidated internal National Assembly rules for violating the constitutional rights of opposition party members. The rule requiring individual

MPs to obtain the permission of the assembly before they could introduce legislation was found contrary to Section 57 of the Constitution which states that '[t]he rules and orders of the National Assembly must provide for . . . the participation in the proceedings of the Assembly and its committees of minority parties represented in the Assembly, in a manner consistent with democracy'. Writing for the majority, the Chief Justice also held that '[a] construction that also recognises an individual competence to initiate or prepare legislation not only accords with the textual meaning of the section but also with the principles of multi-party democracy, representative and participatory democracy, responsiveness, accountability and openness' (Constitutional Court 2012: para. 46; Guardbaum 2019).

Also essential to democracy is the basic civil and political right to freedom of peaceful assembly and association. According to Article 22 of the International Covenant on Civil and Political Rights, everyone shall have the right to freedom of association with others, including the right to form and join trade unions for the protection of one's interests. Accordingly, in 2008 Taiwan's constitutional court, the Council of Grand Justices, declared null and void Articles 2 and 53 of the Civil Associations Act which stipulated that no permission shall be granted for the formation of civil associations that advocate communism or secession. The council found the clauses in conflict with Article 14 of the Constitution, which provides the people with freedom of association. This is to protect the right to form associations, participate in their activities and ensure the sustenance and self-determination of an association's constitution and affairs. The council also argued that freedom of association encourages those with a sense of citizenry to actively participate in socio-economic and political affairs through the formation of civil associations (Judicial Yuan 2008).

Equally fundamental to democracy is freedom of speech. In a democracy everyone has the right to freedom of opinion and expression without interference and to seek, receive and impart information and ideas through any media. In 2007, Colombia's Constitutional Court considered an appeal against a decision by the State Council, the highest administrative tribunal, to impose sanctions against a radio programme on the grounds that it 'was highly destructive and vitriolic to the values and morals of the Colombian youth'. The Constitutional Court held that the decision of the State Council was contrary to the rights to freedom of expression and information. It argued that

> the right to freedom of expression entails a social risk that is implicit in any democratic system. However, forbidding such right on that account would also result in the loss of one of the core principles of a democracy, that is, that in any democratic society, it is preferable to face the consequences resulting from exercising the right to hold opinions without interference, rather than imposing a general restriction on it.
>
> (Constitutional Court 2007)

Finally, as shown in earlier chapters, independent judiciaries support democratic government by testing, through judicial review, whether administrative decisions are consistent with the statutory powers created by legislation. Public policy can also be more fundamentally reviewed by courts empowered to test whether constitutional provisions have been breached by legislative enactment. This draws the judiciary into political controversies in which it is difficult to maintain a truly impartial position, especially when the courts are required to enforce economic, social and cultural rights.

Judicial activism

The powers conferred on the judiciary by the new constitutions of democratizing countries have also prompted unprecedented levels of involvement in the policy-making process. As was seen in Chapter 8, judicial activism extends far beyond the scrutiny of administrative decisions to include guaranteeing human rights, testing the constitutionality of statutes and applying the justices' own constitutional principles. Judicial involvement in policy-making has been encouraged by the acceptance of basic freedoms, usually expressed in terms of fundamental human rights, on which even democratically elected governments should not encroach.

Abstract constitutional review allows some constitutional courts to amend the very rules which define the powers of executive, legislature and judiciary. They may find themselves having to adjudicate when a sovereign democratic legislature has decided that the existing constitution is obsolete, and judging whether a constitutional amendment is so foreign to the original provisions that it is tantamount to replacing them. This raises the question of how far the courts can defend the constitution against the legitimate right of the legislature to amend it. The idea that a constitutional amendment could be found unconstitutional has implications for democracy itself: who should prevail when a legislature seeks to amend the constitution or even replace it with a new one; can an appeal to the principles of the old constitution by the judiciary satisfy those seeking what are perceived to be essential reforms; how far should the current political majority be constrained by a past generation or a judicial elite; can judges avoid referring to their own political values when an authoritarian government, backed by a legislative majority, seeks to limit the rights of individuals and groups?

Judicial review of constitutionality in democratizing countries has drawn the courts into many public policy disputes, even when these have been resolved through the legislative process. This has been encouraged by the protection afforded to human rights in the new constitutions. Constitution protection has been given to an extraordinary range of social, economic and cultural rights: to work, safe and healthy labour conditions, a minimum wage, rest, form and join trade unions, strike, social security, a standard of living sufficient to provide adequate nutrition, clothing, and housing. These 'positive' rights impose duties on governments to provide material benefits to citizens, and their interpretation by the courts inevitably obliges judges to make judgements about public policy. Some legal systems even provide procedural guarantees that have evolved into a right to good administration with far-reaching implications for the judicial review of public administration. In all regions of the world the post-authoritarian constitutions have been notable for the power given to judges to test the conformity of legislation to the protection extended to human rights in the constitution.

Such levels of judicial activism have led to four types of response from governments and commentators: stronger judicial independence (where democracy is more consolidated), policies undermining independence in the illiberal democracies, calls for stronger accountability on the part of judges, and demands for more culturally sensitive systems of justice.

Stronger judicial independence

For the judiciary to enjoy the independence required by such extensive competences, judges have to be impartial and insulated against improper influences. An impartial judge is one who is unbiased in the conduct of hearings and in arriving at a judgement, whether the adjudication is between private parties or disputes between the state and the citizen arising from criminal proceedings or applications for judicial review. Rules ensure that the judicial function is discharged in a way that is only subject to the law. Judges are insulated against improper influences which would prevent them from deciding matters exclusively on the facts and the law.

Insulating judges from pressures brought to bear by those with a vested interest in the outcome of the case not only requires politicians to refrain from interfering in the judicial process. It also requires judges to be inaccessible to attempts by private persons to secure favourable decisions by corrupt means. A range of institutional devices has been created to protect judicial insularity, but especially a measure of self-management, as was shown in Chapters 5 and 6.

Some reforms have fallen foul of the political machinations which threatened that independence in the first place. Political competition is not always as vigorous as it needs to be, and media bias can misinform the public about improper influences on judicial decision-making. The power of executives relative to legislatures is often disproportionate in new democracies, making interference in the judiciary easier. Despite national and international condemnation of the intimidation of judges and other members of the legal profession, the resources needed to improve the security of courts often fall short of what is required.

The behaviour of politicians is far more difficult to reform than administrative arrangements, pointing to the importance of electoral competition to enable those who use their parliamentary support to threaten judicial independence to be disciplined by the electorate. The accountability of executives, ministers of justice and governing parties is crucial to judicial independence. Political developments, notably strength of electoral competition and the political vitality of civil society, may be more important than the constitutional positioning of the judiciary to the preservation of judicial independence. The choice of electoral system then becomes relevant, given that proportional representation may make it more difficult for the executive to affect the careers of individual judges in ways designed to secure a subservient judiciary. An electoral system leading to coalition government provides some protection against parliamentary majorities that support the partisan interests of ministers of justice in their dealings with the judiciary. Partisan interference in judicial decision-making becomes riskier, electorally.

If the role of the executive in managing the judiciary and organizing judicial careers is subject to effective legislative oversight, the system can guard against the politicization of judicial management with its adverse consequences for the independence and impartiality of the judiciary. The accountability of the executive for judicial administration both informs the electorate and raises public confidence in the rule of law. The rule of law is served by such accountability but also helps consolidate democracy by structuring a reasonable separation of powers.

However, political development, especially the consolidation of democracy, and the organization of the judiciary are in a reciprocal relationship. Viable electoral competition requires a transparent political executive and effective legislative oversight so that political accountability can be effective. The organization of the judiciary is an important part of such transparency and oversight. By holding the elected and appointed officials of the state to account, and guaranteeing free and fair elections, an independent judiciary protects the political rights of the citizen against the abuse of authority when crucial electoral choices are being made, including those whose effect is to support the rule of law.

Earlier chapters have shown how reforms aimed at judicial behaviour have tried to improve the capacity of the judiciary to provide an environment in which fair adjudication is open to all equally. Capacity-building has taken the form of performance evaluation, institutional modernization and training. Protection against biased proceedings has included the introduction of trial by jury, widely regarded as a means of building public trust in the rule of law and the new democratic regime. The problem of biased judges has been tackled by the risky process of lustration and by the altogether more acceptable method of appeals to higher courts. Codes of conduct for members of the judiciary have been adopted to shore up judicial independence. Corruption is being addressed by institutional changes but is a problem which often needs a totally new relationship between the judiciary and civil society. Once again political reform is arguably more important to judicial independence than changes to personnel and process, crucial though these are.

Independence undermined

We have seen how the impartiality of the judiciary has frequently been compromised by the too-common propensity among political leaders in the illiberal post-authoritarian regimes to interfere in judicial decision-making, through judicial selection, control of a judge's career or pressure on individual judges in specific cases. The values associated with judicial independence have proved extremely difficult to secure in practice.

Constitutional provisions regarding the judiciary can often be contrasted with the day-to-day practice of politics and legal proceedings. Many countries, where constitutions guarantee the rule of law, the separation of powers, judicial independence, equality before the law and other fundamental rights, as well as the accountability of public officials to the law, experience in practice varying levels of political interference in the judicial process. Often constitutional provisions themselves give the executive too much power over the judiciary while at the same time enshrining the principle of judicial independence.

In addition, in many transitional states, the ideal of 'due process', entailing the impartial application of the laws, the availability of appropriate remedies, provision for appeals, access to legal assistance, and open and efficient judicial procedures, either has not been effectively pursued or has been intentionally disregarded. Legal proceedings are then tainted by disregard for the rules of evidence (including fabricated testimony and evidence obtained under duress) and inadequate legal representation. Judicial proceedings are further biased by failures to presume innocence in criminal cases, follow the rules of natural justice or treat like cases alike by discriminating on unreasonable grounds.

We have also seen how judicial independence can be compromised by a failure to provide adequate funding, by state-sponsored intimidation and by limitations on the scope of judicial review. Judiciaries rendered inefficient by under-resourcing cannot deliver the quality of justice expected from independent courts. Fair and impartial decision-making can also be nullified by a failure on the part of the relevant authorities to comply with the decisions of the courts. The use of exceptional courts raises questions about the effect on judicial independence of fashionable alternatives to conventional courts, especially when these dispense with the rules of natural justice in pursuit of informality, accessibility and traditional or religious customs.

It has proved equally hard to ensure the insularity of the judiciary from inappropriate influences on individual judges. The benefits of judicial independence are lost when there is bias within the judiciary itself, whether from hostility towards the new democracy and the role of the judiciary within it, ideological beliefs or partisan affiliations. And judicial corruption completely destroys any hope of impartial adjudication and equality before the law.

Independence and accountability

The arrangements for constitutional and administrative review by the judiciary have been made so robust under the new democratic regimes that judicial review is increasingly seen as demanding greater accountability on the part of the judiciary itself. When judges use their discretion in the interpretation and development of legal rules, they contribute to the formation of public policy as well as to the adjudicatory function of government. Judges are then accused of encroaching upon the legitimate authority of elected legislatures. Policies in many fields of government are influenced by judicial decisions. Judicial activism is bound to bring the judiciary into conflict with the political executive on occasion.

Consequently, judicial independence is increasingly perceived as having to be 'balanced' by judicial accountability. In practice, however, the main problem with judicial accountability is finding ways to isolate accountability relationships from political manipulations which threaten the rule of law. This in turn entails holding the judiciary accountable only for those aspects of the judicial process for which it is responsible and ensuring that the executive is held to account when it seeks to control the judiciary in ways which are incompatible with the rule of law. The importance of the political accountability of the executive branch to the legislature, and of public opinion articulated by organized civil society, shows that the stronger the democracy, the greater the likelihood that the right balance between judicial independence and accountability will be maintained.

However, in too many transitional states the political context needed for effective judicial accountability is simply not there. Even where significant progress has been made in securing impartial adjudication in the courts, politicians continue to politicize legitimate attempts to balance judicial independence with judicial accountability. When judges develop public policy beyond the limits acceptable to governments and parliaments there remains a tendency to manipulate the judicial process rather than revise the law through legislation.

The challenge within democracies is to strike a balance between restricting the power of judges to thwart the will of parliament by imposing their own ideological standards upon the law, and guaranteeing the impartiality of judges when resolving conflicts, whether between citizens and the state or between private litigants. On the one hand, members of the political executive will always be tempted to influence the decisions of the courts, especially when the government's policies are at stake. On the other hand, the ability of judges, through constitutional review, interpretation of statute or application of precedent, to make law rather than just apply it to specific cases, will affect the relationship between executive and judiciary in all political systems.

Adherence to the separation of powers, though an admirable principle to embody in constitutions because of its association with judicial independence, is impossible to maintain in practice. There may not be overlapping membership between executive and judiciary, as there often is between executive and legislature, but an executive never abdicates all responsibility for the judiciary, not least because it is likely to be held politically accountable for some of its shortcomings. Presidents or ministers of justice exercise powers of appointment to varying degrees under different types of constraint of varying effectiveness. There can never be a complete absence of relationships between the judiciary and other branches of the state. The key challenge in democracies is to find relationships that do not damage the judiciary's role as an independent constraint on unconstitutional and illegal use of executive power.

Such relationships are dependent upon democratic politics with which judicial independence reciprocates. An independent judiciary secures the rights which enable citizens to participate fully in the political process and protects them against the abuse of power by legislatures and executives. In return, the democratic political process makes it electorally damaging for the party of government to manipulate the judiciary for its own political ends. If there is a significant electoral price to pay for interference in the judicial process, judges are more likely to be able to exercise their powers independently and impartially. The executive also has a powerful incentive to ensure that the judiciary functions in an unbiased and efficient manner. It follows, however, that governments supported by large legislative majorities may be motivated to ensure that the judiciary does not develop into the effective opposition which parliament lacks.

A universal rule of law?

One problem with judicial reform for a number of commentators is that often it is assumed, especially by the providers of foreign aid and technical assistance, that a reform can benefit all judicial systems, regardless of the local social and political context. Local cultural characteristics should, it is argued, be allowed to shape the changes needed to improve judicial systems. So, for example, sensitivity to the local context has become part of World Bank thinking on judicial reform (Faundez 2010). Promoting the rule of law, and the institutions that support it, is dismissed as a one-size-fits-all approach, the implementation of which 'lacks the social, historical and cultural connection to the people who are primarily affected by the transition. It is based on the faulty belief that what has worked in a few developed and industrialised countries will work elsewhere' (Vieille 2012: 64). The implication here is that the values and principles that constitute the rule of law are not absolutes but may need to be qualified in order to fit particular cultural imperatives.

There are grave dangers inherent in this approach to judicial reform. First, the basic civil rights enshrined in the constitutions of transitional states and fundamental to the rule of law should be regarded as universal. Even in countries where political leaders (usually with their own authoritarian power rather than justice in mind) claim that particular historical, cultural or religious values should prevail over Western ones, it is also usually admitted that full, universal human rights are desirable as soon as economic and social development permits their observance. It is also noticeable that political activists confronted by state repression advocate support for fundamental and universal human rights that are dependent on the rule of law.

Second, it is by no means clear what rule of law principles can be safely sacrificed in the interest of cultural adaptation. In which social groups are there people who do not deserve a fair trial by unbiased and honest judges? Under what circumstances is arbitrary political power preferable to the absolute supremacy of regular law? Who benefits from legal impunity given to perpetrators of human rights violations? There is no scope for cultural relativism if the rule of law is based on principles deemed to be universal, including the accountability of government officials, individuals and private entities to the law; the requirement for laws to be clear, publicized, stable, just and evenly applied, protecting fundamental rights; fair processes by which laws are enacted, administered and enforced; and the delivery of justice by competent, ethical and independent justices who are of sufficient number, have adequate resources, and reflect the make-up of the communities they serve (WJP 2015).

Third, the parts of the justice sector most likely to reflect cultural particularities are the customary or religious mechanisms used for dispute resolution as an alternative to the ordinary courts. The proponents of this growing trend see customary or traditional methods of adjudication as familiar, time honoured, swift and cheap. While there is an obvious place for some specialized courts, especially when they offer greater informality and lower costs than the ordinary courts, it is imperative that they are demonstrably fair in their procedures. Too many customary devices have a record of violating natural justice: 'In some countries, the tribal, clan, or village chiefs responsible for customary dispute resolution pay little regard to basic human-rights norms. In others, they are effectively pressed to adhere to such norms' (Youngs 2015: 150). Often traditional procedures are used because the universal qualities of the ordinary courts have broken down (through underfunding, inefficiency or corruption), rather than because the values embodied in conventional courts have been dismissed as a 'Western' concept.

Democracy and judicial independence

However controversial the level of judicial activism is thought to be in any given country, it remains the case that the more mature the democracy, the more likely it is that the judiciary will be independent. The average 'judicial independence' score provided by the World Economic forum declines steadily as one moves from mature democracies to authoritarian states (see Figure 10.1).[1]

Judicial independence has sometimes been seen as a threat to democracy. Judges have been accused of being 'enemies of the people', usurpers of democracy, unaccountable elites and 'juristocracies', guilty of 'creeping assaults' on the constitution. Such charges are made largely by authoritarians and illiberal democrats, rather than political leaders seeking to preserve democratic values and institutions.

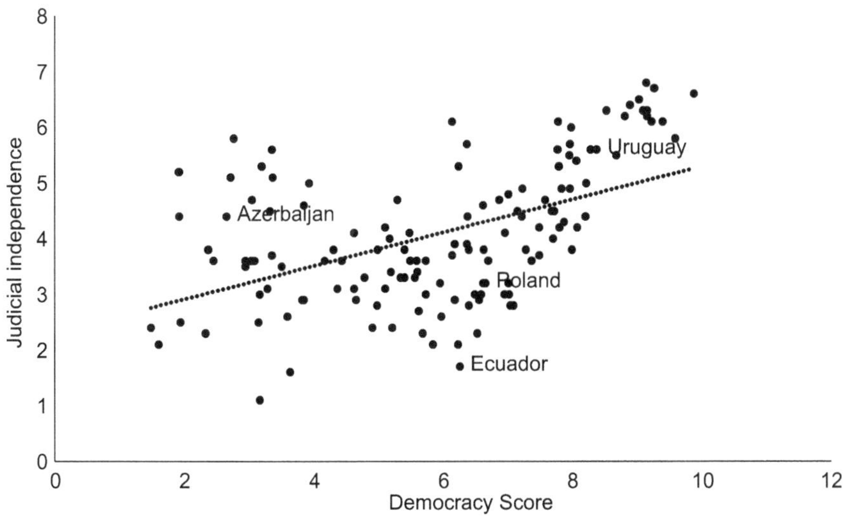

Figure 10.1 Democracy and Judicial Independence, 2018

The abuse of the judiciary is quickly followed up not only by attempt to bring it under political and ideological control but also by assaults on other democratic institutions, especially civil society, political opposition and the independent media: '[D]ominant political party ruling groups have used specific constitutional amendments to weaken the possibility of judicial independence and to establish a politics of institutional and political co-optation' (Castillejos-Aragon 2021: 347–348).

The claim that judges undermine democracy by replacing their policy decisions with those of elected representative is made by the leaders of illiberal governments intent on suppressing opposition, limiting civil rights, violating the rule of law, and distorting the democratic process in order to prolong their own tenure in office. Governments have sought to control the judiciary not to preserve democracy but to ensure favourable rulings when critics seek protection from the courts of their fundamental rights. Judges have been captured because they have defended the law and the constitution, not violated them. They have been drawn into the policy-making process on an unprecedented scale because the rights enshrined in constitutions leave few areas of economic and social policy immune from judicial review, not because intrusive judges have exercised illegitimate powers.

Most of the countries experiencing the greatest difficulties are those which were believed to have found a democratic alternative to the authoritarianism which had characterized past regimes. However, there have been signs recently that the rate of democratic decline, that has led since 2000 to a decline in political rights and civil liberties in a majority of the world's states, might have slowed, if not halted. The popular demand for governments that respect human rights remains strong. Support for populist leaders has declined since 2019 in Mexico, the Czech Republic and Chile. Populist parties have seen their support decline in Hungary, Poland and Brazil. Voters in Brazil, South Africa and Poland have increasingly rejected populist ideology (Foa et al. 2022). Opposition parties have begun to build alliances to compete more effectively against autocrats, as in the Czech Republic and Hungary (Roth 2022). In 2020 South Korea and Taiwan were classified as 'full democracies' by the Economist Intelligence Unit. Improvements in the electoral process and pluralism resulted in more democratic political institutions in Malaysia. Support for democracy and participation in lawful demonstrations increased in Poland. Public support for democracy grew in Albania as the government undertook electoral reforms to bring election laws in line with EU standards. Electoral fairness and transparency improved in Ukraine (EIU 2021).

However, threats to judicial independence remain even when democracy appears to be gaining strength. While the Mexican Supreme Court is generally regarded as independent, a number of justices appointed in 2021 were viewed as too close to the government, raising concerns about diminished autonomy. In the Czech Republic the judiciary is largely independent, but political interests may interfere with due process. Judicial independence remains a matter of concern in Hungary. In Poland the government has asserted control over the judiciary. The judiciary in Brazil is largely independent but is inefficient and subject to politically motivated intimidation and other external influences, especially in rural areas. The South African courts operate with substantial independence, but shortages of judicial staff and financial resources undermine defendants' due process rights, including the right to a timely trial and legal counsel. Many on remand are detained beyond the legal maximum. In South Korea the judiciary is generally considered to be independent, but senior judges have been involved in corruption scandals in recent years. In Albania the courts are subject to political pressures, public trust in the judiciary is low and corruption remains a serious problem. The Malaysian judiciary is compromised by extensive executive influence with courts frequently issuing arbitrary or politically motivated verdicts in high-profile cases. Several laws undermine due process. Reforms aimed at corruption and politicization of Ukraine's courts have been disappointing. Only in Chile and Taiwan are the judiciaries free from political interference, and constitutional guarantees concerning due process in civil and criminal matters generally upheld.

Independent courts must be part of any democratic rejuvenation, supporting the institutions that form the basis of the democratic state: a vibrant civil society, free and fair elections, representative legislatures, a free mass media and the rule of law. The judiciary can then expect to benefit from the genuine political competition which is needed if judicial independence is to be protected.

Note

1 The scores for 'Judicial Independence' are taken from the World Economic Forum's Executive Opinion Survey in *The Global Competitiveness Report 2017–2018*, Geneva: World Economic Forum, 2019, Table 1.06. A score of 1 indicates that the judiciary is 'heavily influenced' by members of government, citizens or firms, and 7 indicates the judiciary is 'entirely independent'.

The 'democracy' ranking is taken from the Economist Intelligence Unit's *Democracy Index 2018*, London: The Economist Intelligence Unit Limited, 2019, pp. 36–40. The index of democracy, on a 0-to-10 scale, is based on the ratings for 60 indicators grouped in five categories: electoral process and pluralism, civil liberties, the functioning of government, political participation and political culture. The overall index of democracy is the simple average of the five category indexes.

References

Ahmed, Z. S. and M. J. Stephan (2010), 'Fighting for the rule of law: civil resistance and the lawyers' movement in Pakistan', *Democratization*, vol. 17, no. 3.

Castillejos-Aragon, M. (2021), 'The role of lawyers in mobilizing for judicial independence: how to take back the court?' in S. Shetreet, H. Chodosh and E. Helland (eds.), *Challenged Justice: In Pursuit of Judicial Independence*, Leiden: Brill.

Constitutional Court (2007), *Decision T-391 of May 22, 2007*, Bogota: The Constitutional Court of Colombia.

Constitutional Court (2012), *Oriani-Ambrosini, MP v Sisulu, MP Speaker of the National Assembly (Case No. CCT 16/12)*, Braamfontein: Constitutional Court of South Africa.

Constitutional Court (2013), *Jealousy Mbizvo Mawarire V Robert Gabriel Mugabe N.O., Morgan Richard Tsvangirai N.O., Arthur Guseni Oliver Mutambara N.O., Welshman*

Ncube, the Attorney-General, Judgment No. CCZ 1/13, Harare: Constitutional Court of Zimbabwe.
Dixon, R. (2017), 'Constitutional design two ways: constitutional drafters as judges', *Virginia Journal of International Law*, vol. 57, no. 1.
EIU (2021), *Democracy Index 2020*, London: Economist Intelligence Unit.
Ellmann, S. (2016), 'The struggle for the rule of law in South Africa', *New York Law School Law Review*, vol. 60, no. 1.
Faundez, J. (2010), 'Rule of law or Washington consensus: the evolution of the World Bank's approach to legal and judicial reform' in A. Perry-Kesaris (ed.), *Law in the Pursuit of Development*, London: Routledge.
Foa, R. S., X. Romero-Vidal, A. J. Klassen, J. F. Concha, M. Quednau and L. S. Fenner (2022), *The Great Reset Public Opinion, Populism, and the Pandemic*, Cambridge: Centre for the Future of Democracy.
Frankel, M. E. (2018), 'Concerning the role the judiciary may serve in the proper functioning of a democracy' in I. P. Stotzky (ed.), *Transition to Democracy in Latin America: The Role of the Judiciary*, Abingdon: Routledge.
Guardbaum, S. (2019), 'Pushing the boundaries: judicial review of legislative procedures in South Africa', *Constitutional Court Review*, vol. 9, no. 1.
Im, H. and H.-K. Kim (2014), 'Revisiting the constitutionality of the voting rights of overseas Koreans', *Korea Journal*, vol. 54, no. 1.
Judicial Yuan (2008), *The Prohibition Against Associations Advocating Communism or Secession Case*, J.Y. Interpretation No. 644, 20 June.
McBeath, J. (2004), 'Democratization and Taiwan's Constitutional Court', *American Journal of Chinese Studies*, vol. 11, no. 1.
Roth, K. (2022), 'With autocrats on the defensive, can democrats rise to the occasion?' in *World Report 2022*, New York: Human Rights Watch.
Sadurski, W. (2019), 'Polish Constitutional Tribunal under PiS: from an activist court, to a paralysed tribunal, to a governmental enabler', *Hague Journal on the Rule Law*, vol. 11, no. 1.
Saffon, M. P. and N. Urbinati (2013), 'Procedural democracy, the bulwark of equal liberty', *Political Theory*, vol. 41, no. 3.
Scheppele, K. L. (2005), 'Democracy by judiciary: or why courts can be more democratic than parliaments' in A. Czarnota, M. Krygier and W. Sadurski (eds.), *Rethinking the Rule of Law After Communism*, Budapest: Central European University Press.
Shafqat, S. (2018), 'Civil society and the Lawyers' Movement of Pakistan', *Law & Social Inquiry*, vol. 43, no. 3.
Smith, B. C. (2013), *Understanding Third World Politics*, Basingstoke: Palgrave Macmillan.
Solyom, L. (2003), 'The role of Constitutional Courts in the transition to democracy with special reference to Hungary', *International Sociology*, vol. 18, no. 1.
Stotzky, I. P. and C. S. Nino (2018), 'The difficulties of the transition process' in I. P. Stotzky (ed.), *Transition to Democracy in Latin America: The Role of the Judiciary*, Abingdon: Routledge.
Supreme Court of Appeal (2020), *Mutharika & Anor. v Chilima & Anor. (MSCA Constitutional Appeal 1 of 2020)*, Lilongwe: Republic of Malawi Supreme Court of Appeal.
Vanberg, G. (1998), 'Abstract judicial review, legislative bargaining, and policy compromise', *Journal of Theoretical Politics*, vol. 10, no. 3.
Vieille, S. (2012), 'Transitional justice: a colonizing field?', *Amsterdam Law Forum*, vol. 4, no. 3, SSRN: http://ssrn.com/abstract=2154483
WJP (2015), *Rule of Law Index 2015*, Washington: World Justice Project.

Wójcicka, E. (2018), 'The new model for filling senior positions in the civil service in Poland', *Transylvanian Review of Administrative Sciences*, Special Issue on Civil Service Reform.

Youngs, R. (2015), 'Exploring "non-western democracy"', *Journal of Democracy*, vol. 26, no. 4.

Index

For Product Safety Concerns and Information please contact our EU representative GPSR@taylorandfrancis.com
Taylor & Francis Verlag GmbH, Kaufingerstraße 24, 80331 München, Germany

www.ingramcontent.com/pod-product-compliance
Ingram Content Group UK Ltd.
Pitfield, Milton Keynes, MK11 3LW, UK
UKHW020152200926
475702UK00016B/2665

9781032369495